Two Arabic Travel Books

Letter from the General Editor

The Library of Arabic Literature series offers Arabic editions and English translations of key works of classical and pre-modern Arabic literature, as well as anthologies and thematic readers. Books in the series are edited and translated by distinguished scholars of Arabic and Islamic studies, and are published in parallel-text format with Arabic and English on facing pages. The Library of Arabic Literature includes texts from the pre-Islamic era to the cusp of the modern period, and encompasses a wide range of genres, including poetry, poetics, fiction, religion, philosophy, law, science, history, and historiography.

Supported by a grant from the New York University Abu Dhabi Institute, and established in partnership with NYU Press, the Library of Arabic Literature produces authoritative Arabic editions and modern, lucid English translations, with the goal of introducing the Arabic literary heritage to scholars and students, as well as to a general audience of readers.

Philip F. Kennedy
General Editor, Library of Arabic Literature

رحلات

أخبار الصين والهند

لأبي زيد السِيرافيّ

وكتاب أحمد بن فضلان

ابن العبّاس بن راشد بن حمّاد

LIBRARY OF
المكتبة
ARABIC
العربية
LITERATURE

Two Arabic Travel Books

Accounts of China and India

Abū Zayd al-Sīrāfī

Edited and translated by
Tim Mackintosh-Smith

and

Mission to the Volga

Aḥmad ibn Faḍlān

Edited and translated by
James E. Montgomery

Volume editors
Philip F. Kennedy
Shawkat M. Toorawa

NEW YORK UNIVERSITY PRESS
New York and London

NEW YORK UNIVERSITY PRESS
New York and London

Library of Congress Cataloging-in-Publication Data

Two Arabic travel books : accounts of China and India / Abu Zayd al-Sirafi ; edited and translated by Tim Mackintosh-Smith ; Mission to the Volga / Ibn Fadlan ; edited and translated by James E. Montgomery.
pages cm. -- (Library of Arabic literature)
In English and Arabic.
Includes bibliographical references and index.
ISBN 978-1-4798-0350-7 (cl) -- ISBN 978-1-4798-4452-4 (e-book) -- ISBN 978-1-4798-0028-5 (e-book)
1. India--Description and travel--Early works to 1800. 2. China--Description and travel--Early works to 1800. 3. Volga River Region (Russia)--Description and travel--Early works to 1800. I. Mackintosh-Smith, Tim, 1961- editor. II. Montgomery, James E. (James Edward), 1962- editor. III. Sirafi, Abu Zayd Hasan ibn Yazid, active 10th century. Silsilat al-tawarikh. IV. Sirafi, Abu Zayd Hasan ibn Yazid, active 10th century. Silsilat al-tawarikh. English. V. Ibn Fadlan, Ahmad, active 922. Kitab ila malik al-Saqalibah. VI. Ibn Fadlan, Ahmad, active 922. Kitab ila malik al-Saqalibah. English. VII. Title: Accounts of China and India. VIII. Title: Mission to the Volga.
DS409.S5713 2015
915.404--dc23
2014021834

CIP

New York University Press books are printed on acid-free paper, and their binding materials are chosen for strength and durability.

Series design by Titus Nemeth.

Typeset in Tasmeem, using DecoType Naskh and Emiri.

Typesetting and digitization by Stuart Brown.

Manufactured in the United States of America
c 10 9 8 7 6 5 4 3 2 1

Table of Contents

Foreword

This volume brings together the two oldest surviving Arabic travel books, dating from the third/ninth and fourth/tenth centuries. These are also two of the shortest Arabic travel books, but if they are small, their scope is huge and their vision panoramic. They set out from the heart of the Arab-Islamic empire, the hub of the Old World in their time: journeying by land from the caliphal capital of Baghdad and by sea from the great Gulf emporia of Basra and Sīrāf, they visit all seven climes of the ancient geographers, the bands of latitude encircling the inhabited earth. They take us, their readers and fellow travelers, from northern steppes, where rivers and beards freeze and trousers are lined in fur, to steamy equatorial islands, whose inhabitants lack beards, trousers, and any clothes at all. They explore a world and an age in which the political unity of the Islamic empire was fast fragmenting but in which the culture of that empire was going global. Some verses by Abū Dulaf Misʿar ibn Muhalhil, a slightly later traveler, catch the spirit of the time:

To us the whole world's open wide,
  And all that's in it of Islam and non-Islam.
We pass our summers on the snow,
  And winter in the land of ripening dates.

In some ways, Ibn Faḍlān's *Mission to the Volga* and Abū Zayd's *Accounts of China and India* are very different books. One is by a single author and describes a particular journey by caravan and camel-skin raft, a diplomatic mission into the icy heart of the Eurasian landmass. The other is Abū Zayd's compilation of fragments from multiple journeys by many travelers, most of them anonymous merchants who crossed the Indian Ocean and China Sea by dhow and then lived, traded, and sweated, often for years, on its shores. Both books are truncated: while one lacks an ending, the other lacks a beginning.

There are also some remarkable similarities. Both books are written in informal Arabic that sometimes seems closer to a spoken than to a literary record. Both portray an extraordinarily mobile world in which a tailor from Baghdad can end up as the Bulghār king's couturier, a wanderer from present-day Pakistan can end up hanging from a tree in a northern forest, and a refugee from

Basra can drop in, apparently on a whim, on the Tang emperor of China. Both are ethnographic gold mines containing strikingly similar information on the peoples beyond the fringe of the Muslim world: marriage and burial customs, punishments for adultery, personal hygiene and the lack of it, the role of women, burial rites, currencies, royal protocol, religious beliefs, diet; even so abstruse and unexpected a subject as the mass sympathetic suicide of courtiers on the death of their king appears in both works. And both these gold mines were to be extensively worked by other, more famous writers.

The correspondences between the two books are often uncanny, given the difference in geography, but they are not surprising. Both peer through the lens of Islam; they look at similar things and see them in similar ways, sometimes with similar distortions. Faced, on occasion, by the seemingly inexplicable and shocking, they both take refuge in the same Qur'anic phrase, «God is exalted above what the wrong-doers say!» (Q Isrāʾ 17:43) They are all-seeing, but their point of view is hardly that of empirical detachment. And yet it may be no bad thing to look askance, as it were, from a viewpoint of cultural certainty—or at least not when one interprets what one sees with an inquisitive mind (indeed, skewed eyesight and a curious mind are the prerequisite of philosophers, if the French philosopher Fontenelle is right). Such a viewpoint was certainly no bad thing for Herodotus, long before Abū Zayd and Ibn Faḍlān, or for the imperial ethnographers of the Victorian age, long after them. We would be much poorer today without the riches they gathered.

Despite their small size, Ibn Faḍlān's *Mission* and Abū Zayd's *Accounts* have a place among the greatest works in all the literature of travel and observation. It seems appropriate that they should now occupy that place jointly, in this volume. For while they differ in setting and climate, authorship and structure, they complement each other in their interests and attitudes, in the tenor of their curiosity. And there are moments of contact, physical and direct, between the oceanic south and continental north that they describe: the gifts given along the way by Ibn Faḍlān's mission, for example, invariably include *fulful*, pepper, a spice that has brought a little of the heat of the Malabar Coast of India, Abū Zayd's "Land of Pepper," via Basra and the imperial hub of Baghdad, all the way to the frozen lands of the Volga.

Here, at last, these two parts of an old but mobile and interconnected world are brought together for us, its heirs, to explore.

Tim Mackintosh-Smith

Accounts of China and India

In memory of my aunt, Elsie Florence Harrison, who showed me the way that led to Arabia, India, and China

Acknowledgements

I would like to thank in particular: my old friend Dr Ḥasan ʿAbd al-Wahhāb al-Shamāḥī of Ṣanʿāʾ, for helping me tease out some of the knottier problems of the text; Ianthe Maclagan and Tim Morris, for their wonderful hospitality in Oxford and Andalusia; Professor Zvi Ben-Dor Benite, for restoring some especially tricky arabicized Chinese terms to their original forms; the Bibliothèque Nationale de France, for supplying with remarkable speed a superb digital copy of the only known manuscript; and Philip Kennedy, Chip Rossetti, and Gemma Juan-Simó for their unceasing encouragement and editorial support from Abu Dhabi and New York. I am also indebted to the late Professor Sauvaget, whose work on the First Book of the *Accounts* was truly a labor of love, for a number of suggested readings and interpretations.

Introduction

This is a book about an ocean and the lands that lie on its shores, about the ships that cross it and the cargoes they carry. In its own words, it is a book about

> the Sea of India and China, in whose depths are pearls and ambergris, in whose rocky isles are gems and mines of gold, in the mouths of whose beasts is ivory, in whose forests grow ebony, sapan wood, rattans, and trees that bear aloe-wood, camphor, nutmeg, cloves, sandalwood, and all manner of fragrant and aromatic spices, whose birds are parrots and peacocks, and the creeping things of whose earth are civet cats and musk gazelles, and all the rest that no one could enumerate, so many are its blessings.[1]

It might have been the inspiration for John Masefield's quinquireme of Nineveh in his poem "Cargoes," with its

> cargo of ivory,
> And apes and peacocks,
> Sandalwood, cedarwood, and sweet white wine.

(And, yes, there is sweet white wine in this book too, made from the sap of the toddy palm.) But it is about more than that, for there is a whole human landscape: ships' captains and customs men, kings and courtiers, princes and paupers—and a few cannibals and kidnappers, to add spice.

What's more, the book describes a real, live world, almost palpably real, despite the passing of eleven centuries. It is built from facts, not sailors' yarns. As the author says in his closing words, "I have avoided relating any of the sort of accounts in which sailors exercise their powers of invention,"[2] sailors, according to his illustrious predecessor al-Jāḥiẓ, not being "respecters of the unvarnished truth. The stranger the story the more they like it; and, moreover, they use vulgar expressions and have an atrocious style."[3] Reality and solidity are what are implied by the first word of the title: *akhbār*, accounts, are reports from credible witnesses. And each *khabar*, each account, fits in with the others to be assembled into a jigsaw picture of a world not unlike our own, a world on the road to globalization.

It is a short book, but it has a sweeping perspective, from the Swahili coast to a rather mistily glimpsed Korea. It is therefore one of those books that seems bigger than it is. And, like the ports of that immense Afro-Asiatic littoral, its pages are busy with people and piled with goods, not just with the luxuries listed above but also with a priceless cargo of information, especially on China. Here are the first foreign descriptions of tea and porcelain, and a whole panorama of Chinese society, from the Son of Heaven and Confucian ethics down to toilet paper and bamboo urinals.

And all this marvelous, mundane world is contained in the compass of a novella. As its own last words say, *wa-in qalla awlā*:[4] Less is more.

Dating and Authorship

If *Accounts of China and India* is good value in its geographical and material coverage, there is a bonus: it is, in fact, two books.

Book One, according to the author of Book Two, dates to the year 237/851–52.[5] There is no reason to doubt this date, and internal evidence supports it.[6] The author of Book One, however, is unknown. It does not help that the first pages are missing from the only manuscript copy known to have survived; these might have given an author's name. Nor does it help that another writer, Ibn al-Faqīh, a writer much closer in time to the composition of Book One than we are, quoted some of its text with an attribution to one Sulaymān al-Tājir.[7] This Sulaymān the Merchant was undoubtedly one of the informants for Book One; he is the only one mentioned in it by name.[8] Commentators in search of authors have therefore leapt on Sulaymān and credited him with the whole book. It is perfectly usual in Arabic books of the time for their authors to appear in the text, as Sulaymān does, in the third person, as if I were to interject suddenly, "And Tim Mackintosh-Smith said . . ." This is, in itself, no obstacle to the attribution of authorship to Sulaymān, but it is likewise not an argument for it. Much ink has been shed over the question, but, in the end, we have no incontrovertible evidence for Sulaymān or anyone else being the author of Book One.

There is a further possible element of mystery: the author of Book One may have been unknown even to the author of Book Two. It is certainly strange that the latter, in the evaluation of Book One that forms the preamble to his own work,[9] does not say who wrote that earlier book. Later on, when he has another chance to name the author of Book One, he seems intentionally to avoid doing so: he calls him merely "the person from whom that First Book was taken down."[10] To me there seems to be only one entirely cogent reason that the author of Book Two did not mention his predecessor's name, which is that he himself did not know it.

About the author of Book Two there is no doubt. He is there at the outset, staking his third-person claim to authorship in the book's opening words, "Abū Zayd al-Ḥasan al-Sīrāfī said . . ."[11] If we knew nothing else about him, we would know from his surname that he was from—or at least had some connection with— the city of Sīrāf on the Iranian shore of the Gulf, which for much of the third/ninth and fourth/tenth centuries was the most important port for long-distance trade across the Indian Ocean. But we do know a little more, from no less an authority than the great historian–geographer al-Masʿūdī: he met Abū Zayd in Basra and says that he "had moved there from Sīrāf in the year 303 [915–16]." Al-Masʿūdī then gives a lineage for Abū Zayd (in which the names of earlier ancestors show an Iranian ethnic origin) and adds that he was "a man of discrimination and discernment," that is, that he was a man of learning, with a well-developed critical sense.[12]

In contrast to Book One, in Book Two it is the date that is the problem. It was obviously being written well after the end of the Huang Chao rebellion in China, suppressed in 271/884, and some considerable time into the ensuing decades of anarchy; these events are reported near the beginning of the book.[13] Book Two was finished, as will become clear below, by the time al-Masʿūdī was working on his own *Meadows of Gold and Mines of Gems* (*Murūj al-dhahab wa-maʿādin al-jawhar*) in 332/943–44. But that still leaves a wide range of possible dates. We will return to the question.

There is another question to ask and to return to. Immediately after declaring his authorship, Abū Zayd says, "I have examined this foregoing book (meaning the First Book), *having been commanded* to look carefully through it, and to verify the information I find in it," and moreover to supplement it "with other reports . . . known to myself but not appearing in the book."[14] These supplementary accounts grew into Book Two. Abū Zayd undoubtedly wrote Book Two, but who was its instigator, the mysterious figure who commanded or instructed him to do so? If he was some important literary patron, why not commemorate him by name? Why hide him with a passive verb, the "anonymous" voice of the Arabic grammarians? Throughout Book Two, that nameless presence peers over the author's shoulder.

Then again Abū Zayd and his predecessor, the writer of Book One, were, strictly speaking, compilers, not authors. The material of both books came from the informants who contributed their *akhbār*, their eyewitness accounts. Other than Sulaymān the Merchant and a certain Ibn Wahb, whose report of his visit to China is incorporated into Book Two,[15] they too are nameless. But these two suggest identities for the anonymous remainder. The other contributors were almost certainly merchants like Sulaymān (rather than mere yarning sailors); they were probably from the Gulf region—Ibn Wahb was from the Iraqi port city of Basra at its head—and especially from Sīrāf, that great trans-oceanic terminus. Most important, they all seem to have visited and spent time in the places they talk about. There is a glimpse of them as a group at the end of Book Two, where the writer apologizes for his lack of information on al-Sīlā (Korea): "None of our circle of informants has ever made it there and brought back a reliable report."[16] These are the true authors, this circle of ex-expatriates, old China and India hands back home, swapping memories of far-off lands like a coterie of Sindbads—and all the more wonderful for being real characters with real stories.

The Historical Context

Those merchant-informants traveled through an open world. Arab expansion—and especially what could be called the Asianization of the Arab-Islamic polity under the Abbasid dynasty from the mid-second/eighth century on—had thrown open an eastward-facing window of trade and travel. The new age is summed up in a saying attributed to al-Manṣūr, the second Abbasid caliph and builder of Baghdad. Standing on the bank of the river of the recently founded imperial city and watching the silks and porcelain unloading, he exclaimed, "Here is the Tigris, and nothing bars the way between it and China!"[17] At the same time, and at the other end of that eastward way, the Chinese were discovering new far-western horizons, with the Tang-dynasty geographer Jia Dan describing the maritime route to Wula (al-Ubullah, ancient Apologus) at the head of the Gulf, then up to Bangda (Baghdad).[18]

The hemiglobal scope of commerce comes across in the diversity of goods described in the *Accounts*: Indian rhino horn, Tibetan musk, Gulf pearls, Chinese porcelain, Sri Lankan sapphires, Maldivian coir, Arabian and East African ambergris, Abyssinian leopard skins. It also comes across in the sheer mobility of individuals mentioned—people like the merchant from Khurasan in eastern Iran, who "made his way to the land of the Arabs, and from there to the kingdoms of the Indians, and then came to [China], all in pursuit of honorable gain," in his case from selling ivory and other luxury goods. In China, his merchandise was taken illegally by an official, but his case reached the ears of the emperor, who chastised the official concerned: "You . . . wanted [this merchant] to return by way of these same kingdoms, telling everyone in them, 'I was treated unjustly in China and my property was seized by force'!"[19] By rights, the emperor said, the official should have been put to death for his action. The message is plain: bad publicity would damage China's reputation as a stable market and a serious trading partner, and that damage would spread across the whole vast continent of Asia. Then, as now, it was supply and demand that propelled and steered the ship of trade, but it was confidence that kept it afloat.

More literally, however, what drove the ships along the "maritime Silk Road" of the Indian Ocean was the great system of winds with its annual alternating cycle, taking vessels eastward in one season and back west in another—the Arabic for "season," *mawsim*, giving English (via the Portuguese *moução/monção*) its name for that system, "monsoon."[20] The two great termini of the monsoon trade were Sīrāf in the Gulf and the Chinese city of Khānfū—which was, according to Abū Zayd, home to 120,000 foreign merchants in the later third/ninth century;[21] the ports of Kūlam Malī in southwestern India and Kalah Bār on the west coast of the Malay Peninsula were the two major havens and crucial entrepôts along the way. Of these four, Kalah Bār has never been pinpointed, while Kūlam Malī survives, sleepily, as the Keralan town of Kollam; only Khānfū remains the great emporium it was, the Chinese megalopolis of Guangzhou. As for Sīrāf, birthplace of Abū Zayd and, in a sense, of this book, it is now the site of a small village; but the village crouches on the ruins of the palaces of rich ship owners and traders, merchant princes of the monsoon who dined off the finest Chinese porcelain and whose wealth grew ever greater through that climactic third/ninth century.[22]

And then, in the last quarter of that century, disaster struck. As Abū Zayd puts it, "the trading voyages to China were abandoned and the country itself was ruined, leaving all traces of its greatness gone."[23] From 260/874 on, China was convulsed by one of those rebellions that seem to well up there every few centuries; the emperor's fears of instability came home to roost, in the heart of his palace in the Tang capital, Chang'an, captured by the rebel leader Huang Chao in 266/880. As for bad publicity, it could hardly have been worse than news of the wholesale massacre of foreign merchants in Khānfū/Guangzhou. The Gulf's direct seaborne trade with China withered away. "China," Abū Zayd goes on, "has remained in chaos down to our own times."[24] The lesser Indian trade remained, and Gulf merchants still struck deals over Chinese goods, but only at the halfway point of Kalah Bār. Book Two is haunted by the knowledge that the good old days were over.

The Literary and Cultural Context

Books of *akhbār*, oral accounts set down in writing, are very old indeed. An *akhbār* collection on the ancient Arabs attributed to the first/seventh-century ʿAbīd ibn Sharyah is, by some accounts, the oldest extant Arabic book, after the Qur'ān.[25] Moreover, the fact that this ʿAbīd was a professional storyteller demonstrates how the genre sits on the division—or maybe the elision—between spoken and written literature. And if those ancient *akhbār* had as their subject matter pre-Islamic battles and heroes, then the inspiration for the overarching theme of this book is almost equally old. Time and again, the Qur'ān tells its listeners to "go about the earth and look."[26]

Akhbār, then, are supposedly verbatim oral reportage, a secular parallel to the literature of hadith, which records the sayings and doings of the Prophet Muhammad and his Companions. And although a full-scale science of *akhbār* never developed as it did for hadith, there was some attempt at classification. Al-Masʿūdī, for example, identifies two types of oral report, those that are on everyone's tongues and those that have been passed down a chain of narrators.[27] He also neatly defines *akhbār* by what they are not: his own book is one of *khabar*, not of *baḥth* and *naẓar*—that is, it presents facts as they are reported but does not analyze them through research and investigation.[28] In other words, *akhbār*, like journalism today, were seen as the first draft of history—and, in the case of *Accounts of China and India*, of geography, ethnology, economics, zoology, and much else besides.

All this means that there is an immediacy to the information. Particularly in Book Two, there are snippets of "writerly" commentary that stitch together the patchwork of accounts, but most of the text has the feel of having been told and taken down directly. An example is the account, mentioned above, of the aggrieved merchant. First, Abū Zayd has his word as literary anchorman—"The Chinese used to monitor their own system, in the old days, that is, before its deterioration in the present time, with a rigor unheard of elsewhere"—but he then gives the nod to his informant, who launches straight into his tale: "A certain man from Khurasan . . . came to Iraq . . ."[29] And the tale spools out spontaneously, occasionally getting lost in its own subordinate clauses as we all do when we speak. To listen to these accounts is to hear the unedited voice of oral history.

"Unedited" does not mean "unrehearsed": as with all travelers' tales, the accounts had no doubt already acquired a polish in the telling and retelling. Nor is it likely to mean "verbatim," for Abū Zayd and his anonymous predecessor probably further burnished their informants' grammar, syntax, and vocabulary. Despite this, some of the language is slightly wayward. It is not bad Arabic, as the French scholar Ferrand claimed;[30] rather, it preserves features of the spoken Arabic that it represents on the page—even today, actual spoken Arabic is nearly always standardized before it goes down on paper. The multiplicity of contributors and the duality of compilers also make for occasional repetitions and very occasional contradictions.[31] Geographically and thematically, too, although the compilers did their best to organize the material, the book as a whole is no disciplined Baedeker—it has more in common, in fact, with the online, interactive travel websites of our own age—nor, of course, does it have the neatness of a discrete journey by a single traveler. Instead, it weaves the threads and fragments of many journeys together into a text that, for its size, must be one of the richest in all the literature of travel and geography.

There is a danger, with all this richness and denseness, of losing one's audience. The leaps from India to China and back, the excursions to Sarbuzah and the Islands of Silver, the sidetracks into the lives of Shaivite saddhus and *devadasi* prostitutes could all be too disorienting for readers back in Basra or Baghdad. But there are always cultural "navigation aids." Inevitably, some of them do not work for us, the readers of more than a millennium later: who, for example, were the Kanīfiyyah and the Jalīdiyyah, to whom rival Indian gangs are compared?[32] Perhaps the Sharks and the Jets of fourth/tenth-century Iraq; the precise reference seems to be lost. But there is also the enduring cultural compass of Islam and Arabdom.[33] It orients the traveler to what he sees, how he sees it, and how he reports it, and the reader to how he receives the report. It works on many levels, from the way the Chinese urinate (standing, not squatting) and why,[34] to interpretations of Buddhist iconography.[35] This constant guiding presence not only enables the traveler-traders—merchants in musk and silk and porcelain, but also in knowledge—to make cultural translations for their immediate audience back home. For us, their audience removed in time, it points not just to where those travelers got to but also to where they came from.

It also may explain a few cases in which the informants' vision is apparently distorted. An example is that of Ibn Wahb's audience with the Tang emperor. Assuming the meeting did in fact take place—and Abū Zayd, that scholar of discrimination and discernment, accepted that it did—would the emperor, in his palace at the heart of the Middle Kingdom, the navel of the civilized earth, really have viewed Baghdad, the barbarian Bangda, as the center of the world and the Abbasid caliph as above him in the international order of precedence?[36] Perhaps he (or his interpreter) was being exceedingly diplomatic. Or perhaps Ibn Wahb was doing what later, European, writers were to do, notably the author of the travels of Sir John Mandeville, in that dubious knight's even more dubious audience with the Mamluk sultan:[37] using the figure of the wise infidel king to make a point about one's own society.

There was certainly a point to be made in the third/ninth century—that the still young Arab-Islamic civilization of the West had not only joined the club of Asian cultures but had also outstripped its ancient fellow members in global importance. If this is indeed the subtext of that strange imperial pronouncement, then it is made more subtly and more eloquently, not by emperors but by unknown merchants, on every page of this book: for it is a book that tells us, by reflex, so to speak, as much about the energy and enterprise of Islam in that age as it does about China and India.

Abū Zayd and Al-Masʿūdī

Al-Masʿūdī, the Herodotus of the Arabs, as he is often and aptly called, was quoted above on Abū Zayd and on the meaning of *akhbār*. Those quotations are from his main surviving work, *Meadows of Gold and Mines of Gems*. But there is more to be said on the relationship between the two authors and their works, for significant portions of the material in *Accounts of China and India* appear also in the pages of al-Masʿūdī. Who got what from whom?

There is, of course, no question about matter taken from Book One, finished some eighty years before al-Masʿūdī was working on his *Meadows of Gold*. Regarding information appearing in our Book Two and in *Meadows of Gold*, however, the picture is more complicated. Commentators have homed in on the meeting between the two authors, which they have placed in the years soon after Abū Zayd's move to Basra in 303/915–16; the meeting, in Miquel's analysis, enabled Abū Zayd to pass on to al-Masʿūdī the information contained in the full and finished *Accounts*.[38] This looks at first like a reasonable assumption, and it would, if correct, give a rough date of the early 310s/920s for the compilation of our Book Two. Certainly as regards the flow of information, it appears to be from Abū Zayd to al-Masʿūdī: the latter's language is the more polished, his organization of the material much better planned; Abū Zayd's work is the raw original from which he has drawn.[39] The only snag is that in the case of one *khabar*, the macabre story of an Indian who cuts pieces off his own liver before burning himself to death, al-Masʿūdī states that he himself witnessed the scene in India in 304/916–17.[40] If we take al-Masʿūdī's bona fides as read, and if we accept that the details of the story are so bizarre and precise that it is unlikely that another witness would independently have given the story to Abū Zayd, then it seems possible that al-Masʿūdī himself is one of the anonymous informants of the *Accounts*.

To those two pending questions, concerning the date of Book Two and the identity of its patron or instigator, there are no firm answers to be drawn from all this, but there are some comments to be made:

1. The meeting between al-Masʿūdī and Abū Zayd, whenever it happened, does not provide a fixed terminal date for the *Accounts*. The final version of the book might have been put together at any time up until 332/943–44, the year in which al-Masʿūdī was writing his *Meadows of Gold*.
2. There seems to have been a two-way exchange of information between the two men at their face-to-face meeting. Ultimately, however, by far the greater flow of material was from Abū Zayd to al-Masʿūdī.
3. Al-Masʿūdī was a busy writer: *Meadows of Gold*, which runs to over 1,500 pages of Arabic in the edition I have, is the smallest of three compendious works that he wrote (the other two seem to be lost),[41] quite apart from at least one other single-volume book. He would probably have been more than happy to make use of material amassed over the years by Abū Zayd, the patient and discriminating collector of *akhbār*.
4. Lastly—and this is no more than a hunch founded on circumstantial evidence—it might be that al-Masʿūdī himself is that shadowy figure who "commanded" Abū Zayd to check through and supplement Book One, thus providing more rough gems to be mined, cut, polished, and inserted into his own more finely wrought *Meadows of Gold*.

The Literary Legacy

Al-Masʿūdī was not the only writer to delve into the *Accounts*' rich lode of data. Other writers were to draw from it—either directly, via al-Masʿūdī, or via each other—for centuries to come. They include some celebrated names in Arabic geography: Ibn Khurradādhbih, who, as early as the third/ninth century, borrowed from Book One material on the maritime route east; in the fourth/tenth, Ibn al-Faqīh and Ibn Rustah; later on, al-Idrīsī and al-Qazwīnī; and, later still, the ninth/fifteenth-century Ibn al-Wardī.

For centuries, then, the *Accounts* was the mother lode of information on the further Orient. There are several reasons. First, after that catastrophic Chinese rebellion in the later third/ninth century, there was little direct contact between the Arab world and China until the time of the cosmopolitan Mongol dynasty, the Yuan, in the seventh/thirteenth and eighth/fourteenth centuries. In the meantime, concerning the subcontinent of India and the rest of the Indian Ocean world, the only other sources of information were either suspect or, in one case, so abstrusely detailed as to be off-putting.

At the head of the first category is al-Rāmhurmuzī's *Wonders of India* from about the year 390/1000, in which the yarning sailors are finally given their say. In fact, many useful matters of fact do lurk in its picturesque jungles of legend, but a process of fabulation had clearly set in that would reach its climax in the Sindbad tales. Alone in the second category is the work of the highly serious early-fifth/eleventh-century indologist al-Bīrūnī. Faced, however, by chapter headings loaded with Sanskrit terms, such as "An Explanation of the Terms 'Adhimāsa,' 'Ūnarātra,' and the 'Ahargaṇas,'"[42] geographical encyclopedists, such as Yāqūt and al-Qazwīnī, must have scratched their heads.

In contrast, the material of the *Accounts* is reliable, valuable, and accessible. For a true successor to those traveling merchants of information, the Arabic reading world would have to wait until Ibn Baṭṭūṭah in the eighth/fourteenth century. As Miquel has said, that curious, objective, and tolerant traveler is their true heir.[43]

The Legacy Endures

Today, the *Accounts* is not only a major repository of historical information; it also shows us what endures. Much of the book may be literally exotic, but it is also strangely familiar (or, perhaps, familiarly strange): the irrepressible

Indianness of India, with its castes and saddhus and suttees; the industrious orderliness of China, whatever the period and the political complexion, punctuated by paroxysms of revolution. The *Accounts* reminds us how those ancient civilizations mark time by the *longue durée*; how, as Jan Morris has said, "a century . . . [is] an eternity by British standards, a flicker of the eye by Chinese."[44]

Perhaps above all, the *Accounts* shows us a world—at least an Old World—already interconnected. It is composed of meshing economies, in which, even if communications were slower, repercussions of events were no less profound. Because of a rebellion in China, not only does a Tang emperor lose his throne, but the ladies of Baghdad, a 12,000-kilometer journey away, lose their silks,[45] and the brokers and merchant skippers of equally distant Sīrāf—the men who make the cogs of the economy turn—lose their jobs.[46]

Shades, or foreshadowings, of subprime-mortgage default in the United States and real-estate agents fleeing distant Dubai.

A Note on the Text

The Arabic Edition

The printed Arabic edition preserves some nonstandard orthographic features of the manuscript, at least where they do not hinder comprehension. It is hard to determine whether these features can be ascribed to the originally oral nature of the material and/or to that polymorphous creature known as "Middle Arabic," or simply to waywardness of orthography. Some forms are consistent: *jazāyir*, "islands," always appears thus, never in the standard written form *jazā'ir*; this is likely to represent a spoken version. Most of the inconsistencies also have to do with the appearance or nonappearance of *hamzah*s. Two examples suffice: *shay'*, "thing," can appear both with and without its *hamzah*, even in the same phrase. And the word for "(the) pearls" is written in at least three ways. Taking these at face value—whatever sounds the writer intended them to represent—these include *al-lu'luwu*, *al-luwulu'u*, and *al-luwulū*, but never the standard written form *al-lu'lu'u*.

Otherwise, *hamzah*s have been placed on *alif*s, where necessary. A few obvious inconsistencies have been silently corrected: for example, the toponym Lanjabālūs first appears thus; later, when it reappears as two words and with different, and erroneous, pointing, it is brought into conformity with its first appearance. Occasionally, letters in the manuscript are left undotted; dots have been supplied silently where there could be no argument over the correct reading. Quite a lot of the manuscript is vocalized. Significant vocalizations have been retained and others added, where they might help readers.

A few proper names have been amended in the body of the text. My policy has been, where a name seems dubious and a commonly attested form exists, to use that (e.g., the Sea of Lārawī, for the manuscript's Dlāruwī), and where a name is unidentifiable and probably corrupt, to use a likely alternative (e.g., the Indian king Dahmā—probably = Dharma[-pāla]—where the manuscript has Ruhmā). Such changes are few, and all but two are in Book One; they are indicated in the footnotes.

Also indicated in the footnotes are divergences from the previous printed editions referred to, where they are of substance. Another, more occasional function of the footnotes to the Arabic text is to suggest alternative readings for phrases or words whose interpretation is problematic.

Where section titles and divisions appear in the manuscript, these are retained. Many more section divisions have been introduced; all but the shortest sections have been further divided into paragraphs, and extra section titles have been inserted.

The English Translation

The Arabic of the *Accounts* is often compressed, especially in Book One. In a translation that aims for clarity and ease of reading, interpolations are needed. Many are of a minor nature, for example, conjunctions (in which Arabic tends to be poor) and clarifications of whom or what a pronoun refers to. Interpolations of greater substance have at times been necessary to help the text make sense. English versions of two short quotations from the Qurʾān are this translator's own.

The Manuscript

There is a single known manuscript of *Akhbār al-ṣīn wa-l-hind* (catalogued as Arabe 2281 in the Bibliothèque Nationale, Paris). Although this was copied towards the end of the sixth/twelfth century, nearly three hundred years after the book was compiled, it has an air of authenticity: its syntax, grammar, and orthography are not always strictly standard, and this points back to the essentially oral character of the original accounts. In other words, it seems that little attempt has been made by copyists to force the text into a more literary mould. The manuscript is written in a clear and (mostly) easily legible hand. It does, however, lack its first few leaves and has some other obvious lacunae. Also, certain proper names, particularly in Book One, are undoubtedly corrupt.

Previous Arabic Editions

The *Accounts* was first published in 1845 in an edition, with annotated French translation, by Reinaud; the Arabic text of this edition had previously been printed, but not circulated, by Langlès, in 1811.[47] In 1948, Sauvaget published a new edition and translation, with detailed notes, but only of Book One. More recent Arabic editions of Books One and Two together are those of Khūrī (listed in the bibliography under "al-Tājir") and al-Ḥibshī; these appear, however, to derive from the published editions of Sauvaget and Reinaud rather than directly from the manuscript. To the present editor's knowledge, therefore, this is the first entirely new Arabic edition of the *Accounts* in more than two centuries.[48]

Previous Translations

The only other English version of the *Accounts* was published in London in 1733 as *Ancient Accounts of India and China by Two Mohammedan Travellers, Who Went to Those Parts in the Ninth Century*; the translator's name does not appear on the title page. It has been reprinted as recently as 1995, in New Delhi. This version was done, however, not from the Arabic but from a French translation of 1718 by Abbé Eusèbe Renaudot. Sauvaget judged Renaudot's version to be good for its period though marred by "too many errors in reading and interpretation."[49] Despite improvements on the translations of both Renaudot and Reinaud, a new French version published in 1922 by Ferrand was also deemed by Sauvaget to include erroneous readings and interpretations, particularly in the field of geography.[50] This is, therefore, the first new English translation of the *Accounts* in nearly three centuries and the first made directly from the Arabic.

Sigla

ب	Paris MS Arabe 2281
ح	al-Ḥibshī
خ	Khūrī (= al-Tājir in the bibliography)
ر	Reinaud
س	Sauvaget

Notes to the Introduction

1 2.15.2.

2 2.19.1.

3 Pellat, *The Life and Works of Jāḥiẓ*, 172–73.

4 2.19.1.

5 2.1.1.

6 Cf. Sauvaget, *Relation de la Chine et de l'Inde*, xxiv–xxv n. 8.

7 Sauvaget, *Relation*, xix and n. 7.

8 1.3.1.

9 2.1.1.

10 2.15.1.

11 2.1.1.

12 Al-Masʿūdī, *Murūj al-dhahab wa-maʿādin al-jawhar*, 1:145.

13 2.2.1.

14 2.1.1

15 2.4.1.

16 1.10.11.

17 Al-Ṭabarī, quoted in Mackintosh-Smith, *Landfalls*, 170.

18 Quoted in Zhang, "Relations between China and the Arabs in Early Times," 93.

19 2.9.1.

20 Yule and Burnell, *Hobson-Jobson: The Anglo-Indian Dictionary*, s.v. "Monsoon."

21 2.2.1.

22 On excavations at Sīrāf, see Hourani, *Arab Seafaring in the Indian Ocean in Ancient and Early Medieval Times*, 140–41.

23 2.2.1.

24 2.2.2.

25 Adūnīs, *Al-Thābit wa-l-mutaḥawwil*, 4:269 n.12.

26 For example, «Go about the earth and look at how He [God] originated creation.» Q ʿAnkabūt 29:20.

27 Al-Masʿūdī, *Murūj*, 2:228–29.

28 Al-Masʿūdī, *Murūj*, 2:299.

29 2.9.1.

30 Cf. Sauvaget, *Relation*, xxi.

31 E.g., do Indian kings pay their troops (1.7.1), or not (1.10.8)?

32 2.10.2.

33 Miquel (*Géographie humaine du monde musulman*, 1:121) used a different metaphor, of Islam as the watermark running through the pages of the book, "*l'Islam y est toujours vu en filigrane.*" That does not seem to give it enough prominence.

34 2.9.6.

35 2.4.3.

36 2.4.2.

37 Moseley, *The Travels of Sir John Mandeville*, 107–8.

38 Miquel, *Géographie*, 1:121–22 n. 4.

39 Occasionally, there are additional details of substance in al-Masʿūdī's renderings of information in the *Accounts*, such as the term *balānjarī* applied to the suicidal courtiers in India (*Murūj*, 1:211), and the number of Turkic troops fighting against Huang Chao, said to be 400,000 (*Murūj*, 1:139).

40 Al-Masʿūdī, *Murūj*, 1:210–11. Cf. 2.10.1.

41 Al-Masʿūdī, *Murūj*, 1:7–8.

42 Al-Bīrūnī, *Albêrûnî's India*, 424.

43 Miquel, *Géographie*, 1:126.

44 Morris, *Hong Kong*, 230.

45 2.2.1.

46 2.2.3.

47 Sauvaget, *Relation*, xvii.

48 Another edition exists, by Yūsuf al-Shārūnī (Cairo: al-Dār al-Miṣriyyah al-Lubnāniyyah, 1999), but the present editor has been unable to obtain a copy.

49 Sauvaget, *Relation*, xvi.

50 Sauvaget, *Relation*, xvii.

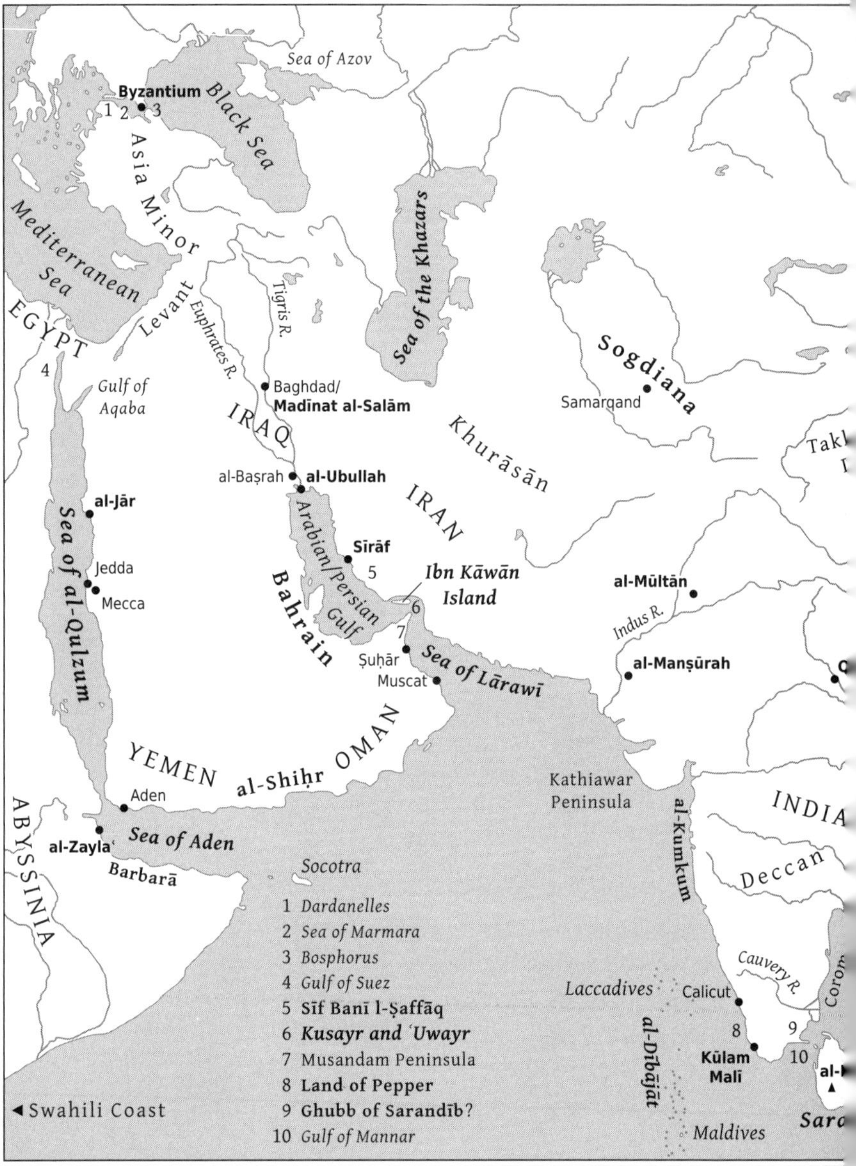

The Lands and Seas of Abū Zayd's *Accounts*

Muscat	Settlement/locality	OMAN	Land/country	*Maldives*	Isla
		Levant	Region/landscape	*Black Sea*	Sea

Obsolete or archaic forms of toponyms, found in the text, are shown in bold (e.g. **al-Jār**). Place names with tentative locations are followed by a question mark (e.g. ***Maljān***?).

0 200 400 600 800 1000 km

Design: Tim Mackintosh-Smith
Cartography: Martin Grosch

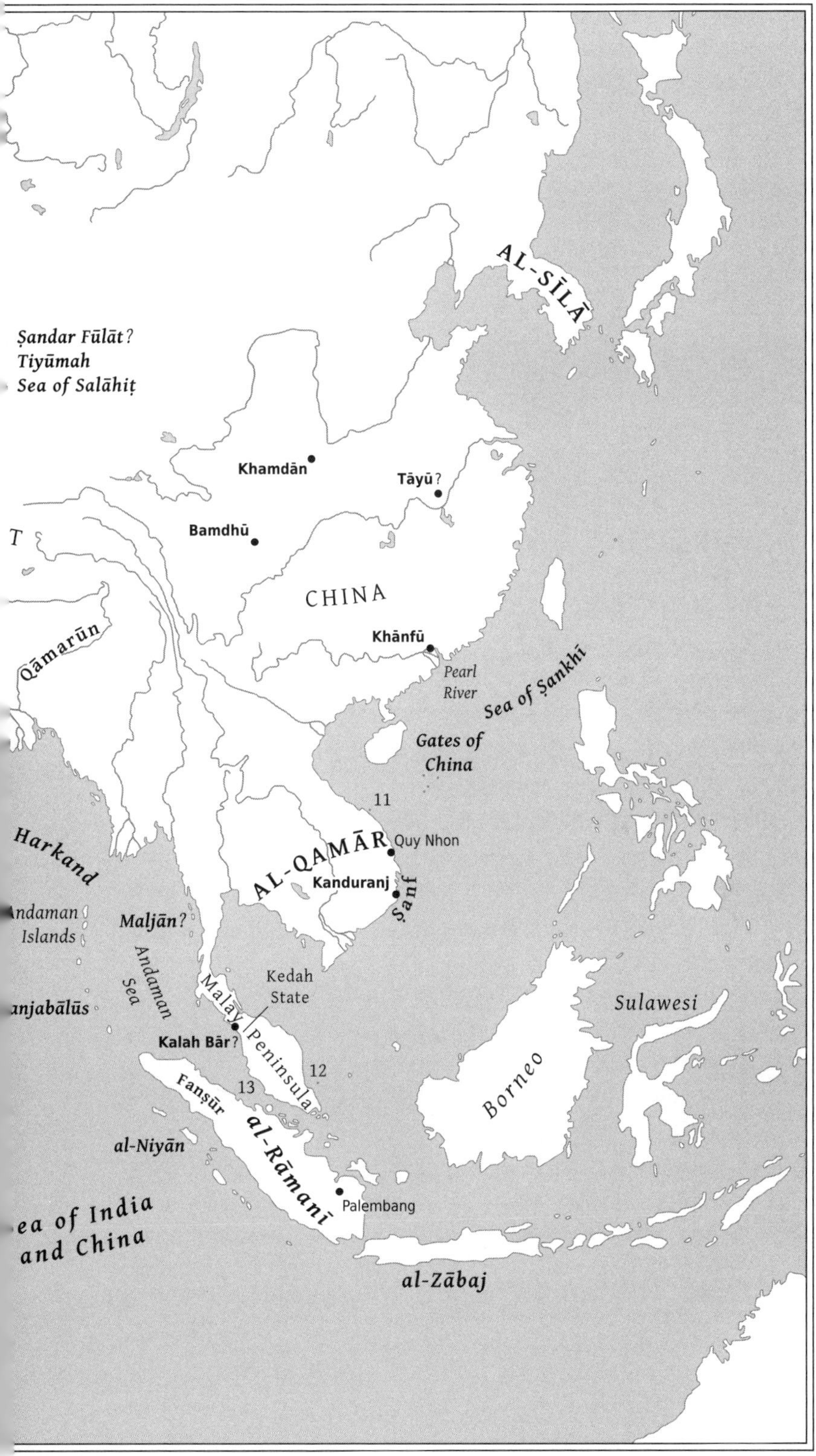

AL-SĪLĀ
Ṣandar Fūlāt?
Tiyūmah
Sea of Salāhiṭ
Khamdān
Tāyū?
Bamdhū
T
CHINA
Qāmarūn
Khānfū
Pearl
River
Sea of Ṣankhī
Gates of
China
11
Harkand
AL-QAMĀR
Quy Nhon
Kanduranj
Ṣanf
Andaman
Islands
Maljān?
Andaman
Sea
Kedah
State
Malay
Peninsula
anjabālūs
Kalah Bār?
12
13
Fanṣūr
al-Rāmanī
al-Niyān
Palembang
Borneo
Sulawesi
Sea of India
and China
al-Zābaj

١،١،١ . . .[١] مثل الشراع. وربّما رفع رأسه . . .[٢] فتراه كالشيء العظيم. وربّما نفخ الماء من فيه فيكون كالمنارة العظيمة. فإذا سكن البحر اجتمع السمك نحواه بذنبه ثمّ يفتح فمه فيُرى السمك في جوفه يغيض كأنّه يغيض[٣] في بير. والمراكب التي تكون في البحر تخافه فهم يضربون بالليل بنواقيس مثل نواقيس النصارى مخافة أن تتّكئ على المركب فتغرقه.

٢،١،١ وفي هذا البحر سمكة اصطدناها يكون طولها عشرين ذراعاً فشققنا بطنها فأخرجنا منها أيضاً سمكة من جنسها. ثمّ شققنا بطن الثانية فإذا في بطنها مثلُها وكلّ هذا حيّ يضطرب يشبه بعضه بعضاً في الصورة. ولهذا السمك الكبير الذي يُدعى الوال[٤] مع عظم خلقه سمكة تُدعى اللَّشَك طولها قدر ذراع فإذا طَغَتْ السمكة وبَغَتْ وآذَتْ السمك في البحر سُلِّطت عليها هذه السمكة الصغيرة فصارت في أصل أذنها ولا تفارقها حتّى تقتلها. وتلتزق بالمركب فلا تقرب المركبَ هذه السمكة الكبيرة فَرَقاً[٥] من الصغيرة.

٣،١،١ وفي هذا البحر أيضاً سمكة يحكي وجهها وجه الإنسان تطير فوق الماء واسم هذا السمك المِيج. وسمك آخر من تحت الماء يرصده حتّى إذا سقط ابتلعه. ويُسمّى هذا السمك العَنقَتُوس. والسمك كلّه يأكل بعضه بعضاً.

١،٢،١ البحر الثالث بحر هَرْكَنْد. بينه وبين بحر لارَوِي[٦] جزاير كثيرة يقال إنّها ألف وتسع ماية جزيرة. وهي فرق ما بين هذين البحرين لاروي وهركند. وهذه الجزاير تملكها

---

١ الجزء الأوّل لـ ب مبتور بما فيه الحديث عن البحر الأوّل وبداية الحديث عن البحر الثاني. ٢ بياض في ب؛ ح وس: [عن الماء]. ٣ خ: يغوص كأنه يغوص؛ س: يغيص كأنّه يغيص. ٤ خ: البال. ٥ س: مرقًا.
٦ ب هنا وفيما بعد: دلارُوى.

Accounts of China and India: The First Book

. . . like a sail.[2] It often raises its head above the water, and then you can see what an enormous thing it is. It also often blows water from its mouth, and the water spouts up like a great lighthouse.[3] When the sea is calm and the fish shoal together, it gathers them in with its tail then opens its mouth, and the fish can be seen in its gullet, sinking down into its depths as if into a well.[4] The ships that sail this sea are wary of it, and at night the crews bang wooden clappers like those used by the Christians, for fear that one of them will blunder into their ship and capsize it.[5] 1.1.1

The Sea of Lārawī[1]

In this sea there is also a kind of fish that reaches twenty cubits in length.[6] We caught one of these and split open its belly. Inside it was another fish of the same genus. We took this second fish out then split its belly open too—and there inside it was yet another fish of the same type! All of them were alive and flapping about, and they all resembled each other in form. This great fish is called the *wāl*. Huge though it is, there is another fish called the *lashak*, about a cubit in length, and if the *wāl* fish becomes so excessively greedy as to endanger the survival of the other fish in the sea, this small *lashak* fish is sent to overcome it. This it does by entering the inner ear of the *wāl* and not letting go until it has caused the *wāl*'s death. The *lashak* also attaches itself to ships, so the great fish do not go near ships, for fear of these smaller fish. 1.1.2

In this sea there is also a kind of fish whose face resembles that of a human and that flies over the water. The name of these fish is *mīj*. Another kind of fish watches out for it from beneath the surface of the water, and when the *mīj* falls back into the water, this second fish swallows it. It is called *ʿanqatūs*. All fish eat each other. 1.1.3

The Sea of Harkand

The third sea is the Sea of Harkand. Between it and the Sea of Lārawī there are many islands. They are said to be 1900 in number, and they are the boundary between these two seas, of Lārawī and Harkand. These islands are 1.2.1

The islands of al-Dībājāt and Sarandīb

امرأة. ويقع في هذه الجزاير عنبر عظيم القدر فتقع القطعة مثل البيت ونحوه. وهذا عنبرٌ ينبت في قعر البحر نباتًا. فإذا اشتدّ هيجان البحر قذفه من قعره مثل الفطر والكمأة. وهذه الجزاير التي تملكها المرأة عامرةٌ بنخل النارجيل. وبُعد ما بين الجزيرة والجزيرة فرسخان وثلاثة وأربعة وكلّها عامرة بالناس والنارجيل. ومالُهم الوَدَع وهذه الملكة تدّخر الودع في خزاينها. ويقال إنّ أهل هذه الجزيرة[1] لا يكون أصنع منهم حتّى أنّهم يعملون القميص مفروغًا منه نسجًا بالكمّين والدِخْرِيصَين والجيب. ويبنون السفن والبيوت ويعملون ساير الأعمال على هذا النسق من الصنعة. والودع يأتيهم على وجه الماء وفيه روح فتؤخذ سعفة من سعف النارجيل فتُطرَح على وجه الماء فيتعلّق فيها الودع. وهم يدعونه الكَبْتَج.[2]

وآخر هذه الجزاير سَرَنْديب في بحر هركند وهي رأس هذه الجزاير كلّها وهم يدعونها الدِيباجات.[3] وبسرنديب[4] منها مغاص اللؤلو بحرها كلّه حولها. وفي أرضها جبل يُدعى الرَهون[5] وعليه هَبَطَ آدم عليه السلام وقَدَمُهُ في صفا رأس هذا الجبل منغمسة في الحجر. في رأس هذا الجبل قدم واحدة ويقال إنّه عليه السلام خطا خطوة أخرى في البحر. ويقال إنّ هذه القدم التي على رأس الجبل نحو من سبعين ذراعًا. وحول هذا الجبل معدن الجوهر الياقوت الأحمر والأصفر والأَسْمانْجُونيّ. وفي هذه الجزيرة مَلِكان. وهي جزيرة عظيمة عريضة فيها العود والذهب والجوهر. وفي بحرها اللؤلو والشَنْك وهو هذا البوق الذي يُنفَخ فيه ممّا يدّخرونه. ٢،٢،١

وفي هذا البحر إذا رُكِبَ إلى سرنديب جزاير ليست بالكثيرة غير أنّها واسعة لا تُضْبَط. منها جزيرة يقال لها الرامِني فيها عدّة ملوك وسعتها يقال ثمانماية أو تسعماية فرسخ وفيها معادن الذهب وفيها معادن تُدعى فَنْصُور يكون الكافور الجيّد منها. ٣،٢،١

١ كذا في ب؛ خ و س: هذه الجزائر. ٢ ح: الكبتح؛ س: الكَسْتَج. ٣ ب: الديبجات. ٤ س: و[بجانب].
٥ ب: الرُهُون.

ruled by a woman. Ambergris of enormous size is washed up on the shores of these islands, and a single piece of it can be as big as a room, or thereabouts. This ambergris grows on the seabed as a plant does, and if the sea becomes rough, it is cast up from the bottom as if it were mushrooms or truffles.[7] These islands that the woman rules are planted with coconut palms. The distance between one island and the next is two, three, or four *farsakh*s, and all of them are inhabited and planted with coconuts. They use cowries for money, and their queen stores them up in her treasuries. It is said that there are no people more skilled in manufacturing than the people of this island group and that they can even produce a finished shirt on the loom, woven complete with sleeves, gores, and a placket at the neck. In their construction of ships and houses, too, as in all their other work, they reach the same level of technical perfection. The cowries, which have an animal spirit,[8] come to them on the surface of the water. A coconut-palm frond is used to collect them: it is placed on the surface of the water, and the cowries attach themselves to it. They call them *kabtaj*.

The last of these islands is Sarandīb, in the Sea of Harkand. It is the chief **1.2.2**
of all these islands, which they call al-Dībājāt. At Sarandīb is the place where they dive for pearls.[9] The sea entirely surrounds the island.[10] In the territory of Sarandīb is a mountain called al-Rahūn. It is on this that Adam descended, eternal peace be upon him, and his footprint is on the bare rock of the summit of this mountain, impressed in the stone. There is only one footprint at the summit of this mountain, but it is said that Adam, eternal peace be upon him, took another step into the sea. It is said, too, that the footprint on the summit of this mountain is about seventy cubits long.[11] Around this mountain lies the area where gems are mined—rubies, yellow sapphires, and blue sapphires. In this island there are two kings.[12] It is a large and extensive island in which aloewood,[13] gold, and gems are to be found, while in the sea surrounding it there are pearls and chanks, which are those trumpets that are blown and which they keep in their treasuries.[14]

The islands of the Sea of Harkand

Crossing this sea to Sarandīb, one finds islands that, although not many, **1.2.3**
are so great in extent that their exact size is unknown. One of them is an island called al-Rāmanī. It is ruled by several kings, and its extent is said to be eight hundred or nine hundred *farsakh*s. It has places where gold is mined and, in an area known as Fanṣūr, sources from which the high-grade sort of camphor comes.[15]

١،٢،٤ ولهذه الجزاير جزاير تليها منها جزيرة يقال لها النِيَان لهم ذهبٌ كثير وأكلُهم النارجيل وبه يتأدّمون ويدّهنون. وإذا أراد أحد منهم أن يتزوّج لم يُزَوَّج إلاّ بِقِحْف رأسِ رجل من أعدايهم. فإذا قتل اثنين زُوِّجَ اثنتين وكذلك إن قتل خمسين زُوِّجَ خمسين امرأة بخمسين قحفاً. وسبب ذلك أنّ أعداءهم كثير فمَن أقدم على القتل أكثر كان رغبتهم فيه أوفر. وفي هذه الجزيرة أعني الرامني فيلة كثيرة وفيها البَقَّم والخيزران وفيها قوم يأكلون الناس. وهي تشرَعُ على بحرين هركند وسَلاهِط.[١]

١،٢،٥ وبعد هذا جزاير تُدعى لَنْجَبالُوس. وفيها خلق كثير عراة الرجال منهم والنساء غير أنّ على عورة المرأة ورقاً من ورق الشجر. فإذا مرّت بهم المراكب جاءوا إليها بالقوارب الصغار والكبار وبايعوا أهلَها العنبر والنارجيل بالحديد وما يحتاجون إليه من كسوة لأنّه لا حرّ عندهم ولا برد.[٢]

ومن وراء هؤلاء جزيرتان بينهما بحر يقال له[٣] أَنْدَمان. وأهلهما يأكلون الناس أحياءً. وهم سود مفلفلو الشعور مناكير الوجوه والأعين طوال الأرجل قدمُ[٤] أحدهم مثل الذراع يعني ذَكَرَه[٥] عراة. ليست لهم قوارب ولو كانت لهم لأكلوا كلّ من مرّ بهم. وربّما أبطأت المراكب في البحر وتأخّر بهم المسير بسبب الريح فينفذ ما في المراكب من الماء فيقربون إلى هؤلاء فيستقون الماء وربّما أصابوا منهم ويفلتون أكثر.

١،٢،٦ وبعد هذه الجزيرة[٦] جبال ليست على الطريق يقال إنّ فيها معادن فضّة. وليست بمسكونة وليس كلّ مركب يريدها يصيبها. وإنّما دلّ عليها جبل منها يقال له الخُشْنامي مرّ به مركب فرأوا الجبل فقصدوا له. فلمّا أصبحوا انحدروا إليه في قارب ليحتطبوا وأوقدوا ناراً فانسكبت الفضّة فعلموا أنّه معدن. فاحتملوا ما أرادوا منه فلمّا ركبوا اشتدّ عليهم البحر فرموا بجميع ما أخذوا منه. ثمّ تجهّز الناس بعد

١ ب: شلاهط. ٢ كذا في ب؛ س: وما يحتاجون من كسوة . . . ولعلّ الصواب: وما يحتاجون إليه من كسوة وهو قليل لأنّه لا حرّ عندهم ولا برد. ٣ كذا في ب؛ س: لهما. ٤ س: فَرْج. ٥ الكلمتان ساقطتان من خ. ٦ كذا في ب؛ خ: هاتين الجزيرتين؛ س: هذه الجزائر.

These large islands have other smaller islands in their vicinity. One of these is an island called al-Niyān, whose inhabitants have much gold. They live on coconuts, also using them as a condiment and as the source of an oil to apply to their skin. If one of them wishes to marry, he is only allowed to do so in return for a skull taken from one of their enemies. If he kills two of the enemy, he marries two women. Similarly, if he kills fifty, he marries fifty woman in return for the fifty skulls. The reason for this is that they have so many enemies that the more of them a man dares to kill, the more desirable they find him. In this island—I mean al-Rāmanī—there are many elephants, and also sapan wood and rattans.[16] There is also a tribe who eat people. The island faces two seas, those of Harkand and Salāhiṭ. 1.2.4

After al-Rāmanī lies a group of islands called Lanjabālūs. In them live a numerous people who are naked, both the men and the women, except that the women have the leaves of trees covering their pudenda. When the merchants' ships pass by, these people come out to them in boats both small and large to barter with the crews, exchanging ambergris and coconuts for iron and such coverings as they need for their bodies, as it is neither hot nor cold in their land.[17] 1.2.5

Beyond these people are two islands separated by a sea that is called Andamān. Their inhabitants eat people alive. They are black and have frizzy hair,[18] hideous faces and eyes, and long feet—the foot of one of them is about a cubit long (meaning his penis)[19]—and they are naked. They have no boats, and if they did, they would eat anyone who passed by them.[20] It sometimes happens that ships make a slow passage and are delayed in their voyage because of unfavorable winds. As a result, the ships' water runs out, and their crews make for these people's islands to get water. When this happens, the islanders often catch some of the crew, although most of them get away.

After this island group, there are some rocky islets lying off the route the ships follow. It is said that there are silver mines in them. They are uninhabited, and not every ship that makes for them is able to find them. In fact they were only discovered when a ship passed one of the islets, which is called al-Khushnāmī, spotted it, and made for it. When day broke, the crew went ashore in a boat to gather firewood. They kindled a fire, and molten silver flowed from the ground, at which they realized that it was a source of the metal. They carried off with them as much as they wanted. When they set sail, however, the sea grew stormy, and they had to throw overboard all 1.2.6

ذلك إلى هذا الجبل فلم يعرفوه. ومثل هذا في البحر كثير لا يُحصى من جزاير ممنوعة لا يعرفها البحريّون فمنها ما لا يقدرون عليه.

وربّما رُءي في هذا البحر سحاب أبيض يظلّ المراكب فيشرع منه لسان طويل رقيق حتّى يلصق ذلك اللسان بماء البحر فيغلي له ماء البحر مثل الزوبعة. فإذا أدركت الزوبعة المركبَ ابتلعته. ثمّ يرتفع ذلك السحاب فيمطر مطرًا فيه قذى البحر فلا أدري أيستقي السحاب من البحر أم كيف هذا. ١،٢،٧

وكلّ بحر من هذه البحار تهيج فيه ريح تثيره وتهيجه حتّى يغلي كغليان القدور فيقذف ما فيه إلى الجزاير التي فيه ويكسر المراكب ويقذف السمك الميّت الكبار العظام. وربّما قذف الصخور والجبال كما يقذف القوسُ السهمَ.

وأمّا بحر هركند فله ريح غير هذه ما بين المغرب إلى بنات نَعْش. فيغلي لها البحر كغليان القدور ويقذف العنبر الكثير وكلّما كان البحر أغزر وأبعد قعرًا كان العنبر أجود. وهذا البحر أعني هركند إذا عظمت أمواجه تراه مثل النار يتّقد. وفي هذا البحر سمك يُدعى اللُخَم وهو سبعٌ يبتلع الناس ...[١]

في أيديهم ...[٢] فيقلّ المتاع. ومن أسباب قلّة المتاع حريق ربّما وقع بخانْفُو[٣] وهو مرفأ السفن ومجتمع تجارات العرب وأهل الصين. فيأتي الحريق على المتاع وذلك أنّ بيوتهم هناك من خشب ومن قنا مشقّق. ومن أسباب ذلك أن تنكسر المراكب الصادرة والواردة أو يُنهَبوا أو يضطرّوا إلى المقام الطويل فيبيعوا المتاع في غير بلاد العرب. وربّما رمت بهم الريح إلى اليمن أو غيرها فيبيعون المتاع هناك. وربّما أطالوا الإقامة لإصلاح مراكبهم وغير ذلك من العلل. ١،٣،١

---

١ هنا نهاية ورقة في ب ويبدو أنّ ورقة أو أكثر قد انبترت من الأصل نظرًا إلى التغيّر المفاجئ لموضوع الحديث في بداية الورقة التالية الموجودة. ٢ غير قابل للقراءة في ب؛ س: في أيديهم كلّ هذه. ٣ ب هنا وفيما بعد: خانفوا.

the silver they had taken. After this, people equipped expeditions to this islet but could not locate it. The sea is full of countless stories like this, of forbidden islands that the sailors cannot find, and of others that can never be reached.

In this sea a white cloud may often be seen casting a shadow over the ships. From it a long thin tongue of vapor emerges and descends until it meets the water of the sea, at which the water boils up like a whirlwind. If this whirlwind makes contact with a ship, it swallows it up. Then the cloud rises, and from it falls rain containing debris from the sea. I do not know if the cloud draws up water from the sea, or how this happens.[21] **1.2.7**

Dangers in the Sea of Harkand

In each of these seas there is a wind that blows up and stirs the water, whipping it up until it seethes like cauldrons on the boil. When this happens, it casts up what it contains on to the islands that are in it, wrecking ships and casting ashore huge great dead fish. At times it even casts up boulders and entire outcrops of rock, as if they were arrows shot from a bow.

The Sea of Harkand, however, has another wind that blows from a bearing between the west and the Big Dipper.[22] This makes the sea seethe like boiling cauldrons and causes it to cast up large quantities of ambergris. The deeper the sea and the lower its bottom lies, the better the ambergris is in quality. And when the waves of this sea—I mean Harkand—grow big, the water seems to you like a blazing fire.[23] In this sea there is a fish called *lukham*, a predator that swallows people . . . [24]

Maritime Commerce between the Arabs and the Chinese

. . . in their hands . . . [25] so that the goods are in short supply. One of the reasons for such a shortage is the frequent outbreak of fire at Khānfū, the port of the China ships and entrepôt of Arab and Chinese trade, and the resulting destruction of goods in the conflagration. This is because their houses there are built of wood and split bamboo. Another reason for shortages is that outbound or returning ships might be wrecked, or their crews might be plundered or forced to put in to some place en route for long periods and thus end up selling their goods somewhere other than in Arab lands.[26] It can happen too that the wind forces them to land in Yemen or elsewhere, and they end up selling their goods there. They might also have to put in somewhere for a long time to repair their ships, or for some other reason. **1.3.1**

The Chinese port of Khānfū

١،٣،٢ وذكر سليمان التاجر أنّ بخانفو وهو مجتمع التجّار رجلاً مسلماً يولّيه صاحبُ الصين الحكمَ بين المسلمين الذين يقصدون إلى تلك الناحية يتوخّى[١] ملك الصين ذلك وإذا كان في العيد صلّى بالمسلمين[٢] وخطب ودعا لسلطان المسلمين وأنّ التجّار العراقيّين لا ينكرون من ولايته شيئاً في أحكامه وعملِه بالحقّ وبما في كتاب الله عزّ وجلّ وأحكامِ الإسلام.

١،٣،٣ فأمّا المواضع التي يردونها ويرقون إليها فذكروا أنّ أكثر السفن الصينيّة تُحمَّل من سِيراف وأنّ المتاع يُحمَل من البصرة وعُمان وغيرها إلى سيراف فيُعبَّى في السفن الصينيّة بسيراف. وذلك لكثرة الأمواج في هذا البحر وقلّة الماء في مواضع منه.

١،٤،١ والمسافة بين البصرة وسيراف في الماءماية وعشرون فرسخاً. فإذا عُبّي المتاع بسيراف استعذبوا منها الماء وخطفوا وهذه لفظة يستعملها أهل البحر يعني يُقلِعون إلى موضع يقال له مَسقَط وهو آخر عمل عُمان. والمسافة من سيراف إليه نحو مايتي فرسخ. وفي شرقيّ هذا البحر فيما بين سيراف ومسقط من البلاد سِيف بني الصَفّاق وجزيرة ابن كاوان.[٣] وفي هذا البحر جبال عُمان وفيها الموضع الذي يُسمّى الدُرْدُور وهو مضيق بين جبلين تسلكه السفن الصغار ولا تسلكه السفن الصينيّة. وفيها الجبلان اللذان يقال لهما كُسَير وعُوَير وليس يظهر منهما فوق الماء إلّا اليسير. فإذا جاوزْنا الجبال صرنا إلى موضع يقال له صُحار عُمان فنستعذب الماء من مسقط من بئر بها. وهناك فية غنم[٤] من بلاد عُمان.

١،٤،٢ فتخطفُ المراكب منها إلى بلاد الهند فتقصد إلى كُولَم مَلِي[٥] والمسافة من مسقط إلى كولم ملي شهر على اعتدال الريح. وفي كولم ملي مَسلَحة لبلاد كولم ملي تجبي[٦]

---

١ ر و س: بتوخّي. ٢ من (الذين يقصدون) حتى (صلّى بالمسلمين) ساقطة من خ. ٣ س هنا وفيما بعد: أبَرْكاوان.

٤ كذا في ب؛ س: فئة غنم؛ ح: [جبل] فية غنم؛ خ: فيه [رعاء] غنم. ٥ ب هنا وفيما بعد في المتن: كوكم ملي؛ وهنا في هامش ب: كُولَم. ٦ ح: تجيء.

Sulaymān the Merchant reported that, in Khānfū, the meeting place of the merchants, there was a Muslim man appointed by the ruler of China to settle cases arising between the Muslims who go to that region, and that the Chinese king would not have it otherwise. At the time of the ʿĪds, this man would lead the Muslims in prayer, deliver the sermon, and pray for the sultan of the Muslims.[27] The Iraqi merchants, Sulaymān added, never dispute any of the judgments issued by the holder of this office, and they all agree that he acts justly, in accordance with the Book of God, mighty and glorious is He, and with the laws of Islam. 1.3.2

Regarding the ports where the merchants regularly go ashore, they have said that most of the China ships[28] take their cargoes on board at Sīrāf. Goods are carried from Basra, Oman, and elsewhere to Sīrāf and loaded there onto the China ships. The reason for this is that, at the other ports on this sea,[29] the water is often too rough and too shallow for the bigger vessels to put in. 1.3.3

Sīrāf in the Arabian/Persian Gulf

The Sea Route from Sīrāf to Khānfū

The sailing distance from Basra to Sīrāf is 120 *farsakh*s. Once the goods have been loaded at Sīrāf, they take on board freshwater there, then they "take off"[30] (an expression used by seamen meaning "set sail") for a place called Muscat. This is at the end of the territory of Oman, the distance there from Sīrāf being about two hundred *farsakh*s. At the eastern end of this sea, the territories between Sīrāf and Muscat include Sīf Banī l-Ṣaffāq and the Island of Ibn Kāwān. Also in this sea are the rocks of Oman.[31] Among them is the place called "the Whirlpool," which is a narrow channel between two rocks through which small ships can pass but not the China ships.[32] Among the rocks of Oman are also the two rocks known as Kusayr and ʿUwayr, of which only small parts appear above the surface of the water. When we have passed all these rocks we reach a place called Ṣuḥār of Oman. Then we take on board freshwater at Muscat, from a well that is there. There are also sheep and goats in plenty for sale, from the land of Oman. 1.4.1

From Basra to Muscat via Sīrāf

From Muscat the ships set sail for the land of India, making for Kūlam Malī. The distance from Muscat to Kūlam Malī is a month, if the wind is constant.[33] At Kūlam Malī there is a guard post belonging to that country that exacts customs duty from the China ships, and there is also freshwater to be had from wells. The sum taken from the China ships is a thousand dirhams, and from other ships it ranges from ten dinars down to one dinar. 1.4.2

From Muscat to Kūlam Malī

السفن الصينيّة وبها ماء عذب من آبار. فيؤخذ من الصينيّة ألف درهم ومن غيرها من السفن ما بين عشرة دنانير إلى دينار.[١] وبين مسقط وبين كولم ملي وبين هركند نحوٌ من شهر. وبكولم ملي يستعذبون الماء.

١،٤،٣ ثمّ تخطف المراكب أي تقلع إلى بحر هركند. فإذا جاوزوه صاروا إلى موضع يقال له لنجبالوس لا يفهمون لغة العرب ولا ما يعرفه التجّار من اللغات. وهم قوم لا يلبسون الثياب بيض كواسج.[٢] وذكروا أنّهم لم يروا منهم النساء وذلك أنّ رجالهم يخرجون إليهم من الجزيرة في زواريق منقورة من خشبة واحدة ومعهم النارجيل وقصب السكّر والموز وشراب النارجيل وهو شراب أبيض فإذا شُرِبَ ساعةَ يؤخذ من النارجيل فهو حلو مثل العسل. فإذا تُرِكَ ساعةً صار شراباً وإن بقي أيّاماً صار خلاًّ. فيبيعون ذلك بالحديد. وربّما وقع إليهم العنبر اليسير فيبيعونه بقطع الحديد. إنّما يتبايعون بالإشارة يداً بيد إذ كانوا لا يفهمون اللغة. وهم حذّاق بالسباحة فربّما استلبوا من التجّار الحديد ولا يعطونهم شيئاً.

١،٤،٤ ثمّ تخطف المراكب إلى موضع يقال له كَلَه بار[٣] المملكة والساحل كُلُّه يقال له بار وهي مملكة الزابَج متيامنة عن بلاد الهند يجمعهم مَلِكٌ. ولباسهم الفُوَط يلبس السَرِي والدنيّ منهم الفوطة الواحدة. ويستعذبون هناك الماء من آبار عذبة وهم يؤثرون ماء الآبار على مياه العيون والمطر. ومسافة ما بين كولم وهي قريبة من هركند إلى كله بار شهر.

ثمّ تسير المراكب إلى موضع يقال له تِيُومة[٤] وبها ماء عذب لمن أراده والمسافة إليها عشرة أيّام. ثمّ تخطف المراكب إلى موضع يقال له كَنْدُرَنْج[٥] عشرة أيّام وفيها ماء عذب لمن أراده. وكذلك جزاير الهند إذا احتُفِرَت فيها الآبار وُجِدَ فيها الماء العذب. وبها جبل مُشْرِف وربّما كان فيه الهُرّاب من العبيد واللصوص.

---

١ س: إلى [عشرين] دينار. ٢ خ: كواشج. ٣ ب: كلاه بار. ٤ ب: بتومة. ٥ ب: كدرنج.

The distance between Muscat and Kūlam Malī and the start of the Sea of Harkand is about a month. In Kūlam Malī they take on freshwater.

1.4.3 *From Kūlam Malī to Lanjabālūs*

Next, the ships "take off"—that is, they set sail—into the Sea of Harkand. When they have crossed it, they reach a place called Lanjabālūs. Its inhabitants do not understand the language of the Arabs or any other language known to the merchants. They are a people who wear no clothes and who have pale skins and sparse beards. The merchants have reported that they have never seen any of the women of this people. This is because it is their men alone who come out from the island in canoes, each hewn out of a single piece of wood, bringing with them coconuts, sugar cane, bananas, and coconut-palm drink. This last product is a whitish-coloured juice, which, if it is drunk as soon as it is tapped from the coconut palm, is as sweet as honey. If it is left for a while, however, it turns into an alcoholic drink; if this is then kept for a few days, it turns into vinegar.[34] All these products they sell in exchange for iron. They often find small amounts of ambergris, and this they also sell for pieces of iron. Their deals are struck entirely by gestures, and payment is made on the spot,[35] as they do not understand the language of the merchants. They are expert swimmers, and they often swim out and carry off the merchants' iron and give them nothing in exchange for it.

1.4.4 *From Lanjabālūs to Kanduranj*

Then the ships set sail for a place called Kalah Bār. Both "kingdom" and "coast" are called *bār*. It is subject to the kingdom of al-Zābaj, which one reaches by veering southward from the land of India. All the people of these regions of Kalah Bār and al-Zābaj are under one king. The dress of the inhabitants consists of waist wrappers,[36] and both their nobles and their lower-class people wear a single wrapper. The crews take on freshwater there from sweet wells, and they prefer the wellwater to springwater and rainwater. The distance to Kalah Bār from Kūlam, which is near the Sea of Harkand, is one month.

Then the ships go on to a place called Tiyūmah, where there is freshwater for anyone wanting it. The distance there from Kalah Bār is ten days. Next, the ships set sail for a place called Kanduranj, ten days distant. There freshwater is to be had by anyone wanting it, and this is the case for all the islands of the Indies—whenever wells are dug, sweet water is found in them. Here at Kanduranj is a mountain overlooking the sea, where fugitive slaves and thieves are often to be found.

ثمّ تسير المراكب إلى موضع يقال له صَنْف[1] مسيرة عشرة أيّام. وبها ماء عذب ومنه يؤتى بالعود الصنفيّ وبها مَلِكٌ. وهم قوم سمر يلبس كلّ واحد منهم فوطتين. فإذا استعذبوا منها خطفوا إلى موضع يقال له صَنْدَر فُولات[2] وهي جزيرة في البحر والمسافة إليها عشرة أيّام وفيها ماء عذب. ثمّ تخطف المراكب إلى بحر يقال له صَنْخِي[3] ثمّ إلى أبواب الصين وهي جبال في البحر بين كلّ جبلين فرجة تمرّ فيها المراكب. ٥،٤،١

فإذا سلّم الله من صندر فولات خطف المركب إلى الصين في شهر إلّا أنّ الجبال التي تمرّ بها المراكب مسيرة سبعة أيّام. فإذا جازت السفينة الأبواب ودخلت الخَوْر صارت إلى ماء عذب إلى الموضع التي[4] ترسى إليه من بلاد الصين وهو يُسمّى خانفو مدينة.[5] وساير الصين فيها الماء العذب من أنهار عذبة وأودية ومسالح وأسواق في كلّ ناحية.

وفيها مدّ وجزر مرّتين في اليوم والليلة. إلّا أنّ المدّ يكون فيما يلي البصرة إلى جزيرة بني كاوان[6] إذا توسّط القمرُ السماءَ ويكون الجزر عند طلوع القمر وعند مغيبه. والمدّ يكون بناحية الصين إلى قريب من جزيرة بني كاوان إذا طلع القمر فإذا توسّط السماءَ جَزَرَ الماء. فإذا غابَ كان المدّ فإذا كان في مقابلة وسطِ السماء جَزَرَ. ١،٥،١

وذكروا أنّ في جزيرة يقال لها ملجان فيما بين سرنديب وكَلَه وذلك من بلاد الهند في شرقيّ البحر قومٌ[7] من السودان عراة إذا وجدوا الإنسان من غير بلادهم علّقوه منكّساً وقطّعوه وأكلوه نيّاً. وعدد هؤلاء كثير وهم في جزيرة واحدة وليس لهم مَلِكٌ. وغذاؤهم السمك والموز والنارجيل وقصب السكّر ولهم شبيه بالغياض والآجام. ٢،٥،١

وذكروا أنّ في ناحية البحر سمكاً صغيراً طيّاراً يطير على وجه الماء يُسمّى جراد الماء. وذكروا أنّ بناحية البحر سمكاً يخرج حتّى يصعد على النارجيل فيشرب ما في النارجيل ٣،٥،١

---

١ ب: صِنف. ٢ س: صنف فولاو. ٣ ب: صنجي. ٤ كذا في ب؛ س: الذي. ٥ كذا في ب.
٦ كذا وفيما بعد في ب والمعروف ما ذكر أعلاه: ابن كاوان. ٧ كذا في ب؛ خ: قوما.

Then the ships go on to a place called Ṣanf, a voyage of ten days. There is freshwater there, and from it the Ṣanfī aloewood is exported. It has a king, and the inhabitants are a brown-skinned people, each of whom wears two waist wrappers. When they have taken on freshwater there, they set sail for a place called Ṣandar Fūlāt, which is an island out to sea. The distance there is ten days, and freshwater is also to be had there. Next, the ships set sail into a sea called Ṣankhī, then on to the Gates of China. These are islets in the sea, with channels between them through which the ships pass. 1.4.5

From Kanduranj to Khānfū

And if God grants a safe passage from Ṣandar Fūlāt, the ships set sail from there to China and reach it in a month, the islets through which the ships must pass being a seven-day voyage from Ṣandar Fūlāt. Once the ships have gone through the Gates and then entered the mouth of the river,[37] they proceed to take on freshwater at the place in the land of China where they anchor, called Khānfū, which is a city. Everywhere in China there is sweet water, from freshwater rivers and valleys, and there are guard posts and markets in every region.

On Tides, and Unusual Phenomena of the Seas

In these seas the tide rises and falls twice a day. In the waters stretching from 1.5.1
Basra to Banū Kāwān Island, however, high tide occurs when the moon is at its height, in the middle of the heavens, and low tide occurs when the moon rises or falls. Conversely, in the seas extending from near Ibn Kāwān Island to the region of China, high tide coincides with the rising of the moon, and low tide occurs when the moon is in the middle of the heavens: when the moon falls the sea rises, and when it returns to a point level with the middle of the heavens, the tide goes out.

Informants have reported that there is an island called Maljān, lying 1.5.2
between Sarandīb and Kalah—in the Indies, that is, in the eastern part of the sea—in which there is a tribe of negroes who are naked and who, if they find anyone from outside their land, hang him upside down, cut him into pieces, and devour him raw. These people are many, and they inhabit a single island and have no ruler. They live on fish, bananas, coconuts, and sugarcane, and in their land are places resembling swamps and thickets.

They have also reported that in a certain part of the sea there are small 1.5.3
flying fish that fly over the surface of the water, called "water locusts,"[38] and that elsewhere in the sea there are fish that come out of the water, climb the coconut palms, drink the sap of the palms, and then return to the water.[39]

من الماء ثمّ يعود إلى البحر. وذكروا أنّ في البحر حيوانًا يشبه السرطان فإذا خرج من البحر صار حجرًا. قال ويُتّخَذُ منه كُحْلٌ لبعض علل العين. وذكروا أنّ بقرب الزابج جبلًا يُسمّى جبل النار لا يُقْدَرُ على الدنوّ منه يظهر منه بالنهار دخان وبالليل لهبُ نار. ويخرج من أسفله عين باردة عذبة وعين حارّة عذبة.

ولباس أهل الصين الصغار والكبار الحرير في الشتاء والصيف. فأمّا الملوك فالجيّد من الحرير ومَن دونهم فعلى قدرهم. وإذا كان الشتاء لبس الرجل السراويلين والثلاثة والأربعة والخمسة وأكثر من ذلك على قدر ما يمكنهم. وإنّما قصدهم أن يدفوا أسافلهم لكثرة الندى وخوفهم منه. فأمّا الصيف فيلبسون القميص الواحد من الحرير ونحو ذلك. ولا يلبسون العمايم. ١،٦،١

وطعامهم الأرزّ وربّما طبخوا معه الكُوشان فصبّوه على الأرزّ فأكلوه. فأمّا الملوك منهم فيأكلون خبز الحنطة واللحم من ساير الحيوان ومن الخنازير وغيرها. ولهم من الفاكهة التفّاح والخوخ والأترجّ والرمّان والسفرجل والكمّثرى والموز وقصب السكّر والبطّيخ والتين والعنب والقثاء والخيار والنبق والجوز واللوز والجِلّوز والفستق والإجّاص والمشمش والغُبَيراء والنارجيل. وليس لهم فيها كثير نخل إلّا النخلة في دار أحدهم. وشرابهم النبيذ المعمول من الأرزّ. وليس في بلادهم خمر ولا تُحمَل إليهم ولا يعرفونها ولا يشربونها. ويُعمَل من الأرزّ الخلّ والنبيذ والناطف وما أشبه ذلك. ٢،٦،١

وليس لهم نظافة ولا يستنجون بالماء إذا أحدثوا بل يمسحون ذلك بالقراطيس الصينيّة. ويأكلون الميتة وما أشبهها ممّا يصنعه المجوس. فإنّ دينهم يشبه دين المجوس. ونساؤهم يكشفن رؤوسهنّ ويجعلن فيها الأمشاط فربّما كان في رأس المرأة عشرون مشطًا من العاج وغير ذلك. ورجالهم يغطّون رؤوسهم بشيء يشبه القلانس. وسُنّتهم في اللصوص أن يُقتَل اللصّ إذا أصيب. ٣،٦،١

They have reported, too, that there is a creature in the sea resembling a crab that turns to stone if it leaves the water; a certain informant said that from this creature an ointment is extracted and used to treat various eye complaints. They have also reported that in the vicinity of al-Zābaj is a rocky island named "the Mount of Fire," near which it is impossible to sail. In the daytime smoke appears from it and at night blazing fire. At its base, cold freshwater comes out of one spring and hot freshwater from another.

The Chinese and Some of Their Customs

The Chinese, whether young or old, wear silk in both winter and summer. **1.6.1**
Their ruling classes wear the finest silk; other classes wear whatever quality they can afford. In winter, the men wear two pairs of trousers, or three, four, five, or even more pairs, according to what they can afford. This they do in order to keep the lower parts of their bodies warm, on account of the prevalence of damp and their fear of its ill effects. In summer they wear a single gown of silk, or something of that sort. They do not wear turbans.

Their staple food is rice. They often cook a sauce to go with it, which they **1.6.2**
pour on the rice before eating it. Their ruling classes, however, eat wheat bread and the flesh of all sorts of animals, including pigs and other such creatures. They have various kinds of fruit—apples, peaches, citrons, pomegranates, quinces, pears, bananas, sugarcane, watermelons, figs, grapes, serpent melons, cucumbers, jujubes, walnuts, almonds, hazelnuts, pistachioes, plums, apricots, serviceberries, and coconuts. Not many date palms are to be found in China, except for the occasional specimen in the garden of a private house. Their drink is a wine made from rice. Grape wine is not to be found in their land, and it is never imported—indeed, they do not know of it and do not drink it. From rice they manufacture vinegar, wine, jellied sweetmeats, and other such products.

The Chinese are unhygienic, and they do not wash their backsides with **1.6.3**
water after defecating but merely wipe themselves with Chinese paper. They eat carrion and other similar things, just as the Magians do; in fact, their religion resembles that of the Magians. Their womenfolk leave their heads uncovered but put combs in their hair, a single woman often wearing twenty combs of ivory and other such materials. Their menfolk, however, cover their heads with something like a cap. In dealing with thieves, their practice is to put them to death if they are caught.

أخبار بلاد الهند والصين أيضاً وملوكها

أهل الهند والصين مُجْمِعون على أنّ ملوك الدنيا المعدودين أربعة. فأوّل من يعدّون ١،٧،١
من الأربعة ملك العرب وهو عندهم إجماع لا اختلاف بينهم فيه أنّه مَلِك أعظم الملوك وأكثرهم مالاً وأبهاهم جمالاً وأنّه ملك الدين الكبير الذي ليس فوقه شيء. ثمّ يعدّ ملكُ الصين نفسَه بعد ملك العرب ثمّ ملك الروم ثمّ بَلْهَرا[١] ملك المُخَرَّمي الآذان.

فأمّا بلهرا هذا فإنّه أشرف الهند وهم له مُقِرّون بالشرف. وكلّ ملك من ملوك ٢،٧،١
الهند متفرّد بمُلكه غير أنّهم مقرّون لهذا فإذا وردت رسله على ساير الملوك صلّوا لرسله تعظيماً له. وهو ملك يعطي العطاء كما تفعل العرب وله الخيل والفيلة الكثيرة والمال الكثير. ومالُه دراهم تُدعى الطاطِريّة وزن كلّ درهمٍ درهمٌ ونصف بسكّة الملك. وتاريخه في سَنة مِن مملكة مَن كان قبله ليس كَسَنة[٢] العرب من عصر النبيّ عليه السلام بل تاريخهم بالملوك. وملوكهم يعمّرون وربّما مَلَكَ أحدهم خمسين سنة وتزعم أهل مملكة بلهرا إنّما يطول مدّة مُلكهم وأعمارهم في المُلك لمحبّتهم للعرب. وليس في الملوك أشدّ حبّاً للعرب منه وكذلك أهل مملكته. وبلهرا اسم لكلّ ملك منهم ككسرى ونحوه وليس باسم لازم. ومُلك بلهرا وأرضه أوّلها ساحل البحر وهي بلاد تُدعى الكُمْكُم متّصلة على الأرض إلى الصين. وحوله ملوك كثيرة يقاتلونه غير أنّه يظهر عليهم.

فمنهم مَلِكٌ يُدعى ملك الجُزُر وهو كثير الجيش ليس لأحد من الهند مثل ٣،٧،١
خيله. وهو عدوّ العرب غير أنّه مقرّ أنّ ملك العرب أعظم الملوك. وليس أحد من الهند أعدى للإسلام منه. وهو على لسان من الأرض وأموالهم كثيرة وإبلهم

١ س هنا وفيما بعد: بَلَّهَرا. ٢ س: كَسُنّة.

Accounts of the Lands of India and China and of Their Rulers

1.7.1 *The four great kings of the world*

The Indians and Chinese are all of the opinion that, of the world's kings, four are to be counted as great. They consider the first of these four to be the king of the Arabs: it is a unanimous opinion among them, about which there is no disagreement, that of the four kings he is the mightiest, the richest in possessions, and the most resplendently fine in appearance, and that he is the king of the great religion to which nothing is superior. The king of China counts himself next in importance after the king of the Arabs, then comes the Byzantine king, and finally Balharā, the king of those Indians who pierce their ears.

1.7.2 *Balharā and his kingdom*

This Balharā is the noblest of the Indians, all of whom acknowledge his nobility. Although each one of the kings in India rules independently, they all acknowledge his superior rank, and when his envoys arrive at the courts of any of the other kings, they make obeisance to them as a mark of honor to Balharā. He is a king who distributes payments to his troops as the Arabs do, and he owns many horses and elephants and possesses great wealth. His coinage is in the form of dirhams called *ṭāṭirī* dirhams, which are one and a half times the weight of dirhams in the coinage of the Arab realm. The coins are dated by the year of each king's reign, counting from the end of his predecessor's reign; in contrast to the Arab practice of dating from the era of the Prophet, eternal peace be upon him, they take their dates from their individual kings. Their kings live long lives, and often one of them will reign for fifty years. The people of Balharā's kingdom assert that their rulers' lengthy reigns and long lives on the throne are due entirely to their fondness for the Arabs. None of the other rulers shows the Arabs such affection as does Balharā, and his people share his fondness for them. "Balharā" is the name given to each of these kings, as is the case with "Kisrā" and so on; it is not a personal name. Balharā's rule covers territories beginning with the coast of the Sea of Lārawī, a region called al-Kumkum, and continues overland as far as China. He is surrounded by other kings who make war on him, but he has the upper hand over them.

1.7.3 *The king of al-Jurz*

Another of the Indian rulers is one called the king of al-Jurz. He has a large army, and none of the other Indian princes has the like of his cavalry. He is the enemy of the Arabs, although he acknowledges the king of the Arabs to be the greatest of rulers. No other Indian is as hostile to Islam as he. He inhabits a peninsula, where his people have great wealth and numerous camels and other beasts. They buy and sell using unworked silver as currency, and it is

ومواشيهم كثيرة. ويتبايعون بالفضّة التبر ويقال إنّ لهم معادن. وليس في بلاد الهند آمن من السرق منها.

١،٧،٤ وإلى جانبه مَلِكُ الطاقى[١] وهو قليل المملكة. ونساؤهم بيض أجمل نساء الهند. وهو ملك موادع لمن حوله لقلّة جيشه. وهو يحبّ العرب كحبّ بلهرا.

١،٧،٥ ويلي هؤلاء مَلِكٌ يقال له دَهْمى[٢] يقاتله ملك الجرز وليس له شرف في المُلك. وهو أيضاً يقاتل بلهرا كما يقاتل ملكَ الجرز. ودهمى هذا أكثر جيشاً من ملك بلهرا ومن ملك الجرز ومن الطاقى ويقال إنّه إذا خرج إلى القتال يخرج في نحو من خمسين ألف فيل. ولا يخرج إلّا في الشتاء لأنّ الفيلة لا تصبر على العطش فليس يسعه إلّا الخروج في الشتاء. ويقال إنّ قصارى عسكره نحوٌ من عشرة آلاف إلى خمسة عشر ألفاً. وفي بلاده الثياب التي ليس لأحد مثلها يدخل الثوب منها في حلقة خاتم دقّةً وحُسناً وهو من قطن وقد رأينا بعضها. والذي يُنْفَق في بلاده الودع وهو عين البلاد يعني ماله. وفي بلاده الذهب والفضّة والعود والثياب الصمر[٣] الذي يتّخذ منه المذابّ.[٤]

١،٧،٦ وفي بلاده البُشان المُعْلَم وهو الكَرْكَدّن له في مقدّم جبهته قرن واحد. وفي قرنه علامةُ صورةٍ خِلْقَةً كصورة الإنسان في حكايته القرن كلّه أسود والصورة بيضاء في وسطه. وهذا الكركدّن دون الفيل في الخلقة إلى السواد ما هو[٥] ويشبه الجاموس قويّ ليس كقوّته شيء من الحيوان. وليس له مفصل في ركبته ولا في يده وهو من لدن رجله إلى إبطه قطعة واحدة. والفيل يهرب منه. وهو يجترّ كما تجترّ البقر والإبل ولحمه حلال قد أكلناه. وهو في هذه المملكة كثير في غياضهم وهو في ساير بلاد الهند غير أنّ قرون هذا أجود. فربّما كان في القرن صورة

---

١ ب هنا وفيما بعد: الطافِق. ٢ ب هنا و فيما بعد: رُهمى. ٣ كذا في ب بدون تحريك؛ س: الصَمَر.
٤ ر: المداب. ٥ كذا في ب؛ ولعلّ الصواب: دون الفيل في الخلقة إلى السواء كما هو.

said that they have mines of silver. Nowhere in the land of India is one safer from robbery than in their territory.

On one side of al-Jurz territory is that of the king of al-Ṭāqā, whose kingdom is small. The women of this land are fair-skinned and are the most beautiful women in India. He is a king who maintains peaceful relations with his neighbors, because his army is small. He shows the same fondness for the Arabs as does Balharā. 1.7.4

The king of al-Ṭāqā

The next kingdom is that of a king called Dahmā. The king of al-Jurz makes war on him, and he does not rank highly as a king.[40] Dahmā also makes war on Balharā as well as on the king of al-Jurz. This Dahmā's army is bigger than those of King Balharā and of the kings of al-Jurz and al-Ṭāqā, and it is said that, when he goes on campaign, he takes about fifty thousand elephants with him. Consequently he campaigns only in winter, because elephants cannot endure a lack of water; he is thus able to go to war only in the wintertime, when enough water is available. Other reports put the maximum number of his troops at about ten thousand to fifteen thousand. In his land, garments are made that have no equal elsewhere: they are so finely and beautifully woven that one of them can be drawn through a finger ring. They are made of cotton, and we have seen one of them. In Dahmā's territory cowries are used for payment, for they are the currency of the land, or, in other words, its money. His territory also produces gold, silver, aloewood, and *ṣamar* cloths, which are made into fly-whisks. 1.7.5

King Dahmā, and the rhinoceros

In Dahmā's land the "marked *bushān*" or rhinoceros is to be found. This animal has a single horn on the front of its forehead, and within this horn is a marking, a naturally-occurring figure depicting the likeness of a human being or some other form. The horn is black throughout, except for this white figure in its interior. This rhinoceros is, by nature, smaller than the elephant but tends to be the same dark color as the elephant.[41] It resembles the buffalo and is so strong that no other animal equals it in strength. It has no knee joints, either in its hind legs or its forelegs, its legs being formed in one piece from the feet to where they join the trunk. An elephant will run away in fear from a rhinoceros. The rhinoceros is a ruminant, like cattle and camels, and its flesh is permissible for Muslims; we have eaten it. The rhinoceros is found in large numbers in this kingdom, living in thickets. In fact, it is present throughout India, but the horns of these animals of Dahmā's realm are of finer quality and often contain the figure of a man, a peacock, 1.7.6

رجل وصورة طاووس وصورة سمكة وساير الصور. وأهل الصين يتّخذون منها المناطق وتبلغ المنطقة ببلاد الصين ألفي دينار وثلاثة آلاف وأكثر على قدر حُسن الصورة. وهذا كلّه يُشترى من بلاد دهمى بالودع وهو عين البلاد.

١.٧.٧ وبعده ملك داخل[١] ليس له بحر يقال له ملك الكاشِبينَ[٢] وهم قوم بيض مخرَّمو الآذان ولهم جمال وهم أصحاب بدو وجبال.

وبعده بحر عليه ملك يقال له القيرنج[٣] وهو ملك فقير فَخُور[٤] يقع إليه العنبر الكثير وله أنياب فيلة وعنده فلفل يؤكل رطباً لقلّته.

وبعد هذا ملوك كثيرة لا يعلم عددهم إلّا الله تبارك وتعالى منهم المُوجَه وهم قوم بيض يشبهون الصين في اللباس ولهم مسك كثير وفي بلادهم جبال بيض ليس شيء أطول منها وهم يقاتلون ملوكاً كثيرة حولهم والمسك الذي يكون في بلادهم جيّد بالغ.

١.٧.٨ ومن ورايهم ملوك المابد[٥] مداينهم كثيرة وهم إلى حيث الموجه وأكثر[٦] من الموجه غير أنّ المابد[٧] أشبهُ بالصين منهم ولهم خدم خصيان مثل الصين عُمّالٌ عليهم وبلادهم تتّصل ببلاد الصين وهم مصالحون لصاحب الصين غير أنّهم لا يسمعون له. وللمابد في كلّ سنة رُسُل إلى ملك الصين وهدايا وكذلك ملك الصين يهدي إليه[٨] وبلادهم واسعة وإذا دخلت رسل المابد بلاد الصين حُفِظوا مخافةَ أن يغلبوا على بلادهم لكثرتهم وليس بينهم وبين بلاد الصين إلّا جبال وعقاب.

---

١ خ: داخلي. ٢ خ: لكشمير؛ س: لَكْشميرُ. ٣ س: التَنْلُوِنْج. ٤ ساقطة في خ؛ و لعلّ الصواب: فَخَّوْر.
٥ س هنا وفيما بعد: المادُبْد. ٦ خ و س: وهم أكْثر. ٧ ب: المابذ. ٨ خ و س: إليهم.

a fish, and other such images. The Chinese use them to make belts, and in China the price of such a belt can reach two or three thousand dinars or more, depending on the fineness of the figure.[42] All of this horn in the Chinese market is bought in Dahmā's land for cowries, which are the currency of the land.

After Dahmā there is a king whose territory lies inland, away from 1.7.7
the sea, called the king of al-Kāshibīn. His people are pale-skinned, have *Other kingdoms*
pierced ears, and are good-looking. Their land includes both open plains and mountains.

After this kingdom, on the sea, comes the territory of a ruler called al-Qyrnj, a king who is poor but proud.[43] Much ambergris is washed up on his shores; his land produces elephants' tusks and a little pepper, but so little that it is eaten while still green.[44]

After al-Qyrnj come so many kings that God alone, blessed and exalted is He, knows their number. One of them rules al-Mūjah, a pale-skinned people whose dress resembles that of the Chinese. They have large amounts of musk, and in their land are white mountains unsurpassed in height. They make war on many kings in the surrounding territories. The musk to be found in their land is of the very highest quality.

Beyond them are the kings of al-Mābud, whose land contains many cities. 1.7.8
Their territory extends as far as that of al-Mūjah, and their people are more numerous than al-Mūjah. The people of al-Mābud, however, resemble the Chinese more closely still; they even have eunuch slaves appointed to tax them, as do the Chinese.[45] Their country adjoins China, and they maintain peaceful relations with the Chinese ruler, although they are not under his control. Every year, al-Mābud sends envoys and gifts to the king of China; similarly, the king of China sends gifts to al-Mābud. Their land covers a wide area. When the envoys from al-Mābud enter Chinese territory they are kept under watch, as they are so many that the Chinese fear they will take over their land. Nothing lies between al-Mābud territory and China but mountains and passes.[46]

ويقال إنّ لملك الصين من أمّهات المداين أكثر من مايتي مدينة ولكلّ مدينة ملك ١،٨،١ وخصيّ وتحت كلّ مدينة مداين. فمن مداينهم خانفو وهي مرسى السفن تحتها عشرون مدينة.

وإنّما تُسمّى مدينةً إذا كان لها الجادَم والجادم مثل البوق يُنفَخ فيه وهو طويل وغلظه ٢،٨،١ ما يجمع الكفّين جميعاً وهو مطليّ بدواء الصينيّات وطوله ثلاثة أو أربعة أذرع ورأسه دقيق بقدر ما يلتقمه الرجل ويذهب صوته نحواً من ميل. ولكلّ مدينة أربعة أبواب[1] فعلى كلّ باب منها من الجادم[2] خمسةٌ تنفخ في أوقات من الليل والنهار. وعلى كلّ مدينة[3] عشرة طبول تُضرَب معه وإنّما يفعل ذلك لتعلم طاعتهم للملك وبه يعرفون أوقات الليل والنهار. ولهم علامات ووزن للساعات.

ومعاملاتهم بالفلوس وخزاينهم كخزاين الملوك وليس لأحد من الملوك فلوس ٣،٨،١ سواهم وهي عين البلاد. ولهم الذهب والفضّة واللؤلؤ والديباج والحرير كلّ ذلك كثير عندهم غير أنّ ذلك متاع والفلوس عين. ويُحمَل إليهم العاج واللبان وسبايك النحاس والذَبَل من البحر وهي جلود ظهور السلاحف وهذا البشان الذي وصفنا وهو الكركدّن يتّخذون من قرونه مناطق. ودوابّهم كثيرة وليس لهم خيل عربيّة بل غيرها ولهم حمير وإبل كثيرة لها سنامان. ولهم الغضار الجيّد ويُعمل منه أقداح في رقّة القوارير يُرى ضوء الماء فيه وهو من غضار.

وإذا دخل البحريّون من البحر قبض الصينيّون متاعهم وصيّروه في البيوت وضمنوا الدرَك إلى ستّة أشهر إلى أن يدخل آخر البحريّين. ثمّ يؤخذ من كلّ عشرةٍ ثلاثةٌ ويُسلَّم الباقي إلى التجّار. وما احتاج إليه السلطان أخذه بأغلى الثمن وعجّله ولم

١ أبواب: ساقطة في ح. ٢ خ: الجوادم. ٣ س: [باب] كلّ مدينة.

China, and the Customs of Its Inhabitants

It is said that the king of China has more than two hundred major cities under his rule, each of which has its own "king" and eunuch chief of finance[47] as well as several lesser cities under its governance. Among their major cities is Khānfū, the port for shipping, which has twenty lesser cities under it. **1.8.1** *The cities of China*

A "city" is only designated as such if it has *jādams*. A *jādam* is an instrument that is blown, like a trumpet but longer, and of such a girth that both hands are needed to grasp and encircle it. It is varnished with the substance used on Chinese lacquerware[48] and reaches three or four cubits in length, with one end narrow enough for a man to place in his mouth; its sound travels about a mile. Every city has four gates, and each is equipped with five *jādams* which are blown at certain times of the night and the day. Each city is also equipped with ten kettledrums, which are beaten when the *jādams* are sounded. The object of all this is to proclaim their obedience to the king; it also enables them to know the times of night and day. In addition, they have indicators to regulate the hours.[49] **1.8.2** *The* jādam

They use copper coins for their transactions, and, although their treasuries are like those of other rulers, no other ruler has copper as the sole currency of his land.[50] They do indeed possess gold, silver, pearls, brocades, and silks, and all in large quantities, but all those are regarded as items of commerce, while the copper coins alone are used as currency. Ivory, frankincense, and copper ingots are imported into China, as well as *dhabl* from the sea, which are the shells from turtles' backs, and the *bushān*, which we have already described, namely, the rhinoceros whose horns they make into belts. Among the many types of animal they use for transport, they do not possess Arab horses but have other breeds instead; they also have donkeys and many two-humped camels. They have a fine type of clay that is made into cups as delicate as glass: when held up to the light, any liquid in them can be seen through the body of the cup, even though it is of clay.[51] **1.8.3** *Currency and commerce in China*

As soon as the sea merchants put in to harbour, the Chinese take charge of their goods and transport them to warehouses, guaranteeing indemnity for up to six months, that is, until the last of the sea merchants arrives.[52] Then, three-tenths of the goods are taken in kind, as duty, and the remainder is returned to the merchants. Any goods that the ruler needs he also takes, but he gives the very highest price for them and pays immediately, so he does no harm to the merchants. Among the goods he buys is camphor, paying fifty

يظلم فيه. ومما يأخذ الكافور المنّا[1] بخمسين فَكّوجاً والفكّوج ألف فلس وهذا الكافور إذا لم يأخذه السلطان يساوي نصف الثمن خارج.[2]

١،٨،٤ وإذا مات الرجل من أهل الصين لم يُدفن إلّا في اليوم الذي مات في مثله من قابل يجعلونه في تابوت ويخلّونه في منازلهم ويجعلون عليه النُورة فتمصّ ماءه ويبقى. والملوك يُجعَلون في الصَبِر والكافور. ويبكون على موتاهم ثلاث سنين ومَن لم يبكِ ضُرِبَ بالخشب كذلك النساء والرجال ويقولون: إنّه لم يحزنك ميّتك. ويُدفَنون في ضريح كضريح العرب. ولا يقطعون عنه الطعام ويزعمون أنّه يأكل ويشرب وذلك أنّهم يضعون عنده الطعام بالليل فيصبحون ولا يجدون منه شيئاً فيقولون قد أكل. ولا يزالون في البكاء والإطعام ما بقي الميّت في منزلهم فيفتقرون على موتاهم فلا يبقى لهم نقد ولا ضيعة إلّا أنفقوه عليه. وقد كانوا قبل هذا يدفنون الملك وما مَلَكَ من آلة بيته من ثياب ومناطق ومناطقهم تبلغ مالاً كثيراً وقد تركوا ذلك الآن وذلك أنّه نُبِشَ بعض موتاهم وأُخِذَ ما كان معه.

١،٨،٥ والفقير والغنيّ من أهل الصين والصغير والكبير يتعلّم الخطّ والكتابة.

١،٨،٦ واسم ملوكهم على قدر الجاه وكبر المداين. فما كان من مدينة صغيرة يُسمّى ملكها طُوسَنج[3] ومعنى طوسنج أقامَ المدينةَ. وما كان من مدينة مثل خانفو فاسم ملكها دِيفُو. والخصيّ يُدعى الطُوقام وخصيانهم منهم مسلولون. وقاضي القضاة يقال له لقشي مامكون[4] ونحو هذا من الأسماء ممّا لا نضبطه.

وليس يُمَلَّك أحد منهم لأقلّ من أربعين سنة يقولون قد حنّكته التجارب.

والملوك الصغار إذا قعد أحدهم يقعد في مدينته على كرسيّ في بَهْوٍ عظيم وبين يديه كرسيّ وتُرفع إليه الكتب التي فيها أحكام الناس ومن وراء الملك رجل قايم

---

١ خ: المنّ. ٢ ح وخ وس: خارجًا. ٣ س هنا وفيما بعد: طسوشي. ٤ س: لُقشي صامكون [شي].

*fakkūj*s for a maund,[53] the *fakkūj* being a thousand copper coins. The same camphor, if the ruler had not bought it, would be worth only half that price on the open market.

When one of the Chinese dies, he is not buried until the anniversary of his death. In the intervening period, they place the body in a coffin and leave it in their house. They put quicklime on the corpse, which absorbs the fluids from it so that it remains uncorrupted; their rulers are embalmed in aloes[54] and camphor. They weep over their dead for three years; all who do not weep, whether women or men, are beaten with wooden staves, and they say to them, "Do you not grieve for your dead?"[55] Eventually the dead are buried in graves like the graves of the Arabs. Up until the time of burial, however, they keep on giving food to the dead person, for they maintain that he eats and drinks: they leave the food by the corpse at night, and when next morning they find none of it left, they say, "He has eaten it." They do not cease weeping over the corpse and giving it food as long as it remains in their house; indeed, they will impoverish themselves for the sake of their dead and will spend every last penny and sell every last plot of land and spend the proceeds to this end. In former times, when they interred a king, they used to bury with him his household possessions, such as robes and belts (their belts being worth large sums of money), but they have now abandoned the practice, because one of these royal dead was dug up and the accompanying goods looted. **1.8.4**

Funerary customs of the Chinese

The Chinese, whether poor or rich, young or old, all learn how to form letters and to write. **1.8.5**

Literacy

The titles of their rulers depend on their rank and on the size of the cities they govern. In the case of a smaller city, its ruler is entitled *ṭūsanj*, the meaning of *ṭūsanj* being, "he set the affairs of the city straight." In the case of a major city like Khānfū, the title of its ruler is *dīfū*. The eunuch chief of finance is called the *ṭūqām*; their eunuchs come from their own people and are deliberately castrated. The chief justice is called *laqshī māmkūn*, and there are other titles of this sort that we cannot set down accurately. **1.8.6**

Rulers and other holders of high office in China

No one is given the office of ruler if he is less than forty years old, for they say of someone of this age, "Experience has taught him."

When one of the lesser rulers sits for a public hearing in his city, he sits on a judgment seat in a large courtyard, with another seat placed before him, and written submissions concerning the legal proceedings of the populace are presented to him. Behind the ruler stands a man called a *līkhū*, and if

يُدعى لِيَخُوا[1] إذا زلّ الملك في شيء ممّا يأمر به وأخطأ ردّه.[2] وليس يعبؤون بالكلام ممّن يرفع إليهم دون أن يكتبه في كتاب. وقبل أن يدخل صاحب القصّة على الملك ينظر في كتابه رجل قايم بباب الدار ينظر في كتب الناس فإن كان فيها خطأ ردّه. فليس يكتب إلى الملك إلّا كاتب يعرف الحكم ويكتب الكاتبُ في الكتاب كَتَبَهُ فلان بن فلان فإن كان فيه خطأ رجع على الكاتب اللومُ فيُضرب بالخشب. وليس يقعد الملك للحكم حتّى يأكل ويشرب لئلّا يغلط. وأرزاق كلّ ملك من بيت مال مدينته.

فأمّا الملك الأكبر فلا يُرى إلّا في كلّ عشرة أشهر يقول: إذا رآني الناس استخفّوا بي والرياسات لا تقوم إلّا بالتجبّر وذلك أنّ العامّة لا تعرف العدل فينبغي أن يُستعمَل معهم التجبّر لنعظم عندها.

وليس على أرضهم خراج ولكنّ عليهم جزية على الجماجم الذكور حسبما يرون من الأحوال. وإن كان بها أحد من العرب أو غيرهم أُخِذَ منه جزية مالِه ليحرز مالَه. ١،٨،٧

وإذا غلا السعر أخرج السلطان من خزاينه الطعام فباعه بأرخص من سعر السوق فلا يبقى عندهم غلاء.

والذي يدخل بيت المال إنّما هو من الجزية التي على رُوسهم وأظنّ أنّ الذي يدخل بيت مال خانفو في كلّ يوم خمسون ألف دينار على أنّها ليست بأعظم مداينهم.

ويختصّ الملك من المعادن بالملح وحشيش يشربونه بالماء الحارّ ويباع منه في كلّ مدينة بمال عظيم ويقال له الساخ وهو أكثر ورقًا من الرَطبة وأطيب قليلاً وفيه مرارة فيُغلى الماء ويُذَرّ عليه فهو ينفعهم من كلّ شيء. وجميع ما يدخل بيت المال الجزية والملح وهذا الحشيش.

---

١ ح: لينجون؛ خ وس: لنجون. ٢ خ: ردَّها.

the ruler makes a slip in any of his pronouncements and gets it wrong, this official rejects the decision. They give no consideration to anything a petitioner has to say unless it is set down in writing. Moreover, before a litigant enters the ruler's presence, his written submission is examined by a man who stands at the palace gate and looks over each person's document; if it contains an error, he rejects it. Consequently only a scribe well acquainted with legal lore will write anything to be submitted to the ruler. Furthermore, he has to write on the document, "Written by So-and-so, son of So-and-so," so that, if it does contain an error, the blame falls on the scribe, and he will be beaten with wooden staves. The ruler never sits in judgment until he has eaten and drunk, lest he judge wrongly. Each ruler's stipend comes from the public treasury of his city.

In contrast to these provincial rulers, the Great King is seen in public only every ten months, for he says, "If the people see me more often, they will look on me with less reverence. Successful rulership calls for a display of kingly pride: the common people have no idea of fairness in a ruler, so a haughty attitude should be adopted towards them in order to increase our importance in their eyes."

1.8.7 *Sources of state income*

Their landed property is not subject to a tax; instead, they themselves are taxed per capita of the male population, according to the authorities' estimation of individual circumstances. In the case of any Arab or other foreigner resident in the land, a tax is paid on his property in order to safeguard that property.

If the price of grain rises too high, the ruler releases stocks from his granaries and sells it at less than the market price, causing the inflation to end.

The income of the public treasury comes from the poll tax. I believe that the daily income of the public treasury in Khānfū is as much as fifty thousand dinars, even though it is not the greatest of their cities.

Among the country's minerals, the ruler has exclusive rights to salt. He also has the rights to a plant that they drink with hot water and that is sold in every city for large sums of money, called *sākh*. It is leafier than alfalfa and a little more aromatic, with a bitterness to it. To prepare it, water is boiled, then the leaves are sprinkled on it, and it serves them as an antidote to all ailments. The entire income of the public treasury consists of the poll tax and the receipts from salt and this plant.

وفي كلّ مدينة شيء يدعى الدّرا وهو جرس على رأس ملك تلك المدينة مربوط ١،٨،٨ بخيط مادٍ على ظهر الطريق للعامّة كافّةً وبين الملك وبينه نحوٌ من فرسخ فإذا حُرِّكَ الخيط الممدود أدنى حركة تحرّك الجرسُ. فمَن كانت له ظلامة حرّك هذا الخيط فيتحرّك الجرسُ منه على رأس الملك فيُؤذن له بالدخول حتّى يُنهِي حاله بنفسه ويشرح ظلامته. وجميع البلاد فيها مثل ذلك.

ومَن أراد سفرًا من بعضها إلى بعض أخذ كتابين من الملك ومن الخصيّ. أمّا ١،٨،٩ كتاب الملك فللطريق باسم الرجل واسم مَن معه وكم عمره وعمر من معه ومِن أيّ قبيلة هو وجميع مَن ببلاد الصين من أهلها ومن العرب وغيرهم لا بدّ لهم أن ينتموا إلى شي يُعَرّفون به. وأمّا كتاب الخصيّ فبالمال وما معه من المتاع. وذلك لأنّ في طريقهم مسالح ينظرون في الكتابين فإذا وَرَدَ عليهم الوارد كتبوا: ورد علينا فلان بن فلان الفلانيّ في يوم كذى وشهر كذى وسنة كذى ومعه كذى[1] لِيَلّا يذهب من مال الرجل ولا من متاعه شيءٌ ضياعًا فمتى ما ذهب منه شي أو مات عُلِمَ كيف ذهب ورُدَّ عليه أو على ورثته من بعده.

وأهل الصين ينصفون في المعاملات والديون.[2] فإذا كان لرجل على رجل ١،٨،١٠ دَينٌ كتب عليه كتابًا وكتب الذي عليه الدين أيضًا كتابًا وعلّمه بعلامة بين[3] أصبعيه الوسطى والسبابة ثمّ جُمِعَ الكتابان فطُويا جميعًا ثمّ كُتِبَ على فصلهما ثمّ فُرِّقَ فأُعطي الذي عليه الدين كتابه بإقراره. فمتى جَحَدَ أحدُهما غريمَه قيل له: أَحْضِرْ كتابك فإن زعم الذي عليه الدين أنّه لا شيء له ودفع كتابه بخطّه وعلامته وذهب كتاب صاحب الحقّ قيل للجاحد الذي عليه الحقّ: أَحْضِرْ كتابًا بأنّ هذا الحقّ ليس

١ يوم كذى ... معه كذى: كذا في ب. ٢ ب: والديوان. ٣ بين: كذا في ب؛ ولعلّ الصواب: تبين.

1.8.8 *The* darā *bell and the investigation of grievances*

In every city there is something called the *darā*. This is a bell hanging over the head of the ruler of the city and connected to a cord stretching until it passes over the middle of the highway, for the use of all the common people; the distance between the ruler and the highway is about a *farsakh*. If the cord is moved, even slightly, the bell moves too. Anyone who has a complaint against injustice moves the cord, causing the bell to move over the ruler's head. The complainant is then permitted to enter the ruler's presence, so that he may deliver in person an account of his circumstances and set forth his grievance. This procedure is in use throughout the land.

1.8.9 *Permits for travel within China*

Anyone wanting to travel from one part of China to another obtains two documents, one from the ruler and one from the eunuch chief of finance. The document from the ruler is a permit for the road, made out in the name of the traveler and those accompanying him, and stating his age and his companions' ages, and the tribe from which he comes: all persons in China, whether of its native population or of the Arabs or other foreigners, are required to declare their ancestral origin from some group with which they may be officially identified. The second document, from the eunuch, concerns the traveler's money and any goods he may have. The reason for this procedure is that there are guardposts on the road where they examine both documents, and, when a traveler arrives at one, they write, "So-and-so, son of So-and-so, of Such-and-such an origin, arrived at our guardpost on the nth day of the nth month of the nth year, accompanied by So-and-so." This is in order that none of the traveler's money or goods should go missing. Whenever anything actually is lost or a traveler dies, the manner in which this occurred will be known and his property returned to him or to his heirs.

1.8.10 *Their fairness in financial dealings and loans*

The Chinese act fairly where financial dealings or debts are concerned.[56] If someone makes a loan to another person, he writes a document to the borrower, obliging him to repay; the borrower also writes a document to the lender, marking it with a mark between his two fingers, the middle and index fingers.[57] The two documents are then placed together and folded in on each other, and an inscription is written across both of them at the place where their edges join. Finally the documents are separated, and the recipient of the loan receives his copy and acknowledges his debt. Subsequently, if one of the parties should repudiate the other, he is told to produce his copy of the document. It may then happen that the debtor maintains that he does not have one, whereupon the creditor's copy (in the debtor's own handwriting and with his mark) can be presented as proof, even if the version written

عليك فمتى ما بيّن عليك صاحب الحقّ الذي جحدتَه فعليك عشرون خشبة على الظهر وعشرون ألف فكّوج فلوساً والفكّوج ألف فلس يكون ذلك قريباً من ألفي دينار والعشرون الخشبة فيها موتُه. فليس يكاد أحد ببلاد الصين يُعطى هذا من نفسه مخافةَ تَلَفِ النفس والمال ولم نرَ أحداً أجاب إلى ذلك. وهم يتناصفون بينهم وليس يذهب لأحد حقّ ولا يتعاملون بشاهد ولا يمين.

وإذا أفلس رجل بمال قوم فحبسه الغرماء بأموالهم عند السلطان أُخِذَ إقراره فإن لبث في السجن شهراً أخرجه السلطان فنادى عليه: إنّ هذا فلان بن فلان أفلس بمال فلان بن فلان. فإن يكن له عند أحد وديعة أو كان له عقار أو رقيق أو ما يحيط بدينه أُخرِجَ في كلّ شهر وضُربَ خشباتٍ على إسته لأنّه أقام في الحبس يأكل ويشرب وله مال فهو يُضرب أقرّ له أحد بمال أو لم يقرّ له فهو يُضرب على كلّ حال يقال: ليس لك عمل إلّا أخْذ حقوق الناس والذهاب بها ويقال له: اِحتِلْ حقوق هؤلاء القوم فإن لم يكن له حيلة وصحّ عند السلطان أنّه لا شيء له دُعي الغرماء فأُعطوا من بيت مال البَغبُون[1] وهو الملك الأعظم وإنّما سُمّي البغبون ومعناه ابن السماء ونحن نسمّيه المَغبُون.[2] ثمّ يُنادَى: مَن بايع هذا فعليه القتل. فليس يكاد يذهب لأحد مال. وإن عُلِمَ أنّ له عند أحد مالاً ولم يقرّ المودع بالمال قُتِلَ بالخشب ولم يُقَلْ لصاحب المال شيء فيُوخذ المال ويُقسَم على الغرماء ولا يبايع بعد ذلك. ١١،٨،١

١ س هنا وفيما بعد: البغبور. ٢ س: المغبور.

by the creditor is, in fact, lost. In such a case, a debtor who still repudiates his creditor will be told, "Produce another document, then, stating that this sum is *not* owed by you. And if you cannot, and the creditor's claim which you have repudiated is shown to be beyond dispute, then you will be made to suffer twenty blows on the back with wooden staves, and to pay twenty thousand *fakkūj*s of copper coins." The *fakkūj* being one thousand copper coins, this fine would amount to around two thousand dinars,[58] while the twenty blows would be enough to kill him. No one in China would willingly bring that upon himself, for fear of ruining both his person and his property, and we have never seen anyone agree to undergo it. Consequently, they act fairly towards each other, with no one ever foregoing his right to be repaid and without recourse to witnesses or oaths in their financial dealings.

If a man incurs the loss of other people's capital and his creditors then have him imprisoned in the ruler's jail pending restitution of their money, an acknowledgement of the debt is first obtained from him. Then, if and when he has remained in jail for a month, the ruler has him brought out and has a public proclamation made over him: "This man, So-and-so, son of So-and-so, has incurred the loss of the capital of So-and-so, son of So-and-so!" And if it then transpires that he has any money deposited with anyone or owns real estate or slaves or anything else that would cover his debt, he is brought out at the end of every subsequent month and beaten a number of times on the buttocks with wooden staves. This is because he has been staying in the jail, eating and drinking at government expense, when in fact he does own property: thus he is beaten, and whether or not anyone acknowledges that the debtor owns property, he is beaten all the same. They say, "Have you nothing better to do than to take what rightfully belongs to others and make off with it?" And they also tell him, "You must have *some* means of finding what you owe those people." But if, in fact, he does have no way out of the situation, and if the ruler is convinced that he really does own nothing, then the creditors are summoned and paid what they are owed from the treasury of the Baghbūn (this is the Great King, but his title is "the Baghbūn," which means "the Son of Heaven"; we Arabic-speakers call him "the Maghbūn"). After this, another public proclamation is made: "Whosoever does business with this bankrupt will be put to death!" As a result, hardly anyone ever loses money in this way. Also, if it emerges that the debtor does indeed have money deposited with someone else, and the latter has not admitted to having it, then that person will be beaten to death with wooden staves. **1.8.11** *Their procedure in cases of bankruptcy*

ولهم حجر منصوب طوله عشرة أذرع مكتوب فيه نقرًا في الحجر ذكر الأدوية والأدواء ١،٨،١٢
داء كذا دواؤه كذا فإذا كان الرجل فقيرًا أُعطي ثمن الدواء من بيت المال.

وليس عليهم خراج في ضياعهم وإنّما يُوخذ من الرؤس على قدر أموالهم وضياعهم. وإذا وُلِدَ لأحد ذَكَرٌ كُتِبَ اسمه عند السلطان فإذا بلغ ثماني عشرة سنة أُخذت منه الجزية. فإذا بلغ ثمانين سنة لم تؤخذ منه جزية وأُجري عليه من بيت المال ويقولون: أخذنا منه شابًا ونُجري عليه شيخًا. وفي كلّ مدينة كتّاب ومعلّم يعلّم الفقرا وأولادُهم من بيت المال يأكلون.

ونساؤهم مكشفات الشعور والرجال يغطّون رؤسهم. ١،٨،١٣

وبها قرية يقال لها تَايُوا في الجبل فَهُم قصرٌ[١] وكلّ قصير ببلاد الصين يُنْسَب إليها.

وأهل الصين أهل جَمال وطول وبياض نقيّ مُشَرَّب حمرةً. وهم أشدّ الناس سواد شعور ونساؤهم يجززن[٢] شعورهنّ.

وأمّا بلاد الهند فإنّه إذا ادّعى رجل على آخر دعوى يجب فيها القتل قيل للمدّعي: ١،٩،١
أتحامله النار فيقول: نعم فتُحمّى حديدة إحماءً شديدًا حتّى يظهر النار فيها ثمّ يقال له: ابسطْ يدك فتوضع على يده سبع ورقات من ورق شجر لهم ثمّ توضع على يده الحديدة فوق الورق ثمّ يمشي بها مقبلاً ومدبرًا حتّى يلقيها عن يده فيؤتى بكيس من جلود فيُدْخِل يده فيه ثمّ يُخْتَم بختم السلطان فإذا كان بعد ثلاث أُتي بأرزّ غير مقشّر فيقال له: افركه فإن لم يكن في يده أثرٌ فَقَدْ فَلَجَ[٣] ولا قتل عليه ويُغرَّم الذي ادّعى عليه

١ خ: قصارٌ. ٢ ب و ر: يجررن؛ ح: يجزُّونَ؛ خ و س: يُجرِينَ. ٣ ح: فلح.

In this case, the owner of the money will not be told anything; his money will be seized and shared out among his creditors, and no one will be permitted to do business with him again.

They have a stone tablet set up, ten cubits tall, on which is written in engraved characters a list of remedies and diseases, each particular disease paired with its appropriate remedy. And if a sick person is poor, he is given the cost of his medicine from the public treasury. **1.8.12**

Government concern for public health and education

They do not have to pay a tax on their land; a poll tax is levied instead, varying according to the amount of landed and other property that they own. When a male child is born to anyone, his name is registered with the ruler, and when he reaches the age of eighteen he has to pay the poll tax. If, however, he lives to the age of eighty, he no longer has to pay the tax; instead, he is given a pension from the public treasury, for they say, "When he was young he paid us a tax; now he is old we pay him a pension." Also, every city has a school and a teacher to teach the poor how to write, and the children of the poor are fed from the public treasury.

Their women go bare-headed, revealing their hair, but their men cover their heads. **1.8.13**

Appearance and dress of the Chinese

There is a village in the mountains in China called Tāyū where the people are short in stature. Every short person in China is said to come from there.

The Chinese are a fine-looking, tall people, with clear, pale complexions tinged with red. No people have blacker hair than they. Their women cut their hair.[59]

India, and Some of the Customs of Its People

Moving now to India, if a man accuses another of an offense for which the mandatory penalty is death, the accuser is asked, "Will you subject the person you have accused to ordeal by fire?" If he agrees to this, a piece of iron is first heated to such a high temperature that it becomes red-hot. The accused man is told to hold out his hand, palm up, and on it are placed seven leaves from a particular tree of theirs; the red-hot iron is then placed on his hand, on top of the leaves. Next, the accused has to walk up and down holding the iron, until he can bear it no longer and has to drop it. At this point, a leather bag is brought out: the man has to put his hand inside this, then the bag is sealed with the ruler's seal. When three days have passed, some unhusked rice is brought, and the accused man is told to husk it by rubbing it between his **1.9.1**

Ordeal by fire

مَنًّا مِن ذهبٍ يقبضه السلطان لنفسه. وربّما أغلوا الماء في قِدْر حديد أو نحاس حتّى لا يقدر أحد يدنو منه ثمّ يُطرَح فيه خاتم حديد ويقال: أَدْخِلْ يدك فتناوَلِ الخاتم وقد رأيتُ من أدخل يده وأخرجها صحيحةً ويُغرَّم المدّعي أيضاً منًّا من ذهب.

٢،٩،١ وإذا مات الملك ببلاد سرنديب صُيِّرَ على عَجَلَة[١] قريباً من الأرض وعُلِّقَ في مؤخّرها مستلقياً على قفاه يجُرُّ شعرُ رأسِه الترابَ عن الأرض وامرأة بيدها مكنسة تحثو التراب على رأسه وتنادي: أيّها الناس هذا ملككم بالأمس قد مَلَكَكم وكان أمرُه نافذاً فيكم وقد صار إلى ما ترون مِن تَرْكِ الدنيا وأَخَذَ روحَه مَلَكُ الموت فلا تغترّوا بالحياة بعده وكلام نحو هذا ثلاثة أيّام. ثمّ يُهيَّأ له الصندل والكافور والزعفران فيُحرَق به ثمّ يُرمى برماده في الريح. والهند كلّهم يحرقون موتاهم بالنار. وسرنديب آخر الجزاير وهي من بلاد الهند. وربّما أُحرِقَ الملك فتدخل نساؤه النار فيحترقن معه وإن شئن لم يفعلن.

٣،٩،١ وببلاد الهند مَن يُنسَب إلى السياحة في الغياض والجبال وقلّ ما يعاشر الناس ويأكل أحياناً الحشيش وثمر الغياض ويجعل في إحليله حلقة حديد لِيلّا يأتي النساء. ومنهم العريان ومنهم من ينصب نفسه للشمس مستقبلها عرياناً إلّا أنّ عليه شيأً من جلود النمور. فقد رأيتُ رجلاً منهم كما وصفت ثمّ انصرفت وعُدتُ بعد ستّ عشرة سنة فرأيته على تلك الحال فتعجّبت كيف لم تَسِلْ[٢] عينُه من حرّ الشمس.

٤،٩،١ وأهل بيت المملكة في كلّ مملكة أهل بيت واحد لا يخرج عنهم المُلك ولهم ولاة عهود. وكذلك أهل الكتابة والطبّ أهل بيوتات لا تكون تلك الصناعة إلّا فيهم. وليس تنقاد ملوك الهند لمَلِكٍ واحد بل كلّ واحد ملكُ بلاده وبلهرا ملك الملوك بالهند. فأمّا الصين فليس لهم ولاة عهود.

---

١ ح: عجله. ٢ خ: تُسْمَلْ؛ س: تَسُلْ.

palms. If after this no mark is found on his hand, he is deemed to have got the better of his accuser, and he escapes execution. Moreover, his accuser is fined a maund of gold, which the ruler appropriates for himself. On some occasions, they heat water in an iron or copper cauldron until it boils so furiously that no one can go near it. An iron finger-ring is then dropped into the water, and the accused man is told to put his hand in and retrieve the ring. I have seen a man put his hand in and bring it out unharmed. In such a case, too, his accuser is fined a maund of gold.

When a king of the land of Sarandīb dies, his corpse is paraded on a low-bedded cart, lying on its back with its head dangling off the rear of the cart, so that the hair drags up dust from the ground. And all the while a woman with a broom sweeps more dust on to the corpse's head and cries out, "O you people, behold your king! Only yesterday he reigned over you, and you obeyed his every word. See now to what he is come and the manner of his going from this world. For the angel of death has taken his soul. Henceforth, let life delude you never more!" These and other such words she declaims, and the obsequies continue for three days. Then a pyre of sandalwood, camphor, and saffron is made ready, and the corpse is burned on it and the ashes scattered to the wind.[60] All the Indians burn their dead on pyres; Sarandīb, the last of the islands,[61] is part of the land of India. At times it also happens that, when a dead king is burned, his womenfolk enter the fire too and are burned alive along with him; but if they wish, they do not do so. 1.9.2

Customs in Sarandīb on the death of a king

There are some in India whose habit is to wander the jungles and hills, seldom mixing with other people. Sometimes they live on leaves and jungle fruits and insert iron rings into the heads of their penises to stop them having sexual intercourse with women. There are some among them who are naked and others who stand upright all day facing the sun, naked too but for a scrap of tiger or leopard skin.[62] I once saw one of these men, just as I have described; I went away and did not return until sixteen years later, and there I saw him, still in the same position. I was amazed at how his eyes had not melted from the heat of the sun.[63] 1.9.3

Indian ascetics

In every kingdom in India, the ruling family belong to a single dynasty from which the royal title never passes to another house; they appoint crown princes.[64] The case is similar with scribes and physicians: they all belong to distinct family lines to which the particular occupation is restricted. The various kings in India do not owe allegiance to a single ruler; instead, each is 1.9.4

Among the Indians, kingship and occupations are hereditary

وأهل الصين أهل ملاهٍ[١] وأهل الهند يعيبون الملاهي ولا يتّخذونها ولا يشربون ١٠١٠،١
الشراب ولا يأكلون الخلّ لأنّه من الشراب. وليس ذلك دِين[٢] ولكنّ أَنَفَةً ويقولون: أيّ ملك شرب الشراب فليس بملك وذلك أنّ حولهم ملوكًا يقاتلونهم فيقولون: كيف يدبّر أمر مُلكِه من هو سكران. وربّما اقتتلوا على المُلك وذلك قليل لم أرَ أحداً غلب أحداً على مملكته إلّا قوم تِلوَ بلاد الفلفل. وإذا غلب ملك على مملكة ولّى عليها رجلاً من أهل بيت المَلِك المغلوب ويكون من تحت يده لا يرضى أهل تلك المملكة إلّا بذلك.

فأمّا بلاد الصين فربّما جارَ الملكُ الذي من تحت يد الملك الأكبر فيذبحونه ويأكلونه. وكلّ من قُتِلَ بالسيف أكل الصينيّون لحمه.

وأهل الصين والهند إذا أرادوا التزويج تهانوا[٣] بينهم ثمّ تهادوا ثمّ يُشْهِرون ٢،١٠،١
التزويج بالصنوج والطبول. وهديّتهم من المال على قدر الإمكان. وإذا أُحضر الرجل منهم امرأةً فبغتْ فعليها وعلى الباغي بها القتل في جميع بلاد الهند وإن زنى رجل بامرأة اغتصبها نفسها قُتِلَ الرجل وحده فإن فَجَرَ بامرأة على رِضى منها قُتِلا جميعاً.

والسَرِقُ[٤] في جميع بلاد الصين والهند في القليل منه والكثير القتل. فأمّا الهند ٣،١٠،١
إذا سرق السارق فلساً فما فوقه أُخذت خشبة طويلة فيُحَدَّد طرفها ثمّ يُقْعَد عليها على إسته حتّى تخرج من حلقه.

وأهل الصين يلوطون بغلمان قد أُقيموا لذلك بمنزلة زواني البِدَدَة.

---

١ ب: ملاهِي. ٢ خ: دينًا. ٣ كذا في ب؛ ح وس: تهانئوا؛ خ: تهانؤوا. ٤ ح: والسرقة؛ ولعلّ الصواب: وعلى السرق.

master of his own country. Balharā, however, is regarded as India's "king of kings."[65] In contrast to the Indians, the Chinese do not appoint crown princes.

Chinese and Indian Customs Compared

The Chinese are fond of musical entertainments; the Indians, however, regard entertainments as shameful and never indulge in them. They do not drink intoxicating drink, either, nor do they consume vinegar, because it is produced from such drink. This is a case not of religious belief but of disapproval. They say, "A king who drinks is not a king at all," the reason being that, in most Indian states, they are surrounded by neighboring kings who make war on them, so they say, "How can someone run a kingdom properly if he is drunk?" Sometimes kings fight each other for the control of a state, but this happens infrequently: I have never seen anyone actually take another king's country by force, except in the case of a people neighboring the Land of Pepper.[66] And if a king does conquer another kingdom, he appoints some member of the defeated king's family to rule it as his puppet,[67] because the people of the kingdom will tolerate no other arrangement. **1.10.1**

Entertainments, wine-drinking, and the execution of unjust rulers

In China, when one of the rulers under the command of the Great King acts unjustly, as sometimes happens, they slay him and eat him. The Chinese eat the flesh of all who are killed by the sword.[68]

Among the Chinese and Indians, when people wish to arrange a marriage they first invite each other to feasts, then they exchange gifts. After this, they make the news of the marriage public by beating cymbals and drums. Their gifts are in the form of money, and the amount depends on what the people concerned can pay. Throughout India, if a man brings a woman home as his wife and she then commits adultery, both she and the adulterer are put to death. If a man forces a woman to have illicit sex with him against her will, he alone is executed; but if he fornicates with her as a consenting partner, they are both put to death. **1.10.2**

Marriage and adultery

In all of China and India the penalty for theft, however great or small, is death. In the case of the Indians, if a thief steals as little as a *fils* or upwards, a long stake is brought, its end is sharpened, and then the thief is impaled on it, backside first, until the point comes out of his gullet.[69] **1.10.3**

Theft and sodomy

The Chinese sodomize boys who are provided for that purpose and are of the same order as female temple prostitutes.[70]

وحيطان أهل الصين الخشب وبناء أهل الهند حجارة وجصّ وآجرّ وطين ٤،١٠،١
وكذلك ربّما كان بالصين أيضاً. وليس الصين ولا الهند بأصحاب فُرُش.

ويتزوّج الرجل من الصين والهند ما شاء من النساء.

وطعام الهند الأرزّ وطعام الصين الحنطة والأرزّ وأهل الهند لا يأكلون الحنطة.

ولا يختتن الهند ولا الصين.

وأهل الصين يعبدون الأصنام ويصلّون لها ويتضرّعون إليها ولهم كُتُبُ دِينٍ.

والهند يطوّلون لحاهم ربّما رأيتَ[١] لحية أحدهم ثلاثة أذرع ولا يأخذون شواربهم. وأكثر أهل الصين لا لحا لهم خِلقةً لأكثرهم. وأهل الهند إذا مات لأحدهم ميّت حلق رأسه ولحيته.

والهند إذا حبسوا رجلاً أو لازموه منعوه الطعام والشراب سبعة أيّام وهم يتلازمون.

ولأهل الصين قضاة يحكمون بينهم دون العُمّال وكذلك أهل الهند.

والنمور والذياب ببلد الصين[٢] جميعاً فأمّا الأُسد فليست بكِلى[٣] الولايتين.

ويُقتَل قاطعُ الطريق.

وأهل الصين والهند يزعمون أنّ البِدَدَة تكلّمهم وإنّما يكلّمهم عِبادهم.[٤]

والصين والهند يقتلون ما يريدون أكلَه ولا يذبحونه فيضربون هامته حتّى يموت.

ولا يغتسل الهند ولا الصين من جنابة. وأهل الصين لا يستنجون إلّا ٥،١٠،١

---

١ ح: أربت. ٢ الصين: كذا في ب؛ ويبدو من نهاية الجملة أن المقصود: الصين والهند. ٣ كذا في ب؛ خ: بكلتي. ٤ ح وخ: عُبّادهم.

The Chinese use wood to build their walls, while the Indians build in stone, gypsum plaster, brick, and mud; these materials are however sometimes used in China also. Neither the Chinese nor the Indians are users of carpets.[71] 1.10.4

Various manners and customs

Chinese and Indian men marry as many women as they like.

The staple food of the Indians is rice, while that of the Chinese is wheat and rice. The Indians do not eat wheat.[72]

Neither the Indians nor the Chinese are circumcised.

The Chinese worship idols, praying to them and beseeching them for favors, and they possess religious texts.

The Indians let their beards grow long, and I have often seen an Indian with a beard three cubits in length. Also, they do not clip their moustaches. In contrast, most Chinese men are beardless by nature, for the most part. When someone in India suffers a bereavement, he shaves his head and his beard.

The Indians, when they imprison someone or keep him in confinement in his house, deny him food and drink for seven days. They are often kept in confinement.

The Chinese have judges who decide civil cases of lesser importance than those heard by provincial governors. The Indians also have such judges.

Leopards, tigers, and wolves are to be found throughout China. There are no lions, however, in either of the two provinces.[73]

Those who "cut the road" are put to death.[74]

Both the Chinese and the Indians assert that their idols speak to them, when, in reality, it is their temple servants who speak to them.

Both the Chinese and the Indians kill animals they intend to eat by bludgeoning them on the head until they die, rather than by cutting their throats, as the Muslims do.

Neither the Indians nor the Chinese bathe themselves when in a state of ritual pollution,[75] and the Chinese use only paper, not water, to clean their backsides after defecating. The Indians, however, bathe daily before eating their morning meal. The Indians do not have sexual intercourse with their women when they are menstruating; indeed, they find them so offensive that they turn them out of the house. The Chinese, on the other hand, 1.10.5

Personal hygiene

بالقراطيس. والهند يغتسلون كلّ يوم قبل الغدا ثمّ يأكلون. والهند لا يأتون النساء في الحيض ويُخرِجونهنّ عن منازلهم تقزّزًا منهنّ. والصين يأتونهنّ في الحيض ولا يُخرِجونهنّ. وأهل الهند يستاكون ولا يأكل أحدهم حتّى يستاك ويغتسل وليس يفعل ذلك أهل الصين.

وبلاد الهند أوسع من بلاد الصين وهي أضعافها وعدد ملوكهم أكثر وبلاد الصين ١٠،١٠،٦
أعمر. وليس للصين ولا للهند نخل ولهم ساير الشجر وثمرٌ ليس عندنا. والهند لا عنب لهم وهو بالصين قليل وساير الفواكه عندهم كثيرة والرمّان بالهند أكثر.

وليس لأهل الصين علم وإنّما أصل ديانتهم من الهند وهم يزعمون أنّ الهند ١،١٠،٧
وضعوا لهم البددة وأنّهم هم أهل الدين. وكلا البلدين يرجعون إلى التناسخ ويختلفون في فروع دينهم.

والطبّ بالهند والفلاسفةُ ولأهل الصين أيضاً طبّ وأكثر طبّهم الكيُّ. ولهم علم بالنجوم وذلك بالهند أكثر. ولا أعلمُ أحداً من الفريقين مسلماً ولا يتكلّم بالعربيّة.

وللهند خيل قليلة وهي للصين أكثر. وليس للصين فيلة ولا يتركونها في بلادهم ١،١٠،٨
تشاؤماً بها.

وجنود ملك الهند كثيرة ولا يُرْزَقون وإنّما يدعوهم الملك إلى الجهاد فيخرجون ينفقون من أموالهم ليس على الملك من ذلك شيء. فأمّا الصين فعطاؤهم كعطاء العرب.

وبلاد الصين أنْزَهُ وأحسن. وأكثر الهند لا مداين لها وأهل الصين في كلّ ١،١٠،٩
موضع لهم مدينة محصّنة عظيمة. وبلاد الصين أصحّ وأقلّ أمراضاً وأطيب هواءً لا يكاد يُرى بها أعمى ولا أعور ولا من به عاهة وهكذا[١] كثير ببلاد الهند.

وأنهار البلدين جميعاً عظام فيها ما هو أعظم من أنهارنا. والأمطار بالبلدين

١ خ: وهذا.

neither stop having sex when their women menstruate nor turn them out. The Indians use tooth sticks, and no one eats before he has cleaned his teeth with one, and washed himself; the Chinese, however, do not do this.

India is greater in extent than China, several times so, and has a greater number of kings. China, though, is more densely inhabited and cultivated.[76] Neither the Chinese nor the Indians have date palms, although they cultivate all other kinds of tree, as well as some types of fruit not to be found in our lands. The Indians, however, do not have grapes, and they are not common in China. All other kinds of fruit are to be found in abundance, although pomegranates are more common in India than in China. **1.10.6**

The relative extent of the two countries, and the varieties of fruit grown in them

The Chinese have no native tradition of religious learning; in fact their religion came from India. They maintain that it was the Indians who introduced the idols to their land and that they, the Indians, were the original people of religion. In both lands, they believe in the transmigration of souls as a basic tenet, although they differ on the resulting details of dogma. **1.10.7**

Religion and science

India is the land of medicine and of philosophers; the Chinese also have medical knowledge. Most of their medicine involves therapeutic burning.[77] In addition, they have a knowledge of astronomy and astrology, although this is more widespread in India.[78] I do not know of a single member of either race who is a Muslim, and Arabic is not spoken.

The Indians possess few horses; they are more common in China. The Chinese, however, do not possess elephants and do not let them remain in their land, as they regard them as ill-omened. **1.10.8**

Horses and troops

The king of India has many troops, but they are not paid as regular soldiers; instead, he summons them to fight for king and country, and they go to war at their own expense and at no cost at all to the king.[79] In contrast, the Chinese give their troops regular pay, as the Arabs do.

China is a more salubrious and finer land than India. In most of the land of India there are no urban settlements, but everywhere you go in China they have a great walled city. Also, China is a healthier country, with fewer diseases and better air: the blind, the one-eyed, and the deformed are seldom seen there, although in India there are plenty of them. **1.10.9**

Cities, diseases, and rivers

In both countries there are big rivers, some of them bigger than our rivers,[80] and both have plentiful rain. India, however, has many desert areas, while all of China is populated and cultivated.

جميعاً كثيرة. وفي بلاد الهند مفاوز كثيرة والصين كلّها عمارة.

وأهل الصين أجمل من أهل الهند وأشْبَهُ بالعرب في اللباس والدوابّ وهم في هيئتهم في مواكبهم شبيه بالعرب يلبسون الأقبية والمناطق. وأهل الهند يلبسون فوطتين ويتحلّون بأَسْوِرة الذهب والجوهر الرجال والنساء. ١،١٠،١٠

ووراء بلاد الصين من الأرض التَغَزْغُز وهم من التُرك وخاقان تُبَّت هذا ممّا يلي بلاد الترك. فأمّا ما يلي البحر فجزاير السِيْلا[١] وهم بيض يهادون صاحب الصين ويزعمون أنّهم إن لم يهادوه لم تمطرهم السماء. ولم يبلغها أحد من أصحابنا فيحكي عنهم. ولهم بُزاة بيض. ١،١٠،١١

تمّ الكتاب الأوّل.[٢]

١ ب: السَيلا. ٢ هنا إضافةٌ إلى متن ب متأخرةٌ عن النسخة الأصليّة: نَظَرَ في هذا الكتاب الفقير محمّد في سنة أحد [كذا في ب؛ ح وخ: إحدى] عشر بعد ألف أحسن الله عاقبتها وما بعدها آمين. أللهمّ اغفر لكاتبه ووالديه والمسلمين.

1.10.10 *Chinese and Indian dress*

The Chinese are better-looking than the Indians and more like the Arabs in their dress and in their choice of mounts; in fact, their style of clothing when they ride out in public is quite similar to that of the Arabs, for they wear long tunics and belts.[81] The Indians, however, wear two waist cloths and adorn themselves with bangles of gold and jewels, the men as well as the women.

1.10.11 *Lands beyond China*

The inland regions beyond China include those of the Taghazghuz, who are a Turkic people, and those of the *khāqān* of Tubbat; these regions adjoin the land of the Turks. In the other direction, that of the ocean, are the islands of al-Sīlā. They are a pale-skinned people who exchange gifts with the ruler of China; they maintain that if they did not keep up this exchange, rain would cease to fall on their land. None of our circle of informants has ever made it there and brought back a reliable report. In the land of al-Sīlā there are white hawks.

Here ends the first book.[82]

الكتاب الثاني من أخبار الصين والهند

١،١،٢ قال أبو زيد الحسن السِيرافيّ: إنّي نظرتُ في هذا الكتاب يعني الكتاب الأوّل الذي أُمِرْتُ بتأمُّله وإثباتِ ما وقفت عليه من أمر البحر وملوكه وأحوالهم وما عرفته من أحاديثهم ممّا لم يَدْخُلْ فيه فوجدت تاريخ الكتاب في سنة سبع وثلاثين ومايتين وأمور البحر في ذلك الوقت مستقيمة لكثرة اختلاف التجّار إليها[١] من العراق. ووجدتُ جميع ما حُكي في الكتاب على سبيل حقّ وصدق إلّا ما ذُكِرَ فيه من الطعام الذي يقدّمه أهل الصين إلى الموتى منهم وأنّه إذا وُضِعَ بالليل عند الميّت أصبحوا فلم يوجد وادّعوا أنّه يأكله فقد كان بلغَنا هذا حتّى وَرَدَ علينا مِن ناحيتهم مَن وثقْنا بخبره فسألناه عن ذلك فأنكره وقال: هي دعوى لا أصل لها كدعوى أهل الأوثان أنّها تكلّمهم.

١،٢،٢ وقد تغيّر بعد هذا التاريخ أمر الصين خاصّةً وحدثت فيه[٢] حوادث انقطع لها الجهاز إليهم وخرب البلد وزالت رسومه وتفرّق أمره وأنا أشرح ما وقفتُ عليه من السبب في ذلك إن شاء الله.

السبب في تغيُّر أمر الصين عمّا كان عليه من الأحكام والعدل وانقطاع الجهاز إليه من سيراف أنّ نابغاً نبغ فيهم من غير بيت المُلك يُعرَف بانشوا[٣] وكان مبتدأ أمره الشطارة والفتوّة وحمل السلاح والعيث واجتماع السفهاء إليه حتّى اشتدّت

١ إليها: كذا في ب. ٢ خ: فيها. ٣ ح و ر: ببابشو.

Accounts of China and India: The Second Book

2.1.1 *Abū Zayd al-Sīrāfī's evaluation of the First Book*

Abū Zayd al-Ḥasan al-Sīrāfī said: I have examined this foregoing book (meaning the First Book), having been commanded to look carefully through it, and to verify the information I find in it about the affairs of the sea and about its kings and their various circumstances,[83] and to compare this information with other reports passed down about these kings, known to myself but not appearing in the book. I found the date of the book to be the year two hundred and thirty-seven [851–52]—a time when maritime business still ran on an even keel, on account of all the toing and froing overseas by merchants from Iraq. I also found that everything recounted in the First Book follows a truthful and veracious line. The only exception is the report about the food the Chinese offer to their dead and which, when they leave it by the corpse at night then find it gone in the morning, they allege the dead person has eaten. This tale had already reached our ears, but we did not know if it was true until someone we trusted as an informant arrived from those parts. When we asked him about the story, he dismissed it as untrue and added, "The allegation is just as baseless as that of the idolators who claim that their idols speak to them."

The Changed Situation in China, and the Cause of It

2.2.1 *The revolution of Huang Chao, and the Khānfū massacre*

Since that above-mentioned date, however, the situation has changed, in China in particular. Because of events that occurred there, the trading voyages to China were abandoned and the country itself was ruined, leaving all traces of its greatness gone and everything in utter disarray. I shall now explain what I have learned concerning the cause of this, God willing.

The reason for the deterioration of law and order in China, and for the end of the China trading voyages from Sīrāf, was an uprising led by a rebel from outside the ruling dynasty known as Huang Chao. At the outset of his career he had been involved in armed banditry and hooliganism, causing general mayhem and attracting a rabble of witless followers. In time, when his fighting capacity, the size of his forces, and his lust for power had grown strong enough, he marched on the great cities of China, among them Khānfū: this

شوكته وكثر عدده واستحكم طمعه فقصد خانفو من بين مدن الصين وهي المدينة التي يقصدها تجّار العرب وبينها وبين البحر مسيرة أيّام يسيرة وهي على وادٍ عظيم وماء عذب فامتنع أهلُها عليه فحاصرهم مدّة طويلة وذلك في سنة أربع وستّين ومايتين إلى أن ظفر بها فوضع السيفَ في أهلها. فذكر أهل الخبرة بأمورهم أنّه قَتَلَ من المسلمين واليهود والنصارى والمجوس سوى من قُتِلَ من أهل الصين مايةً وعشرون[1] ألف رجل كانوا تبوّءوا بهذه المدينة فصاروا بها تجّاراً وإنّما عُرِفَ مقدارُ عدد هذه الملل الأربع لتحصيل أهل الصين بعددهم. وقَطَعَ ما كان فيه[2] من شجر التوت وساير الأشجار وذكرْنا شجر التوت خصوصاً لإعداد أهل الصين ورقه لدود القزّ حتّى تَلِفَ[3] الدود فصار سبباً لانقطاع الحرير خاصّةً عن بلاد العرب.

٢،٢،٢ ثمّ قصد بعد تخريب خانفو إلى بلدٍ بلد فأخربه وعجز مَلِكُ الصين عنه إلى أن قارب مدينة المُلك وتُعْرَف بخمدان فهرب الملك منه إلى مدينة بَمذُو متاخمة[4] لبلاد التبّت فأقام بها. ودامت أيّام هذا النابغ وعظم شأنه وكان قصده ووكده خراب المدن وقَتَلَ أهلها إذ لم يكن من بيت مُلك ومَن يطمع في اتّساق الأمر له فبلغ مِن ذلك مبلغاً فَسَدَ به أمرُ الصين إلى وقتنا هذا.

ولم تزل تلك حالُ هذا النابغ إلى أن كتب ملكُ الصين إلى ملك التغزغز من بلاد الترك وبينهم مجاورة ومصاهرة ووجّه إليه رسلاً يسأله كشفَ هذا الرجل عنه. فأنفذ ملك التغزغز ابناً له إلى هذا النابغ في عدد كثير وجموع وافرة فأزاله بعد حروب متّصلة ووقايع عظيمة فزعم قومٌ أنّه قُتِلَ وزعم آخرون أنّه مات.

٣،٢،٢ وعاد ملك الصين إلى بلده المعروف بخمدان وقد أخربه عليه وعلى سبيل ضعف في نفسه ونقص في أمواله وهلاك قوّاده وصناديد[5] رجاله وكُفاته. وغلب مع ذلك على كلّ ناحية متغلِّبٌ منع من أموالها وتمسّك بما[6] في يده منها. فدعت مَلِكَ الصين الضرورةُ لقصور يده إلى قبول العفو منهم بإظهار الطاعة والدعاء له دون

---

١ خ: عشرين. ٢ فيه: كذا في ب. ٣ ح وخ و ر: يلف. ٤ خ: المتاخمة. ٥ ب: صَنايد. ٦ خ: بها.

city is the destination of Arab merchants and lies a few days' journey from the sea on a great river where the water flows fresh. At first the citizens of Khānfū held out against him, but he subjected them to a long siege—this was in the year 264 [877–78]—until, at last, he took the city and put its people to the sword. Experts on Chinese affairs reported that the number of Muslims, Jews, Christians, and Zoroastrians massacred by him, quite apart from the native Chinese, was 120,000;[84] all of them had gone to settle in this city and become merchants there. The only reason the number of victims from these four communities happens to be known is that the Chinese had kept records of their numbers. Huang Chao also cut down all the trees in Khānfū, including all the mulberry trees; we single out mulberry trees for mention because the Chinese use their leaves as fodder for silkworms: owing to the destruction of the trees, the silkworms perished, and this, in turn, caused silk, in particular, to disappear from Arab lands.

2.2.2 *The progress and eventual defeat of the revolution*

After destroying Khānfū, Huang Chao marched on one city after another, laying waste to each. So powerless was the king of China to withstand him that the rebel eventually closed in on the royal capital, known as Khamdān;[85] the king fled it for the city of Bamdhū on the border of Tibetan territory, and set up his court there. The rebel's power, meanwhile, kept on growing from day to day. His whole aim and purpose was the destruction of cities and the slaughter of their inhabitants, for he did not belong to any royal lineage and therefore could not aspire to gain the throne itself.[86] Moreover, he took his destruction to such extremes that China has remained in chaos down to our own times.

For a time, the rebel's campaign went on unchecked. And then the king of China wrote to the king of the Taghazghuz—a people from the land of the Turks, to whom they are neighbors and kinsmen by marriage[87]—and sent envoys to him, asking him to free him from the curse of Huang Chao. In response, the king of the Taghazghuz dispatched one of his sons against the rebel at the head of a vast number of troops, and, after ceaseless fighting and many great battles, Huang Chao was eliminated. Some people claimed that he was killed, others that he died a natural death.[88]

2.2.3 *The breakup of China and the decline of its foreign trade*

The king of China then returned to his city known as Khamdān, only to find it left in ruins by Huang Chao and to find himself debilitated, his treasury depleted, and his captains, commanders, and capable officers all dead. As a consequence, all the provinces were taken over by warlords: they prevented the central government from gaining access to revenues and kept

السمع والطاعة في الأموال وما كان من الملوك ينفذ فيه. فصارت بلاد الصين على سبيل ما جَرَتْ عليه أحوالُ الأكاسرة عند قتلِ الإسكندر لدارا الكبير وقِسْمتِه أرض فارس على ملوك الطوايف. وصار بعضهم يعضد بعضاً للمغالبة بغير إذن الملك ولا أمره فإذا أناخ القويّ منهم على الضعيف تغلَّبَ على بلاده واجتاح ما فيه[1] وأكل ناسَه كلَّهم وذلك مباح لهم في شريعتهم لأنّهم يتبايعون لحوم الناس في أسواقهم.

وامتدّت أيديهم مع ذلك إلى ظلمِ مَن قصدهم من التجّار. ولمّا حدث هذا فيهم اِلْتَأَمَ إليه ظهور الظلم والتعدّي في نواخذة العرب وأرباب المراكب فألزموا التجّار ما لا يجب عليهم وغلبوهم على أموالهم واستجازوا ما لم يجرِ الرسمُ به قديماً في شيء من أفعالهم. فنزع الله جلّ ذكره البركات منهم جميعاً ومنع البحرُ جانبَه ووقع الفنا بالمقدار الجاري من المدبِّر تبارك اسمه في الربابنة والأدلّاء بسيراف وعُمان.

وذُكِرَ في الكتاب طرفٌ[2] من سنن أهل الصين ولم يُذْكَرْ غيره وهو سبيل المُحْصَن ١،٣،٢
والمُحْصَنة عندهم إذا زنيا القتل وكذلك اللصّ والقاتل. وسبيلهم في القتل أنْ تُشَدّ يدا مَن يريدون قتله شدّاً وثيقاً ثمّ تُطْرَحَ يداه في رأسه حتّى تصيرا[3] على عنقه ثمّ تُدْخَلَ رجله اليمنى فيما ينفذ من يده اليمنى ورجله اليسرى فيما ينفذ من يده اليسرى فتصيرُ قدماه جميعاً من ورايه ويتقبّض ويبقى كالكرة لا حيلة له في نفسه ويستغني

١ فيه: كذا في ب. ٢ خ: وذُكِرَ ... طرفًا. ٣ ح وخ: يصيرا.

hold of all the wealth that was in their hands. Because of the weakness of his own hand, necessity compelled the king of China to accept their excuses; for their part, the warlords feigned obedience to the king and pronounced the customary formulae of allegiance[89] but without actually obeying him in the matter of revenues or in other areas in which provincial rulers had formerly carried out the royal will. Thus China went the way of the Persian emperors when Alexander killed Darius the Great and divided Persia up among factional rulers.[90] Moreover the warlords, acting neither with the king's blessing nor at his bidding, supported each other in their quest for further power: when a stronger one besieged a weaker, he would conquer his territory, annihilate everything in it, and eat all the defeated warlord's people, cannibalism being permissible for them according to their legal code, for they trade in human flesh in their markets.[91]

On top of all this, they extended the hand of injustice against merchants coming to their land. And, in addition to the harm done to the merchants, Arab captains and shipowners began to be subjected to injustices and transgressions. The Chinese placed undue impositions on merchants, seized their property by force, and sanctioned practices in which the custom of former times would in no way have allowed them to engage. Because of this, God—exalted be His name—withdrew His blessings altogether from the Chinese, the sea itself became uncooperative,[92] and ruin befell the ships' masters and pilots of Sīrāf and Oman, as ordained, in the course of events, by God the Ruler, may His name be blessed.

Various Practices and Manufactures of the Chinese

2.3.1 *How criminals are put to death*

One aspect of judicial practice among the Chinese was mentioned in the First Book, but only that one, namely, that married men and women who commit adultery are put to death, as are thieves and murderers. The actual manner of execution is as follows. First, the hands of the man to be executed are firmly bound and pushed over his head, on to the back of his neck; then his right leg is forced through the space formed by his right arm, and his left leg through that formed by his left arm. This means that both his feet are now at his back, and his whole body is compressed and remains like a ball; there is no way he can free himself, and no need of anything to hold him in this position. When he is in this state, his neck becomes dislocated, the vertebrae of his spine are displaced from their supporting tissue, the joints of

عن ممسك يمسكه. وعند ذلك تزول عنقه عن مركبها وتتزايل خرزات ظهره عن بطنها وتختلف وركاه ويتداخل بعضُه في بعض وتضيق[١] نَفَسُه ويصير في حال لو تُرِكَ على ما هو به بعضَ ساعةٍ لَتَلِفَ. فإذا بلغ منه ضُرِبَ بخشبة لهم معروفة على مَقاتِله ضرباتٍ معروفة لا تجاوز فليس دون نفسه شي[٢] ثمّ يُدْفَعُ إلى من يأكله.

٢،٣،٢ وفيهم نساء لا يردن الإحصان ويرغبن في الزنا وسبيل هذه[٣] أن تحضر مجلس صاحب الشُرَط فتذكر زُهْدَها في الإحصان ورغبتها في الدخول في جملة الزواني وتسأل حملها على الرسم في مثلها ومن رسمهم فيمن أراد ذلك من النساء أن تكتب نسبها وحِلْيتها[٤] وموضع منزلها وتُثْبَتَ في ديوان الزواني ويُجْعَل[٥] في عنقها خيطٌ فيه خاتم من نحاس مطبوع بخاتم الملك ويُدْفَع إليها منشور يُذْكَر فيه دخولها في جملة الزواني وأنّ عليها لبيت المال في كلّ سنة كذا وكذا[٦] فلساً وأنّ مَن تزوّجها فعليه القتل فتودي في كلّ سنة ما عليها ويزول الإنكار عنها. فهذه الطبقة من النساء يرُحن بالعشيّات عليهنّ ألوانُ الثياب من غير استتار فيصرن إلى من طَرِيَ[٧] إلى تلك البلاد من الغرباء من أهل الفسق والفساد وأهل الصين فيقمن عندهم وينصرفن بالغدوات. ونحن نحمد الله على ما طهّرنا به من هذه الفتن.

٣،٣،٢ وأمّا تعاملهم بالفلوس فالسبب فيه إنكارُهم على المتعاملين بالدنانير والدراهم وقولهم[٨] إنّ لصّاً لو دخل منزل رجل من العرب المتعاملين بالدنانير والدراهم لتهيّأ له حمل عشرة آلاف دينار ومثلها من الوَرِق على عنقه فيكون فيها عطبُ صاحب المال وإنّ لصّاً لو دخل إلى رجل منهم لم يحمل أكثر من عشرة آلاف فلس وإنّما ذلك عشرة مثاقيل ذهب. وهذه الفلوس معمولة من النحاس وأخلاط من غيره معجونة به والفلس منها في قدر الدرهم البغليّ وفي وسطه ثقب واسع ليفرد[٩] الخيط فيه.

١ ح: يضيق. ٢ شي: ساقطة في خ. ٣ خ: هذا. ٤ وحِلْيتها: كذا في ب ولعلّ المقصود: وحِلْتها.
٥ ح و ر: تجعل. ٦ ب: كذى وكذى. ٧ ح: طرا؛ خ: طرأ. ٨ وقولهم: ساقطة في ح وخ.
٩ ليفرد: قد يكون الصواب حسب ر ليغرز.

his hips are twisted the wrong way around, and all the parts of his frame are compressed into each other: thus his spirit becomes constricted, and if he is left in such a position for even a part of an hour, he will perish. If however he remains alive too long, he is then beaten with a particular wooden stave of theirs, a particular number of times, on the parts of his body where the blows will be fatal; the number of blows is never exceeded, but it is never less than enough to kill him. Then he is given over to those who will eat him.

Among the Chinese are certain women who do not wish to be virtuously married but prefer a life of sexual promiscuity. The practice is for such a woman to go to the office of the chief of police and declare her renunciation of the married life[93] and that she wishes to be entered into the list of harlots and to request that she be subject to the conventions customary for those of her kind. They have a number of conventions with regard to women wishing to lead a promiscuous life. For example, she must record in writing her ancestral descent, her physical appearance,[94] and her place of residence. She is then entered officially in the Register of Harlots, and a cord is placed around her neck from which is suspended a copper tag impressed with the ruler's seal. She is also presented with a written authorization that attests her entry into the list of harlots and states that she must pay such-and-such an amount of copper cash each year to the public treasury;[95] it also states that anyone marrying her is to be put to death. Thereafter, she pays her dues annually, and no opprobrium attaches to her. The women of this class go out in the evenings, dressed in all manner of attire, and unveiled.[96] They go to wanton and licentious foreigners who have arrived in the land, and also to the Chinese themselves, spending the night with them and leaving the following morning. We praise God for the guidance by which He has purified us from such temptations! 2.3.2

The Register of Harlots

Regarding their use of copper coins to transact business, the reason for it is that they look on people who use gold dinars and silver dirhams as mistaken. For they argue that, if a thief enters the house of one of the Arabs who use dinars and dirhams, it is quite possible for him to carry off on his back ten thousand dinars and the same quantity of silver, which would spell ruin for the owner of the money. If a thief enters the house of one of their people, however, he can carry off no more than ten thousand of the copper coins, which are worth only ten *mithqāl*s of gold.[97] These coins are made of copper alloyed with a mixture of other metals. Each of them is the size of a *baghlī* 2.3.3

Chinese copper coinage

وقيمة كلّ ألف فلس منها مثقال من ذهب ويَنْظِمُ الخيطُ منها ألفَ فلس على رأس كلّ ماية عقدة. فإذا ابتاع المبتاع ضياعاً أو متاعاً أو بقلاً فما فوقه دفع من هذه الفلوس على قدر الثمن وهي موجودة بسيراف وعليها نقش بكتابتهم.

وأمّا الحريق ببلاد الصين والبنا وما ذُكِرَ فيه فالبلد مبنيّ على ما قيل من خشب ومن قنا مشبّك على مثال الشقاق القصب عندنا ويُليَّط بالطين وبعلاج لهم يتّخذونه من حبّ الشَهْدانَج فيصير في بياض اللبن تُدْهَن به الجُدُر فيشرق إشراقاً عجيباً. وليس لبيوتهم عَتَبٌ لأنّ أملاكهم وذخايرهم وما تحويه أيديهم في صناديق مركّبة على عجل تدور بها فإذا وقع الحريق دُفِعَت تلك الصناديق بما فيها فلم يمنعها العتب من سرعة النفوذ. ٤،٣،٢

وأمّا أمر الخدم فذُكِرَ مجملاً وإنّما هم ولاة الخراج وأبوابُ المال. فمنهم من قد سُبي من الأطراف فخُصي ومنهم من يخصيه والدُه من أهل الصين ويُهديه إلى الملك تقرّباً به إليه فأمور الملك في خاصّته وخزاينه ومن يتوجّه إلى مدينة خانفو التي يقصد إليها تجّار العرب هَمْ[1] الخدم. ٥،٣،٢

ومن سننهم في ركوب هؤلاء الخدم وملوك ساير المدن إذا ركبوا أن يتقدّمهم رجال بخشب تشبه النواقيس يضربون بها فيُسْمَع من بُعْد فلا يقف أحد من الرعيّة في شيء من ذلك الطريق الذي يريد الخادم أو الملك أن يمرّ فيه ومَن كان على باب دارٍ دخلها وأغلق الباب دونه حتّى يكون اجتياز الخادم أو الملك المُمَلَّك على تلك المدينة وليس في طريقه أحد من العامّة ترهيباً وتجبّراً ولِيَلّا يكثر نظر العامّة إليهم ولا يمتدّ لسان أحد إلى الكلام معهم.

---

١ خ: هُمُ.

dirham and has a hole at its center large enough to take the cord on which the coins are strung. The value of each thousand of these coins is a *mithqāl* of gold: a thousand are strung on the cord, with a knot tied after every hundredth coin. When anyone buys land or any sort of goods or even something as cheap as vegetables, he pays with these copper coins, according to the price of his purchase. They are to be found at Sīrāf and bear a legend in Chinese characters.[98]

Turning to outbreaks of fire in China and the information reported in the First Book about buildings, the cities there are constructed, as stated, of wood and panels of woven bamboo, rather like the reed panels of our lands.[99] The structures are plastered with clay and with a substance peculiar to the Chinese, which they produce from hemp seeds and which turns milk-white: when walls are painted with this, it gleams with extraordinary brightness. The doorways of their houses have no thresholds, because their goods and treasures and all their possessions are kept in chests mounted on wheels, so they can be moved about. If fire breaks out, these chests and their contents can be pushed to safety, with no threshold to impede their swift exit. **2.3.4**

Their manner of saving their possessions in event of fire

On the subject of eunuch slaves, which was mentioned summarily in the First Book, they function as overseers of taxes and as doorkeepers of the treasury. Some of them are of non-Chinese origin, captured in the borderlands, then castrated; others come from the native Chinese population and are castrated by their fathers, then presented by them to the ruler as a means of gaining favor. All matters to do with the ruler's own household and his treasuries, as well as with foreigners arriving in the city of Khānfū (to which the Arab merchants go), all this is the concern of these slaves. **2.3.5**

Eunuch slaves, provincial rulers, and their manner of riding in public

It is a custom of theirs that when these slave officials and the rulers of all the various cities ride out in public, they are preceded by men with wooden instruments like clappers:[100] when they beat them, the sound can be heard from far away, and none of the populace remains on any part of the road along which the slave or the ruler intends to pass. Moreover, anyone who happens to be at the door of his house goes inside and shuts the door behind him until the slave, or the ruler in charge of the city, has passed by. Thus, not a single one of the common people is to be found along their route. The intention is both to impart a sense of fear and awe and to give the commoners no opportunity of gawping at their masters or daring to address them.

ولباس خدمهم ووجوهِ قوّادهم فاخرُ الحريرِ الذي لا يُحْمَل مثله إلى بلاد العرب عندهم ومبالغتهم[١] في أثمانه. وذكر رجل من وجوه التجّار ومَن لا يُشَكُّ في خبره أنّه صار إلى خصيّ كان الملك أنفذه إلى مدينة خانفو لتخيّر ما يحتاج إليه من الأمتعة الواردة من بلاد العرب فرأى على صدره خالًا يشفُّ من تحت ثياب حرير كانت عليه فقدّر أنّه قد ضاعف بين ثوبين منها فلمّا ألحَّ في النظر قال له الخصيّ: أراك تديم النظرَ إلى صدري فَلِمَ ذلك فقال له الرجل: عجبتُ من خال يشفّ من تحت هذه الثياب فضحك الخصيّ ثمّ طرح كمّ قميصه إلى الرجل وقال له: اعددْ ما عليّ منها فوجدها خمسة أقبية بعضها فوق بعض والخال يشفّ من تحتها. والذي هذه صفته من الحرير خامٌ غير مقصور والذي يلبسه ملوكهم أرفعُ من هذا وأعجبُ. ٦،٣،٢

وأهل الصين من أحذق خلقِ الله كفًّا بنقش وصناعة وكلّ عمل لا يتقدّمهم[٢] فيه أحد من ساير الأمم. والرجل منهم يصنع بيده ما[٣] يقدّر أنّ غيره يعجز عنه فيقصد به باب الملك يلتمس الجزاءَ على لطيف ما ابتدع فيأمر الملك بنصبه على بابه مِن وقته ذلك إلى سنة فإن لم يُخْرِجْ أحدٌ فيه عيباً جازاه وأدخله في جملة صنّاعه وإن أُخرِجَ فيه عيبٌ اطّرحه ولم يجازِه. ٧،٣،٢

وإنّ رجلاً منهم صوّر سنبلةً عليها عصفور في ثوب حرير لا يشكّ الناظر إليها أنّها سنبلة وأنّ عصفورًا عليها فبقيت مدّةً وإنّه اجتازَ بها رجل أحدب فعابَها فأُدْخِلَ إلى ملك ذلك البلد وحَضَرَ صانعُها فسئل[٤] الأحدب عن العيب فقال: المتعارَفُ عند الناس جميعاً أنّه لا يقع عصفور على سنبلة إلّا أمالَها وإنّ[٥] هذا المصوِّر صوّر السنبلة قايمةً لا مَيْلَ لها وأثبتَ العصفور فوقها منتصباً فأخطأ. فصُدِّقَ ولم يُثِبِ الملكُ صانعَها بشيء. وقصدُهم في هذا وشِبْهِه رياضةُ مَن

---

١ عندهم ومبالغتهم: كذا في ب؛ وقد يكون تقويم خ على الصواب: مِن عندهم لمبالغتهم. ٢ ح وخ و ر: يقدمهم.
٣ ما: ساقطة في ب. ٤ ح: فسأل. ٥ ح: وأن.

These slave officials of theirs, and their prominent military commanders, dress in silk of exquisite quality, the like of which is never exported to Arab lands because the Chinese themselves pay such inflated prices for it.[101] One of the prominent foreign merchants, a man whose reports are beyond doubt, related that he went to meet a eunuch official whom the Great King had sent to the city of Khānfū to take the pick of certain goods of Arab provenance that he needed. The merchant noticed that on the eunuch's chest was a mole, clearly visible through the silk garments he was wearing, and guessed that the eunuch was wearing a double layer of silk. When he realized that the merchant had been gazing so intently, the eunuch said to him, "I see that you cannot take your eyes off my chest. What is the reason?" The merchant replied, "Because I am amazed at how a mole can be visible through these garments of yours." At this, the eunuch laughed and held out the sleeve of his robe to the merchant: "Count how many I am wearing!" he said. The merchant did so, and found that he was wearing five tunics, one on top of the other; the mole could be seen through them all. Furthermore, the silk described here was of the raw, unbleached sort; the kind worn by their rulers is even more extraordinarily fine. 2.3.6

The diaphanous silks of China

Of all God's creation, the Chinese are among the most dexterous at engraving and manufacturing and at every kind of craft. Indeed, no one from any other nation has the edge on them in this respect. If a Chinese craftsman makes something with his own hands that he thinks no one else would be able to produce, he takes it to the gate of the ruler's palace, hoping that the excellence of his creation will gain him a reward. The ruler then issues instructions for the artefact to be displayed at the gate for a period of a year from the time of its receipt. If during this time no one finds fault with the piece, the ruler will reward its maker and enlist him as one of his recognized artisans; if however a fault is detected, the piece is discarded and the maker receives no reward. 2.3.7

The precise work of Chinese craftsmen

It is said that a certain Chinese craftsman depicted, on a silk robe, an ear of corn with a bird perched on it, in so realistic a way that no one viewing it would have any doubt that it showed an ear of corn with a bird on it.[102] When the piece had been on display for some time, a hunchback passed by and found fault with it. He was admitted into the presence of the ruler of the city; the craftsman was present too. When asked what was wrong with the piece, the hunchback said, "Everyone knows that a bird cannot perch on an ear of corn without making it bend; but the depictor of this scene has shown

يعمل هذه الأشيا ليضطرّهم ذلك إلى شدّة الاحتراز وإعمال الفكر فيما يصنع كلٌّ منهم بيده.

وقد كان بالبصرة رجلٌ من قريش يُعرف بابن وَهْبٍ مِن ولد هَبّار بن الأسود ١،٤،٢
خرج منها عند خرابها فوقع إلى سيراف وكان فيها مركبٌ يريد بلاد الصين. فنزعت به هِمّتُه بالمقدار الجاري على أن ركب في ذلك المركب إلى بلاد الصين ثمّ نزعت به همّته إلى قصد ملكها الكبير فسار إلى خمدان في مقدار شهرين من المدينة المعروفة بخانفو. وأقام بباب الملك مدّة طويلة يرفع الرقاع ويذكر أنّه من أهل بيت نبوّة العرب فأمر الملك بعد هذه المدّة بإنزاله في بعض المساكن وإزاحة علّته فيما يحتاج إليه. وكتب الملك إلى الوالي المستخلف المقيم بخانفو يأمره بالبحث ومَسَئَلة[1] التجّار عمّا يدّعيه الرجل من قرابة نبيء العرب صلّى الله عليه وسلّم. فكتب صاحب خانفو بصحّة نسبه فأذن له ووَصَلَهُ بمال واسع عاد به إلى العراق وكان شيخاً فهِماً.

فأخبرَنا أنّه لمّا وصل إليه وسايَلَهُ[2] عن العرب وكيف أزالوا مُلك العجم فقال[3] له: ٢،٤،٢
بالله جلّ ذكره وبما كانت العجم عليه من عبادة النيران والسجود للشمس والقمر من دون الله. فقال له: لقد غلبَتِ العرب على أجلّ الممالك وأوسعها ريفاً وأكثرها أموالاً وأعقلها رجالاً وأبعدها صوتاً. ثمّ قال له: فما منزلة ساير الملوك عندكم فقال: ما لي بهم علم. فقال للترجمان: قل له إنّا نعدّ الملوك خمسةً فأوسعهم مُلكاً الذي يملك العراق لأنّه في وسط الدنيا والملوك مُحْدِقَةٌ به ونجد اسمه عندنا ملك الملوك وبعده

---

١ ح وخ: ومسألة؛ ر: ومسلة. ٢ ح: وسأله. ٣ فقال: كذا في ب.

the ear of corn standing straight up with no bend to it, and has then stuck the bird standing upright on top of it. That is his mistake." The hunchback was deemed to have spoken the truth, and the ruler gave the artisan no reward. Their aim in this and similar situations is to train the makers of such pieces, so that each one of them will feel compelled to guard carefully against faults and to consider critically what he makes with his own hands.

The Visit of Ibn Wahb al-Qurashī to the King of China

There was a man of Quraysh in Basra known as Ibn Wahb, a descendant of **2.4.1**
Habbār ibn al-Aswad. When the city was destroyed[103] he left it and ended up *Ibn Wahb admitted to the king's presence*
in Sīrāf, where he found a ship about to set sail for China. He was seized by a sudden desire that caused him, as was fated, to travel to China aboard the ship. On arrival he was again seized by a desire, this time to visit the Great King, so he made his way to Khamdān, traveling for about two months from the city known as Khānfū. He lodged by the palace gate for a long time, submitting written requests for an audience in which he stated that he belonged to the family of the Arabs' prophet. Eventually the king commanded that he be given accommodation in one of the official guest houses, and that any needs he lacked should be supplied. The king then wrote to his appointed governor residing in Khānfū, instructing him to make investigations and inquiries among the Arab merchants about Ibn Wahb's alleged kinship with the prophet of the Arabs, God bless him and keep him. When the governor of Khānfū wrote back confirming that this relationship was genuine, the Great King granted Ibn Wahb an audience and gave him a large amount of money, which he brought back to Iraq. This Ibn Wahb was a canny old man.

Ibn Wahb informed us that, when he entered the king's presence, the **2.4.2**
king asked him about the Arabs and how they had brought about the end of *How the Chinese classify world rulers*
the Persian empire. "With the help of God, exalted be His name," Ibn Wahb replied, "and because the Persians worshipped fire and bowed in prayer to the sun and the moon, instead of worshipping God." The king said to him, "The Arabs have indeed conquered the most magnificent of empires, with the most extensive lands for crops and grazing, the greatest wealth, the most intelligent men, and the furthest-flung renown." Then he asked Ibn Wahb, "How are all the kings ranked according to you Arabs?" Ibn Wahb replied, "I know nothing about them." Then the king said to his interpreter, "Tell him that we count five kings as great. The one with the most extensive realm is

ملكُنا هذا ونجده عندنا ملك الناس لأنّه لا أحد من الملوك أَسْوَسُ منّا ولا أضبطُ لمُلكه من ضبطنا لمُلكنا ولا رعيّة من الرعايا أطوع لملوكها من رعيّتنا فنحن ملوك الناس. ومن بعدنا ملك السباع وهو ملك الترك الذي يلينا وبعدهم ملك الفيلة وهو ملك الهند ونجده[1] عندنا ملك الحكمة لأنّ أصلها منهم وبعده ملك الروم وهو عندنا ملك الرجال لأنّه ليس في الأرض أتمّ خلقاً من رجاله ولا أحسن وجوهاً. فهولاء أعيان الملوك والباقون دونهم.

٣،٤،٢ ثمّ قال للترجمان: قل له أتعرف صاحبَك إن رأيتَه يعني رسول الله صلّى الله عليه.[2] فقلتُ: وكيف لي برؤيته وهو عند الله جلّ وعزّ. فقال: لم أُرِدْ هذا إنّما أردتُ صورتَه. فقال: أَجَلْ. فأَمَرَ بِسَفَط فأُخرِجَ فوُضِعَ بين يديه فتناول منه دَرْجاً وقال للترجمان: أَرِهِ صاحبَه فرأيتُ في الدرج صور الأنبيا فحرّكتُ شفتي بالصلاة عليهم ولم يكن عنده أنّي أعرفهم فقال للترجمان: سَلْهُ عن تحريك شفته فسألني فقلتُ: أصلّي على الأنبياء. فقال: من أين عرفتَهم فقلتُ: بما[3] صُوِّرَ من أمرهم هذا نوح في السفينة ينجو[4] بمن معه لمّا أمر الله جلّ ذكره الما فغمر الأرض كلّها بمن[5] فيها وسلّمه ومن معه. فضحك وقال: أمّا نوح فقد صدقتَ في تسميته وأمّا غرق الأرض كلّها فلا نعرفه وإنّما أخذ الطوفانُ قطعة من الأرض ولم يصل إلى أرضنا ولا أرض الهند. قال ابن وهب: فتهيّبتُ الردّ عليه وإقامة الحجّة لعلمي بدفعه ذلك ثمّ قلتُ: هذا موسى وعصاه وبنو إسرائيل. فقال: نَعَمْ على قلّة البلد الذي كان به وفساد قومه عليه. فقلتُ: وهذا عيسى على حمار والحواريّون معه فقال: لقد كان قصير المدّة إنّما كان أمره يزيد على ثلاثين شهراً[6] شيئاً يسيراً.

---

١ ح: ونجد. ٢ ح: عليه وسلّم. ٣ ح: مما. ٤ ب: ينجوا. ٥ ح: ممن. ٦ خ: كان عمره يزيد على ثلاثين سنة.

he who rules Iraq, for he is at the center of the world, and the other kings are ranged around him; we know him by the name 'the King of Kings.' Next comes this king of ours,[104] whom we know by the name 'the King of His People,' for no other king is more astute a ruler than we nor more in control of his realm than we are of ours, and no other populace is more obedient to its kings than ours; we are therefore the Kings of Our People. After us comes 'the King of Beasts,' who is our neighbor the king of the Turks,[105] and after the Turks comes the King of Elephants, that is, the king of India, whom we know as 'the King of Wisdom,' because wisdom originates with the Indians. Finally comes the king of Byzantium, whom we know as 'the King of Men,' for there are no other men on Earth who are more perfect in form than his men, nor any of more handsome countenance. These five are the foremost kings. All the rest are beneath them in rank."

2.4.3 *Portraits of the prophets*

Then the king said to his interpreter, "Say to him, 'Would you recognize your master if you saw him?'", meaning the Prophet of God, God bless him.[106] I replied, "How can I see him, when he is with God, glorious and mighty is He?" "I did not mean that," that king said. "I meant, if you saw his *picture*." To which Ibn Wahb replied that, yes, he would. The king then told them to fetch a certain casket, which was brought out and placed before him. From it he took a scroll, saying to his interpreter, "Show him his master." In the scroll I saw pictures of the prophets, and moved my lips in silent prayer for them.[107] The king had not imagined that I would recognize them, and said to the interpreter, "Ask him why he is moving his lips." He asked me, and I replied, "I am praying for blessings on the prophets." "And how come you can recognize them?" asked the king. "From the circumstances in which they are depicted," I said. "This is Noah in his Ark, saving himself and his people when God, exalted be His name, commanded the waters to inundate the entire Earth and all its inhabitants but preserved Noah and his people." At this the king laughed and said, "Noah you have named correctly. The inundation of the entire Earth, however, we do not acknowledge to be true. For the Flood only affected a part of the Earth; it did not reach either to our land or to India." At this point, Ibn Wahb commented: I was afraid to contradict the king and challenge this statement, as I knew that he would only dismiss my arguments.[108] He then resumed his account: Then I said, "And this is Moses with his staff, and the people of Israel," and the king replied, "So it is, although the land he occupied was a small one, and his people behaved wrongfully towards him." Then I said, "And this is Jesus, mounted

وعَدَّدَ من أمرساير الأنبياء ما اقتصرنا على ذكر بعضه وزعم أنّه رأى فوق كلّ صورة لنبيّ كتابةً طويلة قدّر أنّ فيها ذِكْرُ أسمايهم ومواقع بلدانهم وأسباب نبوّاتهم. ثمّ قال: رأيتُ صورةَ النبيّ صلّى الله عليه وسلّم على جَمَلٍ وأصحابُه محدقون به على إبلهم في أرجلهم نعال عربيّة وفي أوساطهم مساويك مشدودة فبكيتُ. فقال للترجمان: سَلْهُ عن بُكايه فقلتُ: هذا نبيّنا وسيّدنا وابن عمّي عليه السلام. فقال: صدقتَ لقد ملك هو وقومه أجلّ الممالك إلّا أنّه لم يعاين ما مَلَكَ وإنّما عاينه مَن بعده. ورأيتُ صور أنبياء ذوي عدد كثير منهم مَن قد أشار بيده اليمنى وجمع بين الإبهام والسبابة كأنّه يومي في إشارته إلى الحقّ ومنهم قايمٌ على رِجله مشير بأصابعه إلى السماء وغير ذلك زعم الترجمان أنّهم من أنبيايهم وأنبياء الهند.

٤،٤،٢ ثمّ سألني عن الخلفاء وزيّهم وكثير من الشرايع ووجوهها على قدر ما أعلم منها ثمّ قال: كم عمرُ الدنيا عندكم فقلتُ: قد اُختُلِفَ فيه فبعض يقول ستّة آلاف سنة وبعض يقول دونها وبعض يقول أكثر منها إلّا أنّه[1] بيسير. فضحك ضحكاً كثيراً ووزيره أيضاً واقف دلّ[2] على إنكاره ذلك وقال: ما أحسب نبيّكم قال هذا. فزللتُ وقلتُ: بلى هو قال ذلك فرأيتُ الإنكار في وجهه. ثمّ قال للترجمان: قل له ميّزْ كلامَكَ فإنّ الملوك لا تُكَلَّمُ إلّا عن تحصيل أمّا ما زعمتَ أنّكم تختلفون في ذلك فإنّكم إنّما اختلفتم في قول نبيّكم وما قالته الأنبياء لا يجب أن يُختَلَفَ فيه بل هو مُسلَّمٌ فاحذر هذا وشِبْهَه أن تحكيه وذَكَرَ أشياء كثيرة قد ذهبت عنّي لطول العهد.

١ أنّه: ساقطة في ح. ٢ كذا في ب ولعلّ الصواب: وأَقَفَ ودلّ.

on a donkey and accompanied by his disciples," and the king replied, "His time was short, for his career lasted only a little more than thirty months."[109]

Ibn Wahb went on to enumerate the circumstances depicted in the images of all the other prophets, but we have confined ourselves to mentioning only part of what he reported. He also maintained that he saw above each picture of a prophet a long inscription, which he supposed to include their names, the locations of their countries, and the causes of their prophethood. Then he said: I saw the picture of the Prophet Muḥammad, God bless him and keep him, mounted on a camel, with his Companions around him on their camels, with Arab sandals on their feet and tooth sticks stuck in their waistbands, and I wept. The king said to the interpreter, "Ask him why he is weeping." And I replied, "This is our prophet and our master and my cousin, eternal peace be upon him." The king said, "You are correct. He and his people gained possession of the most magnificent of kingdoms. But he never saw his possessions in person; only his successors saw them." Ibn Wahb added: I also saw pictures of other prophets, a great multitude of them: some were shown gesturing with their right hands, the tips of their thumbs and index fingers placed together, as if the gesture were a sign of truth; others were shown standing on their feet and gesturing with their fingers to heaven; and there were yet other poses. The interpreter maintained that all these were their own prophets and those of the Indians.[110]

2.4.4 *A dispute over the age of the world*

The king then questioned me about the caliphs, their appearance, and their mode of dress;[111] he also asked much about our laws and their various aspects, and I replied according to what I knew of them. Then he asked, "How old do you Arabs consider the world to be?" I replied, "The matter has been disputed: some have said six thousand years, some have said less than that, and some have said more, but only a little more." This made him laugh a lot, and his vizier too, who stood beside him, showing his disapproval of what I had said.[112] Eventually he said, "I do not suppose that your prophet said this," whereupon I blurted out,[113] "On the contrary, he *did* say that." However, I saw again the disapproval on his face. He then said to his interpreter, "Tell him, 'You must exercise discretion in what you say, for kings should be addressed only on the basis of properly acquired knowledge. You allege that you Arabs dispute this subject, whereas in fact you have only disputed what your prophet said. What is said by the prophets ought not to become a matter of dispute; rather, it should be accepted without question. Guard, therefore,

٢،٤،٥ ثمّ قال لي: لِمَ عدلتَ عن مَلِكك وهو أقرب إليك منّا داراً ونسباً فقلتُ: بما حدث على البصرة ووقوعي إلى سيراف ونظري إلى مركب ينفذ إلى الصين وما بلغني من جلال مَلِك الصين وكثرة الخير به فأحببتُ الوقوع إلى تلك الناحية ومشاهدتها وأنا راجعٌ عنها إلى بلادي ومُلْكِ ابن عمّي ومُخْبِرٌ بما شاهدتُه من جلال هذا المَلِك وسعة هذه البلاد وسأقول بكلّ حَسَنٍ وأثني بكلّ جميلٍ. فسَرّه ذلك وأمر لي بالجايزة السَنيّة وبحملي على بغال البريد إلى مدينة خانفو وكتب إلى مَلِكها بإكرامي وتقديمي على جميع مَن في ناحيته من ساير الملوك وإقامة النُزُل لي إلى وقت خروجي. فكنتُ في أخصب عيش وأنعمه إلى أن خرجتُ من بلاد الصين.

٢،٤،٦ فسألناه عن مدينة خمدان التي بها المَلِك وصفتها[1] فذكَرَ سعة البلد وكثرة أهله وأنّه مقسوم على قسمين يفصل بينهما شارع طويل عريض فالملك ووزيره وجنوده وقاضي القضاة وخصيان الملك وجميع أسبابه في الشقّ الأيمن منه وما يلي المشرق لا يخالطهم أحد من العامّة ولا فيه شي من الأسواق بأنهار في سككهم مطّردة وأشجار عليها منتظمة ومنازل فسيحة.

وفي الشقّ الأيسر ممّا يلي المغرب الرعيّة والتجّار والمِيرة[2] والأسواق وإذا وَضَحَ النهارُ رأيتَ قَهارِمة الملك وأسبابه وغلمان داره وغلمان القوّاد ووكلايهم من بين راكب وراجل قد دخلوا إلى الشقّ الذي فيه الأسواق والتجّار فأخذوا وظايفهم وحوايجهم ثمّ انصرفوا فلم يعُدْ أحد منهم إلى هذا الشقّ إلّا في اليوم الثاني.

١ ر: وصفها. ٢ خ: الميسرة.

against this and other such talk, lest you utter it again.'" And he said much else besides, but it was so long ago that it has slipped my memory.

The king then said to me, "Why have you turned away from your own king, when he is so much closer to you than we are, both in abode and in blood?"[114] I replied, "Because of what befell Basra and because, when I arrived in Sīrāf, I saw a ship leaving for China. Also, because of what I had heard of the majesty of the king of China and of his bountiful goodness. All this made me long to travel to these parts and see them for myself. Now I shall return from here to my homeland, to the realm of my cousin, and I shall recount what I have witnessed of the majesty of this king and the extent of this country. I will have nothing but good to say, and I shall spare no fine word in my praise." He was delighted by this response, and commanded that I be given a right royal gift, and that I should then be conveyed by post mule to the city of Khānfū. He also wrote to the ruler of Khānfū, instructing him to bestow his own largesse upon me, to give me precedence over all the other rulers in his province, and to provide me with everything a guest could need until the time of my departure. As a result I lived in the greatest possible luxury and comfort until I departed from China. 2.4.5

The generosity of the king of China to Ibn Wahb

We then questioned Ibn Wahb about the city of Khamdān, the seat of the king, and asked him to describe it. He told us of the city's extent and of its large population[115] and said that it was divided into two sectors separated by a long, broad street. The Great King, his vizier, his troops, the chief justice, the king's eunuchs, and all his relations dwell together in the right-hand sector, that is, on the eastern side. There is not a single member of the common populace to be found living among them, and no markets at all. The streets of this sector have streams flowing along them and are lined with trees planted regularly, and it has spacious residences. 2.4.6

The city of Khamdān described

In the left-hand sector, that is, on the western side, are to be found the general populace, the merchants, the provision stores, and the markets. At break of day you will see that the king's stewards and his relations, together with the palace slaves, and the slaves and agents of the army commanders, some mounted, some on foot, have all crossed over to the sector where the markets and the traders are. They get their daily allowances of provisions and whatever else they need, then they leave, and not one of them will return to this sector until the following morning.

وأنّ بهذا البلد من كلّ نزهة وغيضة[١] حسنة وأنهار مطّردة إلاّ النخل[٢] فإنّه معدوم.

١،٥،٢ وممّا حدث في زماننا هذا ولم يعرفْهُ مَن تقدّمَنا أنّه لم يكن أحد يقدّر أنّ البحر الذي عليه بحر الصين والهند يتّصل ببحر الشام ولا يقوم في أنفسهم حتّى كان في عصرنا هذا فإنّه بلغَنا أنّه وُجِدَ في بحر الروم خشبُ مراكب العرب المخروزة التي قد تكسّرت بأهلها فقطّعها الموجُ وساقتها الرياحُ بأمواج البحر فقذفته إلى بحر الخَزَر ثمّ جرى في خليج الروم ونفذ منه إلى بحر الروم والشام. فدلّ هذا على أنّ البحر يدور على بلاد الصين والسِيلا[٣] وظَهرِ بلاد الترك والخزر ثمّ يصبّ في الخليج ويفضي إلى بلاد الشام. وذلك أنّ الخشب المخروز لا يكون إلّا لمراكب سيراف خاصّة ومراكبُ الشام والروم مسمورةٌ غير مخروزة.

وبلغَنا أيضاً أنّه وُجِدَ ببحر[٤] الشام عنبرٌ وهذا من المُستنكَر وما لم يُعرَفْ في قِدَم الدهور. ولا يجوز – إن كان ما قيل حقّاً – أن يكون العنبر وقع إلى بحر الشام إلّا[٥] من بحر عدن والقُلْزُم وهو البحر الذي يتّصل بالبحار التي يكون فيها العنبر لأنّ الله جلّ ذكره قد جعل بين البحرين حاجزاً. بل هو – إن كان صحيحاً – ممّا يقذفه بحر الهند إلى ساير البحار واحداً بعد واحد حتّى يُفضي به إلى بحر الشام.

---

١ ب: وغيظة. ٢ خ: النحل. ٣ ب: السَيلا. ٤ ح: في بحر. ٥ إلّا: كذا في ب ويبدو أنّه يجب حذف الكلمة ليستقيم معنى بقيّة الجملة.

Ibn Wahb added that in this city all kinds of delightful gardens and pleasant wooded glades can be found, with streams flowing through them. But there are no palm trees, for they do not exist there.

How the Seas Are Connected One to Another

Among the discoveries of this age of ours, unknown to our predecessors, is the previously unsuspected fact that the ocean onto which the Sea of China and India opens is connected to the Mediterranean Sea.[116] This is something people would not have credited until our own time, in which news reached us of the discovery in the Mediterranean Sea of planks from the sewn ships of the Arabs.[117] These ships had broken up and their crews had been lost; the waves had pounded their hulls to pieces, and these were then driven by winds and currents which cast the planks into the Sea of the Khazars. From there, the timbers floated through the Gulf of al-Rūm, finally emerging into the Mediterranean Sea.[118] This points to the fact that the ocean turns north around China and al-Sīlā, continues around the back of the lands of the Turks and the Khazars, then debouches through the Gulf of al-Rūm, arriving at the Levant, the reason being that these sewn planks are used only for Indian Ocean ships, and those of Sīrāf in particular. In contrast, the ships of the Levant and of Byzantium are nailed, rather than sewn, together. 2.5.1

News also reached us of ambergris being found in the Mediterranean Sea, a notion that would have been rejected, and indeed was unheard of, in past ages. For it would not be possible (assuming that the report is true) for the ambergris to have reached the Mediterranean Sea except via the Sea of Aden and al-Qulzum—this being the sea connected to the oceans in which ambergris is found—since God, exalted be His name, has placed a barrier between the two seas.[119] Instead, the ambergris (assuming again that the report is correct) must have been among the flotsam that the Indian Ocean cast into those other seas and that floated through them one after another, to arrive eventually in the Mediterranean Sea.

ذكر مدينة الزابج

ثمّ نبتدئ بذكر مدينة الزابج[١] إذ كانت تحاذي بلاد الصين وبينهما مسيرة شهر في البحر وأقلّ من ذلك إذا ساعدت الرياح. ومَلِكُها يُعرَف بالمَهراج ويقال إنّ تكسيرها تسعماية فرسخ وهذا الملك مملَّكٌ على جزاير كثيرة يكون مقدار مسافة مُلكه ألف فرسخ وأكثر. وفي مملكته جزيرة تُعرَف بسَرُبُزة[٢] تكسيرها على ما يذكرون أربع ماية فرسخ وجزيرة أيضاً تُعرف بالرامني[٣] تكسيرها ثمانماية فرسخ فيها منابت البقّم والكافور وغيره. وفي مملكته جزيرة كَلَه وهي المنصّف بين أراضي الصين وأرض العرب وتكسيرها على ما يذكرون ثمانون فرسخاً وبِكَلَه مُجَمَّعُ الأمتعة من الأعواد والكافور والصندل والعاج والرصاص القَلْعِيّ والأبنوس والبقّم والأفاويه كلّها وغير ذلك ممّا يتّسع ويطول شرحه. والجِهاز من عُمان - في هذا الوقت - إليها ومنها إلى عُمان واقعٌ. وأمرُ المهراج نافذٌ في هذه الجزاير وجزيرته التي هو بها في غاية الخصب وعمارتُها منتظمة. ٢.٦.١

وذَكَر من يُوثَق بقوله أنّ الدِيَكة إذا غرّدت في الأسحار للأوقات كتغريدها عندنا تجاوبت إلى ماية فرسخ وما فوقها يجاوب بعضها بعضاً لاتّصال القرى وانتظامها وأنّه لا مفاوز فيها ولا خراب وأنّ المنتقِلَ[٤] في بلادهم إذا سافر وركب الظَهرَ سار إذا شاء فإذا ملّ وكلّ الظهرُ نَزَلَ حيث شاء.

ومن عجيب ما بلغنا من أحاديث هذه الجزيرة المعروفة بالزابج أنّ ملكاً من ملوكهم في قديم الأيّام وهو المهراج وقصره على ثلاج يأخذ من البحر - ومعنى الثلاج وادٍ كدِجلَة مدينة السلام والبصرة يغلب عليه ماء البحر بالمدّ وينضب عنه الما العذب بالجزر - ومنه غدير صغير يلاصق قصر الملك فإذا كان في صبيحة كلّ يوم دخل ٢.٦.٢

١ مدينة الزابج: كذا في ب وفي عنوان هذه الفقرة ويبدو أنّ المقصود: جزيرة الزابج. ٢ ح: بسريرة.
٣ ب:الرامي. ٤ ح: المتنقل.

The Kingdom of al-Mihrāj

Account of the City of al-Zābaj

2.6.1 *Islands in the kingdom of al-Mihrāj, and their products*

Next we will begin an account of the city of al-Zābaj,[120] because it is situated opposite China; the sailing time between the two lands is a month, or less than that if the winds are favorable. The king of al-Zābaj is known as al-Mihrāj; it is said that its extent is nine hundred *farsakh*s,[121] although this king also rules over many other islands, and his entire realm is spread over a distance of a thousand *farsakh*s and more. His kingdom includes an island known as Sarbuzah, whose extent is reported to be four hundred *farsakh*s; also an island known as al-Rāmanī, extending to eight hundred *farsakh*s, which is home to the places where sapan wood, camphor, and other such trees grow. In addition, his kingdom includes the peninsula of Kalah, the halfway point between the lands of China and the land of the Arabs, whose extent is reported to be eighty *farsakh*s. At Kalah is the entrepôt for commodities such as aloewood in its different varieties, camphor, sandalwood, ivory, white lead,[122] ebony, sapan wood, aromatics of all sorts, and other goods that it would take far too long to detail. The trading voyages from Oman go, these days, as far as Kalah, then return from there to Oman.[123] The authority of al-Mihrāj is obeyed throughout these islands. His island of al-Zābaj, which is his seat, is fertile in the extreme and is settled and cultivated in a most orderly manner.

A trustworthy informant reported that, when the cocks of al-Zābaj crow at daybreak to announce the time as they do in our lands, they answer one another over a distance of a hundred *farsakh*s and more, relaying the call one to another, so continuous are the villages and so regularly dispersed. He reported, too, that there are no barren areas on the island, nor any signs of dilapidation. He also said that when anyone traveling around their land sets out on his mount, he goes as far as he pleases, but if he gets bored or his mount tires, he can break his journey wherever he wishes.[124]

2.6.2 *The Pool of the Kings, and the manner in which they hoarded gold*

One of the more extraordinary reports that has reached us from this island known as al-Zābaj tells of one of their kings—al-Mihrāj, that is—in days long past. His palace overlooked a *thalāj* leading to the sea, *thalāj* meaning the tidal reach of a river such as the Tigris of Madīnat al-Salām and Basra, which fills with seawater at high tide and through which freshwater trickles out when the tide is low. Connected to this was a small pool, immediately adjoining the royal palace. Every morning, the king's steward

قَهْرَمانُ الملك ومعه لَبِنَةٌ قد سبكها من ذهب فيها أمنا[١] قد خفي عنّي مبلغُها فيطرحها بين يديّ الملك في ذلك الغدير. فإذا كان المدّ علاها وما كان مجتمعاً معها من أمثالها وغَمَرَها[٢] فإذا كان الجزر نضب عنها فأظهرها فلاحَتْ في الشمس والملك مطّلع عليها عند جلوسه في المجلس المطلّ عليها. فلا تزال تلك حالُه[٣] يطرح في كلّ يوم في ذلك الغدير لبنة من ذهب ما عاش ذلك الملك من الزمان لا يُمَسُّ شيءٌ منه. فإذا مات الملك أخرجها القايمُ من بعده كلّها فلم يدع منها شيئاً وأُحْصِيَتْ ثمّ أُذيبَتْ وفُرِّقَتْ على أهل بيت المملكة رجالهم ونسايهم وأولادهم وقوّادهم وخدمِهم على قدر منازلهم ورسومٍ لهم في كلّ صنف منهم فما فَضَلَ بعد ذلك فُضَّ على أهل المَسْكَنة والضعف. ثمّ دُوِّنَ عددُ اللبن الذهب ووزنُها وقيل إنّ فلاناً مَلَكَ من الزمان كذا وكذا[٤] سنة وخلّف من لبن الذهب في غدير الملوك كذا وكذا[٥] لبنة وإنّها فُرِّقَت بعد وفاته في أهل مملكته فالفخرُ عندهم لمن امتدّت أيّامُ مُلكه وزاد عددُ اللبن الذهب في تَرِكَتِه.

٢،٧،١ ومن أخبارهم في القديم أنّ ملكاً من ملوك القَمار وهي الأرض التي يُجْلَبُ منها العود القماريّ وليست بجزيرة بل هي على ما يلي أرض العرب وليس في شي من الممالك أكثر عدداً من أهل القمار وهم رجال[٦] كلّهم يحرّمون الزنا والأنبذة كلّها فلا يكون في بلادهم ومملكتهم شيء منه[٧] وهي مسامِتةٌ لمملكة المهراج والجزيرة المعروفة بالزابج[٨] وبينهما مسافة عشرة أيّام إلى عشرين يوماً عرضاً في البحر إذا كانت الريحُ متوسّطةً.

---

١ أمنا: كذا في ب أي أمناء جمعُ من جموع كلمة مَنّ الوزن المعروف؛ خ: أمنان. ٢ ح: غمرها. ٣ ح: حالة.
٤ ب: كذى. ٥ ب: كذى. ٦ ب: رجاله؛ ح وخ: رحّالة؛ ر: رحالة؛ ويمكن قراءتها أيضًا: رجّالة.
٧ منه: كذا في ب. ٨ ح هنا وفيما بعد: الزابج.

would bring an ingot of gold which he had caused to be cast, several maunds in weight (I was not told how many); as the king looked on, the steward would place the ingot in the pool. When the tide came in, the water covered this and the other ingots collected together with it, and submerged them; when the tide went out, the water seeped away and revealed the ingots; they would gleam there in the sunlight, and the king could watch over them when he took his seat in the hall overlooking them. He continued thus, his steward placing an ingot of gold in the pool every day for as long as that particular king lived, and not an ingot in the hoard would be touched. On the death of the king and subsequent kings, however, his successor would remove all the ingots, leaving not a single one. They would then be counted, melted down and shared out among the royal family, men, women, and children, as well as among their army commanders and slaves, each according to his rank and to the accepted practice for each class of recipients. Any gold left over afterwards would be distributed to the poor and needy. Finally, the number and weight of the gold ingots were recorded, so that it might said that So-and-so's reign had lasted for such-and-such a number of years and that he had left such-and-such a number of gold ingots in the Pool of the Kings and that they had been shared out after his death among the people of his kingdom. The longer a king reigned and the more ingots he left on his death, the greater his glory in the people's eyes.

The Land of al-Qamār and the Stupidity of Its King

2.7.1 *Description of the land of al-Qamār*

One of their accounts of the past concerns one of the kings of al-Qamār. This is the land from which Qamārī aloewood is exported; it is not an island, for it is situated on the continental landmass extending from the land of the Arabs. No other kingdom at all has a greater population than that of al-Qamār. They are men[125] who all regard adultery and all types of wine as prohibited, and nothing of this sort is to be found in their land and their kingdom. Al-Qamār is situated opposite the kingdom of al-Mihrāj and, to be precise, opposite the island known as al-Zābaj; the sailing time to cross the open sea between them is between ten and twenty days, given a moderate wind.

2.7.2 *The wish of the king of al-Qamār, and how al-Mihrāj heard of it*

It is said that the king in question ascended the throne of al-Qamār, in days long past, when he was still an impetuous youth.[126] One day he was sitting in his palace; this overlooked a flowing river of freshwater, like the Tigris of Iraq, and was a day's journey from the sea. His vizier was with

فقيل إنّ هذا المَلك تقلّد المُلكَ على القمار في قديم الأيّام وهو حدثٌ متسرّعٌ وإنّه ٢،٧،٢
جلس يوماً في قصره - وهو مُشرفٌ على وادٍ يجري بالما العذب كدجلة العراق وبين قصره والبحر مسيرة يوم - ووزيره[١] بين يديه. إذ قال لوزيره وقد جرى ذِكرُ مملكة المهراج وجلالتها وكثرة عمارتها وما تحت يده من الجزاير: في نفسي شهوةٌ كنتُ أُحبُّ بلوغَها. فقال له الوزير وكان ناصحاً وقد علم منه السرعةَ: ما هي أيّها الملك. قال: كنتُ أحبّ أن أرى رأس المهراج ملك الزابج في طَستٍ بين يديّ. فعلم الوزير أنّ الحسد أثار هذا الفكر في نفسه فقال: أيّها الملك ما كنتُ أحبّ أن يحدّثَ الملكُ نفسَه بمثل هذا إذ لم يجرِ بيننا وبين هولاء القوم لا في فعلٍ ولا في حديثٍ تِرَةٌ ولا رأَينا منهم شرّاً وهم في جزيرة نائية غير مجاورة لنا في أرضنا ولا طامعين في مُلكنا وليس ينبغي أن يقف على هذا الكلام أحدٌ ولا يُعيد المَلِكُ فيه قولاً.

فغضب ولم يسمع من الناصح وأذاع ذلك لقوّاده ومَن كان يحضره مِن وجوه أصحابه. فتناقلته الألسنُ حتّى شاع واتّصل بالمهراج وكان جَزلاً متحرّكاً محنّكاً قد بلغ في السنّ مبلغاً متوسّطاً فدعا بوزيره وأخبره بما[٢] اتّصل به وقال له: ليس يجب - معما[٣] شاع من أمر هذا الجاهل وتمنّيه ما تمنّاه بحداثة سنّه وغِرّته وانتشارِ ذلك من قوله - أن نُمسِكَ عنه فإنّ ذلك ممّا يَفُتُّ في عضد المُلك وينقصه ويضع منه. وأَمرَهُ بستر ما جرى بينهما وأن يُعِدَّ له ألف مركب من أوساط المراكب بآلاتها ويندبَ لكلّ مركب منها من حَمَلَة[٤] السلاح وشجعان الرجال مَن يستقلّ به. وأظهر أنّه يريد التنزُّهَ في الجزاير التي في مملكته وكتب إلى الملوك الذين في هذه الجزاير وهم في طاعته وجملته بما عزم عليه من زيارتهم والتنزّه بجزايرهم حتّى شاع ذلك وتأهّبَ مَلِكُ كلّ جزيرة لِما يصلح للمهراج.

---

١ ح: ووزيرة. ٢ ح: مما. ٣ ح: مما. ٤ ح و ر: جملة.

him, and they had been speaking of the kingdom of al-Mihrāj—of how magnificent it was, and how densely populated and cultivated, and of how many islands were under al-Mihrāj's rule—when the king said to the vizier, "There is something I yearn for with all my soul and that I have been longing to see fulfilled." The vizier, a wise counselor who already had experience of the king's rashness, replied, "And what may that be, Your Majesty?" The king said, "I have been wanting to see the head of al-Mihrāj, the king of al-Zābaj, placed before me in a basin of brass." The vizier realized that it was envy that had stirred this idea in the king's soul, and he said, "Your Majesty, I would rather not have heard His Majesty saying such things to himself. For there is no current cause, either in deed or word, for any quarrel between us and those people, and they have done us no wrong. They are not neighbors to our land but live in an island far away from us, and they harbor no designs on our kingdom. It would therefore be inappropriate if these words of His Majesty's were communicated to any other person, nor should His Majesty mention the matter again."

The king, however, was enraged at this and would not listen to his counselor. Instead, he made his wish public knowledge among the commanders of his army and those of his most prominent companions at court. Tongues wagged, word spread, and it eventually reached the ears of al-Mihrāj himself. The latter was a man of sound judgement, swift action, and considerable experience, and had reached middle age. He summoned his own vizier and informed him of what he had heard, saying, "With all this talk circulating about that idiot and about that wish of his, inspired by his youth and recklessness—indeed, with his very words being repeated everywhere—we must not refrain from action. For if we did, it would weaken the strong arm of our rule and leave it diminished and enfeebled." He then instructed the vizier to keep what had passed between them secret but, at the same time, to make ready a thousand ships of middling size, all equipped for war, and to appoint an independent commander to each ship from among the arms-bearing men and brave warriors. The king, meanwhile, put it about that he intended to go on a pleasure cruise through the islands of his realm; he wrote to the local rulers in these islands, who were all loyal members of his circle, telling them of his decision to visit them and enjoy himself in their islands. Word duly spread of the intended tour, and the ruler of each island made preparations to give al-Mihrāj an appropriate reception.

فلمّا استتبّ أمرُه وانتظم دَخَلَ في المراكب وعبر بها وبالجيش إلى مملكة القمار. ٣،٧،٢
وهو وأصحابُه أهل سواكٍ دايم يفعل الرجل منهم ذلك في اليوم مرّاتٍ وسواكُ كلّ واحد منهم معه لا يفارقه أو مع غلامه.[١] فلم يشعر به ملك القمار حتّى هجم على الوادي المفضي إلى دار ملك القمار فطرح[٢] رجاله فأحدقوا به على سبيل غرّة فأخذه واحتوى على داره وطار أهل المملكة من بين يديه. فأمر بالنداء بالأمان وقعد على السرير الذي كان يجلس عليه ملك القمار وقد أخذه أسيرًا فأحضره وأحضر وزيره.

فقال لملك القمار: ما حَمَلَكَ على تمنّي ما ليس في وسعِك ولا لك فيه حظّ لو نِلْتَه ولا أوجبه سببٌ يسهّل السبيل إليه. فلم يُحِرْ[٣] جوابًا. ثمّ قال له المهراج: أمّا أنّك لو تمنّيتَ - معما[٤] تمنّيتَه من النظر إلى رأسي في طستٍ بين يديك - إباحةَ أرضي ومُلكَها أو الفسادَ في شيء منها لَاستعملتُ ذلك كلَّه فيك لكنّك تمنّيتَ شيئًا بعينه فأنا فاعِلُه بك وراجعٌ إلى بلدي من غير أن أمدّ يدًا إلى شيءٍ من بلادك ممّا جلّ ودقّ لتكونَ عِظةً لِمَن بعدك ولا يتجاوزَ كلٌّ قدرَه وما قُسِمَ له وأن يستغنمَ العافيةَ مِن لبستِهِ.[٥] ثمّ ضَرَبَ عنقه.

ثمّ أقبل على وزيره فقال له: جُزِيتَ خيرًا مِن وزير فقد صحّ عندي أنّك أشرتَ على صاحبك بالرأي لو قُبِلَ منك فانظرْ مَن يصلح للمُلك مِن بعد هذا الجاهل فأقِمْه مقامه.

وانصرف من ساعته راجعًا إلى بلاده من غير أن يمدّ هو ولا أحد من أصحابه ٤،٧،٢
يده إلى شي من بلاد القمار. فلمّا رجع إلى مملكته قعد على سريره وأشرف على غديره ووضع الطست بين يديه وفيها رأس ملك القمار وأحضر وجوهَ مملكته

---

١ وهو وأصحابه ... غلامه.: يبدو أنّه قد حصل تحريف في هذه الجملة يجعلها كأنّها دخيلة أو أنّه قد سقط كلامٌ ما كان يبرّر وجودها هنا. ٢ ح وخ و ر: وطرح. ٣ ر: يجر. ٤ ح: مما. ٥ كذا في ب ولعلّ المقصود: مَن لَبَّسْتَهُ.

When all was ready and in order, the king embarked with his fleet and sailed with it and his army across to the kingdom of al-Qamār. He and his companions are constant users of tooth sticks, every man cleaning his teeth with one several times a day; each man keeps his tooth stick with him and is never separated from it, or he keeps it with his slave.[127] The king of al-Qamār, meanwhile, had no inkling of what was happening, until, all of a sudden, al-Mihrāj burst into the river leading to the royal palace of al-Qamār. He landed his men, they surrounded the king of al-Qamār by surprise, and al-Mihrāj captured him and took over his palace. The king of al-Qamār's courtiers and officials fled before their master's eyes; al-Mihrāj, however, had it proclaimed that all would be under his protection. He then sat upon the throne[128] on which the captured king of al-Qamār had previously sat and had the captive and his vizier brought before him. 2.7.3

Al-Mihrāj's punishment of the king of al-Qamār

"Whatever drove you," he asked the king of al-Qamār, "to wish for something you were incapable of achieving, which would have brought you no good fortune even if you had attained it, and when there was nothing to make you set out on such a course in the first place?" To this the king of al-Qamār had no response. Al-Mihrāj continued, "Now, had you wished—along with your wish to see my head placed before you in a basin of brass—to make free with my land and take it over or to cause mischief in any part of it, then I would have done all that to *you*. But your wish was for something specific. So I shall now do this thing to you, then return to my country without laying hands on anything in your land, whether great or small. This is so you will be an example to warn those that come after you, so that no one should seek to exceed the bounds of his allotted abilities, and so that everyone should instead make the most of being free from such confusion."[129] Having said this, he had the head of the king of al-Qamār cut off.

Al-Mihrāj then turned to the executed king's vizier and said, "May God reward you for being so excellent a vizier. For I have ascertained that the advice you gave your master was sound—if only he had taken it. Consider now who will be fit to succeed that idiot as king, and install him in his place."

Al-Mihrāj then departed immediately on the voyage back to his country; neither he nor anyone from his force had laid hands on anything in the land of al-Qamār. When he arrived back in his kingdom, he sat upon his throne, surveyed his pool,[130] and had the basin of brass put before him in which the head of the king of al-Qamār had been placed. He then summoned 2.7.4

The return home of al-Mihrāj

وحدّثهم بخبره والسبب الذي حمله على ما أقدم عليه فدعا له أهلُ مملكته وجزوه خيرًا. ثمّ أَمَرَ بالرأس وغُسِلَ وطُيِّبَ وجَعَلَه في ظرفٍ وردّه إلى الملك الذي قام بالأمر ببلاد القمار من بعد الملك المقتول. وكتب إليه: إنّ الذي حملني على ما فعلناه بصاحبك بَغْيُه علينا وتأديبُنا لأمثاله وقد بَلَغَنا منه ما أراده بنا ورأينا ردّ الرأس إليك إذ لا دَرَكَ لنا في حبسه ولا فخر بما ظفرنا به منه.

واتّصل الخبرُ بملوك الهند والصين فعَظُمَ المهراجُ في أعينهم. وصارت ملوك القمار من بعد ذلك كلّما أصبحت قامت وحوّلت وجوهها نحوَ بلاد الزابج فسجدت وكفّرت للمهراج تعظيمًا له.[1]

وساير ملوك الهند والصين يقولون بالتناسخ ويدينون به. وذكر بعض مَن يوثق ١،٨،٢
بخبره أن ملكًا من ملوكهم جَدَّرَ[2] فلمّا خرج من الجُدَريّ نَظَرَ في المرآة فاستقبح وجهه فأبصر ابنًا لأخيه فقال له: ليس مثلي أقام في هذا الجسم على تغيُّره وإنّما هو ظرفٌ للروح متى زال عنه عاد في غيره فقُمْ بالمُلك فإنّي مزيلٌ بين جسمي وروحي إلى أن أنحدِرَ في جسمٍ غيره. ثمّ دعا بخنجر له مشحوذٍ قاطعٍ فأمر به فحُزَّ رأسُه ثمّ أُحرِقَ.

---

١ له: ساقطة في ح. ٢ ب: جُدِّرَ.

the prominent men of his kingdom, told them the story of the head, and explained what had led him to undertake such a venture. On hearing this, the dignitaries of the realm prayed God to reward him for what he had done. The king then gave orders for the head to be washed and embalmed with perfumes; he had it placed in a casket, and sent it back to the new ruler who had succeeded the executed king on the throne of the land of al-Qamār. With it he wrote a letter: "I was induced to act as we did with your former master by his outrageous threat to us and by the need to punish such behavior in others; for we had been told of what he wished to do to us. We have decided, however, to restore his head to you, because keeping it locked up here would achieve no end and because the goal we have already gained through it can bring us no more glory."

The news of al-Mihrāj's deed reached the kings of India and China, and his importance swelled in their eyes. And, ever after, when the kings of al-Qamār rose in the morning, they would stand and turn their faces towards the land of al-Zābaj, then bow and prostrate themselves to al-Mihrāj, out of reverence to him.

The Belief of the Eastern Kings in the Transmigration of Souls

All the kings of India and China believe in the transmigration of souls and **2.8.1**
hold it as an article of faith. A trustworthy informant reported that one of their kings in these lands was afflicted by smallpox. When he had recovered, he looked in the mirror and thought how hideous his face had become.[131] Seeing one of his brother's sons, he said to him, "It is not for the like of me to dwell in this body, now it is so changed. The body is, after all, a mere receptacle for the soul; when the soul passes out of it, it returns in another receptacle. You must be king in my place, for I shall now disjoin my soul from my body, until such time as I alight in another body." He then called for a dagger of his that had a particularly sharp edge, and commanded that his head be severed with it. He was duly decapitated, then his corpse was burned.

رجعٌ إلى أخبار الصين

ذكرُ[1] بعض أمورهم

كان أهل الصين من شدّة التفقّد لأمرهم في قديم أيّامهم وقبل تغيّره في هذا ١،٩،٢
الوقت على حالة لم يُسْمَعْ بمثلها. وقد كان رجل من أهل خُراسان ورد العراق فابتاع متاعاً كثيراً وخرج إلى بلاد الصين. وكان فيه بخلٌ وشحٌّ شديدٌ فجرى بينه وبين خصيّ للملك - كان أنفذه[2] إلى خانفو (وهي المدينة التي تقصدها تجّار العرب) لأخذِ ما يحتاج إليه ممّا يرد في المراكب وكان هذا الخصيّ من أجلّ خدم الملك وإليه خزائنُه وأموالُه - مشاجرةٌ في أمتعة العاج وغيره امتنع من[3] بيعها حتّى شَرِقَ الأمرُ بينهما. وحمل الخصيّ نفسَه على انتزاع خيار الأمتعة التي كانت معه واستهان بأمره.

فشَخَصَ مستخفياً حتّى ورد خمدان وهو بلد الملك الكبير في مقدار شهرين من الزمان وأكثر فخرج إلى السلسلة التي وُصِفَت في الكتاب. وسبيل من حرّكها على الملك الكبير أن يُباعَدَ إلى مسيرة عشرة أيّام على سبيل النفي ويؤمر بحبسه هناك شهرين ثمّ يُخرجه ملكُ تلك الناحية ويقول: إنّك تعرّضتَ فيه بوارُك[4] وسفكُ دمك إن كنتَ كاذباً وإذ كان الملك قد قرّب لك ولأمثالك من وزرايه وملوكه مَن لا يعوزك الانتصافُ بهم. واعلم أنّك متى وصلتَ إلى الملك فلم يكن ما تظلمتَ منه ممّا يجب في مثله الوصول إليه فليس دون دمك شيء لِيَلّا يُقْدِمَ على ما أقدمتَ كلُّ مَن يهمّ بمثله فاستَقِلْ نُقَلَكَ[5] وامضِ لشأنك. فإنْ استقال ضُرِبَ[6] خمسين خشبة ونُفِيَ إلى البلاد التي منها قَصَدَ وإن أقام على تظلُّمِه وَصَلَ. ففُعِلَ ذلك بالخراسانيّ فأقام على[7] ظلامته والتمس الوصول.

---

١ ح: وذكرُ. ٢ ح: أنفده. ٣ ح: عن. ٤ تعرّضتَ فيه بوارُك: كذا في ب وقد يكون تقويم ح على الصواب: تعرّضتَ لِما فيه بوارُك؛ خ: تعرّضتَ إلى ما فيه بوارُك. ٥ خ: فاستَقِلْ نُقِلَّكَ (بتشديد اللام الثانية وفتحها).
٦ ح: ضربه. ٧ تظلّمه ... على: ساقط في خ.

Accounts of China Continued

Various Matters Relating to the Chinese

The Chinese used to monitor their own system—in the old days, that is, before its deterioration in the present time—with a rigor unheard of elsewhere. An example of this is the story of a certain man from Khurasan who came to Iraq, bought a large quantity of goods, and took them out to China. He was of a miserly and exceedingly avaricious nature, and a dispute arose between him and one of the Great King's eunuchs, who had been sent by his master to Khānfū (the city to which the Arab merchants go) to get various items the king required from among the goods imported on Arab ships; this eunuch was one of the king's most respected slaves and was in charge of the royal treasuries and other property. The dispute was over certain ivory and other goods, which the merchant held out against selling at the price offered until things reached a heated impasse, at which the eunuch took it upon himself to seize by force the pick of the merchant's goods, and treated him with contempt. 2.9.1

The concern of their kings for investigating merchants' complaints

Following this, the Khurasani set out incognito and traveled to Khamdān, the Great King's capital, taking two months and more on the journey. On his arrival, he went to the chain attached to the bell that was described in the First Book.[132] Now, the procedure for anyone who pulls the chain to ring the bell hanging over the Great King is as follows. He is first removed to a place ten days' journey distant, by way of banishment, and ordered to be placed under detention there for two months. At the end of that period, the ruler of the province concerned brings him out of detention and says to him, "You have exposed yourself to the risk of your own perdition and the shedding of your blood, if it emerges that you have been lying. For the Great King has already given you and your like direct access to ministers and provincial rulers of his, through whom it is not difficult for you to obtain justice. You must be aware that, if you take your case to the Great King and it transpires that your complaint is not grave enough to entail an appeal to him, then the outcome will be nothing less than your death: this is to deter everyone else who might consider a similar course of action from daring to do what you have dared. Retract your complaint, therefore, so that we may release you; go back to your own business." If the complainant then withdraws his case, he is dealt fifty blows with a wooden stave and deported to his country of origin; if, however, he decides to pursue his complaint, he is admitted to

فبُعِثَ به ووَصَلَ إلى الملك. فسايَلَهُ[1] الترجمان عن أمره فأخبره بما جرى عليه من الخادم وانتزاعه من يده ما انتزع. وكان الأمر فيه قد شاع بخانفو وذاع فأمر الملك بحبس الخراسانيّ وإزاحة علّته في مطعمه ومشربه وتقدّم إلى وزيره في الكِتّاب إلى العمّال بخانفو بالفحص عمّا ادّعاه الخراسانيُّ وكَشْفِه والصدق عنه وأمر صاحبَ الميمنة والميسرة وصاحب القلب بمثله وهؤلا الثلاثة عليهم يدور بعد الوزير أمرُ جيوشه ويثق بهم على نفسه وإذا ركب بهم لحربٍ[2] أو غيره كان كلّ واحد منهم في مرتبته. فكتب كلّ واحد منهم وقد كشف عن الأمر بما وقف به على صحّة الدعوى من الخراسانيّ. فتتابعت به الأخبار عند الملك من كلّ جهة فأُشْخِصَ الخصيُّ فلمّا ورد قبض أمواله ونزع خزائنه من يده. وقال له: كان حقُّك القتل إذ[3] عرّضتَني لرجل قد سلك من خراسان وهي على حدّ مملكتي وصار إلى بلاد العرب ومنها إلى ممالك الهند ثمّ إلى بلدي طلباً للفضل فأردتَ أن يَعُودَ مجتازاً بهذه الممالك ومَن فيها فيقول: إنّي ظُلِمْتُ ببلاد الصين وغُصِبْتُ[4] مالي. لكنّي أتجافى عن دمك لقديم حُرَمَتِك وأُوَلّيك تدبيرَ الموتى إذ عجزتَ عن تدبيرِ الأحياء. وأمر به فجعله في مقابر الملوك يحرسها ويقوم بها.

ومن عجيب تدبيرهم في قديم الأيّام دون هذا الوقت أمرُ الأحكام وجلالُها في صدورهم واختيارهم لها مَن لا يخالج قلوبهم الشكُّ في علمه بشرايعهم وصدقِ لهجته وقيامِه بالحقّ في كلّ أحواله وتجنُّبِه الإغماض عمّن جلّ مقدارُه حتّى يقع الحقُّ موقعه ويكون عفيفاً عن أموال أهل الضعف وما يجري على يده. ٢،٩،٢

[1] ح: فسأله. [2] ح: بحرب. [3] ح و ر: إذا. [4] ح: وغصب.

the Great King's presence. This procedure was followed with the Khurasani; he persisted in his complaint and requested an audience.

He was thus duly dispatched and entered the king's presence. The interpreter questioned him about his case, and the Khurasani told him how the eunuch slave had mistreated him and had snatched his property out of his hands. Meanwhile, the affair of the Khurasani had already become public knowledge in Khānfū, and news of it had spread through the city. The king therefore ordered that the Khurasani be detained and supplied with all necessary food and drink; at the same time, he instructed his vizier to write to the government representatives in Khānfū, telling them to investigate the Khurasani's allegation and to ascertain the truth of the matter. He also ordered similar investigations to be undertaken by the commanders of the right and left wings of the army and the commander of the center; after the vizier, it is upon these three that control of the king's forces devolves: he trusts them with his life, and if he rides out with them to do battle or for some other purpose, each one of them rides with him, in rank. Eventually each one of these officers wrote independently to the Great King, having uncovered enough evidence about the matter to apprise himself of the truth of the Khurasani's allegation. Other similar reports on the case kept reaching the king from every quarter, and the eunuch was summoned. When he appeared, the king seized his property and deprived him of control over his own treasuries. He then said to him, "You deserve to be put to death. For you exposed me to the risk of losing face on account of a man who journeyed from Khurasan, on the border of my kingdom, and made his way to the land of the Arabs, and from there to the kingdoms of the Indians, and then came to my land, all in pursuit of honorable gain—and whom you then wanted to return by way of these same kingdoms, telling everyone in them, 'I was treated unjustly in China, and my property was seized by force'! But I am loath to shed your blood, if only because you have enjoyed my protection for so long. Instead, I shall appoint you to manage the dead, because you have failed in your management of the living." And the king commanded that the eunuch be given a position guarding and overseeing the royal cemeteries.

Another example of their admirable governance in the old days (but not in this time) was the status of the law and the high regard they had for it in their hearts. They would select someone to dispense the law only if they had no doubt in their minds about his knowledge of their legal code, the truth of his words, the correctness of his conduct in all his affairs, and his refusal to turn **2.9.2**

The chief justice of China

فإذا عزموا على تقليد قاضي القضاة أنفذوه قبل تقليده إلى جميع البلدان التي هي أعمدة بلادهم حتّى يقيم في كلّ بلد شهرًا أو شهرين فيبحث عن أمر أهله وأخبارهم ورسومهم ويعلم مَن يجب قبولُ قولِه منهم معرفةً يستغني بها عن المَسْئَلة.[١] فإذا سُلِكَ به هذه الأمصار ولم يبقَ في المملكة بلدٌ جليلٌ إلّا وَطِئَهُ رحل إلى دار المملكة ووُلِّيَ قضاء القضاة وجُعِلَ إليه اختيارُهم فيليهم. وعِلمُه بجميع المملكة ومَن يجب أن يُقَلَّدَ في كلّ بلدٍ مِن أهله أو غيرهم علمُ مَن يستغني بعلمه عن الرجوع إلى مَن لعلّه أن يميلَ فيه أو يقولَ بغير الحقّ فيما سُئِلَ[٢] عنه. ولا يتهيّأ لأحد من قضاته أن يكاتبه بشي قد عَلِمَ خلافَه أو يزيله عن جهته.

ولقاضي القضاة مُنادي[٣] في كلّ يوم على بابه[٤] يقول: هل مِن متظلِّمٍ على الملك المستور عن عيون رعيّته أم مِن أحد من أسبابه وقوّاده وساير رعيّته فإنّي أنوبُ في ذلك كلِّه عنه لِما بَسَطَ به يدي وقلّدني يقول ذلك ثلاثًا لأنَّ المُلْكَ في عَقْدِهم أنّ المَلِكَ لا يزول عن موضعه حتّى تَنْفُذَ الكتبُ من دواوين الملوك بالجَوْرِ المصرَّح وأن يُهْمِلَ أمرَ الحكم والحكّام؛ وأنّه متى تَحَفَّظَ[٥] مِن هذين الأمرين فلم تنفذ الكتبُ من الدواوين إلّا بالعدل ولم يَلِ الحكم إلّا مَن يقوم بالحقّ فالمُلْكُ منتظِمٌ.

فأمّا خراسان ومتاخمتها لبلاد الصين فالذي بينها وبين الصُغْد مسيرة شهرين ٢،٩،٣
إلّا أنّه في مفازة ممتنعة ورمال منتظمة لا ما فيها ولا أودية لها ولا عمارة بقُربها فهو السبب المانع من هجوم أهل خراسان على بلدهم. وأمّا ما كان من الصين يلي[٦] مغرب الشمس وهو الموضع المعروف بمذو[٧] فهو على حدود التبّت والحروب بينهم متّصلة.

---

١ ح وخ: المسألة. ٢ ح: يُسأل؛ خ: سُيِلَ؛ ر: يُسُل [كذا]. ٣ ح: منادٍ. ٤ ح: ينادي على بابه.
٥ خ: تحنّثَ. ٦ خ: على. ٧ ب وح و ر: بمذو.

a blind eye to the misdeeds of those of high status—their intention being that right be done wherever it is due, and that their judges should have no designs on the property of the vulnerable or on any sums passing through their hands.

When they decide to appoint a chief justice, they send him, before his appointment, on a tour of all the cities that are the chief ones in their land. The object is for him to stay in each city for a month or two, looking into the affairs of its inhabitants, hearing their reports, and learning about their customary practices; also, it is so that he can get to know directly which citizens are trustworthy in what they say[133] and will thus not need to ask intermediaries. When he has been taken around these provincial capitals and none of the great cities of the kingdom remains unvisited, he makes his way to the royal palace to be installed as chief justice; their selection of him is now confirmed, and he takes up their appointment. Moreover, he is now fully acquainted with the entire kingdom and with which of the citizens or others in each city should be appointed as provincial judges. This sort of personal knowledge saves him from having to seek advice on such appointments from those who, when questioned, may be biased or untruthful in their replies. Besides, none of his provincial judges will subsequently be prepared either to write reports to him containing anything contrary to the facts he knows, or to omit mention of such facts from their side.

Every day, the chief justice has a crier proclaim these words at his gate: "Does any of you have a complaint for the king who is veiled from his subjects' eyes, or against one of the king's relations or his commanders or any other of his subjects? For it is I who am deputed by him to deal with all such grievances, by virtue of the power he has placed in my hands and the office with which he has invested me!" He proclaims this three times. The reason is that, according to their understanding of the monarchy, the king will only be deposed when reports of flagrant injustice arrive from the offices of provincial rulers and when the king himself neglects the law and those who dispense it. Equally, they believe that, as long as the king guards against these two failings—with the result that official reports bring news only of just administration and that only those who act rightly are appointed to be judges—then the monarchy will maintain its proper harmony.[134]

Regarding Khurasan and its proximity to the land of China, between the latter and Sogdiana there is a journey of two months. The way, however, is via a forbidding desert of unbroken sand dunes in which there are no water sources and no river valleys, with no habitation nearby.[135] This is what **2.9.3**

China's western borders and neighboring countries

٤،٩،٢ وقد رأينا ممّن دخل الصين ذكَرَ أنّه رأى رجلاً حمل على ظهره مِسْكاً في زِقٍّ وورد من سَمَرْقَنْد راجلاً يقطع بلداً بلداً من مدن الصين حتّى صار إلى خانفو وهو مجتمع التجّار القاصدين من سيراف. وذلك أنّ الأرض التي بها ظِبا المسك الصينيّ والتبّت أرضٌ واحدة لا فرق بينهما فأهل الصين يجتذبون ما قَرُبَ منهم من الظباء[1] وأهل التبّت ما قرب منهم. وإنّما فَضَلَ[2] المسكُ التبّتيّ على الصينيّ بحالتين إحديهما[3] أنّ ظبيَ المسك يكون في حدّ التبّت رعيُه[4] من سُنْبُل الطِيب وما يلي أرض الصين منها رعيه ساير الحشايش. والحالة الأخرى تركُ أهل التبّت النوافج بحالها[5] وغشُّ أهل الصين لِما وقع إليهم منها وسلوكُهم أيضاً في البحر وما يلحقهم من الأنداء[6] فإذا تَرَكَ أهلُ الصين المسك في نوافجه وأُودِعَتْ البَرانيَّ واستُوثِقَ منها وَرَدَ[7] أرضَ العرب كالتبّتيّ في جودته.

وأجودُ المسك كلّه ما حَكَّهُ الظبيُ على أحجار الجبال إذ كان مادّةً[8] تصير في سُرّته وتجتمعُ[9] دماً عَبِيطاً كاجتماع الدم فيما يعرض من الدمامل فإذا أَدركَ حكَّهُ وأضجرَه[10] فيُفْرِعُ[11] إلى الحجارة حتّى يخرقه فيسيل ما فيه فإذا خرج عنه جفّ واندمل وعادت المادّةُ تجتمع فيه من[12] ذي قبل. وللتبّت رجال يخرجون في طلب هذا ولهم به معرفة فإذا وجدوه التقطوه وجمعوه وأودعوه النوافجَ وحُمِلَ إلى ملوكهم. وهو نهاية المسك إذ كان قد أدرك في نوافجه على حيوانه وصار له فضلٌ على غيره من المسك كفضل ما يدرك من الثمار في شجرِه[13] على ساير ما يُنْزَعُ منه قبل إدراكه.

١ من الظباء: ساقطة في خ. ٢ خ: فضلُ. ٣ كذا في ب؛ خ: إحداهما. ٤ ح: رعية. ٥ ح وخ و ر: في حالها. ٦ ح: الأيذاء [كذا]؛ ر: الافداء. ٧ ب وح وخ و ر: وورد؛ ويجب حذف الواو الأولى ليستقيمَ المعنى. ٨ ح وخ: مادّةٌ. ٩ ح وخ و ر: ويجتمع. ١٠ خ: وأجْره. ١١ ب: فيَفرِع؛ خ: فيفرغ. ١٢ خ: مثل. ١٣ ح: شجرة.

prevents the people of Khurasan from launching an assault on China. Turning to the part of China lying in the direction of the setting sun, namely the place known as Bamdhū, this is located on the borders of Tibet, and fighting never ceases there between the Chinese and the Tibetans.

We have seen one of the people who entered China, who reported that he saw a man carrying on his back a skin bag filled with Tibetan musk; this man had come on foot from Samarqand, passing through one Chinese city after another until he finally arrived in Khānfū, the meeting place of merchants coming from Sīrāf. This journey was possible because the land that is home to the gazelles that produce Chinese musk is one and the same land with Tibet: the Chinese catch the gazelles nearest to them, and the Tibetans those nearest to them.[136] Furthermore, the superiority of Tibetan musk to Chinese is due to only two factors. The first of these is the fact that musk gazelles in the Tibetan borderlands graze on Indian spikenard,[137] whereas those in the region neighboring China graze on other kinds of herbage. The second factor is the Tibetans' practice of leaving the musk pods in their natural state.[138] The Chinese, in contrast, adulterate the musk pods that they get hold of; there is the additional factor of their using the maritime route to export the musk and the exposure to moist vapors that this incurs. If the Chinese were to leave the musk intact in its pods and then place the pods in earthenware pots, sealing them securely, then their musk would be of the same quality as Tibetan musk when it reached Arab lands.[139] 2.9.4 *Musk and its origin*

The best musk of all in quality is that which the gazelle has rubbed onto stones in the mountains.[140] Musk is a substance that goes to the gazelle's navel and gathers there like uncoagulated blood, just as blood itself gathers in the superficial parts of boils. When the swollen pod "ripens," the gazelle rubs it against stones and chafes it until the musk starts to ooze out on to the stones; the gazelle eventually bursts it, and its contents flow out. When all the musk has come out, the pod dries up and scabs over, then the substance begins to gather in it as before. The Tibetans have men who go out in search of this musk deposited on stones and who have expert knowledge of it. When they find some, they pick it off the stone, gather it together, and pack it into empty musk pods; it is then taken to their kings. This is the very best musk of all, because it has ripened in its pods on the living animal. It is superior to other sorts of musk, in the same way that fruit ripened on the tree is superior to all other fruit that is picked before it is ripe.

وغير هذا من المسك فإنّما يصاد بالشَرَكِ المنصوب أو السهام وربّما قُطِعَت النوافج عن الظبي قبل إدراك المسك فيها وعلى أنّه إذا قُطِعَ عن ظبايه كان كَرِيهَ الرايحة مدّةً من المُدد حتّى يجفّ على الأيّام الطويلة وكلّما جفّ استحالَ حتّى يصير مسكًا. وظبي المسك كساير الظباء عندنا في القَدّ واللون ودقّة القوايم وافتراق الأظلاف وانتصاب القرون وانعطافها ولها نابان دقيقان أبيضان في الفكّين قايمان في وجه الظبي طولُ كلّ واحد منهما مقدار فِتْرٍ ودونه على هيئة ناب الفيل فهو الفرق بينها وبين ساير الظباء.

٢،٩،٥ ومكاتبات ملوك الصين لملوك أمصارهم وخصيانهم على بغال البريد مُجَزَّزَة[١] الأذناب على سبيل بغال البريد عندنا على سكك معروفة.

٢،٩،٦ وملوك[٢] أهل الصين معما وصفناه[٣] مِن أمرهم يبولون من قيام وكذلك ساير رعيّتهم من أهل بلادهم. فأمّا الملوك والقوّاد والوجوه فلهم أنابيب من خشب مدهونة طول كلّ خشبة منها ذراع وفي الطرفين ثقبتان تتّسع العليا للحَشَفَة فيقف على رجله إذا أراد البول ويباعدها عن نفسه ويبول فيها[٤] ويزعمون أنّ ذاك[٥] أصحّ لأجسامهم وأنّ ساير ما يعتري من وجع المثانة والبول من الاستحجار فيها إنّما هو من الجلوس للبول وأنّ المثانة لا تطفو[٦] بما فيها إلّا مع القيام لذلك.

٢،٩،٧ والسبب في تركهم الشعورَ على رُوسهم[٧] - أعني الرجال - امتناعُهم من تدوير رأس المولود وتقويه[٨] كما يستعمل العرب وقولُهم إنّ ذاك[٩] ممّا يزيل الدماغ عن حاله[١٠] التي خُلِقَ عليها وإنّه يُفسِد الحاسّة المعروفة. فرؤسهم[١١] مضطربة يسترها الشعر ويُعفّي عليها.

١ ح وخ: مجهَّزة. ٢ وملوك: ساقطة في ح وخ و ر. ٣ ح: مهما وصفناهم. ٤ وفي الطرفين ... ويبول فيها: ساقطة في خ. ٥ ح وخ و ر: ذلك. ٦ ب: تطفوا؛ ح: تصفوا. ٧ ح وخ: رؤوسهم. ٨ ر: وتقويمه (ولعلّها المقصود). ٩ خ: ذلك. ١٠ ح: حالة. ١١ ح وخ: فرؤوسهم.

Except for this kind, all musk is from gazelles that are trapped in enclosures of nets staked upright or hunted with arrows, and often the pods are cut out of the gazelle before the musk in them has ripened. Besides, when it is cut out of the gazelles, it retains an unpleasant odor for a certain time, until it dries, this taking a long period of days; as it dries out, its substance changes and turns into musk. The musk gazelle itself resembles the other types of gazelle found in our lands, both in size and color, and has similarly slender legs and cloven hoofs, and horns that rise straight and then curve in a similar way.[141] However, the musk gazelle has a pair of slender white tusks, one on each side of its lower jaw, standing up in front of its face; the length of each is about the distance between the tips of a man's thumb and index finger when stretched apart, or less than that, and its shape is that of an elephant's tusk in miniature.[142] This is the difference between the musk gazelle and other gazelles.

The correspondence of the Great Kings of China with the rulers of their provincial capitals and with their eunuch officials goes on post mules. These have their tails clipped in the manner of our post mules[143] and follow recognized routes. **2.9.5** *Post mules*

Further to what we have already said in description of the rulers of the Chinese is the fact that they urinate from a standing position; so too do all those of their subjects who belong to the native population.[144] The rulers themselves, the army commanders and the other people of high rank use tubes of lacquered wood, each a cubit in length and with a hole at either end, the upper one big enough for the user to insert the head of his penis: when he wants to urinate, he stands on his feet, aims the tube away from himself, and urinates through it. They maintain that this method is healthier for their bodies, that the pain from bladder stones felt in the bladder itself and during urination is entirely due to the practice of squatting to urinate, and that the bladder allows its contents to well up and flow out only when one urinates standing.[145] **2.9.6** *The Chinese manner of urination*

The reason they let their hair grow on their heads—I mean the men—is the fact that they do not believe in "rounding" the heads of new-born babies and letting them harden, as is practiced by the Arabs.[146] They say that the practice is one of the causes of the brain becoming displaced from the position in which it was created and that it interferes with the normal faculties of sensation. As a result, their heads are covered in bumps, which their hair covers up and hides from view. **2.9.7** *The reason Chinese men let their hair grow*

فأمّا المناكح ببلاد الصين - وهم شعوب وقبايل كشعوب بني اسرائيل والعرب ٢،٩،٨ وبطونها يتعارفون ذاك بينهم - ولا[1] يزوّج أحدٌ منهم قريباً ولا ذا نسبٍ ويتجاوزون ذلك حتّى لا تتزوّج القبيلة في قبيلتها مثال ذلك أنّ بني تَميم لا تتزوّج في تميم ورَبيعة لا تتزوّج في ربيعة وإنّما تتزوّج ربيعة في مُضَر ومضر في ربيعة ويدّعون أنّ ذلك أَنْجَبُ للولد.

بعض أخبار الهند

في مملكة بلهرا وغيره من ملوك الهند مَن يحرق نفسه بالنار وذلك لقولهم بالتناسخ ٢،١٠،١ وتمكُّنِه في قلوبهم وزوالِ الشكّ فيه عنهم.

وفي ملوكهم مَن إذا قعد للمُلك طُبِخَ له أرزٌ ثمّ وُضِعَ بين يديه على ورق الموز وينتدب من أصحابه الثلاثماية والأربعماية باختيارهم لأنفسهم لا بإكراهٍ مِن الملك لهم. فيعطيهم الملك من ذلك الأرزّ بعد أن يأكل منه ويتقرّب رجلٌ منهم فيأخذ منه شيئاً يسيرًا فيأكله فيُلْزَمُ كلُّ مَن أكل من هذا الأرزّ إذا مات الملك أو قُتِلَ أن يحرقوا أنفسهم بالنار عن آخرهم في اليوم الذي مات فيه لا يتأخّرون عنه حتّى لا يبقى منهم عين ولا أثر.

وإذا عزم الرجل على إحراق نفسه صار إلى باب الملك فاستأذن ثمّ دارَ في الأسواق وقد أُجِّجَتْ له النار في حطبٍ جَزْلٍ كثيرٍ عليها رجالٌ يقومون بإيقادها حتّى تصير كالعقيق حرارةً والتهاباً ثمّ يعدو[2] وبين يديه الصنوجُ[3] دايرًا في الأسواق وقد احتوشَه أهلُه وقرابتُه وبعضهم يضع على رأسه إكليلاً من الريحان يملأُوه[4] جمرًا ويصبّ عليه السَنْدَرُوس وهو مع النار كالنفط ويمشي وهامتُه تحترق وروايحُ لحم

---

[1] ولا: كذا في ب؛ ولعلّ المقصود: فلا. [2] ب: يعدوا. [3] خ: ثمّ يُعِدونَ بينَ يديهِ الصنوجَ. [4] يملأُوه: كذا في ب؛ ح: يملؤه؛ خ: يملأُه.

Regarding the choice of spouses in China, the Chinese are made up of different peoples and tribes (just as the Israelites and Arabs are peoples and subtribes) all recognizing one another among themselves.[147] None of the Chinese, however, is ever married to a near relation or to anyone sharing the same immediate lineage; indeed, they take this even further, to the extent that members of a particular tribe will never marry within that tribe. The Arab equivalent would be for members of Tamīm never to marry within Tamīm, and for Rabīʿah never to marry within Rabīʿah; instead, Rabīʿah would only marry spouses from Muḍar, and Muḍar from Rabīʿah. The Chinese claim that this produces better-developed offspring. 2.9.8

Choice of spouses among the Chinese

Further Accounts of India

In the kingdom of Balharā and those of other Indian rulers, there are people who burn themselves to death with fire. This stems from their belief in the transmigration of souls, which has so firm a place in the hearts, and from their desire to banish from themselves any doubts about it. 2.10.1

The Indians who burn themselves to death

Certain kings of theirs, when they ascend the throne, have rice cooked for them and placed before them on banana leaves. The new king invites three or four hundred of his companions—they come of their own free choice, not under any compulsion from the king—and gives them some of the rice, having first eaten some himself; one by one they come up to him, take a little of the rice, and eat it. It then becomes obligatory for all those who have eaten some of this rice, when the king dies or is killed, to burn themselves to death by fire. This they must do to the last man, and on the very day of the king's death, without delay, until not a single one of them remains, or even a trace of them.

If someone from the general populace makes up his mind to burn himself to death, he first goes to the gate of the king's palace to ask permission to do so, then he goes around in the markets. In the meantime a fire has been kindled for him in a huge great pile of firewood; there are men in charge of this who stoke the flames until they blaze red-hot, as red as carnelian. The man then begins to run around the markets, preceded by people clashing cymbals and surrounded by members of his family and close kin. One of these now places on his head a wreath made from aromatic plants, fills the space in the center of it with burning embers, and sprinkles them with sandarac, which has the same effect on fire as does naphtha.[148] The man walks on, the crown

رأسه تفوح[1] وهو لا يتغيّر[2] في مشيته ولا يظهر منه جزعٌ حتّى يأتي النارَ فيثب فيها فيصير رماداً.

فذكَرَ بعضُ مَن حَضَرَ رجلاً منهم يريد دخول النار أنّه لمّا أشرف عليها أخذ الخنجر فوضعه على رأس فؤاده فشَقَّه بيده إلى عانته ثمّ أدخل يده اليسرى فقبض على كبده فجذب منها ما تهيّأ له وهو يتكلّم ثمّ قطع بالخنجر منها قطعةً فدفعها إلى أخيه استهانةً بالموت وصبراً على الألم ثمّ زجّ بنفسه في النار إلى لعنة الله.

٢،١٠،٢ وزعم هذا الرجل الحاكي أنّ في جبال هذه الناحية قوماً من الهند سبيلهم سبيل الكنيفيّة والجليديّة عندنا في طلب الباطل والجهل وبينهم وبين أهل الساحل عصبيّة. وأنّه لا يزال رجل من أهل الساحل يدخل الجبل فيستدعي مَن يصابره على التمثيل بنفسه وكذلك أهل الجبل لأهل الساحل. وأنّ رجلاً من أهل الجبال صار إلى أهل الساحل لمثل ذلك فاجتمع إليه الناس بين ناظرٍ ومتعصّبٍ فطالَبَ أهلَ العصبيّة بأن يصنعوا مثل ما يصنع فإن عجزوا عنه اعترفوا بالغلبة. وأنّه جلس عند رأس منابت القنى[3] وأَمَرَهم باجتذاب قناةٍ من تلك القنى - وسبيله سبيل القصب في الِتفافِهِ وأصله مثل الدنّ وأغلظ وإذا حُطَّ رأس القناة استجابت حتّى تقارب الأرض فإذا تُرِكَتْ عادت إلى حالها - فجُذِبَ رأس قناة غليظة حتّى قربت منه ثمّ شدّ بها ضفايره شدّاً وثيقاً ثمّ أخذ الخنجر وهو كالنار في سُرعتها فقال لهم: إنّي قاطعٌ رأسي به فإذا بانَ عن بدني فأطلقوه من ساعته فسأضحكُ إذا عادت القناةُ برأسي إلى موضعها وتسمعوا قهقهةً يسيرةً. فعجز أهل الساحل عن أن يصنعوا مثل ذلك. ولقد أخبرنا بهذا من لا نتّهمه وهو اليوم متعارفٌ إذ كانت هذه البلاد من الهند تقرب من بلاد العرب وأخبارها متّصلة بهم في كلّ وقت.

[1] ب: يفوح. [2] ح: يتعثّر. [3] ح: القنا هنا وفيما بعد.

of his head ablaze and giving off the reek of burning flesh, but he does not alter his pace or show any fear, until at last he reaches the pyre, leaps into the flames, and is burned to ashes.

An informant who was present when one of these men was intending to enter the fire reported that, when he was on the point of doing so, the man took a dagger, placed the point of it at the top of his abdomen[149] and, with his own hand, ripped himself open down to below the navel. He plunged his left hand into his innards, grasped his own liver and pulled out as much as he could, speaking all the while, then sliced off a piece of the liver and handed it to his brother—all to demonstrate his contempt of death and his ability to bear pain—and finally launched himself into the flames and into God's damnation.

2.10.2

Rival gangs among the Indians, and their extraordinary challenges to each other

This same informant also maintained that, in the uplands of this region, live a group of Indians who, in their pursuit of the pointless and idiotic, resemble the Kanīfiyyah and the Jalīdiyyah in our lands, and that they and the coastal people are gang rivals. Men from the coast, the informant stated, continually go to the uplands and challenge the uplanders to match them in trials of endurance; similarly, the uplanders go and challenge the men of the coast. For example, an uplander went to the coastal people to issue such a challenge. A crowd gathered around him, some of them onlookers and some of them gang members. The uplander demanded that the gang members do what he was about to do; if they could not, they would have to admit defeat. The challenger then went and sat at the edge of some bamboo thickets and told the people to bend one of the bamboo stems downwards. Now, these bamboos are all tangled together like reeds, but their bases are as thick as large storage jars, or thicker;[150] if the top of a bamboo is pushed downwards, the stem will respond by bending nearly to the ground, and if it is let go, it will spring back to its upright position. So the top of a thick bamboo was duly bent down until it was by the man. He then tied his long plaited hair to the stem with a tight knot, took a dagger—theirs have blades that cut as swift as fire—and said to the onlookers, "I am going to cut off my head with this dagger. The moment it is separated from my body, let it go. And as soon as the bamboo has sprung back to its upright position, taking my head with it, I will laugh out loud, and you will hear a short burst of chuckling." The men of the coast were unable to emulate his act.[151] We have heard this account from someone we do not suspect of lying; indeed, the story is now common knowledge, because these regions of India are close to Arab lands, and such accounts reach the Arabs from there all the time.

٢،١٠،٣ ومن شأنهم إذا أخذَتِ السنُّ من رجالهم ونسايهم وضعفت حواسُّهم أن يطالب مَن صار في هذه الحال منهم أهلَه بطرحه في النار أو تغريقه في الما ثقةً منهم بالرجعة. وسبيل موتاهم الإحراق.

٢،١١،١ وقد كان بجزيرة سرنديب وبها جبل الجوهر ومغاص اللؤلؤ وغيرُه يُقدِمُ الرجل الهنديّ على دخول السوق ومعه الجزبي[١] وهو خنجر لهم عجيب الصنعة مُرهَفٌ فيضرب بيده إلى أجلّ تاجر يقدر عليه ويأخذ بتلابيبه ويَشهَرُ الخنجر عليه ويُخرجه عن البلد في مجمع من الناس لا يتهيّأ لهم فيه حيلة وذلك أنّه متى أُريدَ انتزاعُه منه قتل التاجرَ وقتل نفسه. فإذا خرج عن البلد طالَبَه بالفدية وتبِعَ التاجرَ[٢] مَن يفتديه بالمال الكثير. فدام ذلك بهم مدّة من الزمان حتّى مَلَكَهم ملكٌ أمر بمن فعل ذلك من الهند أن يؤخذ على أيّة حالٍ كان ففُعِلَ ذلك فقتل الهنديُّ التاجرَ وقتل نفسه. فجرى هذا على جماعة منهم وتَلِفَتْ فيه أنفسُ الهند وأنفسُ العرب فلمّا وقع البأس انقطع ذلك وأَمِنَ التجّارُ على أنفسهم.

٢،١١،٢ والجوهر الأحمر والأخضر والأصفر مخرجُهُ[٣] من جبل سرنديب وهي جزيرة وأكثر ما يظهر لهم في وقت المدود يدحرجُهُ الما عليهم من كهوف ومغارات ومسايل مياه لهم عليها أرصادٌ للمَلِك. وربّما استنبطوه أيضاً كما تستنبَطُ المعادن فيخرج الجوهر مُلْصَقاً بالحجارة فيُكسَرُ عنه.[٤]

٢،١١،٣ ولملك هذه الجزيرة شريعة ومشايخ لهم مجالس كمجالس محدّثينا يجتمع إليهم الهند فيكتبون عنهم سِيَرَ أنبيايهم وسنن شرايعهم. وبها صنمٌ عظيم من ذهبٍ إبريزٍ يُفرِط البحريّون في مبلغ وزنه وهياكلُ قد أُنفِقَ عليها أموال عظيمة. وبهذه الجزيرة

١ ح وخ: الجربى. ٢ التاجر: ساقطة في خ. ٣ ح: مخرجة. ٤ كذا في ب؛ خ: فتكسَرُ عنه.

It is a feature of the Indians, when old age saps the strength of their men and women and their faculties become impaired, that someone in this state will ask his family to put him alive on a pyre or drown him in water, such is their trust in the return of their souls to another body. Their custom is to cremate the dead. 2.10.3

Voluntary euthanasia among the elderly

Accounts of the Island of Sarandīb and of the Region of al-Aghbāb, Which Faces It

In the island of Sarandīb (where the mountain of gems, the pearl fishery, and so on are situated) certain Indian men[152] used to make so bold as to go into the market armed with the *jazbī*, a type of dagger of theirs, superbly crafted and finely honed; they would lunge at the most eminent merchant they could get hold of, grab him by the collar, pull the dagger on him, then march him out of town—and all in the middle of a crowd of people who could do nothing at all to stop him, because, if they tried to snatch the merchant from him, the abductor would kill both his captive and himself. Once away from town, the abductor would demand a ransom from the merchant, and someone would come after the latter and pay a large sum of money to secure his release. These kidnappings went on for a period of time, until a king ascended the throne who gave orders that any Indian committing this crime should be captured, whatever the cost. This was acted upon, and the Indian kidnapper would kill the merchant and then himself. The same happened to a considerable number of them, and the lives of both the Indian kidnappers and the Arab merchants were lost as a result. Then, when fear had befallen everyone, the abductions ceased, and the merchants felt safe again. 2.11.1

The abduction of merchants

The source from which their red, green, and yellow gemstones emerge is the Mountain of Sarandīb.[153] Sarandīb is an island, and the gems mostly appear to the people at times when the tide is high: water causes the stones to tumble down to them out of their caves, grottos, and watercourses, and these places are kept under surveillance by the king. Also, they sometimes mine the gems in the same way that minerals are mined; they come out embedded in rock, which has to be chipped away. 2.11.2

Gemstones and how they obtain them

The king of this island has a code of religious law and a corps of legal scholars specializing in it: they hold sessions like those of our scholars of hadith, in which the Indians[154] gather to take down from the scholars' dictation the lives of their prophets and the laws contained in their legal codes. 2.11.3

Religions in Sarandīb

جمعٌ من اليهود كثير ومن ساير المِلَل وبها أيضاً ثَنَوِيّة والملك يبيح لكلّ فريق منهم ما يتشرّع به.

٢،١١،٤ وتحاذي[١] هذه الجزيرة أغبابٌ واسعةٌ - ومعنى الغِبّ[٢] الوادي العظيم إذا أَفْرَط في طوله وعرضه وكان مصبُّه إلى البحر - يسير المجتازون في هذا الغبّ المعروف بغبّ سرنديب شهرين وأكثر في غياض ورياض وهَوا معتدلٍ. وفي فوّهة هذا الغبّ البحرُ المعروف بهركند. وهو نَزِهٌ[٣] المكان الشاة فيه بنصف درهم وما يشرب جمعٌ من الرجال من الشراب المطبوخ من عسل النخل[٤] بحَبّ الداذيّ[٥] الرطب بمثل ذلك.

٢،١١،٥ وأكثر أعمالهم القمار بالديكة والنرد. والديكة عندهم عظيمة الأجسام وافرة الصَياصي يستعملون لها من الخناجر الصغار المرهفة ما يُشَدّ على صياصيها ثمّ تُرسَل. وقمارهم في الذهب والفضّة والأرضين والبنات[٦] وغير ذلك فيبلغ الديكُ الغالبُ جملةً من الذهب.

وكذلك لعبُهم بالنرد دايم على خطرٍ واسعٍ حتّى أنّ أهل الضعف منهم ومَن لا مال له ممّن يذهب إلى طلب الباطل والفتوّة ربّما لاعَبَ في أنامله فيلعبُ وإلى جنبه شي قد جُعِلَ فيه من دهن الجوز أو دهن السمسم - إذ كان الزيت معدوماً عندهم - وتحته نارٌ تحميه وبينهما فأسٌ صغيرة مشحوذة. فإذا غلب أحدُهما صاحبَه وضع يده على حجرٍ وضرب القامرُ بالفأس أنملةَ المقمور فأبانها ووضع المقمورُ يده في الدهن وهو في نهاية الحرارة فيكويها. ولا يقطعه ذاك عن المعاودة في اللعب فربّما افترقا وقد بطلت أناملُهما جميعاً.

ومنهم من يأخذ الفتيلة فينقعها في الدهن ثمّ يضعها على عضو من أعضايه ويشعل النار فيها فهي تحترق ورايحة اللحم تفوح وهو يلعب بالنرد لا يظهر منه جزعٌ.

---

١ ح وخ و ر: محاذي. ٢ كذا في ب هنا وفيما بعد؛ والمتعارف عليه الغُبّ بالضمّ. ٣ ح: نزةُ. ٤ ح وخ و ر: النحل. ٥ الداذيّ: كذا في ب؛ وهو الذاذيّ. ٦ ح وخ و ر: والنبات.

There is also a huge idol of pure gold, about whose weight sailors make stupendous claims, and temples on which huge sums of money are spent.[155] On this island, too, are large communities of Jews and followers of other religions, as well as Dualists. The king permits each of these denominations to live by its own laws.

2.11.4 *The Ghubb of Sarandīb, and the blessings of that land*

Facing this island are some wide *ghubb*s, *ghubb* meaning the course of a large river, provided it is extremely long and broad and has an outflow to the sea. People going along the particular *ghubb* known as the Ghubb of Sarandīb can travel for two months and more through woods and meadows where the climate is moderate. At the mouth of this *ghubb* lies the sea known as Harkand. It is a salubrious place; a sheep costs half a dirham there, and the drink prepared from palm "honey" with fresh hypericum seeds costs the same.[156]

2.11.5 *Gambling among the people of this land*

Their most frequent occupation is gambling at cock fights and backgammon. Their cocks have large bodies and well developed spurs; in addition, the people make use of sharpened miniature daggers, which they lash on to the birds' spurs before letting them loose. They gamble for gold, silver, land, slavegirls,[157] and other stakes, and a champion cock can be worth a huge amount of gold.

Similarly, their backgammon games are always played for very high stakes, to the extent that the indigent and penniless types among them, if they are the sort who go looking for ways to waste time and display their machismo, sometimes gamble their own fingertips away. This type of gambler, when he plays, keeps a container beside him into which walnut or sesame oil has been poured—olive oil is not to be found in their land—and beneath which a flame burns, heating the oil; between the two players lies a small, sharp ax. When one of them defeats his fellow player, the latter puts his hand on a stone, then the winner strikes one of the loser's fingertips with the ax and chops it off. The loser then dips his hand in the oil, which is now extremely hot, and cauterizes it. Nor does this stop him going back to the game; indeed, the players sometimes part having both lost all their fingertips.

Some players will also take the wick of a lamp, soak it thoroughly in the oil, place it on one of their limbs, then set fire to it. The wick smoulders away and the smell of burning flesh wafts about, while the player continues his backgammon game apparently undismayed.

٦،١١،٢ والفساد في هذا الموضع فاشٍ في النساء والرجال غير محظور حتّى أنّ تجّار البحر ربّما دعا الواحدُ منهم ابنةَ مَلِكِهم فتأتيه إلى غياضهم بِعِلم أبيها. وكان مشايخ أهل سيراف يمنعون من الجهاز إلى هذه الناحية وخاصّةً الأحداثَ.

١،١٢،٢ وأمرُ اليسارة التي تكون ببلاد الهند – وتفسيرها المطر – فإنّهم[١] يدوم عليهم في الصيف ثلاثة أشهر تِباعًا ليلاً ونهارًا لا يُمسِكُ الشتاءُ[٢] عنهم بتّةً. وقد استعدّوا قبل ذلك لأقواتهم فإذا كانت اليسارة أقاموا في منازلهم لأنّها معمولة من خشبٍ مكنّسةُ[٣] السقوف مظلّلةٌ بحشائش لهم فلا يظهر أحد منهم إلّا لمهمّ على أنّ أهل الصناعات يعالجون صنائعهم في هذه الأماكن هذه المدّة. وربّما عفنت أسافلُ أرجلهم في هذا الوقت.

بهذه اليسارة عيشُهم وإذا لم تكن هلكوا لأنّ زراعتهم الأرزُّ لا يعرفون غيره ولا قُوتَ لهم سواه إنّما يكون في هذا الوقت في حرامات[٤] لهم طريحًا لا يحتاجون إلى سقي ومعاناة ومعنى الحرامات منابت الأرزّ عندهم. فإذا انكشفت السماء عنهم بلغ الأرزّ النهاية في الريع والكثرة. ولا يُمطَرون الشِتا.

٢،١٢،٢ وللهند عُبّاد وأهل علم يُعرَفون بالبراهمة وشعراء يغشَون الملوك ومنجّمون وفلاسفة وكهّان وأهل زَجْرٍ للغربان[٥] وغيرها وبها سحرة وقوم يُظْهِرون التخاييل ويُبْدِعون فيها وذلك بقَنَّوج خاصّةً وهو بلد عظيم في مملكة الجرز.[٦]

٣،١٢،٢ وبالهند قوم يُعرَفون بالبيكرجيّين[٧] عُراةٌ قد غطّت شعورُهم أبدانَهم وفروجَهم وأظفارهم مستطيلة[٨] كالحِراب إذ كانت لا تُقَصُّ إلّا ما ينكسر منها وهم على

---

١ ح وخ: فإنّه. ٢ ح: لا تمسكُ السماء. ٣ مكنّسة: كذا في ب؛ ولعلّ المقصود: مكنّنة أي ذات كُنّن بارزة.
٤ خ: حزامات. ٥ خ: للعريان. ٦ ح و ر: الجوز؛ خ: الحوز. ٧ ب: البيكرحيّين. ٨ ب: مُستطلية.

Sexual immorality is rife in this place, among both women and men, and is not prohibited. It even happens that one of the seagoing merchants will sometimes invite a daughter of the king of these people to an assignation, and she will come to him in the forests, with the full knowledge of her father. The religious scholars in Sīrāf used to forbid their people from going on trading voyages to this region, and particularly the young men. 2.11.6

The sexual immorality of the people of this land

General Accounts of India Continued

Concerning the *yasārah* that occurs in India, meaning the monsoon rain, it falls on their land continuously throughout the summer, for three consecutive months, night and day, the rainfall never letting up at all.[158] They lay in their basic provisions in advance of it, and, when the *yasārah* comes, they stay put in their houses, because they are solidly built of wood and have roofs which they keep swept with brooms[159] and which are thatched with certain types of native grass. No one ventures out, except for some pressing need; craftsmen, however, ply their trades in these places throughout the period of the rains. Sometimes the soles of their feet rot in this season. 2.12.1

Monsoon rains and the cultivation of rice

Their livelihood depends on this *yasārah*; if it fails, they perish. This is because they grow rice alone: they know no other crop, and have no other staple food. The rice grows only at this time in their *ḥarāms*, thrown down haphazardly, with no need for them to irrigate it or take care of it (*ḥarāms* meaning "rice fields" in their language). When their skies become clear at the end of the monsoon rains, the rice is at its most abundant and plentiful. In winter, no rain falls on their land.

Among the Indians are religious devotees and men of learning known as brahmans, as well as poets who frequent the courts of kings, astrologers, philosophers, soothsayers, and those who take auguries from the flight of crows and other birds.[160] In India there are also conjurors and illusionists who are masters of their art; they are particularly to be found at Qannawj, a large city in the kingdom of al-Jurz. 2.12.2

Brahmans, conjurors, and others

In India there is a group known as the *bīkarjīs*. They are naked, although their hair is so long that it covers their upper bodies and pudenda. They let their fingernails grow as long as spearheads, for they are never clipped, or only if they get broken, and they live a life of wandering. Each of them wears a cord around his neck from which a human skull is suspended. When one of them becomes unbearably hungry he stops at the door of one of the Indians, 2.12.3

The bīkarjīs

سبيل سياحة. وفي عنق كلّ رجل منهم خيط فيه جمجمة من جماجم الإنس[١] فإذا اشتدّ به الجوع وقف بباب بعض الهند[٢] فأسرعوا إليه بالأرزّ المطبوخ مستبشرين به فيأكل في تلك الجمجمة فإذا شبع[٣] انصرف فلا يعود لطلب الطعام إلّا في وقت حاجته.

٢،١٢،٤ وللهند ضروبٌ من الشرايع يتقرّبون بها زعموا[٤] إلى خالقهم - جلّ الله وعزّ عمّا يقول الظالمون علوًّا كبيرًا - منها أنّ الرجل يبتني في طُرُقهم الخانَ للسابلة ويقيم فيه بقّالاً يبتاع المجتازون منه حاجتهم ويقيم في الخان فاجرةً من نساء الهند يُجْرِي[٥] عليها لينالَ منها المجتازون وذاك عندهم ممّا يُثابون عليه.

وبالهند قِحاب يُعْرَفون[٦] بقحاب البُدّ والسبب فيه أنّ المرأة إذا نذرت نذرًا وولِدَ لها جاريةٌ جميلة أتت بها البدّ وهو الصنم الذي يعبدونه فجعلتها له. ثمّ اتّخذت لها في السوق بيتًا وعلّقت عليه سترًا وأقعدتها على كرسيّ ليجتاز بها أهل الهند وغيرهم من سائر الملل ممّن يتجاوز في دينه فتُمكِّنُ من نفسها بأُجرة معلومة. وكلّما اجتمع لها شي من ذلك دفعته إلى سَدَنة الصنم ليُصْرَفَ في عمارة الهيكل. واللهُ جلّ وعزّ نحمده على ما اختار لنا وطهّرنا من ذنوب الكَفَرة به.

٢،١٢،٥ فأمّا الصنم المعروف بالمُولْتان وهو قرب المنصورة فإنّه يُقْصَد من مسيرة أشهر كثيرة ويحمل الرجل منهم العود الهنديّ القامَرُونيّ - وقامَرُون بلد يكون فيه فاخر العود - حتّى يأتي به إلى هذا الصنم فيدفعه إلى السدنة لبخور الصنم. ومن هذا العود ما قيمة المنا[٧] منه مايتا[٨] دينار وربّما خُتِمَ عليه فانطبع الخاتمُ فيه لِلُدُونَتِهِ فالتجّار يبتاعونه من هولاء السدنة.

٢،١٢،٦ وبالهند عبّاد في شرايعهم يقصدون إلى الجزاير التي تحدثُ في البحر فيغرسون بها النارجيل ويستنبطون بها المياه للأجر وإن يجتاز بها المراكب فتنال منها.

---

١ ح وخ: الأنس. ٢ ح: الهنود. ٣ ح و ر: أشبع. ٤ ح: فيما زعموا. ٥ ح: يجريء. ٦ يُعْرَفون: كذا في ب. ٧ خ: المن. ٨ ح: مائتي.

and they rush out to him bringing cooked rice, for they regard his coming as a blessing. He eats the rice out of the skull, and when he has had enough he goes away and will not ask for food again until he feels the need for it.

The Indians have various sorts of religious practices by which they propitiate, or so they claim, their Creator—glorious is God, and exalted far beyond what the evildoers say![161] One of these practices is for someone to build a roadside shop for travelers and to install in it a shopkeeper from whom passers-by can buy what they need and to install in the same shop an Indian woman as a prostitute. The builder of the shop pays her expenses, and passing travelers can enjoy her favors. This "benefaction" they consider an act for which they will be divinely rewarded. **2.12.4** *Roadside prostitutes and "idol prostitutes"*

In India there are also prostitutes known as "idol prostitutes."[162] The reason for this is that, if a woman who has made a vow gives birth to a pretty baby daughter, she takes it to the *budd*—that is, the idol that they worship—and dedicates her daughter to it.[163] In time, she finds her daughter a room in the market, hangs a curtain over the door, and sits the girl on a chair in front of the curtain. This is so that Indians and others of all sects may call on her—those, that is, who allow themselves such license in their religion—and the girl will make herself available for a standard fee. Whenever her takings reach a certain amount, she hands them over to the idol's sacristans to be spent on the fabric of the temple. And God, glorious and mighty is He, we praise for the guidance He chose for us and by which He purified us from the sins of the unbelievers!

Regarding the idol known as al-Mūltān, which is near al-Manṣūrah, devotees will travel for many months to visit it. A visitant will carry with him Indian aloewood of the Qāmarūnī variety (Qāmarūn is a region in which excellent aloewood is found) in order to bring it to this idol and present it to the sacristans for the censing of the idol. This aloewood can be worth two hundred dinars a maund,[164] and it is sometimes so saturated with resin that one can press a seal ring into the wood and it will retain the impression. Merchants buy it from these sacristans.[165] **2.12.5** *The idol of al-Mūltān*

In India there are certain pious people whose religious practices include that of traveling to the islands that are created in the sea, planting coconut palms on them and providing sources of freshwater, all with a view to divine reward. If ships put into these islands, they can enjoy the benefits of the palms. Indeed, in Oman there are shipwrights who travel to these islands **2.12.6** *The blessings of the coconut palm*

وبُعمان مَن يقصد إلى هذه الجزاير التي فيها النارجيلُ ومعهم آلات النجارة[١] وغيرها فيقطعون من خشب النارجيل ما أرادوا فإذا جفّ قُطِعَ ألواحاً ويفتلون من لِيفِ النارجيل ما يخرزون به ذلك الخشب ويستعملون منه مركباً وينحتون منه أدقالاً وينسجون[٢] من خوصه شراعاً ومن ليفه خراباتٍ وهي القلوس عندنا. فإذا فرغوا من جميعه شُحِنَت المراكب بالنارجيل فقُصِدَ بها عمان فبِيعَ وعظمت بَرَكَتُه ومنفعته إذ كان جميعُ ما يتّخذ منه غيرَ محتاج إلى غيره.

١،١٣،٢ وبلاد الزَنْج واسعة وكلّ ما ينبت فيها من الذُرة وهو أقواتهم وقصبُ السكّر وسايرُ الشجر فهو أسود عندهم. ولهم ملوك يغزو[٣] بعضهم بعضاً وعند ملوكهم رجال يُعْرَفون بالمخرَّمين قد خُرِّمَت أنوفهم ووُضِعَ فيها حلق ورُكِّبَ في الحلق سلاسل فإذا كانت الحرب تَقَدَّموا وقد أخذ بطرف كلّ سلسلة رجل يجذبها ويصدّه عن التقدّم حتّى تَسْفُرَ السفراء بينهم وإن[٤] وقع الصلح وإلّا شُدَّت تلك السلاسل في أعناقهم وتُرِكوا والحرب فلم تقم لهم[٥] قايمة ولم يزل أحدهم عن مركزه دون أن يُقْتَلَ.

وللعرب في قلوبهم هيبة عظيمة فإذا عاينوا رجلاً منهم سجدوا له وقالوا: هذا من مملكةٍ ينبت بها شجر التمر لجلالة التمر عندهم وفي قلوبهم.

٢،١٣،٢ ولهم الخُطَبُ وليس في الأمم كخطبايهم بألسنتهم. وفيهم من يتعبّد ويستتر بجلد نمر أو جلد قرد ويأخذ بيده عصا ويقبل نحوَهم فيجتمع إليه منهم جمع فيقف على رجله يوماً إلى الليل يخطب عليهم ويذكّرهم بالله جلّ ذكره ويصف لهم أمور مَن هلك منهم.

---

١ ح وخ و ر: النجّار. ٢ وينسجون: في هامش ب بخطّ الناسخ، تصحيحاً لـ (يفتلون) في المتن. ٣ ب: يغزوا.
٤ وإن: كذا في ح وخ؛ ر: فان؛ غير واضحة في ب. ٥ ح: له.

where the coconut palms are, bringing with them carpentry tools and other equipment. They fell as much coconut wood as they want; when it is dry, it is sawn into planks. Next, using the coconut fiber, they twist enough cordage to sew together the planks they have sawn, and use them to build the hull of a ship.[166] They then hew masts from the coconut wood, weave sails from its fronds, and use its fiber to twist what they call *kharābāt*, which are cables in our parlance. When they have finished all this, the ships are loaded with coconuts and sailed to Oman, where the nuts are sold. The blessings and advantages of the coconut palm are great indeed, for all these products come from it and do not need to be supplemented from any other source.

The Land of the Zanj

The land of the Zanj is extensive. All the millet that grows there and is their staple food, as well as the sugar cane and other plants—all their varieties of these crops are black in color. They are ruled by kings who raid each other. These kings have warriors known as the Pierced Ones, whose noses are pierced and fitted with rings to which chains are attached. In time of war they advance; each chain, however, has a man holding on to the other end of it and tugging at it—this is to hold the warriors back from advancing until envoys have gone out to mediate between the two sides. If peace is made, there the matter ends; if not, the warriors are let loose with the chains bound around their necks, and battle is joined. Nothing can stand up to these fighters, and nothing less than death itself will cause one of them to desert his post. **2.13.1**

Crops, warriors, and the awe in which the Arabs are held

The Zanj feel great awe in their hearts for the Arabs. If they catch sight of an Arab, they prostrate themselves before him and say, "This man is from a kingdom where the date tree grows!" This is because of the prestige that dates enjoy, both in their land and in their hearts.

The Zanj have a talent for sermons; indeed, no other nation has preachers like theirs, when they preach in their own tongues. There are those of them who devote themselves to a life of piety; wearing the skin of a leopard or a monkey and holding a staff, such a man will approach the people, and a crowd will gather around him. He will then stand there, remaining on his feet all day until nightfall, preaching to them, calling on them to keep God in their minds—may His honorable name be exalted—and describing to them the fate of their people who have died. **2.13.2**

Zanj preachers

ومن عندهم تُحْمَل النمور الزنجيّة وفيها حُمرة وهِجانة ولها كِبَر وسعة.

وفي البحر جزيرة تُعْرَفُ بسُقُوطَرا[1] وبها منابت الصِبْر الأُسْقُوطَريّ وموقعها قريب من بلاد الزنج وبلاد العرب. وأكثر أهلها نصارى والسبب في ذلك أنّ الإسكندر[2] لمّا غلب على مُلْكِ فارس كان يكاتبه معلّمُه أرِسْطُوطالِيس فيعرّفه ما وقع عليه من الأرضين فكتب إليه يؤكّد عليه في طلب جزيرة في البحر تُعْرَفُ بسقوطرا وأنّ بها منابت الصبر وهو الدواء الأعظم الذي لا تتمّ الإيارَجاتُ إلّا به وأنّ الصواب أن يُخْرِجَ[3] مَن كان في هذه الجزيرة ويقيمَ فيها مِن اليونانيّين مَن يحوطها ليُحْمَلَ منها الصبرُ إلى الشام والروم ومصر. فبعث الإسكندر فأخرجَ أهلَها عنها وأنزلَ جمعاً من اليونانيّين فيها وتَقَدَّمَ إلى ملوك الطوايف - إذ كانوا عند قَتْله دارا الكبير طَوْعَ يده - بالاحتفاظ بهم. فكانوا في صيانةٍ حتّى بعث الله عيسى عليه السلام فبلغ مَن بهذه الجزاير من اليونانيّة أمرُه[4] فدخلوا في جملة ما دخلت فيه الرومُ من التنصّر. وبقاياهم بها إلى هذا الوقت مع ساير مَن سكنها من غيرهم. ١،١٤،٢

ولم يَذكر في هذا الكتاب يعني الكتاب الأوّل ما تَيامَنَ من البحر عند خروج المراكب من عمان وأرض العرب[5] وتوسُّطِهم للبحر الكبير وإنّما شُرِحَ فيه ما تَياسَرَ[6] منها[7] إذ كان فيه بحر الهند والصين وفيه كان مقصدُ مَن كَتَبَ ذلك الكتابُ عنه. ١،١٥،٢

ففي هذا البحر الذي عن يمين الهند للخارج[8] عن عمان بلادُ الشِحْر وهي منابت ٢،١٥،٢

١ بسُقُوطَرا: كذا في ب؛ والمتعارف عليه سُقُطْرَى أو سُقُطْرا أو سُقُطْرة. ٢ ح وخ و ر هنا وفيما بعد: اسكندر.
٣ ب: تخرجَ. ٤ خ: أمرَهُ. ٥ ب: العَر. ٦ ح: تيسر. ٧ منها: كذا في ب. ٨ ب وح و ر: الخارج.

It is from their land that Zanjī leopards are exported.[167] They are notable for their reddish color and excellent breeding, as well as for their ample size.

The Island of Socotra

In the sea lies an island known as Socotra, where the Socotri aloes grow;[168] 2.14.1
it is situated near both the land of the Zanj and the land of the Arabs. Most of its inhabitants are Christians. The reason for this is that, when Alexander conquered the empire of Persia, his tutor Aristotle would write to him to inform him of the various lands he had come across in his researches. In the course of this correspondence, Aristotle wrote to Alexander telling him that he should seek out an island in the sea known as Socotra, and that it was where aloes grow, aloes being the sovereign remedy without which no laxative is complete. The correct course of action, Aristotle advised, was to expel the inhabitants of the island and to resettle it with Greeks who could keep guard over it, so that the aloes could be exported from there to the Levant, Asia Minor,[169] and Egypt. Alexander therefore dispatched a force, expelled the islanders, and settled a body of Greeks on the island. He also gave orders to the factional rulers in Persia[170]—who, following the death of Darius the Great at his hands, were as yet obedient to his commands—to keep the settlers under their protection. The position of the settlers thus remained secure. In time, when God sent Jesus as a prophet, eternal peace be upon him, news of his mission reached the Greeks living on these islands[171] and they, along with the mass of the Romans, adopted Christianity. Their remaining descendants live on the island to this day, alongside other races who have settled there.[172]

Seas and Lands Lying West of the Gulf of Oman

In this book, meaning the First Book, the author did not mention the seas 2.15.1
that lie to starboard of ships when they leave Oman and the land of the Arabs and sail out into the middle of the ocean. Only those seas lying to port were covered—that is, those comprising the Sea of India and China—for that was the intention of the person from whom that First Book was taken down.[173]

On this sea that extends to starboard of India, from the viewpoint of a ship 2.15.2
leaving Oman,[174] lies the land of al-Shiḥr. In it are the places where frankincense grows, and it is one of the territories of ʿĀd, Ḥimyar, Jurhum, and the

The coasts between al-Shiḥr and al-Zaylaʿ

اللبان وأرض من أراضي عاد وحِمْيَر وجُرْهُم والتَبابِعة. ولهم ألسنةٌ بالعربيّة عاديّة قديمة لا يعرف أكثَرها العربُ وليست لهم قرى وهم في قشفٍ وضيقِ عيشٍ إلى أن تنتهي أرضهم إلى أرض عَدَن وسواحل اليمن وإلى جُدّة ومن جدّة إلى الجار إلى ساحل الشأم ثمّ يُفضي إلى القلزم وينقطع البحر هناك - وهو حيث يقول الله جلّ ذكره: ﴿وَجَعَلَ بَيْنَ ٱلْبَحْرَيْنِ حَاجِزًا﴾. ثمّ ينعرج البحر من القلزم على أرض البَرْبَر ثمّ يتّصل بالجانب الغربيّ الذي يقابل أرض اليمن حتّى يمرّ بأرض الحبشة - التي تُجْلَبُ جلود النمور البربريّة منها وهي أحسن الجلود وأنقاها - والزَيْلَع وفيها العنبر والذبل وهو ظهور السلاحف.

٣،١٥،٢ ومراكب أهل سيراف إذا وصلت في هذا البحر المتيامن عن بحر الهند فصارت إلى جدّة أقامت بها ونُقِلَ ما فيها من الأمتعة ألتي تُحْمَلُ إلى مصر في مراكب القلزم إذ كان لا يتهيأ لمراكب السيرافيّين سلوكُ ذلك البحر لصعوبته وكثرة جباله النابتة فيه وأنّه لا ملوك في شيء من سواحله ولا عمارة وأنّ المركب إذا سلكه احتاج في كلّ ليلة إلى أن يطلب موضعاً يستكنّ فيه خوفاً من جباله فيسير النهارَ ويقيم الليلَ. وهو بحر مظلم كريه الروائح لا خَيْرَ في بطنه ولا ظهره وليس كبحر الهند والصين الذي في بطنه اللؤلؤ والعنبر وفي جباله الجوهر ومعادن الذهب وفي أفواه دوابّه العاج وفي منابته الأبنوس والبقّم والخيزران وشجر العود والكافور والجوزُبَوّا والقرنفل والصندل وساير الأفواه الطيّبة الذكيّة وطيوره الففغى - يعني الببّغاوات - والطواويس وخرشات[1] أرضه الزَبَاد وظبا المسك وما لا يحصيه أحد لكثرة خيره.

١،١٦،٢ فأمّا العنبر وما يقع منه إلى سواحل هذا البحر فهو شي تقذفه الأمواج إليه ومبدأه[2] من بحر الهند على أنّه لا يُعْرَفُ مخرجه غير أنّ أجوده ما وقع إلى بَرْبَرا وحدود بلاد

١ ح: حرشات. ٢ ب: مبدأوه؛ خ: مبدوءه.

Tubbaʿs. The people there speak ancient ʿĀdite dialects of Arabic, and the Arabs do not understand most of their speech.[175] They have no settlements, even as small as villages, and live harsh and straitened lives. Their territory continues up to that of Aden and the coasts of Yemen; the coast then continues to Jidda, and from Jidda to al-Jār and the coast of al-Shaʾm. The coast then carries on to al-Qulzum, and there the sea comes to an end;[176] it is the place about which God, may His honorable name be exalted, said in the Qurʾan, «And He has placed between the two seas a barrier.»[177] The coast of the sea then turns back from al-Qulzum towards the land of the Barbar and connects with the western side of the Sea of al-Qulzum, which faces the land of Yemen. It continues past the land of Abyssinia—from where Barbarī leopard skins are exported, which are the best and most flawless skins available—then passes al-Zaylaʿ, where ambergris and *dhabl* (turtle shells) are to be found.

If the ships of the Sīrāfīs reach this sea that lies to starboard of the Sea of India and then go on to Jidda, they remain there; meanwhile, cargoes of theirs bound for Egypt are transferred to the ships of al-Qulzum. The reason is that the Sīrāfīs' vessels are not suited to sailing this sea of al-Qulzum, because of the difficulty of navigating it and the numerous rocks that protrude from its waters; in addition, there are no kings[178] and no inhabited places anywhere on its shores. Ships sailing this sea must look for a place to take shelter every night, for fear of the rocks in it, so they sail only by day and anchor at night. It is a dismal, hostile, and malodorous sea,[179] and there is no good to be found in its depths or on its surface, unlike the Sea of India and China, in whose depths are pearls and ambergris, in whose rocky isles are gems and mines of gold, in the mouths of whose beasts is ivory, in whose forests grow ebony, sapan wood, rattans, and trees that bear aloewood, camphor, nutmeg, cloves, sandalwood, and all manner of fragrant and aromatic spices, whose birds are *fafaghā* (parrots, that is) and peacocks, and the creeping things of whose earth are civet cats and musk gazelles, and all the rest that no one could enumerate, so many are its blessings. **2.15.3**

The perils of the Sea of al-Qulzum, and the blessings of the Sea of India and China

Ambergris and Whales

On the subject of ambergris, such as that which is cast up on the shores of this sea on the western side of the Sea of India, it is a substance that is driven there by the waves but originates further out in the Sea of India, although it is not known where it emerges from.[180] The finest quality is the sort that is **2.16.1**

الزنج والشحر وما والاها وهو البَيْض المدوّرُ الأزرقُ. ولأهل هذه النواحي نُجُبٌ يركبونها في ليالي القمر ويسيرون بها على سواحلهم قد رِيضَتْ[١] وعُرِّفَتْ طلب العنبر على الساحل فإذا رآه النجيبُ بَرَكَ بصاحبه فأخذه. ومنه ما يوجد فوق البحر ويزن وزناً كثيراً وربّما كان كهيئة الثور ودونه فإذا رآه الحوت المعروف بالبال[٢] ابتلعه فإذا حصل في جوفه قَتَلَهُ وطفا الحوت فوق الماء. وله قومٌ يراعونه في قوارب قد عرفوا الأوقات التي يوجد فيها هذه الحيتان المبتلعة العنبر فإذا عاينوا منها شيئاً اجتذبوه إلى الأرض بكلاليب حديد فيها حبال متينة تنشبُ في ظهر الحوت فيشقّوا عنه ويُخرجوا[٣] العنبر منه. فما كان يلي بطنَ الحوت فهو المَنْدُ الذي فيه سُهُوكَةٌ وسَمَكِيّةٌ[٤] موجودة عند العطّارين بمدينة السلام والبصرة وما لم تصل إليه سهوكةُ الحوت كان نقيّاً جدّاً.

وهذا الحوت المعروف بالبال ربّما عُمِلَ من فقار ظهره كراسي يقعد عليها الرجل ويتمكّن. وذكروا أنّ بقرية من سيراف على عشرة فراسخ تُعْرَف بالتاين بيوتٌ عاديّةٌ لطافٌ سقوفُها من أضلاع هذا الحوت. وسمعتُ مَن يقول إنّه وقع في قديم الأيّام إلى قرب سيراف منه واحدةٌ فقصد للنظر إليها فوجد قوماً يصعدون إلى ظهرها بسلّمٍ لطيف. والصيّادون إذا ظفروا بها طرحوها في الشمس وقطعوا لحمها وحفروا له حُفَراً يجتمع فيها الوَدَك ويُغرَفُ من عينها - إذا أذابتها الشمسُ - الودكُ بالحِرارِ[٥] ويُجَمَعُ فيباعُ على أرباب المراكب ويُخْلَط بأخلاط لهم يُمْسَحُ بها مراكبُ البحر يُسَدُّ به خَرْزُها ويسدّ أيضاً ما ينفتق من خرزها فيباع ودكُ هذا الحوت بجملة من المال.

---

١ ب: رُيضَت. ٢ ب: بالتال هنا وفيما بعد. ٣ خ: فيشقونه ويخرجون. ٤ ب: وسمكة؛ ح وخ و ر: وسمكته.
٥ ح وخ: أذابَتِ الشمسُ الودكَ بالحرارِ؛ ر: أذابتها الشمس الودك بالحرارة.

cast up at Barbarā and on the shores bordering the land of the Zanj, as well as at al-Shiḥr and the adjoining coast: it is found in the form of "eggs,"[181] rounded and bluish-gray. The people of these regions have thoroughbred camels, and on moonlit nights they mount them and ride out along their shores; the camels are specially trained and taught how to scan the shore for ambergris, and, when they spot some, they kneel so that their riders can dismount and pick it up. Ambergris is also found floating on the surface of the sea in lumps of great weight, sometimes up to the size of a bull. If the whale known as the *bāl* sees this floating ambergris, it swallows it;[182] when it reaches its stomach it causes the death of the whale, which then floats on the surface of the water. There are people who keep a lookout for this from boats and who know the times when these ambergris-swallowing whales are to be found. When they catch sight of one, they haul it ashore with iron grapnels attached to stout ropes, which stick into the whale's back, in order to cut it open and extract the ambergris from it. Any of the ambergris that has been in contact with the whale's stomach is *mand*, the sort with the rancid and fishy smell[183] stocked by the druggists in Madinat al-Salām and Basra; any ambergris uncontaminated by the rancidness of the whale's stomach will be extremely pure.

Sometimes the vertebrae of this whale known as the *bāl* are used to make seats: a person can sit on one of these and fit snugly into it. Informants have reported, too, that at a village ten *farsakh*s distant from Sīrāf, known as al-Tāyin, there are some ancient small houses roofed with the bones of this whale.[184] I also heard someone say that, in days of old, one of these whales was washed up near Sīrāf; he went to have a look at it and found people climbing on to its back with a small ladder. If fishermen get hold of one, they leave it in the sun, cut up its flesh, and dig trenches for this flesh so that the whale oil will accumulate in them. The oil is also scooped out of the whale's eye with jars, once the eye has been melted by the sun.[185] All this oil is collected and sold to the owners of ships; it is then mixed with various other ingredients that they use and daubed on the hulls of the seagoing ships to seal the seams in the planking and to seal any places where the seams have come apart.[186] The oil of this whale fetches a considerable sum of money.

ذكر اللؤلؤ

بَدؤُ خلقِ اللؤلؤ بلطيف تدبير الله تبارك اسمه وهو عزّ وجلّ يقول: ﴿سُبْحَانَ ٱلَّذِي خَلَقَ ٱلْأَزْوَاجَ كُلَّهَا مِمَّا تُنبِتُ ٱلْأَرْضُ وَمِنْ أَنفُسِهِمْ وَمِمَّا لَا يَعْلَمُونَ﴾. فاللؤلؤ يبتدئ في مثل قَدَرِ الأَنْجُذانة[1] وعلى لونها وفي هيئتها وصغرها وخفّتها ورقّتها وضعفها فيطير على وجه الماء طيراناً ضعيفاً ويسقط على جوانب مراكب الغاصة ثمّ يشتدّ على الأيّام ويعظم ويستحجر فإذا ثقل لزم قعر البحر ويغذو[2] بما الله أعلم به وليس فيه إلّا لحمة حمراء كمثل اللسان في أصله ليس لها عظم ولا عصب ولا فيها عِرق. وقد اختلفوا في بدء اللؤلؤ فقال قوم إنّ[3] الصدف إذا وقع المطرُ ظَهَرَ على وجه البحر وفتح فاه حتّى يقطر فيه من المطر فيصيرُ حَبّاً. وقال آخرون إنّه يتولّد من الصدفة نفسها وهو أصحُّ الخبرين لأنه ربّما وُجِدَ في الصدفة وهو نابتٌ لم ينقلع فيُقْلَع وهو الذي تسمّيه تجّار البحر اللؤلؤَ القِلَعَ والله أعلم. ٢.١٧.١

ومن عجايب ما سمعنا من أبواب الرزق أنّ أعرابيّاً ورد البصرة في قديم الأيّام ومعه حبّة لؤلؤ تساوي جملة مال فصار بها إلى عطّار كان يألفه فأظهرها له وسايَلَهُ[4] عنها وهو لا يعرف مقدارها فأخبره أنّها لؤلؤة. فقال: ما قيمتُها. قال:ماية درهم. فاستكثر الأعرابيّ ذاك وقال: هل أحد يبتاعها منّي بما قلتَ. فدفع له العطّار ماية درهم فابتاع بها ميرةً لأهله وأخذ العطّار الحبّة فقصد بها مدينة السلام فباعها بجملة من المال واتّسع العطّار في تجارته. ٢.١٧.٢

[1] ب وح و ر: الأنجُدانة؛ خ: الأمجدانة. [2] ب: ويغذوا. [3] إنّ: ساقطة في ح وخ. [4] ح: وسأله.

An Account of Pearls

The genesis of pearls comes about under the beneficent direction of God, may His name be blessed. For it is He that says in the Qur'an, mighty and exalted is He, «Glory be to Him who has created all the pairs of that which the earth sends forth, and of humankind themselves, and of that which they do not know.»[187] When pearl oysters first come into being, they are similar in size to an asafoetida leaf and of similar color, shape, smallness, lightness, delicacy, and fragility.[188] While in this state, they flit over the surface of the water until they alight on the sides of the pearl divers' boats. With the passing days, they grow stronger and bigger, and gradually turn hard like stone. When they are heavy enough, they sink and attach themselves to the seabed; God knows best what they get their sustenance from. The oysters contain nothing but a piece of pinkish flesh, like a tongue, attached to the base of their shells, with neither bone nor sinew and having no vein in it. Opinions have differed as to how the pearl first comes into being. Some have said that when rain falls, the oysters appear on the surface of the water and open their mouths; this is so that drops of rain will fall into them and become pearls. Others have said, however, that the pearls are generated from the oyster itself. This is the more accurate of the two accounts, because pearls are often found in the oyster when they are still sprouting up and have not yet become separated from the nacreous lining of the shell. They are pried off by the pearlers and are what the seagoing merchants term "pried pearls."[189] And God knows best which of the two accounts is correct. **2.17.1** *The formation of pearls*

Among the various amazing accounts we have heard of how God sustains His creatures in unexpected ways[190] is that of a bedouin who, in days of old, arrived in Basra with a pearl that was worth a large amount of money. He took it to a druggist of his acquaintance, showed it to him, and asked him what it was; he himself had no idea of its value. The druggist told him that the object was a pearl. "What is it worth?" the bedouin asked. "A hundred dirhams," the druggist replied. The bedouin thought this an enormous sum. "Would anyone actually give me that much for it?" he asked. The druggist immediately paid him a hundred dirhams, and the bedouin went off and bought provisions for his family. The druggist, meanwhile, took the pearl to Madīnat al-Salām and sold it there for a large amount of money, with which he was able to expand his business. **2.17.2** *The tale of the oyster and the fox*

فذكر العطّار أنّه سأل الأعرابيّ عن سبب اللؤلؤة فقال: مررتُ بالصَمّان - وهي من أرض البحرين بينها وبين الساحل مُدَيدة قريبة - ورأيتُ في الرمل ثعلباً ميتّاً على فيه شي قد أطبق عليه فنزلتُ فوجدتُ شيئاً كمثل الطبق يلمع جوفُه بياضاً ووجدتُ هذه المُدَحْرَجة فيه فأخذتُها. فعلم أنّ السبب في ذلك خروجُ الصدفة إلى الساحل تستنشق الريح وذاك[1] من عادة الصدف فمَرَّ بها الثعلبُ فلمّا عاين اللحمة في جوفها وهي فاتحةٌ فاها وَثَبَ بسرعته فأدخل فاه في الصدفة[2] وقبض على اللحمة فأطبقت الصدفة على فيه. ومن شأنها إذا أطبقت على شيء وأحسّت بيد تلمسها لم تفتح فاها بحيلة حتّى تُشَقَّ من آخرها بالحديد ضَنّاً[3] منها باللؤلؤة وصيانةً لها[4] كصيانة المرأة لولدها. فلمّا أخذت بنفس الثعلب أَمْعَنَ في العَدْوِ يضرب بها الأرض يميناً وشمالاً إلى أن أخذت بنفسه فمات وماتت وظَفِرَ بها الأعرابيُّ فأخذ ما فيها وساقَهُ اللهُ إلى العطّار فصارت له[5] رزقاً.

١،١٨،٢ وملوك الهند تلبس الأقراط من الجوهر النفيس في آذانها المركَّبِ في الذهب وتضع في أعناقها القلايد النفيسة المشتملة على فاخر الجوهر الأحمر والأخضر واللُولؤ ما يعظُمُ قيمتُه ويجلُّ مقدارُه[6] وهو اليَوْمَ كنوزهم وذخائرهم وتلبسه قوّادهم ووجوههم. والرئيس منهم يَركَبُ على عنق رَجُلٍ منهم وعليه فوطة قد استتر بها وفي يده شي يُعْرَف بالجِتْرة[7] وهي مظلّة من ريش الطواويس ويأخذها[8] بيده فيتّقي بها الشمسَ وأصحابُه محدقون به.

٢،١٨،٢ ومنهم صِنْفٌ لا يأكل اثنان منهم في غَضارة واحدة ولا على مايدة واحدة

١ ح وخ و ر: وذلك. ٢ ح وخ: الصدف. ٣ ح: ظنًا. ٤ ب: له. ٥ بها ... فصارت له: ساقط في ح وخ. ٦ خ: ولجُلِّ مقدارِهِ. ٧ بالجِترة: كذا في ب؛ ح وخ: بالجترة. ٨ ح وخ: يأخذها.

The druggist mentioned that he asked the bedouin how he had come by the pearl. "I was passing al-Ṣammān," the bedouin told him—this being part of the land of Bahrain,[191] a short distance from the seashore—"when I saw a fox lying dead on the sand. I noticed that something had attached itself to the fox's muzzle, so I went down to it and found the thing was like a dish with a lid, all gleaming white inside. Then I found this round thing in it, and I took it." On hearing this, the druggist realized what had happened. The oyster had left the sea and gone on to the shore to sniff the wind, as oysters are accustomed to do. The fox had passed by and spotted the piece of flesh inside the oyster's open mouth, and had then pounced with all swiftness, stuck its muzzle in the oyster and sunk its teeth into the flesh inside. At this the oyster had snapped shut on the fox's muzzle. (It is in the nature of oysters, if they have thus clamped shut on something and then sense a hand touching them, that nothing will induce them to open their mouths—until, that is, they are split apart with an iron blade: this is the oyster's way of holding on to its pearl and protecting it, as a mother protects her baby.) When the oyster had begun to suffocate the fox, the fox had rushed about, hitting the oyster on the ground, right and left. Eventually the oyster had succeeded in suffocating the fox; the fox had died, and the oyster had died too. Then the bedouin had got hold of the oyster and taken the pearl that was in it, and God had led him to the druggist. And thus the oyster proved to be the bedouin's windfall.

Further Accounts of Indian Customs

The kings of India wear in their ears pendants of precious gems set in gold **2.18.1** and adorn their necks with precious necklaces comprising magnificent red and green gems and pearls, all of which are enormously costly and valuable and which today represent their treasure and their reserves of wealth; the commanders of their armies and other prominent men also wear such jewelry. The most important Indian dignitaries ride about on men's backs, wearing nothing but a waist cloth to make themselves decent, and holding a thing known as a *chatrah*,[192] which is a parasol of peacock feathers that they carry to protect themselves from the sun. Thus they ride, surrounded by their entourage.

Their habit of adorning themselves with gems and of carrying parasols

There is a class of Indians of whom two will not eat together out of the **2.18.2** same dish or even at the same table; they would consider it a most dreadful disgrace to do so. If they came to Sīrāf and one of the prominent merchants

Some customs concerning food

يجدون ذلك عيباً فاحشاً. فإذا وردوا سيراف فدعاهم وجهٌ من وجوه التجّار وكانوا ماية نفس أو دونها أو فوقها احتاج أن يضع بين يدي كلّ رجل منهم طبقاً فيه ما يأكله لا يشاركه فيه سواه. وأمّا ملوكهم في بلادهم ووجوههم فإنّه يُتَّخَذ لهم في كلّ يوم موايدُ يُسَفُّ خوص النارجيل سفّاً ويُعْمَلُ منه كهيئة الغضار والصحاف فإذا أُحْضِرَ الغدا[1] أكلوا الطعام في ذلك الخوص المسفوف فإذا فرغوا من غدائهم[2] رُمِيَ بتلك المايدة والغضار المسفوف من الخوص معما[3] بقي من الطعام إلى الماء واستأنفوا من غدهم مثله.

٢،١٨،٣ وكان يُحْمَلُ إلى الهند في القديم الدنانير السِنْديّة فيباع الدينار بثلاثة دنانير وما زاد. ويُحْمَلُ إليهم الزُمُرُّد الذي يرد من مصر مركّباً في الخواتيم مصوناً في الحِقاق. ويحمل البُسَّذ[4] وهو المرجان وحجرٌ يقال له الدَهْنَج ثمّ تركوه.

٢،١٨،٤ وأكثر ملوكهم يُظْهِرون نساهم إذا جلسوا لمن دخل إليهم من أهل بلدهم وغيرهم لا يُحْجَبْن عن النظر إليهنّ.

٢،١٩،١ فهذا أجمل ما لَحِقَه الذُكْرُ في ذلك الوقت على سعة أخبار البحر مع التجنّب لحكاية شيء ممّا يكذب[5] فيه البحريّون ولا يقوم في نفس المرء صدقُهُ والاقتصار من كلّ خبر على ما صحّ منه وإن قلّ أَولى. والله الموفّق للصواب.

والحمد لله ربّ العالمين وصلواته على خيرته من خلقه محمّد وآله أجمعين وهو حسبُنا ونعمَ الناصر والمُعين.[6]

---

١ ح وخ: الغذاء. ٢ ح: غذائهم؛ خ: غذايهم. ٣ ح: مهما. ٤ ب: البُسَدُّ. ٥ ب: يَكْذِنُ.
٦ في هامش ب: قُوبِلَ بالمنتسخ [خ: بالمتنسَّخ] منه في صفر سنة ٥٩٦ [ح: ٥٩٤] والله الموفّق.

invited them to a meal—even as many as a hundred of them, or less, or more—the host would have to place a dish in front of each man, with his own food in it, so that no one else would have to share it with him.[193] In the case of kings and other important people in their own country, new tables are provided for them every day, and the fronds of coconut palms are woven together and made into the equivalent of crockery and serving dishes. When the main meal is served, they eat their food off these woven palm fronds, and, when they have finished their meal, both the table and the woven palm-frond "crockery" are thrown, together with any remaining food, into water. The following day they start all over again with fresh utensils.

2.18.3 *Dinars and gemstones exported to India*

In the past, Sindī dinars used to be exported to the Indians; the exchange rate for one of them was three standard dinars and more. Emeralds originating in Egypt are exported to them, set in signet rings and encased in small boxes. *Bussadh* (coral) is also exported there. A stone called *dahnaj* used to be exported there, too; then they abandoned it.

2.18.4 *The display in public of royal ladies*

Most of the kings of India, when they hold audiences, have their womenfolk with them on public display, to be seen by all comers whether native or foreign. They are not concealed from view.

Afterword to the Second Book

2.19.1 *Abū Zayd's afterword*

This Second Book, then, is the best part of what my memory has been able to recollect at the time, given the wide range of accounts of the sea.[194] I have avoided relating any of the sort of accounts in which sailors exercise their powers of invention but whose credibility would not stand up to scrutiny in other men's minds. I have also restricted myself to relating only the true contents of each account—and the shorter the better.[195] And God it is who guides us to what is correct.

And praise be to God, Lord of the universe, and may His blessings be upon the choicest part of His creation, Muḥammad, and on all his family. God is our sufficiency and our best support and aid.[196]

Notes

1 The English-language synopses and chapter headings have been supplied by the editor-translator and are not part of the original Arabic text.

2 The opening pages of the book are lost, including the section on the First Sea (i.e., the Arabian/Persian Gulf; cf. al-Masʿūdī, *Murūj*, 1:149) and the beginning of that on the Second Sea. Here the author is describing a whale.

3 *Minārah*, "lighthouse," is also used for (and is the origin of the English word) "minaret." Whales spray water from their blowholes, not from their mouths.

4 Some whales do indeed smack the water with their tails, to stun and concentrate their prey before swallowing them, a behavior known as "kick feeding." Recent studies have regarded it as a learned behavior unique to North Atlantic humpback whales (http://www.internationalwhaleprotection.org/forum/index.php?/topic/3057-chapter-86-the-tail/).

5 *Nawāqīs*, wooden clappers, were used in Eastern churches as "bells" (Ibn Baṭṭūṭah, *Travels*, 2:470 n. 214).

6 The length of a cubit was subject to local variation. Taking it as 47.5 centimeters (a general standard for a builder's cubit, cf. Serjeant and Lewcock, *Ṣanʿāʾ*, 468), this would make the *wāl* 9.5 meters long.

7 The real origin of ambergris, a valuable fixative for perfumes, is even stranger: it is a waxy substance exuded by the intestines of sperm whales, usually as a result of irritation caused by the undigested beaks of cuttlefish or giant squid (Cheung and DeVantier, *Natural History*, 212).

8 That is, they are animals, not plants.

9 The most celebrated pearl fisheries were in the Gulf of Mannar, in northwestern Sri Lanka (Tennent, *Ceylon*, 2:560).

10 Unless the reading is defective, this seems to mean that open sea surrounds it so that it has no near neighbors, unlike the Maldives and Laccadives.

11 Seventy cubits (ca. 33 m.) is a huge exaggeration. Ibn Baṭṭūṭah (*Travels*, 4:854) gives eleven spans (ca. 2.25 m.). Skeen (*Adam's Peak*, 203) found the alleged footprint to be five feet seven inches (ca. 1.70 m.) long.

12 The reference to two kings alludes to the age-old division of influence between Sinhala and Tamil rule in Sri Lanka.

13 Aloewood is the fragrant and highly prized resinous heartwood of trees of the genus *Aquilaria*.

14 Arabic *shank* is the same word as English "chank" (*Turbinella rapa*). Chank fishing remained a government monopoly into the nineteenth century (Tennent, *Ceylon*, 2:556).

15 The use of *maʿādin*, usually meaning "mines, sources of minerals," for camphor as well as gold may suggest that the writer believed camphor to be of mineral origin. The substance, although crystalline, comes from the camphor tree.

16 *Caesalpina sappan* produces a valuable red dye (Yule and Burnell, *Hobson-Jobson*, s.v. "Sappan-Wood"). Rattans are various types of pliable cane.

17 An interpolation may have occurred (*ilayhi min* instead of simply *ilā*). Without it, the sense would agree with the rest of the paragraph: "And they do not need coverings for their bodies, because it is neither hot nor cold." Alternatively, a phrase may have been omitted, and the original may have read along these lines: "and such coverings as they need for their bodies, *and these are few*, as it is neither hot nor cold in their land."

18 Literally, "peppercorn-like."

19 The parenthetical comment is strange, although it may be that *qadam* (foot) is used here as a slang term for the penis.

20 The accusation of cannibalism persisted into the time of Marco Polo (*Travels*, 2:309) and beyond.

21 The most powerful types of waterspout, such as that described here, are tornadoes occurring over the sea. Although they do not in fact draw up water, they can pose a danger to smaller craft.

22 That is, from the northwest, the Big Dipper (Arabic *banāt al-naʿsh*) being the seven brightest stars in Ursa Major, the prominent constellation in the northern sky.

23 A reference to phosphorescence, a common phenomenon in Indian Ocean waters.

24 Apparent lacuna in text, perhaps caused by a missing leaf or leaves.

25 Text defective.

26 Given the distance from the Arabian/Persian Gulf to China and the risk of missing the right sailing season (*mawsim*, the origin of "monsoon") for a particular stage of the voyage, it was possible to be held up by adverse winds for many months.

27 Prayers for the Muslim ruler, pronounced during the sermon at Friday congregational worship and at the two ʿĪds, or festivals, were a sign of political allegiance to him.

28 As Hourani points out (*Arab Seafaring*, 75), "China ships," that is, large vessels from the Gulf specializing in the China trade, is more accurate than "Chinese ships," ships from China. Cf. the term "Indiamen" for European ships involved in the East India trade.

29 That is, the Arabian/Persian Gulf.

30 The verb *khaṭifa* most commonly means "to take quickly and unexpectedly, to snatch." Although "to set sail" is among its classical senses (Lane, *Lexicon*, s.v. *khaṭifa*) it is a rare one, which "take off" attempts to reflect.

31 Jibāl 'Umān is literally "the mountains of Oman." At sea, however, a *jabal* can be anything from a flat coral island to a towering rock stack. Here, part of the fjord-like coast of the Musandam Peninsula and its outlying islets may be intended.

32 This *durdūr* (whirpool) is described in greater detail by al-Idrīsī (*Nuzhah*, 1:164). It is not specifically mentioned in the later navigational texts, although Aḥmad ibn Mājid warns of "strong currents" in these waters (Tibbetts, *Arab Navigation*, 213).

33 From here on, the sailing times appear to include the time needed to put into port, do business, load supplies, etc. For comparison, *Sohar*, a sailing ship constructed on the lines of early Arab vessels, took twenty-eight days from Muscat to Calicut (not far north of Kollam), including a stop of some days for repairs in the Laccadives (Severin, *Sindbad Voyage*, 6).

34 The alcoholic version of the drink is the Anglo-Indian "toddy."

35 "Payment . . . on the spot" is the classical sense of *yadan bi-yad*, literally "hand in hand" (Lane, *Lexicon*, s.v. *yad*).

36 Arabic *fūṭah*, the Malay *sarong*.

37 The Zhu Jiang, or Pearl River.

38 In contrast to the earlier reference (1.1.1) in which flying fish are given a Persian name for "locust," here the usual Arabic word, *jarād*, is used.

39 This palm-climbing "fish"—the Arabic word being used here to mean "sea creature"—must be the aptly named coconut crab.

40 Does this reflect a difference in caste from the other Indian princes? *Sharaf*, the "high rank, nobility" that Dahmā lacks and in which his fellow-king Balharā excels, is often a matter of ancestry.

41 The Arabic which this last phrase tentatively translates is obscure. A small emendation, however, could make the sentence read: "By nature this rhinoceros [ranges from being] smaller than the elephant up to the same [size] as it." This statement would be no stranger than the claim, below, that the animal has no joints in its legs. In Ibn Baṭṭūṭah's equally strange perception (*Travels*, 3:596) the rhinoceros is "smaller than an elephant, but its head is many times bigger than an elephant's head."

42 Such belts, in vogue under the Tang dynasty, were of leather decorated with rhinoceros-horn plaques (Sauvaget, *Relation*, 54).

43 The word *fakhūr*, "proud," is voweled as such in the manuscript but may be a scribal error for *fa-khawr*, "and then [comes] a bay/estuary," that is, where the ambergris of the next phrase is found.

44 This suggests that there is not enough pepper to be dried for storage and/or export and that it is eaten fresh as a local delicacy.

45 In China, eunuch officials were in charge of taxes and financial affairs in general (see below, 2.3.5).

46 That is, al-Mābud is the last of the kingdoms before one reaches Chinese territory.

47 "King" in the sense of "[provincial] ruler"; hereafter "ruler" is used to translate it. On eunuch officials, see above, n. 45.

48 *Ṣīniyyāt* (chinaware) most frequently refers, as in English, to ceramics. Here, however, Chinese lacquerware is probably intended (cf. Sauvaget, *Relation*, 56 n.33.3). The instrument's length of 3–4 cubits equals about 142.5–190 cm.

49 Literally, "They have indicators and regulation for the hours." Public water clocks were known in Tang Dynasty China.

50 "Copper coins," Arabic *fulūs* (sg. *fils*), are small copper-alloy coins of low value, pierced in the middle for stringing on a cord, and later known in English as "cash."

51 This succinct description is, apparently, the first known one of porcelain in a text from the West (Sauvaget, *Relation*, 57 n. 34.5).

52 The indemnity granted to the sea merchants (literally "sea men", i.e., traders from overseas) presumably guarantees compensation for any harm befalling their goods while in the government warehouses. The point of the six-month delay is that, at the end of that period, contrary winds mean no more merchants will come until the following sailing season; releasing all the goods into the market simultaneously means that their prices can be controlled.

53 The Anglo-Indian "maund," Arabic *mann(ā)*, is a unit of weight that varies greatly. That here intended is probably a little more than two pounds (1 kg.) (Yule and Burnell, *Hobson-Jobson*, s.v. "Maund").

54 Not, here, the fragrant wood (see n. 13 above), but the juice of succulent plants of the genus *Aloe*.

55 The implication being, "Well, you'll grieve for them *now*!" Three years was the official period of mourning for a deceased parent (Whitfield, *Silk Road*, 146).

56 Some phrases in the following paragraph are open to different interpretation. It is not always entirely clear which of the two parties the various pronouns and verbs refer to; the problem is exacerbated by the text's customarily compressed wording, as well as by some loose syntax.

57 The sense of a mark made *bayna*, "between," two fingers is not clear. The historian Rashīd al-Dīn (d. 718/1318) mentions outlines of fingers traced as identifying marks in China; there is also evidence of the use, as early as the Tang Dynasty, of fingerprints as marks (Yule, *Cathay*, 3:123–24). If the latter is intended here, then various emendations

might be proposed for *bayna*, e.g., *tubayyinu/tubīnu*, "showing clearly," or even *banāni*, "of the fingertips of."

58 Going by the (correct) information given below (2.3.3), namely that one *fakkūj* equals about one dinar, the figure here should be amended to twenty thousand dinars.

59 Reading *yajzuzna*, "cut, crop" (although other readings are possible). The implication is not that they have their hair cut *off*, but rather that it is cut and styled, unlike, say, Arab women, who allow their hair to grow freely. Cf. the illustration of Tang women's hairstyles in Whitfield, *Silk Road*, 145.

60 The foregoing passage on royal funeral rites appears, with a few additions, in *Murūj al-dhahab* (al-Masʿūdī, 1:83–84), introduced by the words, "I have seen in the land of Sarandīb . . . that when a king of theirs dies . . ." Given that al-Masʿūdī clearly borrowed the account, the phrasing is more than a little arch, with its suggestion, if not categorical statement, that he witnessed the scene himself.

61 That is, the last of the Dībājāt (today's Laccadives, Maldives, and Sri Lanka) when approached from the Arabian/Persian Gulf. Cf. 1.2.1, above.

62 "Tiger or leopard" is Arabic *numūr*, which can refer to either or both.

63 *Tasil . . . min*, "melted from," might possibly be amended to *tusmal . . . min*, "been put out by."

64 The appointment of crown princes would facilitate succession in the ruling dynasty.

65 As indicated above (1.7.1), he is "king of kings" not in the imperial sense, but rather in that of "king senior in precedence."

66 That is, the Malabar Coast of southwestern India, corresponding approximately with the modern state of Kerala.

67 "As his puppet": the Arabic phrase is, literally, "from under his hand."

68 There is evidence that certain body parts of executed criminals were indeed eaten and that the practice continued down at least to the nineteenth century (Sauvaget, *Relation*, 64 n. 56.2).

69 A slightly different style of impalement was described by Ibn Baṭṭūṭah (*Travels*, 4:806) as the penalty, in southwestern India, for stealing a single coconut.

70 *Zawānī l-bidadah*, literally "the harlots of the idols," are the women known in India as *devadasis*. See also 2.12.4 below.

71 "Neither . . . nor . . . are users of carpets," Arabic *laysa . . . bi-ʾaṣḥābi furshin*. Sauvaget (*Relation*, 65 n. 61.1) and his predecessors have taken *fursh* to mean "wives, concubines," a euphemistic usage: *fursh* are "mats, carpets, mattresses, furnishings, beds," and thus, by extension, "bed*fellows*." It seems preferable, however, to take the phrase as belonging to the section on buildings and to translate it as some sort of literal furnishing. "Carpets"

may well be the intention, as their absence would be of particular interest to an Arabic reader for whom carpets were ubiquitous.

72 A good example of how the informants' purview did not extend to the inland, wheat-eating areas of northern India.

73 "The two provinces"—*al-wilāyatayn* (an unusual word to refer to the two countries)—suggests that the previous sentence should end "China *and India.*" "Leopards, tigers" at the beginning of that sentence again gets around the multiple meanings of *numūr* (see n. 62, above).

74 In the Islamic legal context, probably intended here too, "those who 'cut the road'" include rebels and other malefactors as well as highway robbers.

75 *Janābah* is a state of bodily pollution, most commonly caused by sexual activity. For a Muslim, it necessitates washing the entire body before one is permitted to pray.

76 "More densely inhabited and cultivated": *aʿmar* means either or both; one might also add "and built up."

77 In the Chinese context, therapeutic burning, Arabic *kayy*, is probably the practice known as moxibustion. Another form, still occasionally practiced in the Arab world, involves burning the patient with small branding irons on certain parts of the body.

78 *ʿIlm al-nujūm*, "the science of the stars," is another of those single terms that has more than one meaning in present-day English—hence "astronomy and astrology."

79 If by this singular "king of India" Balharā is meant, the information here would contradict the earlier statement (above, 1.7.1) that he pays his troops.

80 "Our rivers," given the context, probably includes the Tigris and the Euphrates.

81 This may be a reference to the long belted tunic in vogue under the Tang Dynasty and called the *hufu*, or "foreigner's robe." Cf. the illustrations in Whitfield, *Silk Road*, 89 and 107.

82 Here, in the margin of the manuscript, is a note added, in a poor hand, some four hundred years after the book was copied: "This book was checked by al-Faqīr Muḥammad in the year 1011 [1602–3], may God bless with goodness the year that follows and those that come after. Amen. And may God forgive the writer of these lines his sins, and those of his parents too, and of all the Muslims."

83 "Its kings" is shorthand for "the kings of its islands and of the lands on and beyond its shores."

84 Al-Masʿūdī (1:138) puts the number of foreigners killed in Khānfū at 200,000.

85 Huang Chao took the imperial capital, Chang'an, in the fall of 267/880 (Whitfield, *Silk Road*, 150).

86 Huang Chao did in fact proclaim himself emperor.

87 "They are . . . kinsmen by marriage": it is not wholly clear whether the relationship is between the Chinese and the Taghazghuz, or between the Taghazghuz and the rest of the Turks. If the former is meant, however, the phrase probably refers to marriages contracted earlier in the third/ninth century between women of the Tang imperial family and chiefs of the Turkic Uighurs, the Taghazghuz of the text (cf. Whitfield, *Silk Road*, 95 and 98).

88 The son of "the king of the Taghazghuz" was, in fact, the son of a chieftain of a powerful Turkic tribe, the Shatuo/Shato. This commander is known to the Chinese histories as Li Keyong. Al-Masʿūdī (*Murūj*, 1:139) gives the number of troops under his command as 400,000. Huang Chao is usually said to have cut his own throat before he could be captured, in the summer of 271/884 (Whitfield, *Silk Road*, 152).

89 "Pronounced the customary formulae of allegiance": literally, "prayed for him [sc. at Friday prayers]," in an Islamic context, the usual way of publicly declaring official fealty to the caliph.

90 "Factional rulers" is either a reference to the satraps through whom Alexander ruled Persia or to his generals who were to squabble over his empire as a whole after his death. (Below, 2.14.1, the phrase clearly refers to the satraps.)

91 Cf. n. 68, above.

92 "The sea itself became uncooperative": the phrase is taken from a saying, attributed to ʿAlī ibn Abī Ṭālib, predicting economic disaster.

93 A slightly ironical sense of *zuhdahā*, "her renunciation," which normally refers to the renunciation of earthly pleasure for a life of pious asceticism.

94 *Ḥilyatahā*, translated here as "her physical appearance," more often means "her ornaments, her jewelry," etc., and might do so here. Alternatively, it could be a slip for *ḥillatahā*, "her [city] quarter."

95 Revenues could be considerable: high-class courtesans, known as "mistresses of the table," would charge sixteen thousand copper cash per evening (Whitfield, *Silk Road*, 147).

96 "All manner of attire": Arabic *alwān* means both "types, sorts, manners" and "colors." The latter may be implied here too.

97 The weight of one thousand copper cash was more than than 1.5 pounds (0.68 kg.) (Whitfield, *Silk Road*, 173).

98 Chinese coins have indeed turned up in the excavations at Sīrāf (Whitehouse, "Siraf," 143).

99 *Shiqāq*, "panels," are usually the pieces of heavy hair cloth that go together to make a tent. Here, however, they are clearly the panels of woven reed used in the reed architecture of southern Iraq, where the author lived.

100 On wooden clappers, see n. 5 above.

101 As it stands, the Arabic is slightly defective in the latter part of this sentence. The translation depends on a minor amendment.

102 Presumably, Abū Zayd included the second part of this sentence for the benefit of his Muslim readers who were not generally accustomed to seeing images of living creatures or only to seeing stylized depictions of them.

103 Basra was destroyed in 257/871, during the so-called Zanj Rebellion.

104 Presumably, the king refers to himself in the third person here because he is telling the interpreter what to say; immediately below, he returns to the first person. (In any case, this whole section containing Ibn Wahb's report is especially inconsistent in its use of grammatical persons and pronouns.)

105 Al-Masʿūdī explains in a parallel passage (*Murūj*, 1:143) that this is because the Turks are "the beasts of mankind."

106 To a Muslim readership the question would not seem strange: the Islamic aversion to depicting living beings applies in particular to the prophets, and, in the case of the Prophet Muḥammad, amounts to an outright ban.

107 It is customary for Muslims to utter a short prayer of blessing whenever a prophet is mentioned.

108 As a Muslim, Ibn Wahb would have believed that the Qur'anic/biblical Flood covered the whole earth.

109 "Thirty months" is a reflection of the relatively short public ministry of Jesus, beginning with his baptism.

110 The poses described are reminiscent of those of some of the figures of the Buddha and the Bodhisattvas, as depicted in Tang Dynasty images.

111 *Ziyy* is yet another word with more than one distinct sense in English, "outward appearance" and/or "clothing."

112 As it stands in the manuscript, the meaning of the second part of the sentence is a little obscure. With a small emendation to the Arabic it could mean, " . . . and his vizier too, and he scoffed and made it quite clear that he disapproved of what I had said."

113 "I blurted out": literally, "I [i.e., my tongue] slipped, and I said."

114 "Both in abode and in blood": literally, "in dwelling and in kinship."

115 In the later third/ninth century, Chang'an covered an area of about thirty square miles (ca. 78 sq. km.) and had a population of nearly two million (Whitfield, *Silk Road*, 146).

116 The Mediterranean is called here "the Sea of al-Shām" (i.e., of the Levant), in the next sentence "the Sea of al-Rūm" (of the Romans/Byzantines), and, a little further on, by both names together. The English name is used to avoid confusion. The Sea of China and India is the Indian Ocean; the ocean into which it leads is the Pacific.

117 The ships of the Arabs and other seafaring peoples of the western Indian Ocean were constructed without nails: the planks of the hulls were drilled, the corresponding holes of adjacent planks were "sewn" tightly together with coir rope, and all the seams and holes were thoroughly caulked. Severin (*Sindbad Voyage*, ch. 3) describes this ancient shipbuilding technique in detail. See also 2.12.6, below.

118 Abū Zayd has arrived at the right conclusion—that the Mediterranean Sea and Indian Ocean are connected—but by a very wrong route. Al-Masʿūdī, who drew on this passage, was well aware that the Caspian Sea does not connect with any other sea (*Murūj*, 1:125); he, too, suggests that the sewn planks must have floated around the north of the Eurasian landmass but implies that they entered the Mediterranean through the Strait of Gibraltar (*Murūj*, 1:163).

119 In this foregoing sentence, it seems that the word "except" is a slip and should be omitted, given the existence of the "barrier" (now penetrated by the Suez Canal) between the Red and Mediterranean Seas.

120 "The city of al-Zābaj," here and in the section title above, seems to be a slip for "The island of al-Zābaj."

121 "Extent" is used, here and below, to translate *taksīr*, properly speaking, "area." Nine hundred square *farsakh*s, however, is only a fraction of the actual area of Java, but it would be a far more accurate figure for the sailing distance *around* Java and the associated chain of islands to the east, and this may be what is intended.

122 *Al-raṣāṣ al-qalʿī* is commonly glossed as white lead, or cerussite, the main use of which was as a pigment. Yule and Burnell, however, argue (*Hobson-Jobson*, s.v. "Calay") that tin is meant.

123 That is, since the disturbances in China, Kalah [Bār] is the easternmost point to which Arab ships sail.

124 That is, there is no need to travel long stages, as in most of the land of the Near East, because accommodation, food, etc., are available everywhere.

125 "They are men": reading *rijāl*. Other readings are possible, including *raḥḥālah*, "[frequent] travelers," and *rajjālah*, "travelers/fighters on foot."

126 What historical basis the following story may have (if any) is unclear. It could, however, be a mythicized memory of incursions into Cambodia at the end of the eighth century AD by the Sailendra dynasty of Java.

127 It is hard to explain the presence of this sentence. It may be corrupt, or a copyist may have inadvertently omitted words that would have given it context.

128 Properly speaking, "the throne," *al-sarīr*, is a low dais or divan such as the *gaddi* of Indian rulers.

129 This last phrase is obscure. With a small emendation to the voweling, the Arabic might mean, "so that those whom good health has clothed should make the most of it."

130 The Pool of the Kings, in the story above (2.6.2). On al-Mihrāj's throne, see n. 113, above.

131 That is, his face was now disfigured by smallpox scars.

132 See 1.8.8 above. In a parallel passage in al-Masʿūdī (*Murūj*, 1:141), the aggrieved Khurasani does not resort to ringing the bell but rather to wearing a garment of a particular type of red silk.

133 Trustworthy and thus, as becomes clear below, worthy of appointment as provincial judges.

134 This is a neat summary of Confucian concepts of government.

135 The desert is the Taklamakan.

136 The musk "gazelles" (in English musk "deer") are in fact neither true deer nor gazelles but belong to their own family, the *Moschidae*.

137 A Himalayan plant of the valerian family, from whose rhizome a costly perfume was made.

138 Musk is a secretion deposited in glands, the musk "pods," situated between the male animal's navel and its genitalia.

139 Clearly, Tibetan musk was imported into the Arab world overland and was thought to be a variety different from Chinese musk, which came by sea.

140 The musk deer does, in fact, rub its musk glands against trees and stones, to mark its territory and/or to attract mates. Whether this would deposit a harvestable amount of musk is to be doubted.

141 In fact, musk deer have neither horns nor antlers.

142 The "tusks" are, in fact, in the upper jaw and are elongated canines up to about seven centimeters long that point downward. *Fitr*, the Arabic unit of length translated as "the distance . . . stretched apart," is sometimes expressed in English as a "small span."

143 "Clipped": perhaps "docked."

144 All Abū Zayd's readers, male as well as female, would have squatted to urinate.

145 The phrase "allows its contents to well up," Arabic *ṭafū bi-mā fīhā*, might be used of a scum rising to the surface in a cooking pot. The implication is that the noxious contents of the bladder can only be expelled in this way.

146 "Rounding" babies' heads, that is, molding them into an evenly spherical shape while they are still malleable, is still practiced by the Arabs and other peoples and can be achieved by gentle binding and/or ensuring that the baby does not always sleep in the same position. Most if not all of Abū Zayd's male readers would have kept their heads shaved or worn their hair short.

147 An allusion to Q Ḥujurāt 49:13, which states that God has made mankind into "peoples and tribes, that you may recognize one another." (Is there an implied hint, in "among themselves," of " . . . even if all the Chinese look the same to us non-Chinese"? The prejudice is an old one.) In contrast to the Chinese practice described in this section, Arabs will marry as close a relative as a first cousin.

148 Sandarac is the resin of a coniferous tree of the cypress family.

149 Literally, "at the head of his heart/internal organs."

150 The storage jar called in Arabic *dann* is a type of large amphora.

151 The text does not say so, but we must assume he did it.

152 "Indian men": clearly, here and below, local inhabitants of Sarandīb are meant. From the end of this section, it seems that the merchants involved were Arabs.

153 "The Mountain of Sarandīb" could stand for the highlands of Sri Lanka as a whole but means, in general, Adam's Peak (see text, 1.2.1). The passage that follows implies a belief that tidal fluctuations had an affect on the level of subterranean water inland.

154 See n. 151, above, first sentence.

155 The idol of gold is a recurring theme in descriptions of Sarandīb (cf. Ibn Baṭṭūṭah on Dondra, *Travels*, 4:855–56, which may refer to the statue mentioned in this passage). Abū Zayd's reluctance to give a weight for it reflects his policy to avoid "sailors' yarns" (see text, 2.19.1).

156 *Hypericum* is a genus of shrubs also known as St. John's wort. Regarding the first ingredient of the drink, other editions read *ʿasalu l-naḥl*, "bee honey," for the *ʿasalu l-nakhl*, "palm 'honey,'" of the manuscript. The dot of the *kh* is, admittedly, tentatively written in the manuscript, but it is far more likely to be correct, given the tradition of palm tapping in the region (cf. Yule and Burnell, *Hobson-Jobson*, s.v. "Jaggery").

157 Other editions read *al-nabāt*, "plants, vegetation," where this editor reads *al-banāt*, "girls." The dots in the manuscript are too equivocally placed for a categorical decision, but the latter seem a more enticing prize.

158 "Rainfall" here is *shitāʾ*, meaning also "winter." At the end of this section, however, *shitāʾ* is used to signify the season.

159 "Roofs which they keep swept with brooms" is the immediately apparent meaning and hardly appropriate, given that the roofs are thatched. By reading *mukannanah* for *mukannasah*, however, the meaning would be "roofs with overhanging eaves," which would make more sense.

160 Taking auguries from the flight of birds, a practice called *zajr*, was a feature of ancient Arab life, which still has its Indian counterparts.

161 Cf. Q Isrāʾ 17:43.

162 See n. 70, above.

163 The sense of the "vow" is that the woman has made a request to the deity and has promised to dedicate to it any daughter she may give birth to, if her request is fulfilled.

164 See n. 53, above.

165 The implication being that the sacristans are corrupt.

166 See n. 117, above, on sewn ships.

167 Unless the text is defective, the animals themselves are intended here, not their skins.

168 See on aloes n. 53, above. Socotri aloes were supposedly the most efficacious as a medicine.

169 Asia Minor: Arabic al-Rūm, literally "[the land of] the Romans," but probably used here in the sense current in Abū Zayd's time, "[the land of] the Byzantines."

170 See on these factional rulers n. 90, above.

171 "These islands": the plural may be a slip, but there are, in fact, several lesser islands associated with Socotra, two of which currently have small populations.

172 Writing in the sixth century AD, the Alexandrian traveler Cosmas Indicopleustes (quoted in Cheung and DeVantier, *Natural History*, 228) noted the presence of Greek-speaking Christians on Socotra, whose ancestors, he says, were sent by Alexander's successors in Egypt, the Ptolemies.

173 This statement of Abū Zayd's may be taken to imply that he himself did not know the identity of the compiler of the First Book. See above, 5–7.

174 "To starboard of India, from the viewpoint of a ship leaving Oman" is a sailor's periphrasis for "To the west of India."

175 Six non-Arabic languages, classed as the Modern South Arabian group, are still found in the region. Each of the three major ones, Mehri, Soqotri, and Shehri, has tens of thousands of speakers, the others far fewer. Although they share features with ancient South Arabian languages such as Sabaic, it is now thought that they are not directly derived from them.

176 That is, the sea extends no further north.

177 Q Naml 27:61.

178 By "no kings," Abū Zayd means that there are no (civilized) kingdoms.

179 "Dismal, hostile": Arabic *muẓlim* is both "dark" and "full of difficulties, evils."

180 It was thought that ambergris exuded or grew from the seabed (cf. 1.2.1, above).

181 That is, ovoid lumps.

182 In 1.1.1, above, the similar term *wāl* may have signified the tiger shark. *Bāl* here is definitely the whale, specifically the ambergris-producing sperm whale. The substance forms in the whale's own gut, rather than being swallowed (see n. 7, above).

183 "Fishy smell" depends on a tentative reading.

184 Ibn Baṭṭūṭah (*Travels*, 2:391) also mentions houses on the southern Arabian coast built/roofed with "fish bones"; remains of such structures are still to be seen (Mackintosh-Smith, *Travels with a Tangerine*, 264). Abū Zayd's "ancient" houses are literally "'Ādite," that is, ascribed to the ancient people, ʿĀd.

185 The oil scooped from the whale's eye must be sperm oil, a liquid wax obtained from cavities in the sperm whale's head. The oil of the previous sentence is extracted from the blubber of various whale species. In the Gulf, the heat of the sun alone might have been enough to render it, as the text implies, without the need for heating the blubber, as practiced by whalers in cooler climates.

186 To seal gaps, the oil would of course have been used in conjunction with caulking.

187 Q Yā Sīn 36:36.

188 The comparison is with *anjudhānah*, glossed in its plural form by al-Muẓaffar (*Al-Muʿtamad*, 9) as the leaves of asafoetida, a plant with both culinary and medicinal uses. Presumably Abū Zayd or his informant was thinking of the dried leaves familiar to cooks and apothecaries of the time.

189 "Pried pearls" are what English terms "blister pearls."

190 "How God sustains His creatures in unexpected ways": more literally, "doorways/openings [that lead] to divinely provided sustenance (*rizq*)." At the end of the section, *rizq* is translated more loosely still, as "windfall."

191 *Ṣammān* in general signifies an area of low rugged hills; this particular one was nine days' journey from Basra (Yāqūt, *Muʿjam al-buldān*, 3:481). At this period, the name "Bahrain" included both the islands known by the name today and a large area of the adjacent mainland.

192 *Chatrah* (in which the text carefully specifies the consonant *ch*, alien to standard Arabic) is the Sanskrit *chattra*, "umbrella."

193 Abū Zayd's readers, when dining in company, would have eaten from communal dishes regardless of the class or status of their companions.

194 As above (see n. 83), "the sea" is shorthand for the sea itself, the islands in it, and the lands on and beyond its shores.

195 As the English saying goes, less is more.

196 Here follows a note by the copyist: "This copy was checked against the original from which it was made, in Safar of the year 596 [November–December 1199]. And God it is who guides."

Glossary of Names and Terms

ʿĀd a prehistoric proto-Arab people often mentioned in the Qurʾan.

Aden ancient trading port in the southwestern Arabian Peninsula, near the mouth of the Red Sea.

Aden and al-Qulzum, Sea of the Gulf of Aden and the Red Sea. "Al-Qulzum" is an arabicization of Clysma, the Greek name of an ancient port on the Gulf of Suez.

al-Aghbāb plural of Ghubb. See Ghubb of Sarandīb.

Andamān Sea the Andaman Islands in the Bay of Bengal are still known by the same name. The application of the name to the sea separating the islands, as in the text here, may reflect an old usage, or it may be a copyist's error.

Alexander Alexander III ("the Great"), 356–323 BC, king of Macedon and conqueror of a mainly Asian empire including Persia.

ʿanqatūs unidentified, and voweling uncertain. Al-Idrīsī (*Nuzhah*, 1:65), who drew on the present text, has *ʿanqarīs* as the name of a fish in the Sea of Lārawī.

Aristotle Greek philosopher and scientist, 384–322 BC, and tutor to Alexander (q.v.), when the latter was crown prince of Macedon.

Baghbūn an error for Baghbūr (often spelled Faghfūr), from Persian *baghpūr*, "son of the divinity" (Polo, *Travels*, 2:148 n. 1). The Arabic-speakers' (intentionally jocular?) version, al-Maghbūn, would mean "the Defrauded One, the Dupe."

baghlī dirham an early type of dirham (q.v.) supposedly named after al-Baghl, a Jewish master of the mint in the Umayyad period (Ḥibshī, *Riḥlat al-Sīrāfī*, 58 n. 1). It was a third heavier than the later standard dirham.

Balharā from Prakrit *ballaha-rāya*, "well-beloved king," a title of various monarchs in the Deccan (Sauvaget, *Relation*, 51 n. 25.1).

Bamdhū possibly a corruption of "Shamdū" but, in any case, a version of the name Chengdu, capital of Sichuan province, to which the Tang emperor Xizong removed his court during the occupation of Chang'an by Huang Chao.

Banū Kāwān Island see Ibn Kāwān Island.

Barbar by "the land of the Barbar" Abū Zayd means that of the Somalis and related people—the "Barbarah" of the Arab geographers and of Ibn Baṭṭūṭah (*Travels,* 2:373)—rather than that of the Berbers (the Arabic spelling is the same). The "Barbarī leopard skins" mentioned presumably take their name from the region of their export, not from that of their stated origin, Abyssinia. The northern Somali port of Berbera preserves the old name; Abū Zayd's "Barbarā," rather than signifying this port in particular, probably means the same as "the land of the Barbar."

Barbarā see Barbar (last sentence).

Basra city in southeastern Iraq, on the Shaṭṭ al-ʿArab waterway.

bīkarjī seemingly a garbled and arabicized version of Sanskrit *vairāgika,* "ascetic," or some derivation from it. Cf. also the note on *bīkūr/baykūr* in al-Rāmhurmuzī, *ʿAjāʾib al-hind,* 194–95.

budd from Persian *but,* "idol."

bushān probably from Sanskrit *viṣāna,* "horn."

bussadh (spelled *busadd* in the manuscript) preferred by al-Bīrūnī, in his book on precious stones (*Kitāb al-jamāhir,* 137), to the more common *murjān* as the term for coral.

Dahmā a emendation of the manuscript's "Ruhmā." "Dahmā" is, in turn, a plausible arabicization and shortening of *Dharma-pāla,* title of a king prominent in northern India in the early ninth century.

dahnaj the deep-green copper-bearing mineral malachite (Persian *dahnah*).

darā a Persian word for "bell."

Darius the Great here referring to Darius III, the last Achaemenid ruler of Persia (r. 336–330). "The Great" is more usually the epithet of Darius I.

al-Dībājāt Islands the archipelagos of the Maldives and Laccadives (Lakshadweep) in the Arabian Sea. "1900" is too many; the actual number is between 1200 and 1300.

dīfū Chinese *tai fu,* title of a high-ranking governor (Sauvaget, *Relation,* 58 n. 37.2).

dinar the standard gold coin, for many centuries, of much of the Islamic world. Its official weight was about 4.25 grams.

dirham the standard silver coin, for many centuries, of much of the Islamic world. Its weight varied between 2.5 grams and 3 grams.

Dualists known also as Manicheans, from the name of the founder of their religion, Mani (third century AD). Their dualism was a belief in a primeval and eternal conflict between the powers of light and darkness.

fafaghā cognate with the standard Arabic word for a parrot, *bab[b]aghā'* (used in the text in a plural form, *babbaghāwāt*, to gloss it), and perhaps a dialect variant.

fakkūj a term, of uncertain origin, for a string of one thousand copper "cash." It was worth, according to Book Two (2.3.3), about a *mithqāl* of gold—a weight equal to that of one dinar. This corresponds approximately with the Chinese silver equivalent in value, the *liang* (Yule and Burnell, *Hobson-Jobson*, s.v. "Tael"). Professor Zvi Ben-Dor Benite suggests that *fakkūj* may be a distortion of *fang kongqian*, a generic term for "cash" in premodern China (personal communication).

Fanṣūr the region of Barus, on the west coast of Sumatra (cf. Tibbetts, *Arab Navigation*, 490).

al-Faqīr Muḥammad unknown. *Al-faqīr* is, in general, a pious epithet—"he who is in need [of God's mercy]"—and was used by Sufis leading lives of poverty.

farsakh a linear measure (Persian *parasang*) of about 5.77 kilometers but varying considerably according to local usage (Ibn Baṭṭūṭah, *Travels*, 1:34 n. 93).

fils any small copper coin, including the Chinese currency known as "cash."

Fire, Mount of it is impossible to know which of the many active volcanoes in the Indonesian Archipelago is intended here.

Gates of China the Paracel Islands, a group of low-lying coral islands and reefs in the South China Sea, now administered by China.

Ghubb of Sarandīb the editors of al-Rāmhurmuzī discuss (*'Ajā'ib*, 274–75) the identity of the (plural) Ghubbs of Sarandīb mentioned in that work but do not locate them any more precisely than in the Coromandel region of southeastern India, in the modern states of Andhra Pradesh and Tamil Nadu. The great length of the Ghubb in our text—two months' travel—suggests a network of waterways; if a single river is meant, it may be the Cauvery, which is more than 750 kilometers long.

Habbār ibn al-Aswad a tribesman of Quraysh (q.v.), who was a contemporary and a distant cousin of the Prophet Muḥammad.

hadith accounts of the utterances and deeds of the Prophet Muḥammad and his Companions.

ḥarām probably from Sanskrit *ārāma*, "garden" (cf. *jarām* in al-Rāmhurmuzī, *ʿAjāʾib*, 195).

Harkand, Sea of the Bay of Bengal.

Ḥimyar name of a South Arabian people and of the last indigenous power to rule Yemen before the coming of Islam.

Huang Chao in the manuscript "Bānshū," probably an error for "Yānshū." Leader of a rebellion (874–84) that seriously weakened the power of the Tang Dynasty. Although the rebellion was eventually put down, the Tang never fully recovered.

Ibn Kāwān Island the Iranian island of Qishm (Tibbetts, *Arab Navigation*, 447), south of Bandar ʿAbbās and west of the Strait of Hormuz. The name is the usual Arabic deformation of the island's pre-Islamic name, Abarkāwān (Sauvaget, *Relation*, 42 n. 13.5). On occasion, the name appears, further deformed, as "Banū Kāwān."

Ibn Wahb al-Qurashī traveler from Basra, known only from this text and others deriving from it.

jādam modern Chinese *haotong*, "signaling tube," Tibetan *r gyadung* (Sauvaget, *Relation*, 56 n. 33.3).

Jalīdiyyah see Kanīfiyyah.

al-Jār former Red Sea port, now the site of the city of Yanbuʿ, in present-day Saudi Arabia.

jazbī voweling conjectural. This may represent a non-Arabic word; other possible readings include *jurbī*, which could conceivably be a corruption of *jurī/churī*, the latter being the Sanskrit word for "knife." (The Sanskrit term is arabicized by al-Masʿūdī, *Murūj*, 1:210, as *jurīʾ*.) However, because the verb *jazaba* is a southern Arabian dialect variant of standard Arabic *jazama*, "to cut, lop" (Piamenta, *Dictionary*, s.v. *jazama*), and *jazbī* would be a plausible formation from it, it is also possible that the term here is an Arabic one.

Jidda Red Sea port in present-day Saudi Arabia, the nearest seaport to Mecca.

Jurhum ancient South Arabian tribe, who, for a time, controlled pre-Islamic Mecca.

al-Jurz the Gurjaras. By the mid-ninth century, the Gurjaras controlled much of northern India. The reference to their king inhabiting a peninsula—literally, "a tongue of land"—may refer to the original Gurjara homelands, which included, along with the Indus Valley, the Kathiawar Peninsula.

kabtaj this may be a version of some word cognate with the Sanskrit name for the cowry, *kaparda* (Yule and Burnell, *Hobson-Jobson,* s.v. "Cowry"). Van Der Lith and Devic discuss the word at length (al-Rāmhurmuzī, *ʿAjāʾib,* 216–17) but inconclusively.

Kalah, Peninsula of the Malay Peninsula, or some portion of it, and the location of Kalah Bār (q.v.). Opinions probably varied at different periods as to whether it was a peninsula or an island (Arabic *jazīrah* can serve for both).

Kalah Bār on the west coast of the Malay Peninsula. Its exact location is unknown, but a form of the first part of the name may survive in that of the Malaysian state of Kedah. "Bār" derives ultimately from Sanskrit *vāra,* "district."

Kanduranj this seems to be a version of "Panduranga," the modern Phan Rang, a major city of the kingdom of Champa, located on the south coast of Vietnam.

Kanīfiyyah this and the associated term Jalīdiyyah probably refer to two rival gangs in Iraq. Ḥibshī (*Riḥlat al-Sīrāfī,* 79 n. 2) suggests amending the reading of the former to "Katīfiyyah" and deriving it from *katīf,* a broad-bladed sword; the second term he associates (79 n. 3) with the verb *jālada,* "to fight with a sword." Following Ḥibshī, the terms might thus be rendered "the Broadswordsmen" and "the Fencers." Equally tentative is a reference in Bosworth (*The Mediaeval Islamic Underworld,* 1:43–44 n. 117) to the two gangs (whose names are, however, read slightly differently) as "the Khulaidiyya, 'those condemned to perpetual imprisonment' (?), mentioned [by al-Jāḥiẓ] as a group of beggars or brigands . . . and linked with the Katīfiyya/Kutaifiyya, perhaps those chained up by their shoulders (*aktāf*) or in irons (*katāʾif*)." There are, however, other possible derivations (*kanīf* is, inter alia, "a lavatory"; *jalīd,* applied to a person, means "tough").

al-Kāshibīn Ferrand takes this as a corruption of Lakṣmipura, the name of a town in eastern Assam (Sauvaget, *Relation,* 54 n. 29.1).

Khamdān the usual Arabic version of the name of the Tang Dynasty imperial capital, Chang'an, now called Xi'an.

Khānfū the Chinese city of Guangzhou. The Arabic name probably reflects a shortened version of the old official name of the city, Guangzhou-fu (Yule and Burnell, *Hobson-Jobson,* s.v. "Canton").

khāqān a Turkic royal title. Its application to the ruler of Tibet shows that information about that country arrived via Turkic intermediaries.

kharābāt specified by Tibbetts (*Arab Navigation*, 55) as "anchor ropes." The term is still in use.

Khazars, Sea of the the Caspian Sea. The Khazars were a Turkic people living in the lower Volga basin.

Khurasan a large province in northeastern Iran.

al-Khushnāmī unidentified. The word is from Persian and means "of good name."

Kisrā title of the pre-Islamic Persian kings, arabicized from "Khusraw."

Kūlam Malī Kollam, in the Indian state of Kerala.

al-Kumkum Sanskrit Konkaṇa, the low-lying part of the western coast of India between Goa and Gujarat (Yule and Burnell, *Hobson-Jobson*, s.v. "Concan").

Kusayr and ʿUwayr Yāqūt (*Muʿjam*, s.v. "Kusayr") points out that the names of these dangerous rocks are derived from the words for "breaking" and "spoiling." They belong to a group of islets lying off the tip of the Musandam Peninsula and known as "Salāmah and her Daughters" (Ibn Baṭṭūṭah, *Travels*, 1:409–10 n. 144).

Lanjabālūs Islands the Nicobar Islands.

laqshī mamkūn a slightly deformed arabicization of Chinese *lüshicanjun* (Professor Zvi Ben-Dor Benite, personal communication). Professor Benite adds that there is a confusion in our text over the nature of this office, which, under the Tang Dynasty, was associated with a military rather than a judicial function.

Lārawī, Sea of the Gulf of Oman and the northern part of the Arabian Sea.

lashak possibly from a non-Arabic word, but cf. the later Arabic name for the remora fish, *luzzāq*, connected with the verb *laziqa*, "to stick" (Tibbetts, *Arab Navigation*, 288). As reflected by another of its English names, "shark sucker," the remora does attach itself to sharks, but its relationship with them tends to be commensal, not destructive.

līkhū Sauvaget (*Relation*, 59 n. 38.4) reads *lnjūn*, with the first letter unvocalized, and equates with a title given to high-level secretaries.

lukham sharks in all their varieties.

al-Mābud reading conjectural. Sauvaget (*Relation*, 55 n. 32.1) derives the name from Tibetan *smad bod*, a term for the eastern part of Tibet.

Madīnat al-Salām "The City of Security, of Peace," an alternative name for Baghdad.

Maghbūn see Baghbūn.

Magians that is, Zoroastrians. The comparison in the text between Chinese and Zoroastrian beliefs reflects the hazy notions many Muslims held about the latter.

Maljān Island unidentified, and first vowel uncertain. Sauvaget (*Relation*, 46 n. 18.1) suggests a connection with the name of the Mergui Archipelago, off the coast of Burma. Perhaps more evocative of the Arabic is the name of the largest island in the group, Mali Kyun.

mand al-Muẓaffar (*Al-Muʿtamad*, 339 and 340) lists *mandah* as low-grade, black ambergris used to adulterate the more valuable grades.

al-Manṣūrah founded as their capital in the second/eighth century by the Muslim conquerors of Sind, it was located in southern present-day Pakistan.

al-Mihrāj voweled thus in the manuscript. An arabicization, probably via Persian, of the Indian title "Maharaja." The rulers referred to here are probably those of the Sailendra kingdom, based in Java between the first/seventh and fifth/eleventh centuries.

mīj a Persian word for "locust" (Sauvaget, *Relation*, 34 n. 3.1). The Arabic name *jarād al-baḥr*, "sea locusts," sometimes applied elsewhere to prawns/shrimps, is used in southern Arabia for flying fish (Tibbetts, *Arab Navigation*, 286 n. 74).

mithqāl a unit of weight equivalent to that of a dinar (q.v.).

Muḍar in traditional genealogy, the progenitor of an eponymous major tribe, one of the two main branches of the so-called ʿAdnānī or Northern Arabs; the other branch is named for Rabīʿah.

al-Mūjah apparently the ethnic group known in Chinese as the Miao, or Miaozhu, found in southern China and neighboring regions (Professor Zvi Ben-Dor Benite, personal communication).

al-Mūltān (usual later Arabic form "Multān") Multan, an ancient city in central present-day Pakistan. The phrase in the text could be understood as "the [well-]known idol of al-Mūltān," but it seems more likely that Abū Zayd regarded the name as that of the idol first (and the place second). The idol in question was a representation of the solar deity Surya or Aditya (al-Bīrūnī, *Albêrûnî's India*, 100).

al-Niyān Island Pulau Nias, called locally Tanö Niha, off the west coast of Sumatra.

al-Qamār the usual Arabic name in old texts for the region including present-day Cambodia. It is cognate with the name of the most prominent people of the region, the Khmer.

Qāmarūn the Kamrup region of Assam (cf. Ibn Baṭṭūṭah's "Kāmarū," *Travels,* 4:869).

Qannawj Kannauj, on the Ganges, in present-day Uttar Pradesh.

al-Qulzum see Aden and al-Qulzum, Sea of.

Quraysh Arab tribe centered on Mecca, to which the Prophet Muḥammad belonged.

al-Qyrnj voweling and interpretation uncertain; possibly located in what is now Burma (Myanmar).

Rabīʿah in traditional genealogy, the progenitor of an eponymous major tribe, one of the two main branches of the so-called ʿAdnānī or Northern Arabs; the other branch is named for Muḍar.

al-Rahūn Sripada or Adam's Peak, a mountain and pilgrimage site in Sri Lanka. Cf. Ruhuna Raṭa, the ancient Pali name for southern Sri Lanka (Skeen, *Adam's Peak,* 22).

al-Rāmanī Island seemingly a corruption of "Lāmurī" (or some variant), the name of a port in or near the Aceh region of Sumatra but applied by early writers to Sumatra as a whole (al-Tājir, *Akhbār al-ṣīn wa-l-hind,* 104–5).

al-Rūm, Gulf of "The Gulf of the Romans/Byzantines," which, in Abū Zayd's hazy understanding, appears to include not only the Bosphorus, the Sea of Marmara, and the Dardanelles but also the Black Sea and the Sea of Azov.

sākh the passage here describing it is the first correct foreign mention of tea. As it stands, the Arabic name is presumably a corruption of the Chinese *cha* (or some dialect variant). The original Arabic form may have been (by simple rearrangement of dots) *shāj,* with the *j* pronounced, as it is in several Gulf dialects, as a *y*; cf. the later standard Arabic *shāy.*

Salāhiṭ, Sea of the Malacca Strait. From *selat,* the Malay term for "strait" (Hourani, *Arab Seafaring,* 71).

ṣamar at first sight, from Sanskrit *camara,* "fly whisk." The traditional *camara,* however, is made from a yak's tail, so other explanations may be in order.

Samarqand ancient trading city of Sogdiana (q.v.), now the second-largest city in Uzbekistan.

Ṣandar Fūlāt Sauvaget (*Relation,* 45–46 n. 16.4) sees this as a copyist's error for (although it may be a mariners' version of) the name Ṣanf Fūlāw, "the island of Champa," Fūlāw representing *pulau,* the Malay word for "island." Possibly one of the Vietnamese group still known as Cu Lao Cham, "the Cham[pa] Islands," near the mainland port of Hoi An, or the island of Ly Son, about one hundred kilometers to the southeast.

Ṣanf the Arabic approximation of "Champa," the name of the ancient kingdom in the coastal region of what is now Vietnam. The text seems to indicate a particular port by the name, but its location is unclear. The main port of Champa in the central coastal region of Vietnam was near the present-day town of Quy Nhon.

Ṣankhī, Sea of the northern part of the South China Sea. Probably from Chinese *san hai*, "huge sea."

Sarandīb the most common name for Sri Lanka in early Arabic texts.

Sarbuzah voweled thus by Yāqūt (*Muʿjam*). Its location has been much discussed, especially by the editors of al-Rāmhurmuzī (*ʿAjāʾib*, 247–53), who identify it with Palembang, in southeastern Sumatra. Given that Sumatra is already represented in our text by the island of al-Rāmanī and that Sarbuzah is itself said to be a large island, it should perhaps be sought elsewhere. Borneo has also been suggested as a possibility. At the risk of adding to the confusion, Sulawesi, on the grounds both of its name and its size, might also be a contender.

al-Shaʾm otherwise written al-Shām and translated elsewhere as "the Levant." In the context of a description of the Red Sea and neighboring coasts, "the coast of al-Shaʾm" must refer to the Gulf of Aqaba.

al-Shiḥr now the name of a town on the south coast of Yemen but formerly denoting a region including much of the southern coast of the Arabian Peninsula and its hinterland.

Sīf Banī l-Ṣaffāq a coastal region (*sīf*, meaning "shore") in southern Iran, between Sīrāf (q.v.) and Qishm (see Ibn Kāwān Island, above) (Bosworth, "The Nomenclature of the Persian Gulf," 83). Yāqūt has "Sīf Banī l-Ṣaffār" (*Muʿjam*).

al-Sīlā the early Arabic name for Korea, from the Silla dynasty who ruled it until the tenth century AD. The reference to Korea as "islands" might be translated as "peninsula and adjoining islands," but, as the text implies, notions of the country's geography were hazy.

Silver, Islands of unidentified.

sindī dinars dinars (q.v.) of Sind, which is, properly speaking, the territory on the Indus below the Punjab (Yule and Burnell, *Hobson-Jobson*, s.v. "Sind").

Exactly what coins are intended is unclear, although large gold coins were used in the area before the Islamic period, and the imported coinage may have catered to local tastes.

Sīrāf until its near-destruction by an earthquake in 366-67/977 (Hourani, *Arab Seafaring*, 78) the chief port on the Iranian side of the Arabian/Persian Gulf, south of Shīrāz. Sīrāf was the origin of Abū Zayd, author of the second part of this work.

al-Sīrāfī, Abū Zayd al-Ḥasan see Introduction, 6–7.

Socotra (also written in English as Soqotra and Suqutra) The largest island in the Arab world, belonging to Yemen and lying off the Horn of Africa.

Sogdiana ancient name for a Central Asian land east of Khurasan (q.v.) and centered on Samarqand (q.v.).

Sulaymān the Merchant although the single mention of him in the earlier part of the text suggests that he was an informant, Sulaymān al-Tājir ("the Merchant") was credited by the geographer Ibn al-Faqīh as its author or compiler (al-Tājir, *Akhbār*, 11 and 12). More recent commentators have disagreed with this ascription. See also Introduction, 5.

Taghazghuz voweled thus in the manuscript. An arabicization of the Turkic name Toquz Oghuz, "the Nine Oghuz [Tribes]," a group including the Turkic people known today as Uighurs.

Tamīm in traditional genealogy, a descendant of Muḍar (q.v.). In the text, the name is used as an alternative to Muḍar as a tribal name.

al-Ṭāqā the manuscript has "al-Ṭāfiq." Al-Ṭāqā is Sauvaget's suggested emendation (*Relation*, 52 n.27.1); it may reflect "Ṭakka," the name in Indian sources of a kingdom in the upper reaches of the Chenab and Ravi rivers.

ṭāṭirī dirhams the phrase is repeated by other authorities who have drawn on this text, but there is no convincing explanation for it. Yule and Burnell (*Hobson-Jobson*, 896) cite *tetari* as a Mingrelian term for a silver coin. The reference here could be to the coinage of the Shahi dynasty of Kabul and Gandhara, often imitated at this period by other North Indian kingdoms, its standard silver denomination being, as the text suggests, considerably heavier than the Islamic dirham.

al-Tāyin (the "i" is conjectural) unidentified.

Tāyū identified by Sauvaget (*Relation*, 62 n. 49.1) as Taihu, in southwest Anhui province. Later reports of alleged Chinese "pygmies" include one, emanating from approximately this region of China, in the purported travels of Sir John Mandeville (Moseley, *Travels*, 139–40).

thalāj first vowel conjectural. As used in the text, the word signifies the tidal reach of a river, or a tidal basin. An arabicization derived ultimately from Sanskrit *talāga*, explained by the editors of al-Rāmhurmuzī (*ʿAjāʾib*, 195) as "lagoon"; cf. also modern Indonesian *telaga*, "lake, pond."

Tiyūmah Island Tioman, now part of the southeastern Malaysian state of Pahang.

Tubbaʿ a personal name (but considered by later Arab writers to be a title) of some of the later kings of Ḥimyar (q.v.).

Tubbat Tibet.

ṭūqām Chinese *tujian*, director-in-chief of the eunuch hierarchy (Professor Zvi Ben-Dor Benite, personal communication).

ṭūsanj Professor Zvi Ben-Dor Benite suggests that this may represent the second and third elements of the longer term *jieduzhangshuzhi*, "a versatile and ubiquitous title" that came, in post-Tang times, to mean "prefectural secretary" (personal communication).

wāl cf. *awāl*/*afāl* in al-Masʿūdī (*Murūj*, 1:108), often assumed to be a whale. In view of the information given here (and allowing for some exaggeration in measurement) the tiger shark, which can exceed six meters in length, might be a likelier candidate.

yasārah feasibly a corruption of *bas[h]ārah*, which might, in turn, be an arabicization (with metathesis) of a word derived from *varṣā*, Sanskrit for "rain"; this suggestion is, however, highly tentative. Because both *yasārah* and *bashārah* have meanings in Arabic—"ease of living" and "good tidings," respectively—what might be called "semantic assimilation" may be involved here. Al-Masʿūdī (*Murūj*, 1:148) uses the same term and mentions a verb derived from it, *yassara*, "to spend the rainy season."

al-Zābaj Java. The name is probably an arabicized version of the early form "Jāwaga" (Yule, *Cathay*, 1:127 n. 6).

Zanj the usual Arabic word for the black peoples of East Africa south of the equator.

al-Zaylaʿ usually Zaylaʿ; also spelled Zeila. Town on the northern coast of Somalia, near the border with Djibouti, formerly the principal port of the region.

Bibliography

Adūnīs [Adonis]. *Al-Thābit wa-l-mutaḥawwil.* 10th ed. 4 vols. Beirut: Dār al-Sāqī, 2011.

Bīrūnī, Abū Rayḥān Muḥammad ibn Aḥmad al-. *Albêrûnî's India.* Translated by Edward C. Sachau. New Delhi: Rupa, 2002. Originally published London: Trübner, 1888.

Bīrūnī, Abū Rayḥān Muḥammad ibn Aḥmad al-. *Kitāb al-Jamāhir fī maʿrifat al-jawāhir.* Beirut: ʿĀlam al-Kutub, 1984.

Bosworth, Clifford Edmund. *The Mediaeval Islamic Underworld.* 2 vols. Leiden: E.J. Brill, 1976.

Bosworth, Clifford Edmund. "The Nomenclature of the Persian Gulf." *Iranian Studies* 30, nos. 1/2 (1997): 77–94.

Cheung, Catherine, and Lyndon DeVantier. *Socotra: A Natural History of the Islands and Their People.* Hong Kong: Odyssey Books and Guides, 2006.

Ḥibshī, ʿAbdallāh al-, ed. *Riḥlat al-Sīrāfī.* Abu Dhabi: al-Mujammaʿ al-Thaqāfī, 1999.

Hourani, George F. *Arab Seafaring in the Indian Ocean in Ancient and Early Medieval Times.* Revised and expanded by John Carswell. Princeton: Princeton University Press, 1995.

Ibn Baṭṭūṭah, Muḥammad ibn ʿAbdallāh. *The Travels of Ibn Baṭṭūṭa: A.D. 1325–1354.* Translated by H. A. R. Gibb and C. F. Beckingham. 4 vols. London: Hakluyt Society, 1958–94.

Idrīsī, Muḥammad ibn Muḥammad al-. *Kitāb Nuzhat al-mushtāq fī ikhtirāq al-āfāq.* 2 vols. Cairo: Maktabat al-Thaqāfah al-Dīniyyah, n.d.

Lane, Edward William. *Madd al-qāmūs: An Arabic-English Lexicon.* 8 vols. New Delhi: Asian Educational Services, 1985. Originally published London: Williams and Norgate, 1863–93.

Mackintosh-Smith, Tim. *Travels with a Tangerine: A Journey in the Footnotes of Ibn Battutah.* London: John Murray, 2001.

Mackintosh-Smith, Tim. *Landfalls: On the Edge of Islam with Ibn Battutah.* London: John Murray, 2010.

Masʿūdī, ʿAlī ibn al-Ḥusyan al-. *Murūj al-dhahab wa-maʿādin al-jawhar.* Edited by Muḥammad Muḥyī l-Dīn ʿAbd al-Ḥamīd. 4 vols. Beirut: Dār al-Maʿrifah, n.d.

Miquel, André. *Géographie humaine du monde musulman.* 2nd ed. 2 vols. Paris: Mouton, 1973.

Morris, Jan. *Hong Kong.* New York: Vintage Books, 1989. Originally published London: Penguin, 1988.

Moseley, C. W. R. D., ed. and trans. *The Travels of Sir John Mandeville.* London: Penguin, 1983.

Muẓaffar al-Ghassānī, Yūsuf ibn ʿUmar ibn ʿAlī ibn Rasūl al-Malik al-. *Al-Muʿtamad fī l-adwiyah al-mufradah*. Edited by Muṣṭafā al-Saqqā. Beirut: Dār al-Maʿrifah, n.d.

Pellat, Charles, ed. and trans. (into French). *The Life and Works of Jāḥiẓ*. Translated (into English) by D. M. Hawke. London: Routledge and Kegan Paul, 1969.

Piamenta, Moshe. *Dictionary of Post-Classical Yemeni Arabic*. 2 vols. Leiden: E. J. Brill, 1990.

Polo, Marco. *The Travels of Marco Polo*. Translated and annotated by Henry Yule (3rd ed., revised by Henri Cordier). 2 vols. New York: Dover Publications Inc., 1993. Originally published London: John Murray, 1929.

Rāmhurmuzī, Buzurg ibn Shahriyār al-. *ʿAjāʾib al-hind*. Edited by P. A. Van Der Lith and translated by L. Marcel Devic. Leiden: E. J. Brill, 1883–86.

Reinaud, Joseph Toussaint, ed. and trans. *Relation des voyages faits par les Arabes et les Persans dans l'Inde et à la Chine* (Arabic text originally edited by Louis-Mathieu Langlès). 2 vols. Paris: Imprimerie Royale, 1845.

Renaudot, Eusèbe, trans. (into French; English trans. from French by anon.). *Ancient Accounts of India and China by Two Mohammedan Travellers, Who Went to Those Parts in the 9th Century*. London: Samuel Harding, 1733.

Sauvaget, Jean, ed. and trans. *Relation de la Chine et de l'Inde, rédigée en 851*. Paris: Belles Lettres, 1948.

Serjeant, R. B., and Ronald Lewcock, eds. *Ṣanʿāʾ: An Arabian Islamic City*. London: World of Islam Festival Trust, 1983.

Severin, Tim. *The Sindbad Voyage*. London: Hutchinson 1982.

Skeen, William. *Adam's Peak*. New Delhi: Asian Educational Services, 1997. Originally published Colombo: W. L. H. Skeen, 1870.

Tājir, Sulaymān al- (attributed) and Abū Zayd al-Sīrāfī. *Akhbār al-ṣīn wa-l-hind*. Edited by Ibrāhīm Khūrī. Beirut: Dār al-Mawsim li-l-Iʿlām, 1411/1991.

Tennent, James Emerson. *Ceylon*. 2 vols. New Delhi: Asian Educational Services, 1999. Originally published London: Longman, Green, Longman, and Roberts, 1859.

Tibbetts, G. R. *Arab Navigation in the Indian Ocean Before the Coming of the Portuguese*. London: Royal Asiatic Society, 1971.

Whitehouse, David. "Siraf: A Medieval Port on the Persian Gulf." *World Archaeology* 2, no. 2 (October 1970): 141–58.

Whitfield, Susan. *Life Along the Silk Road*. London: John Murray, 2000. Originally published London: John Murray, 1999.

Yāqūt al-Ḥamawī, *Muʿjam al-buldān*. Edited by Farīd ʿAbd al-ʿAzīz al-Jundī. 7 vols. Beirut: Dār al-Kutub al-ʿIlmiyyah, n.d.

Yule, Henry. *Cathay and the Way Thither*. 2nd edition. Revised by Henri Cordier. 4 vols. New Delhi: Munshiram Manoharlal, 1998. Originally published London: The Hakluyt Society, 1916.

Yule, Henry, and A. C. Burnell. *Hobson-Jobson: The Anglo-Indian Dictionary*. 2nd ed. Edited by W. Crooke. Ware, UK: Wordsworth, 1996. Originally published London: John Murray, 1903.

Zhang Jun-yan. "Relations between China and the Arabs in Early Times." *Journal of Oman Studies* 6, no. 1 (1983): 91–109.

Mission to the Volga

For Josh, for the journey

Acknowledgements

I first read sections of Ibn Faḍlān's book as an undergraduate at the University of Glasgow, in the company of John N. Mattock, a guide well seasoned in the classical Arabic tradition. When I began teaching at the University of Oslo in 1992, it seemed only natural that I should guide my students through the description of their Viking forebears. I have read the text in the company of many students at Oslo and Cambridge over the years and learned much from their insights. I would like to thank them all. I can no longer recall what is mine and what is theirs. I guess that's the camaraderie of the road. The same is true of the audiences at the many institutions where I have talked about Ibn Faḍlān and his journey over the years.

When I finished *The Vagaries of the Qaṣīdah* in 1997, I was keen to take a holiday from pre-Islamic poetry, and Ibn Faḍlān's text seemed like just the site I was looking to visit. I did not intend my stay there to become permanent but, in odd ways, it has. Over the years I have written articles and encyclopedia entries, given papers and radio talks, and received many emails and phone calls from those who have also fallen under the spell of the text. I especially remember the Icelander who lost his patience with me when I tried to explain that Crichton's *Eaters of the Dead* was a fantasy novel. Of course, I was hoist with my own petard some years later, when, in the days before library catalogues could be searched electronically, I tried in vain to locate a reference to an article in a journal. I had scribbled it on a piece of paper with no indication as to where I had come across it. After an hour among the catalogues and stacks I realized that the reference was spurious and that it had come from Crichton's preface to the novel!

I have kept up my interest in Ibn Faḍlān as a hobby over the years. I have never found the time to learn Russian, so I knew that I was not the person to do justice to the text and its abundant scholarship. So, I have tried, with my edition and translation, to furnish a new generation of scholars with the basic equipment and the grid references they need to find their way through Ibn Faḍlān's strange but enthralling world.

Many companions have helped me along the way. An old friend, Geert Jan van Gelder, reviewed my first draft a decade ago and, as is his wont, saved me on many occasions from having egg on my chin before I even left the house. A new friend, Shady Hekmat Nasser, advised on orthography. Thorir Jonson Hraundal, of Reykjavik University, helped with the Glossary and the Further Reading. I am delighted that Ibn Faḍlān has afforded us the opportunity to develop our friendship over the years. Maaike van Berkel gave me a copy of her excellent PhD thesis.

Most of the work on this volume has been done on flights between London and Abu Dhabi or New York, in the InterContinental Hotel Abu Dhabi, and in various restaurants, hotels, and bars in Greenwich Village and SoHo. I would like to thank the staff of the InterCon and the cabin crews of Etihad and Virgin Airways who looked after me so well. I can well imagine how envious but dismissive of these luxuries Ibn Faḍlān would be.

Over the years the village of Embsay in Yorkshire has been a welcome retreat where I can combine walking and writing. David and Julie Perrins are wonderful hosts. The Chancellors, Nigel and Christina, took Yvonne and me around the Gulf of Bothnia in their boat and introduced us to the magic of the Finnish sauna. We also managed to explore a Viking cemetery together, despite the depredations of man-eating Finnish insects.

My family has always given me everything I needed, whatever jaunt I was off on.

Philip Kennedy and I have been swapping traveler's tales of our mishaps in the Arabic literary tradition for thirty years. In the company of our editor comrades, we are happily trying to redraw the map of Arabic literary creativity by means of the Library of Arabic Literature. My fellow editors on the board of Library of Arabic Literature are a constant reminder to me of how far I still have to travel in order to master Arabic and English.

And last but by no means least, I owe a special debt to my project editor Shawkat Toorawa. He and I have worked on this volume on and off whenever we happened to be together over the last eighteen months and most recently in Abu Dhabi in February 2014. There was a delightful incongruity about discussing the frozen wastelands of the Ustyurt beside the pool at the InterCon. And, as with all adventures, my memories of our collaboration will remain with me forever.

Despite such generous guidance and company, I am only too conscious of how often I have stumbled and slipped in my edition, translation and notes. Sometimes I just never learn.

Introduction

On Thursday, the twelfth of Safar, 309 [June 21, 921], a band of intrepid travelers left Baghdad, the City of Peace. Their destination was the confluence of the upper Volga and the Kama, the realm of the king of the Volga Bulghārs. They arrived at the court of the king on Sunday, the twelfth of Muharram, 310 [May 12, 922]. They had been on the road for 325 days and had covered a distance of about 3,000 miles (4,800 km). They must have managed to travel on average about ten miles a day.

The way there was far from easy. The province of Khurasan was in military turmoil. There were many local potentates, such as the Samanid governor of Khwārazm, who were often lukewarm in their support for the caliphate in Baghdad: our travelers had to secure their permission to continue. The Turkish tribes who lived on the Ustyurt plateau, on the eastern shores of the Caspian Sea, were mostly tolerant of Muslim merchants, but they were proudly independent and suspicious of outside interference. The Khazars, who controlled the delta where the Volga flowed into the Caspian, had always defied Muslim control. And there was the terrain and the weather: deserts, mountains, rivers, snows, and bitter cold.

Why would someone want to make such a journey in the early fourth/tenth century, from the luxurious splendor of caliphal Baghdad to a billet in a yurt among the Bulghārs, a semi-nomadic Turkic tribe?

Some months before the travelers left, a missive had reached the court of Caliph al-Muqtadir (295–320/908–32). The king of the Volga Bulghārs had embraced Islam. He was asking to be accepted as one of the caliph's loyal emirs—the caliph's name would be proclaimed as part of Friday prayers in Bulghār territory. The king petitioned the caliph to send him instruction in law and in how he and his people were to correctly perform religious devotions as proper Muslims. He also asked that the caliph bestow enough funds on him to enable him to construct a fort and thus protect himself against his enemies.

The petition was granted, and arrangements were made to meet the king's request. A diplomatic mission was assembled to visit the king and formally recognize him and his people as members of the Islamic community.

We know about the events and its actors from a remarkable book by Aḥmad ibn Faḍlān, a member of the mission. Yet all of the members of the diplomatic mission remain shrouded in obscurity, especially the book's author.

Sadly our other extant sources make no mention of this adventure. We rely exclusively on the information provided in the book to enable us to reconstruct the composition of the embassy. The only other early source that mentions any of the characters involved is an annalistic chronicle known as *Experiences of Nations, Consequences of Ambition* (*Tajārib al-umam wa-ʿawāqib al-himam*), by the civil servant, philosopher, and historian Miskawayh (d. 421/1030), and, even then, not in the context of the embassy but of the affairs of the reign of al-Muqtadir.

Dramatis Personae

It is difficult to work out from Ibn Faḍlān's book who took part in the mission and who played what part.

1. The Representative: Nadhīr al-Ḥaramī. The man placed in charge of the embassy, who did not actually travel, was the official assigned to recruit the personnel and finance the mission. He seems to have enjoyed al-Muqtadir's confidence, and it is likely, from his name "al-Ḥaramī," that he was a eunuch who guarded the harem. In addition to organizing the embassy, he entrusted it with (at least) two letters: one was addressed to Atrak ibn al-Qaṭaghān, the field marshal of the Ghuzziyyah (Oghuz Turks), along with several gifts; the other was addressed to the king of the Bulghārs. It is clear from the account that Nadhīr had been in communication with the field marshal and with the Bulghār king. His relationship with the Ghuzziyyah is based on their host-friend system, described in the text, and the Bulghār king had written to him asking for more medication (this is an otherwise unattested detail that features prominently in some non-Arabic accounts of the Bulghārs' conversion to Islam).
2. The Envoy: Sawsan al-Rassī. Sawsan is bound to Nadhīr as his freed man. Sawsan's name "al-Rassī" is obscure but may indicate that he was of Turkic or other Central Asian origin. Sawsan would presumably have been well acquainted with the geopolitics of the region. We discover, when the embassy leaves al-Jurjāniyyah for the Ustyurt, that he is accompanied by a brother-in-law, who is not mentioned elsewhere in the account.

3. The Local Expert: Takīn al-Turkī. Takīn (the name is a Turkic honorific) was well acquainted with and known in the area. The *khwārazm-shāh*, the Samanid governor of Khwārazm, recognizes him and refers to him as a slave-soldier and notes that he had been involved in the arms trade with the Turks, suspecting that he is the prime mover behind the mission. On the Ustyurt, we meet him chatting with a fellow Turk, and, in the enforced stay in Bulghār, he informs Ibn Faḍlān of the presence there of a giant from the land of Gog and Magog.
4. The Soldier: Bārs al-Ṣaqlābī. Bārs may have been the Samanid commander, the chamberlain of Ismāʿīl ibn Aḥmad and governor of al-Jurjāniyyah, who defected, in 296/908–9, with a force of some 4,000 Turkish slave-troops from the Samanids to Baghdad. Ibn Faḍlān's account provides no substantial information on him.
5. The Financier: A further member of the mission is Aḥmad ibn Mūsā al-Khwārazmī, who is appointed as the agent for the estate from which the mission is to receive its principal funds. Unaccountably, he leaves Baghdad later than the embassy and is easily thwarted in his attempts to reach Bukhara. The mission, therefore, must proceed without the funds the king of the Bulghārs so badly wanted.
6. The vizier Ḥāmid ibn al-ʿAbbās, who otherwise does not feature in our account, has entrusted the mission with a letter for the king.
7. The king is represented by a Khazar: ʿAbdallāh ibn Bāshtū, the Bulghār envoy, was a Muslim of Khazar origin, who may, according to some scholars, have been involved in the dissemination of Islam throughout Volga Bulgharia. The French scholar of Ibn Faḍlān, Marius Canard, thinks he is a political refugee from Khazaria and sees in his ethnic identity a clear indication that Khazar enmity was the occasion of the Bulghār petition.[1] From his actions in Khwārazm, it is clear that ʿAbdallāh's advice was respected by the mission.
8. The jurists and the instructors. These nameless individuals are an enigma. When the mission is about to set out from al-Jurjāniyyah, we discover that there is only one instructor and one jurist. The jurist and the instructor decide not to continue to Bulghār territory. No reason is given.
9. The retainers or slave-soldiers. It also appears, from the report of the departure from al-Jurjāniyyah, that the mission was accompanied by retainers or slave-soldiers (*ghilmān*), who likewise do not continue. This is the sole reference to them in the account.

10. The guide. The mission picks up a guide named Falūs, from al-Jurjāniyyah. It is not clear whether this guide also acts as the *tarjumān*, the interpreter.
11. The interpreter. Ibn Faḍlān mentions "the interpreter" in twelve paragraphs: §§19, 20, 30, 31, 38, 40, 45, 47, 61, 84, 85, 88. It is unclear how many interpreters there are. The king's interpreter was presumably ʿAbdallāh ibn Bāshtū al-Khazarī, whom he sent to Baghdad with his petition, although the text does not say that he fulfilled this function for the king. We also meet Takīn al-Turkī acting in the role of interpreter. Were there more interpreters, one the mission brought along with it as the "guide" from al-Jurjāniyyah and one serving the king of the Bulghārs? The interpreter not only translates on behalf of the embassy but also provides cultural commentary on some of the phenomena and customs observed by Ibn Faḍlān.
12. And so to Ibn Faḍlān, a figure who, like a wandering archetype, turns up in the most unexpected places and in the most unexpected guises. Who was Ibn Faḍlān? As is so often the case, it is easier to begin with who he was not. He was not an Arab merchant, or the leader of the mission, or the secretary of the mission, or a jurist. He was neither the figure inspired by the *Arabian Nights*, whom Michael Crichton created in his novel *The Eaters of the Dead* (1976), nor the Hollywood realization played by Antonio Banderas in the movie *The Thirteenth Warrior* (1999). He was not a Greek resident of Baghdad who had been converted to Islam and held a position of trust at the court of Caliph Muqtadir. In fact, we have only his own words to go by: his role was to ensure that protocol was observed; to read the letters of the caliph, the vizier, and Nadhīr, the representative of the king of the Bulghārs; and to present formally the gifts intended to honor the hosts of the mission. That he was educated is clear from his duties, and the instruction in Islamic law that he delivers to the Muslims of Bulghār would not have been beyond the ken of any reasonably educated Muslim. The king of the Bulghārs treats him as an Arab, though some scholars prefer to see him as a non-Arab Muslim.

At one stage of reading this book, I liked to imagine Ibn Faḍlān as a character not unlike Josiah Harlan, a nineteenth-century American Quaker adventurer in Afghanistan, whose life has now been entertainingly written by Ben Macintyre in *Josiah the Great: The True Story of the Man Who Would Be King*. As Macintyre's title intimates, Harlan is the inspiration for Rudyard Kipling's short story,

The Man Who Would Be King (first published in *The Phantom Rickshaw*, 1888), wonderfully filmed by John Huston in 1975 with Michael Caine and Sean Connery. Then when I read J. M. Coetzee's remarkable *Waiting for the Barbarians*, I thought I could hear echoes of Ibn Faḍlān in the actions and behavior of Coetzee's Magistrate.

Yet Harlan, Coetzee's Magistrate, and Kipling's Peachey Carnehan and Daniel Drahot are weak adumbrations of Ibn Faḍlān. Ibn Faḍlān is a voice, or, rather, a series of voices: the voice of reason, when faced with his colleagues' obduracy; the voice of decorum and dignity, and often of prudery, when confronted by the wilder excesses of Turkic behavior; the voice of shock, when horrified by the Rūs burial rite. Yet he is also the voice of curiosity, when exposed to the myriad of marvels he witnesses; the voice of candor, when he reveals how he is out-argued by the Bulghār king; and the voice of calm observation, as he tries to remain unperturbed so many miles from home, on the fringes of Muslim eschatology, in the realm of Gog and Magog.

There is something quintessentially human about this series of voices. Like all of us, Ibn Faḍlān can be one person and many simultaneously. He is able to entertain contradictions, as we all are. Our sense of his humanity is highlighted by his avoidance of introspection. He is not given to analysis, whether self-analysis or the analysis of others. He strives to record and understand what he has observed. He regularly fails to understand, as we all do, and sometimes, defeated by what he has observed, he indulges his sense of superiority, as we all do. But he is not convincing when he does so. I find Ibn Faḍlān the most honest of authors writing in the classical Arabic tradition. His humanity and honesty keep this text fresh and alive for each new generation of readers fortunate to share in its treasures.

My earlier comparison with Kipling is instructive in other ways. Like so much of Kipling's work, for example, the nature of what might loosely be referred to as the imperial experience is at the heart also of Ibn Faḍlān's account—nowhere more acutely, perhaps, than when he is bested in a basic legal disputation (*munāẓarah*) by the Bulghār king or when a Bāshghird tribesman notices our author watching him eating a louse and provocatively declares it a delicacy. And just as Kipling's English mirrors the wit and pace of the table talk enjoyed in the Punjab Club, Ibn Faḍlān's Arabic may perhaps mirror the conversational idioms of his intended audience (or audiences). There is mystery here though. Ibn Faḍlān's audience remains as elusive as do he and the members of the mission, for his work disappears completely without a trace until, several centuries later, the geographer and lexicographer Yāqūt quotes it on his visit to Marw and Khwārazm. In Islamic scholarship, for an author to be read was for that author to be reproduced and quoted. There is no indication that Ibn Faḍlān's work was ever read before Yāqūt!

Turmoil

The world Ibn Faḍlān lived in and traveled through was in turmoil. The caliphal court, the treasury, the vizierate, the provinces, Baghdad's population, religious sectarianism—everything was in a state of upheaval. In Ibn Faḍlān's account we read of the strange surprises and uncustomary peoples he encountered, but he says almost nothing about Baghdad. As Baghdad and the caliphal court provide the religio-political context for the mission, no matter how eastward looking it may be, it is worth visiting Baghdad in the early fourth/tenth century.

Baghdad was the Abbasid capital founded by Caliph al-Manṣūr in 145/762, with its Round City known as the City of Peace (*Madīnat al-Salām*), a Qur'anic echo at its spiritual heart. The Baghdad of the early fourth/tenth century is the Baghdad of al-Muqtadir's reign. At the age of thirteen, al-Muqtadir was the youngest of the Abbasids to become caliph, and he remained caliph for some twenty-four years, with two minor interruptions totaling three days.

A period of stability and possibly even prosperity, one might imagine—but not according to modern scholarship, which views al-Muqtadir's caliphate as an unmitigated disaster, a period when the glorious achievements of his ancestors such as Hārūn al-Rashīd were completely undone.[2] State and caliphal treasuries were bedeviled by chronic lack of funds, with variable revenues from tax and trade. Caliphs and their viziers were constantly caught short of ready money. The fortunes of the recent caliphs had teetered constantly on the brink of bankruptcy.

Upon al-Muqtadir's accession to the caliphate, the rule of al-Muktafī (289–95/902–8) had witnessed a revival in the establishment of caliphal control. The western provinces, Syria and Egypt, had been brought into line, the Qarmaṭians had been defeated by Waṣīf ibn Sawārtakīn the Khazar (294/906–7), and the coffers of the treasury were adequately stocked, to the sum of 15 million dinars.[3]

During al-Muqtadir's caliphate, however, the center once again began to lose its grip on the periphery. Egypt became the private preserve of the rival Faṭimid caliphate, Syria began to enjoy the protection of the Kurdish Ḥamdanid dynasty, and the Qarmaṭian threat erupted once more, in a series of daring raids on cities and caravans, culminating in the theft of the Black Stone from the Kaaba in 317/930, by the Qarmaṭian chieftain Abū Ṭāhir Sulaymān. The eastern provinces had already consolidated the autonomy of their rule. Armenia and Azerbaijan had become the exclusive domains of the caliphally appointed governor Muḥammad ibn Abī l-Sāj al-Afshīn, until his death in 288/901. Transoxania and, by 287/900, Khurasan were under Samanid rule, and Sīstān was the seat of the Ṣaffarids (247–393/861–1003), founded by the coppersmith Yaʿqūb ibn al-Layth, a frontier warrior (*mutaṭawwiʿ*) fighting the unbelievers to extend the rule of Islam.

In 309/921, the year the Volga mission left Baghdad, al-Muqtadir's reign did enjoy some military success, when Mu'nis, the supreme commander of the caliphal armies, was invested with the governorship of Egypt and Syria, and the Samanids gained an important victory over the Daylamites of Ṭabaristān and killed al-Ḥasan ibn al-Qāsim's governor of Jurjān, the redoubtable Daylamite warlord Līlī ibn al-Nuʿmān, near Ṭūs, an event to which Ibn Faḍlān refers (§4).

The treasury's fiscal and mercantile revenues were heavily dependent on the success of the caliphal army, and no stability could be guaranteed. Apparently al-Muqtadir did not care in the least about stability: he is reputed to have squandered more than seventy million dinars.[4]

The dazzling might and splendor of the imperial Baghdad of al-Muqtadir's reign were fabulously encapsulated in his palace complexes. I like in particular the spectacular Arboreal Mansion. This mansion housed a tree of eighteen branches of silver and gold standing in a pond of limpid water. Birds of gold and silver, small and large, perched on the twigs. The branches would move, and their leaves would move as if stirred by the wind. The birds would tweet, whistle, and coo. On either side of the mansion were arranged fifteen automata, knights on horseback, who performed a cavalry maneuver. The lavishness of this craftsmanship and the ingenuity of its engineering match the opulence of the caliphal architectural expenditure for which al-Muqtadir was rightly famed. The Arboreal Mansion was just one of the many awe-inspiring sights of the caliphal complex (which included a zoo, a lion house, and an elephant enclosure) on the left bank of the Tigris: one observer reckoned it to be the size of the town of Shiraz.

Al-Muqtadir remained caliph for many years, and his longevity was accompanied by a decline in administrative consistency. Fourteen different administrators held the office of vizier during the period. This was one of the secrets behind the length of al-Muqtadir's rule: he, with the complicity of his bureaucracy, was following the precedent set by Hārūn al-Rashīd when, in 187/803, Hārūn so spectacularly and inexplicably removed the Barmakid family from power. The financial expedient of *muṣādarah* ("mulcting": the confiscation of private ministerial fortunes, a procedure usually accompanied by torture and beating) contributed to these changes, with courtly conspiracy and collusion the order of the day. We have an example of this in Ibn Faḍlān's account, for the funds to cover the construction of the fort in Bulghār territory were to be acquired from the sale of an estate owned by a deposed vizier, Ibn al-Furāt (§§3, 5).

Baghdad, with its population of between a quarter and half a million people in the fourth/tenth century, was the world's largest consumer of luxury goods, and trade was buoyant, but it was also a city on the brink of lawlessness and anarchy. It was poorly managed, food supplies were unreliable, famine was a regular occurrence, and prices were high. There were sporadic outbreaks of disease, largely because of the floods occasioned by municipal neglect of the irrigation system.

Factionalism was commonplace, and religious animosities, especially those between the Shiʿi community and the Ḥanbalite Sunnis, under the energetic direction of the theologian and traditionist al-Ḥasan ibn ʿAlī ibn Khalaf al-Barbahārī (d. 329/941), frequently erupted into violence. Although doctrinally quietist and sternly opposed to formal political rebellion, the Ḥanbalites, followers of Aḥmad ibn Ḥanbal (d. 241/855), did not disregard divergent expressions of Islamic belief or public displays of moral laxity. They took to the streets of Baghdad on several occasions to voice their disapproval of the corruption of the times. The great jurist, exegete, and historian al-Ṭabarī (d. 310/923) is thought to have incurred their wrath when he pronounced a compromise verdict on a theological dispute concerning the precise implications of Q Isrāʾ 17:79:

> Strive through the night—as an offering in hope that your Lord may raise you to a praiseworthy place.

This verse had been adopted by al-Barbahārī as a slogan, following the realist and anthropomorphic exegesis of it advocated by his teacher, al-Marwazī (d. 275/888). According to the Ḥanbalites, the verse declared that God would physically place Muḥammad on His throne on Judgment Day—anything less was tantamount to heresy. According to several sources, Ḥanbalite animosity to al-Ṭabarī persisted until his death, when a mob gathered at his home and prevented a public funeral being held in his honor. Al-Ṭabarī was buried in his home, under cover of darkness.

Ḥanbalite agitation was at its most violent in 323/935, when the caliph al-Rāḍī (r. 322–29/934–40) was compelled formally to declare Ḥanbalism a heresy and to exclude the Ḥanbalites from the Islamic community.

And then the authorities had al-Ḥallāj to contend with. Abū l-Mughīth al-Ḥusayn ibn Manṣūr, known as al-Ḥallāj, "the Wool-Carder," was a charismatic Sufi visionary. In the markets of Baghdad he preached a message of God as the One Truth, the Only Desire. He installed a replica of the Kaaba in his house and passed the night in prayer in graveyards. He appealed to the populace to kill him and save him from God, and, in a fateful encounter in the Mosque of al-Manṣūr in Baghdad, he is said to have exclaimed, "I am the Truth." In other words, he shouted, he had no other identity than God.

The administration was terrified of the revolutionary appeal of al-Ḥallāj and considered him a threat to the stability of the empire. He was arrested and an inquisition held. His main opponents were Ibn al-Furāt and Ḥāmid ibn al-ʿAbbās, both of whom feature in Ibn Faḍlān's account. (It was one of Ibn al-Furāt's estates that was to fund the building of the Bulghār fort, and Ḥāmid ibn al-ʿAbbās provided the mission with a letter for the king of the Bulghārs.) It was a singular event to see both men in agreement in their opposition to al-Ḥallāj. They so hated one another that, when Ibn al-Furāt had been accused of financial corruption and removed from the vizierate, Ḥāmid, who was to replace him, was restrained from a vicious attempt to pull out Ibn al-Furāt's beard! Al-Ḥallāj was executed on March 26, 922, two months before the mission reached the Bulghārs.[5]

It was from this "City of Peace" that the embassy departed, following the Khurasan highway, but the first leg of their journey was fraught with danger. They made their way to Rayy, the commercial capital of al-Jibāl province. In military terms, this was one of the most hotly contested cities in the whole region. In 311/919, two years before the departure of the mission, Ibn Faḍlān's patron Muḥammad ibn Sulaymān had been killed in a failed attempt to oust the Daylamite Aḥmad ibn ʿAlī from control of the city. Aḥmad ibn ʿAlī was later formally invested by Baghdad as governor of Rayy (307–11/919–24). At the time of the mission, then, the caliphate, the Samanids, and the Zaydī Daylamites were engaged in constant struggle for control of the region.

There were other powerful local actors at work in the area, too. Ibn Abī l-Sāj, the governor of Azerbaijan, was a force to be reckoned with. So too was Ibn Qārin, the ruler of Firrīm and the representative of the Caspian Zaydī *dāʿī* al-Ḥasan ibn al-Qāsim. Al-Ḥasan ibn al-Qāsim was the successor to al-Uṭrūsh ("the Deaf") (d. 304/917), restorer of Zaydī Shiʿism in Ṭabaristān and Daylam. Both were powerful men hostile to Abbasids and Samanids. This is why Ibn Faḍlān notes, with some relief, that Līlī ibn Nuʿmān, a Daylamite warlord in the service of al-Uṭrūsh and al-Ḥasan ibn al-Qāsim, had been killed shortly before the embassy reached Nishapur (§4), and why he points out that, in Nishapur, they encountered a friendly face in Ḥammawayh Kūsā, Samanid field marshal of Khurasan. The mission thus made its way briskly through a dangerous region and, in order to proceed to Bukhara, successfully negotiated its first major natural obstacle, the Karakum desert.

Such was the world in which the caliphal envoys lived and against which Ibn Faḍlān would measure the peoples and persons he met on his way to the Volga.

Why?

Why did Caliph al-Muqtadir agree to the king's petition? What did the court seek to achieve? What were the motives behind the mission? The *khwārazm-shāh* in Kāth (Khwārazm) (§8) and the four chieftains of the Ghuzziyyah assembled by Atrak ibn al-Qaṭaghān (§33) are suspicious of Baghdad's interest in spreading Islam among the Bulghār. The Samanid emir shows no interest in the mission. He was still a teenager, after all (§5). Should we be suspicious too or emulate the teenage emir?

The king asked the caliph for instruction in Islamic law and ritual practice, a mosque and a *minbar* to declare his fealty to the caliph as part of the Friday prayer, and the construction of a fort. The Baghdad court's reasons for acceding to the request are not specified. There is no discussion in the account of the lucrative trade route that linked Baghdad, Bukhara, and Volga Bulgharia; of the emergence of the Bulghār market as a prime source of furs and slaves; or of the Viking lust for silver dirhams that largely fuelled the northern fur and slave trade. Yet there are hints. We learn of the political and religious unrest in Khurasan (bad for the secure passage of trade goods), of the autonomy of the Samanid emirate in Bukhara, and of how jealously the trade links between Bukhara, Khwārazm, and the Turks of the north were protected by the Samanid governor of Khwārazm.

Scholars have speculated on the motives of the mission. Was it intended somehow to bypass the Samanid emirate and secure the Bulghār market for Baghdad? International diplomacy did not exist in isolation but was in many ways the official handmaiden of mercantile relations. Trade was fundamental to the economies of the northern frontier and also a factor in the commission of the embassy: a fort, along the lines of Sarkel on the Don, would have provided the Muslims with a stronghold from which to resist the Khazars and control the flow of trade through the confluence of the Volga and the Kama and would have been a statement of Islamic presence in the area. Or is this speculation just the imposition on the fourth/tenth century of our own obsessions with economic viability?

For Shaban, this diplomatic adventure was a "full-fledged trade mission . . . a response to a combined approach by Jayhānī and the chief of the Bulghār." Shaban thinks the Volga mission was a cooperative venture between the Samanids and Abbasids masterminded by al-Jayhānī, an assertion for which there is no shred of evidence. He reasons that the Samanids needed allies to help control the Turkic tribes north of Khwārazm.[6]

Togan, who discovered the Mashhad manuscript in 1923, suggested that conversion to Islam as conceived and practiced by the caliphal court in such a distant outpost of the empire would have acted as a corrective to Qarmaṭian propaganda, to Zoroastrian prophecies of the collapse of the caliphate at the hands of the Majūs (a name, in Arabic texts of the period, for fire-worshippers, i.e., both Zoroastrians and Vikings!), and to Shiʿi missionary activity, and would have countered the spread of any of these influences among the already volatile Turkic tribes.[7] Togan was a Bashkir Bolshevik who had fallen out with Lenin over policies concerning Togan's native Tataristan and was living in exile in Iran. It is hardly surprising that he read the mission in such richly ideological terms.

According to one commentator, the court must have reasoned that, by controlling how the Volga Bulghārs observed Islamic ritual, it could control their polity, a position that owes more to modern notions of political Islam than to an understanding of the fourth/tenth century.[8]

Do we need to be so suspicious? Of course, the religious overtones of the king's petitions were sure to appeal to the caliph and his court. Here was a foreign ruler who had embraced Islam, requesting religious instruction, as well as the construction of a mosque and a *minbar* from which he could acknowledge the caliph's suzerainty, and seeking assistance against unspecified enemies, presumably the Khazars, although the Rus' always represented a threat.

The construction of a fort on the Volga bend would have followed the precedents set by both Rørik's hill-fort, built by the Rus', and Sarkel, built on the Don by the Byzantines for the Khazars.

It might be helpful to take a brief look at some disparate examples of the Christian ideology of trade, travel, warfare, and expansion. In 1433, Dom Manuel justifies the Portuguese voyages of discovery:

> not only with the intention that great fame and profit might follow to these kingdomes from the riches that there are therein, which were always possessed by the Moors, but so that the faith of Our Lord should be spread through more parts, and His Name known.[9]

Jonathan Riley-Smith has argued that religion and self-interest were inseparable in the outlook of the early Crusaders.[10] Stephen Greenblatt discusses the "formalism" of Columbus's "linguistic acts," and Margarita Zamora draws attention to the equal weight given spiritual and worldly (i.e., commercial) ambitions in the "Letter to the Sovereigns."[11] Christopher Hill has been the most persistent and persuasive exponent of the religiosity of the seventeenth-century Puritan worldview, in which every aspect of man's behavior is seen through a religious prism.[12] In the wake of the feting of William Dampier upon the publication of his *New Voyage round the World* in 1697, the Royal Society urged seamen to greater scientific precision in their journals, "to improve the stock of knowledge in the world and hence improve the condition of mankind."[13] And by improving "the condition of mankind," we can savor the ambiguity between Enlightenment reason and the *mission civilatrice* that would come with conversion to Christianity.

It is muddle-headed to consider religious motives as mere justification for interference in "foreign" affairs. The caliphal court would not have known what we mean by these distinctions. Such a line of reasoning attempts to separate and differentiate between a mutually inclusive set of notions: missionary activity, conversion, trade, and expansion of the caliphate.

What I am advocating is respect for the integrity of Ibn Faḍlān's account. To be sure, it is in many ways a bizarre book. It has no textual analogues, no other works from the third/ninth or fourth/tenth centuries we can compare it with. Its obsession with eyewitness testimony, connected ultimately with the practice of, and requirements for, giving witness in a court of law, is almost pathological. It contains many wonderful encounters, conversations, dialogues, and formal audiences—and we hear so many non-Muslims speak, from tribesmen of the Ghuzziyyah and the Bulghār king to the Rūs who mocks Ibn Faḍlān for the primitiveness of his religious observances. On top of all this, it is a cracking good read. I hope others enjoy reading it as much as I have enjoyed editing and translating it and, along the way, kept alive my boyhood love of adventure stories.

A Note on the Text

The Texts

The Arabic text of Ibn Faḍlān's book exists in two formats: as part of a manuscript contained in the library attached to the Mausoleum of the imam ʿAlī al-Riḍā in Mashhad, Iran, discovered in 1923 by A. Zeki Validi Togan; and as five quotations in Yāqūt's *Geographical Dictionary* (*Muʿjam al-buldān*).[14] The relationship between the Arabic of the Mashhad manuscript and Yāqūt's quotations is not clear.

I. The Mashhad Manuscript

The version of the text contained in the Mashhad manuscript is part of a volume containing four works donated to the library as a *waqf* bequest in 1067/1656–57 by a certain Ibn Khātūn. It contains 212 folios, is written in a clear *naskh* hand, nineteen lines to each folio, and is undated. There is no indication of the identity of the individual who commissioned the compilation. The manuscript is incomplete: the text of Ibn Faḍlān contains the first few lines of an account of the Khazars, but the last extant folio is damaged, and some material has clearly been lost. Furthermore, the last extant folios of the manuscript, containing Ibn Faḍlān's description of the Rūs, have been severely damaged and are illegible in many places.

The manuscript contains copies of: two travelogue epistles by the globetrotter and poet Abū Dulaf Misʿar ibn Muhalhil al-Khazrajī (fl. 331–41/943–52);[15] an excerpt from Ibn al-Faqīh al-Hamadhānī's (fl. late 3rd/9th c.) *Kitāb al-buldān* (*Book of Places*); the account of Ibn Faḍlān. It is evident, however, that the general geographical focus of the volume is east of Baghdad, in Khurasan, Transoxania, and Central Asia.

I have not examined the manuscript in person. Three photographic reproductions are available in: *Majmūʿ fī l-jughrāfiyā mimmā allafahu Ibn al-Faqīh wa-Ibn Faḍlān wa-Abū Dulaf al-Khazrajī*, edited by Fuat Sezgin, with Mazen Amawi, Carl Ehrig-Eggert, and Eckhard Neubauer (1994); in Kovalevskiĭ, *Kniga*

(1956); and in Czeglédy, "Zur Meschheder Handschrift" (1950–1). I have relied principally on Kovalevskiĭ's reproduction.

The Mashhad copy of Ibn Faḍlān's book is messy. It displays the standard avoidance of *hamzah*, disregard for the rules governing the use of numbers—as far as I can see only a few of the numbers given in the manuscript are grammatically correct—and the cheerful neglect of whether verbs in the imperfective should, for example, be dotted as third person masculine or feminine singular or first person plural. There are also occasions when the syntax of the text copied in the manuscript may raise an eyebrow of the reader expecting *fuṣḥā* Arabic. And this is to say nothing of the numerous foreign words and names with which Ibn Faḍlān's account is so liberally scattered.

The section of the manuscript containing Ibn Faḍlān's account has been edited numerous times and has been the subject of many studies. The editions of Togan, *Reisebericht* (1939), and al-Dahhān, *Risālah* (1959), are especially important and should be used with the articles by Ritter, "Zum Text von Ibn Faḍlān's Reisebericht" (1942), Dunlop, "Zeki Validi's Ibn Faḍlān" (1947–52), and Czeglédy, "Zur Meschheder Handschrift" (1950–1). Also relevant is the extensive commentary by Kovalevskiĭ, *Kniga*.[16]

II. Yāqūt's Muʿjam al-buldān

The geographical dictionary of Yāqūt (d. 626/1229) includes excerpts from Ibn Faḍlān's book in six lemmata:

1. Itil: Wüstenfeld 1.112.16–113.15 = Mashhad 208a.4–208b.9 → §68 of the present edition.
2. Bāshghird: Wüstenfeld 1.468.17–469.15 = Mashhad 203a.7–203b.3 → §§37–38 of the present edition.
3. Bulghār: Wüstenfeld 1.723.6–19 = Mashhad 196b.18–197a.12; 1.723.19–725.4 = Mashhad 203b.5–204b.7; 1.725.5–726.16 = 205b.1–206a.12; 1.726.16–727.1 = 206b.2–10; 1.727.2–3 = 206b.14–16; 1.727.3–10 = 206b.17–207a.5; 1.727.10–12 = 207a.9–11; 1.727.12–13 = 207a.16–17; 1.727.14–21 = 207b.4–11; → §§1–4, 39–44, 48, 51, 53–56, 59, 61–63 respectively of the present edition.
4. Khazar: Wüstenfeld 2.436.20–440.6 (only 2.438.11–14 matches the extant text in the Mashhad manuscript) = Mashhad 212b.15–19 → §90 of the present edition (and §§90A–98 of the Khazar section appended to the present edition).

5. Khwārazm: Wüstenfeld 2.484.10–485.23 = Mashhad 198a.17–199a.3 → §§8–11 of the present edition.
6. Rūs: Wüstenfeld 2.834.18–840.12 = Mashhad 209b.17–212b.15 → §§74–89 of the present edition.

I have not consulted any manuscripts of Yāqūt's work but have relied exclusively on Wüstenfeld's edition.

III. The Mashhad Manuscript and Yāqūt Compared

Yāqūt frequently remarks that he has abbreviated Ibn Faḍlān's account, occasionally criticizes him, and expresses disbelief in his version of events. He stresses that his quotation of Ibn Faḍlān's passage on the Rūs is accurate and implies that it is a verbatim quotation. This raises, in my mind, the possibility that Yāqūt may not be quoting Ibn Faḍlān so accurately in the other five lemmata. And a close comparison between the passage on the Rūs in both sources reveals that, here too, Yāqūt's quotation may not, strictly speaking, be verbatim but may have been subjected to modification, paraphrasing, and rewording. (I say "may have been" because it is likely that Yāqūt was quoting from an ancestor to the actual Mashhad manuscript.) Furthermore, on two occasions, in the lemma devoted to the Khazars, Yāqūt confuses quotations drawn from al-Iṣṭakhrī's mid-fourth/tenth century work *Kitāb al-Masālik wa-l-mamālik* (*The Book of Highways and Kingdoms*) with the quotation he took from Ibn Faḍlān.

When the Arabic of the Mashhad manuscript is compared with the Arabic of the same passages recorded by Yāqūt, the differences between them, in their linguistic chastity, are evident. Of course, I have not consulted the manuscripts of Yāqūt's text, so my impression may be the result of the editorial work carried out by Wüstenfeld, though the differences comprise syntax as well as orthography and grammar. My impression—and I say this without having completed a thorough analysis of the data and as someone who is not a specialist in historical linguistics—is that the closest analogue to the Arabic of the Mashhad manuscript is a nonformal type of Arabic that often bears comparison with that variety of the language generally denoted as "Middle Arabic."

I am unable to say whether or not the Arabic of the Mashhad manuscript represents the Arabic of Ibn Faḍlān. Despite this, my working hypothesis has been that the Mashhad manuscript may represent a version of the text written (or dictated) in an idiom (perhaps spoken) that is not a fully inflected *ʿArabiyyah*. The syntax is often loose—indeed, it can be quite "rough and ready." Several words suggest an idiomatic and spoken usage, such as *wāfā* in the sense of to arrive, *jāza* used with the meaning of *jā'a*, *laysa* as an undeclined negative, and *ṣāra* for *sāra*.

Because the Arabic of the Mashhad manuscript is rough and ready and the Arabic of Yāqūt's versions is formal and chaste, editors, confronted by divergences between the two sources, tend to allow Yāqut's versions to dominate the Mashhad manuscript. Editions (and translations) of the manuscript are thus repeatedly altered and replaced or supplemented by the readings of Yāqūt. The result is that the versions of Ibn Faḍlān's book in circulation are ones that, whenever possible, jettison the Mashhad manuscript in favor of Yāqūt's versions. So, for all the attention it has attracted from scholars, the Mashhad manuscript has not really been viewed as anything other than a poor substitute for a lost, more pristine original, shards of which can be gleaned from Yāqūt's quotations.

When editing the work and working from the assumption that the Mashhad manuscript may be closer to the Arabic that Ibn Faḍlān wrote than are Yāqūt's quotations, I have often found myself concluding that Ibn Faḍlān was indeed using an informal type of Arabic, one less chaste than the rarified *ʿArabiyyah* we expect from classical writers. In fact I found myself wondering what precisely standard Arabic usage might have been for an official such as Ibn Faḍlān, writing in the early fourth/tenth century. In other words, I found myself asking, does the Mashhad manuscript preserve a type of unpolished and private-life writing that we sometimes encounter in Arabic?[17] Or does this use of a non-formal Arabic indicate that Ibn Faḍlān was not a proper scholar but rather an individual who wrote on the margins of scholarship? Should we study this work as an early (fourth/tenth century) example of Middle Arabic?

IV. The Present Edition

In view of these intuitions, my approach to the Mashhad manuscript is informed by the conviction that it warrants serious and close attention. My edition of the manuscript—note that this is an edition of the manuscript and not a transcription—does not automatically emend the Arabic of the manuscript in favor of the Arabic given by Yāqūt or in preference for proper usage. As a rule of thumb, if I have the sense that the Arabic works, however loosely that working may be in terms of syntax, I have let it stand. I have not automatically presumed the ubiquity of mistakes in reading the skeleton or the diacritical pointing of a word (*taṣḥīf*) or the corruption of words or phrases by altering the skeleton (*taḥrīf*).

I first tried to mount a defense of the manuscript reading; if I concluded that the pointing or the wording of the manuscript worked, I would let it stand. I have, however, tried not to let any obvious grammatical or syntactical howlers remain in the edited text (even when they represent standard Middle Arabic practice). In such cases I have erred on the side of caution and noted in the apparatus when the manuscript has been corrected. I have followed standard modern Arabic orthographical practices. All the *hamzah*s and *alif*s missing from the manuscript, for example, have been added.

Although I have endeavored to keep the apparatus as light as possible, and while the apparatus does not list every instance of the usual slips and mistakes encountered in manuscripts, such as undotted or incorrectly dotted verbal prefixes, loose usage in writing numerals, and so on,[18] the apparatus does record many of the instances when Yāqūt's versions differ from the Mashhad manuscript and those occasions when I have felt it necessary to normalize the syntax (e.g., when chaste Arabic usage requires the subjunctive and not, as is common in Middle Arabic, the imperfective after the conjunction *ḥattā*).

In my use of Yāqūt's versions I have made one important exception—in the passage on the Rūs, when the manuscript is lacunose, in order to fill in the gaps of the Mashhad manuscript I relied on Yāqūt's Arabic more than was the case for his other lemmata. In such cases, I have included in the apparatus the lacunose reading of the Mashhad manuscript. And for the sake of completeness, I added a supplement to the truncated Mashhad manuscript in the form of the continuation of the passage on the Khazars as given by Yāqūt in his *Muʿjam al-buldān*. In my edition and translation, I make it clear that this is so by ending the text when the manuscript ends and then repeating the passage from the manuscript in the continuation of the passage I have taken from Yāqūt; see §§90 and 90A–98.

The current edition of Ibn Faḍlān's book conforms to the standards set by the Library of Arabic Literature. Therefore, in view of the nonformal Arabic of the manuscript, my edition has basically become a hybrid—it recognizes, to a limited extent, the nonformal features of the Arabic of the text contained in the Mashhad manuscript but corrects many of these features in order to produce a modernized version of the work that does not violate completely what we expect of *fuṣḥā* Arabic. The majority of my corrections has been recorded in the apparatus, in order that the linguist interested in nonformal Arabic and in Middle Arabic can follow the choices I have made. The scholar in me, however, could not let the situation rest there. On the website of the Library of Arabic

Literature, I make available an alternate edition of the Mashhad manuscript that does not correct the grammatical and syntactical peculiarities (e.g., I have not corrected any of the numbers) and preserves many of the orthographical practices of pre-modern Arabic (especially the absence of *hamzah*, the writing of terminal *yā'*, the regular omission of long *ālif*, the inconsistent dotting of *tā' marbūṭah*, etc.). I have also appended to this critical edition a short list of the features of the manuscript consistent with the characteristics of Middle Arabic. I hope that one day the Arabic of the Mashhad manuscript will secure the attention of a specialist. In the interim, I trust I have made enough materials available to the community.

For the sake of completeness and in order to make clear the differences between Yāqūt's versions and the work as copied in the Mashhad manuscript, the Arabic texts of Yāqūt's quotations from Ibn Faḍlān are reproduced from Wüstenfeld's edition, translated into English and made available on the Library of Arabic Literature website; I repeat, I have not consulted any of the manuscripts of Yāqūt's *Mu'jam al-buldān* but have relied instead on Wüstenfeld's edition. A concordance of manuscript folios, al-Dahhān's pagination, and the paragraph numbering of the current edition is also posted on the website. Finally, I make available on the website a shortened version of the text, an experiment in reconstructing what I like to imagine may represent the logbook that I think Ibn Faḍlān might have kept while on his travels.

Names

One of the wonderful things about Ibn Faḍlan's account is that we get to hear about so many unfamiliar places and, in the process, are introduced to many Turkic terms transcribed (presumably aurally and phonetically) into Arabic, and to listen to so many non-Arabs speak, via the intermediary of the translator(s) Ibn Faḍlān used. Of course, this abundance of transcriptions is rarely graphically straightforward.

There is confusion surrounding the "correct" form of the toponyms and Turkic titles in which the text abounds. Whenever possible in my edition I have relied on the many studies of Turkic names and titles by scholars such as Peter Golden. The onomastic challenge is especially acute in the riverine topography of the journey from the Ghuzziyyah to the Bulghārs: §§34–38. A uniform solution to these names proved impossible, so I decided to apply a principle of minimal intervention. When the identity of the river proposed by scholars seemed close to the form of the word as written by the Mashhad scribe I accepted the reconstructed identification but made as few changes as possible to the form of the name given in the manuscript. The principle of minimal intervention means, for example, that the word *swḥ* becomes *sūḥ* and not *sūkh*, and *bājāʿ* does not become *bājāgh*. Please note, however, that *ḥ*j* became *jaykh* (the "*" is used here and in a few other cases to represent an undotted consonant in the manuscript that could be read as *bāʾ*, *tāʾ*, *thāʾ*, *nūn*, or *yāʾ*). I have avoided, wherever possible, the addition of vowels to the consonantal skeleton of these names in Arabic. On one occasion I could not decide whether the word *smwr* masked *s-mūr* or *s-mawr*, so I let it stand.

This procedure of minimal intervention is not an argument for the onomastic accuracy of the manuscript. There has undoubtedly been considerable corruption in transmission, and the scribe of the Mashhad manuscript is not always as reliable as we might like. The procedure is simply a not very subtle solution to an impasse. I use the Extended Glossary of Names and Places posted on the Library of Arabic Literature website to discuss Turkic terms and names and to survey the identifications offered by scholars.

In the two cases in which we are fortunate to have lemmata in Yāqūt's *Muʿjam al-buldān* (Itil and Arthakhushmīthan), I have adopted his orthography and vocalization.

The Translation

Ibn Faḍlan's text is brisk and characterized by narrative economy. I wanted my English to be the same. My translation aspires to lucidity and legibility. James E. McKeithen's excellent PhD thesis (Indiana University, 1979) will satisfy the reader in search of a crib of the Arabic. There are two other translations into English, by Richard N. Frye (2005) and by Paul Lunde and Caroline Stone (2012). They are both admirable in their way: Frye's is very useful for the studies he provides alongside the translation, and Lunde and Stone have produced a nicely readable version of the work. Both, however, effectively promote a version of Ibn Faḍlān's text dominated by Yāqūt's quotations.

I have also added to the translation some headers, toponyms, and ethnonyms that help identify the principal agents and locations of the action, including the Arabic title that introduces the passage on the Khazars taken from Yāqūt.

The Guide to Further Reading is intended to provide readers, students, and scholars interested in studying the work further with a representative catalogue of secondary scholarship on Ibn Faḍlān and his world. For ease of reference, it is therefore organized according to subject. I hope this will be a useful study aid to what can sometimes be a complicated bibliographical tumult.

I have also prepared two glossaries, one for the book and one for the Library of Arabic Literature website. The Extended Glossary on the website is intended as a repository of information that, in a publication intended for an academic audience, might be included in the form of annotations to the text. This approach has the added advantage of keeping to a minimum both the glossary for the book and the annotation to the translation. Each website glossary entry includes key references to the copious annotations provided by the scholars who have edited and/or translated the work. I hope that, in this way too, this version of the glossary can become a useful study aid.

Notes to the Introduction

1 *Relation*, 51.

2 Zetterstéen and Bosworth, "al-Muḳtadir," 542; Kennedy, *The Prophet and the Age of the Caliphates*, 188.

3 See Kennedy, *Prophet*, 187; Zetterstéen and Bosworth, "al-Muktafī."

4 Zetterstéen and Bosworth, "al-Muḳtadir."

5 Massignon and Gardet, "al-Ḥallādj̲," 102; Massignon, *Hallāj. Mystic and Martyr.*

6 Shaban, *Islamic History: A New Interpretation*, 2:149–51.

7 *Reisebericht*, 1939, xx-xxvii.

8 Bukharaev, *Islam in Russia*, 39.

9 Subrahmanyam, *The Career and Legend of Vasco da Gama*, 170.

10 Riley-Smith, "The State of Mind of Crusaders to the East, 1095–1300."

11 Greenblatt, *Marvelous Possessions*, 53–85; Zamora, "Christopher Columbus's 'Letter to the Sovereigns.'"

12 Hill, *The English Bible and the Seventeenth Century Revolution*, 34.

13 Edwards, *The Story of the Voyage*, 26–27.

14 There are also some passages translated into Persian and quoted in *Haft iqlīm* (*Seven Climes*) of Amīn Rāzī, from the late tenth/sixteenth century, and *ʿAjāʾib al-makhlūqāt* (*The Wonders of Creation*) of Najīb Hamdhānī (also known as Aḥmad Ṭūsī), from the second half of the eleventh/seventeenth century. They are not included in this study. The translation by Marius Canard, *Ibn Fadlân: Voyage*, renders some key passages into French.

15 On Abū Dulaf and his epistles, see V. Minorsky, "Abū Dulaf."

16 I have not been able to use this commentary because I do not read Russian.

17 See Reynolds (ed.), *Interpreting the Self*, for further discussion of this kind of private-life writing. Fragments of a diary covering the period 1 Shawwāl, 460–14 Dhu l-Qaʿdah, 461/3 August, 1068–4 September, 1069, written by an otherwise obscure scholar named Ibn al-Bannāʾ, have survived: see the translation by Makdisi, "Autograph Diary."

18 To have noted each and every divergence would have produced a cumbersome and tedious apparatus criticus. The reader who wants a list of all the idiosyncracies, errors, and slips will find them included in the diplomatic edition on the Library of Arabic Literature Web site and in the edition by Kmietowicz, Kmietowicz, and Lewicki, *Źródła arabskie do dziejów słowiańszczyzny*, 77–84.

Ibn Faḍlān's Route to the Volga

Route of journey with stop

Lake with river

BULGHĀR Tribe

Karakum Landscape

0 200 400 600 800 km

Design: James Montgomery
Cartography: Martin Grosch

كتاب أحمد بن فضلان

١ هذا كتاب أحمد بن فضلان بن العبّاس بن راشد بن حمّاد مولى محمّد بن سليمان رسول المقتدر إلى ملك الصقالبة[١] يذكر فيه ما شاهد في بلد الترك والخزر والروس والصقالبة والباشْغِرْد وغيرهم من اختلاف[٢] مذاهبهم وأخبار ملوكهم وأحوالهم في كثير من أمورهم.

٢ قال أحمد بن فضلان لمّا وصل كتاب الحسن بن يِلْطَوار[٣] ملك الصقالبة إلى أمير المؤمنين المقتدر يسأله فيه البعثة إليه ممّن يفقّهه في الدين ويعرّفه شرائع الإسلام ويبني له مسجدا وينصب له منبرا ليقيم عليه الدعوة له في بلده وجميع مملكته ويسأله بناء حصن يتحصّن فيه من الملوك المخالفين له أجيب[٤] إلى ما سأل من ذلك وكان السفيرَ فيه[٥] نذير الحرميّ فنُدبتُ أنا لقراءة الكتاب[٦] عليه وتسليم ما أُهدي إليه والإشراف على الفقهاء والمعلّمين وسبّب له بالمال المحمول إليه لبناء ما ذكرناه وللجراية على الفقهاء والمعلّمين على الضيعة المعروفة بأرْثَخُشْمِيثَن[٧] من أرض خوارزم من ضياع ابن الفرات.

٣ وكان الرسولَ إلى المقتدر من صاحب الصقالبة رجل يقال له عبد الله بن باشْتُوا الخزريّ والرسول من جهة السلطان سوسن الرسّيّ مولى نذير الحرميّ وتَكِين التُرْكيّ وبارِس الصقلابيّ وأنا معهم على ما ذكرت فسلّمت إليه الهدايا له ولامرأته ولأولاده وإخوته وقوّاده وأدوية كان كتب إلى نذير يطلبها.

٤ فرحلنا من مدينة السلام يوم الخميس لإحدى عشرة ليلة خلت من صفر سنة تسع وثلاثمائة فأقمنا بالنَهْرَوان يوما واحدا ورحلنا مجدّين حتّى وافينا الدَسْكَرة فأقمنا

---

١ الجملة (إلى ملك الصقالبة) مكتوبة في الحاشية. ٢ الأصل: اخلاف. ٣ الأصل: بلطوار؛ ياقوت: ألمس بن شلكي بلطوار؛ الدهّان: ألمش بن شلكي يلطوار. ٤ ياقوت: فأجيب. ٥ ياقوت: السفير له. ٦ الأصل: فندت انا لقراة الكتاب. ٧ الأصل: ارنخشمثين.

Mission to the Volga

This is the written account of Aḥmad ibn Faḍlān ibn al-ʿAbbās ibn Rāshid[1] ibn Ḥammād, the envoy of al-Muqtadir to the king of the Ṣaqālibah. His patron was Muḥammad ibn Sulaymān.[2] It records his observations in the realm of the Turks, the Khazars, the Rūs, the Ṣaqālibah, the Bāshghird, and other peoples. It also includes reports of their various customs and ways of living, their kings, and many other related matters, too. 1

Aḥmad ibn Faḍlān said:[3] In the letter of al-Ḥasan, son of Yilṭawār, the king of the Ṣaqālibah, which al-Muqtadir the Commander of the Faithful received, the king petitioned al-Muqtadir to send people to instruct him in law and acquaint him with the rules of Islam according to the sharia, and to construct a mosque and build a *minbar* from which he could proclaim al-Muqtadir's name throughout his kingdom. He also beseeched him to build a fort to protect him against the kings who opposed him. His requests were granted. 2

Baghdad

The representative of the king of the Ṣaqālibah at court was Nadhīr al-Ḥaramī.[4] I, Aḥmad ibn Faḍlān, was delegated to read al-Muqtadir's letter to him, to present him with the official gifts designated, and to supervise the jurists and instructors. Nadhīr identified a fixed sum of money to be brought to him, to cover the construction costs and to pay the jurists and instructors. These expenses were to be covered by Arthakhushmīthan, one of the estates of Ibn al-Furāt in Khwārazm. The envoy from the king of the Ṣaqālibah to the caliph was a man named ʿAbdallāh ibn Bāshtū al-Khazarī. The caliph's envoy was Sawsan al-Rassī. Sawsan's patron was Nadhīr al-Ḥaramī. Takīn al-Turkī, Bārs al-Ṣaqlābī, and I accompanied him. As I said, I was charged with the following responsibilities: I presented him with the official gifts for him, his wife, children, brothers, and commanders. I also handed over the medication that the king had requested, in writing, from Nadhīr.[5] 3

We traveled from Baghdad, City of Peace, on Thursday, the twelfth of Safar, 309 [June 21, 921]. We stayed one day in Nahrawān, then rode hard until we reached al-Daskarah, where we stayed three days. Then we traveled without delay or diversion and came to Ḥulwān, where we stayed two days. 4

بها ثلاثة أيّام ثمّ رحلنا قاصدين لا نكون على شيء حتّى صرنا إلى حُلْوَانَ فأقمنا بها يومين وسرنا منها إلى قِرْمِيسِينَ فأقمنا بها يومين ثمّ رحلنا فسرنا حتّى وصلنا إلى هَمَذَانَ فأقمنا بها ثلاثة أيّام ثمّ سرنا حتّى قدمنا سَاوَةَ فأقمنا بها يومين ومنها إلى الرَيّ فأقمنا بها أحد عشر يوما ننتظر أحمد بن عليّ أخا صعلوك لأنّه كان بخُوار الريّ ثمّ رحلنا إلى خوار الريّ فأقمنا بها ثلاثة أيّام ثمّ رحلنا إلى سِمْنَانَ ثمّ منها إلى الدامَغان وصادفنا بها ابن قارن من قِبَل الداعي فتنكّرنا في القافلة وسرنا مجدّين حتّى قدمنا نيسابور وقد قُتل لِيلي بن نعمان فأصبنا بها حَمَّوَيْه كُوسا صاحب جيش خراسان ثمّ رحلنا إلى سَرَخْسَ ثمّ منها إلى مَرْوَ ثمّ منها إلى قُشْمِهَانَ وهي طَرَف مفازة آمُل فأقمنا بها ثلاثة أيّام نُزيح الجمال لدخول المفازة ثمّ قطعنا المفازة إلى آمل ثمّ عبرنا جَيْحُون وصرنا إلى آفرن[1] رباط طاهر بن عليّ.

ثمّ رحلنا إلى بَيْكَنْدَ ثمّ دخلنا بخارى وصرنا إلى الجيهانيّ وهو كاتب أمير خراسان ٥
وهو يدعى بخراسان الشيخ العميد فتقدّم بأخذ دار لنا وأقام لنا رجلا يقضي حوائجنا ويريح عللَنا في كلّ ما نريد فأقمنا أيّاما ثمّ استأذن لنا على نصر بن أحمد فدخلنا إليه وهو غلام أمرد فسلّمنا عليه بالإمرة وأمرنا بالجلوس فكان أوّل ما بدأنا به أن قال كيف خلّفتم مولاي أمير المؤمنين أطال الله بقاءه وسلامته في نفسه وفتيانه وأوليائه فقلنا بخير قال زاده الله خيرا ثمّ قرئ الكتاب عليه بتسليم أرْثَخُشميثن[2] من الفضل بن موسى النصرانيّ وكيل ابن الفرات وتسليمها إلى أحمد بن موسى الخوارزميّ وإنفاذنا والكتاب إلى صاحبه بخوارزم يتْرُكَ العَرَض لنا والكتاب بباب التُرْك بِبَذْرَقَتِنا وتَرْك العرض لنا فقال وأين أحمد بن موسى فقلنا خلّفناه بمدينة السلام ليخرج خلفنا لخمسة أيّام فقال سمعا وطاعة لما أمر به مولاي أمير المؤمنين أطال الله بقاءه.

قال واتّصل الخبر بالفضل بن موسى النصرانيّ وكيل ابن الفرات فأعمل الحيلة ٦
في أمر أحمد بن موسى وكتب إلى عمّال المُعاوِن بطريق خراسان من جند سرخس إلى بيكند أن أذكوا العيون على أحمد بن موسى الخوارزميّ في الخانات والمراصد وهو

---

١ كما في الأصل. ٢ الأصل: ارتخشمثين.

From there we traveled to Qirmīsīn, where we stayed another two days, and next arrived at Hamadhān, where we stayed three days. We traveled to Sāwah and, after two days, on to Rayy, where we stayed eleven days, until Aḥmad ibn ʿAlī, the brother of Ṣuʿlūk, had left Khuwār al-Rayy. Then we traveled to Khuwār al-Rayy itself and three days later to Simnān, then on to al-Dāmghān, where our caravan happened to encounter Ibn Qārin, who was preaching on behalf of the *dāʿī*. We concealed our identity and hurried to Nishapur, where we met Ḥammawayh Kūsā, the field marshal of Khurasan. Līlī ibn Nuʿmān had just been killed. Then we proceeded to Sarakhs, Marw, and Qushmahān, at the edge of the Āmul desert. We stayed three days there and changed camels for the desert journey. We crossed the desert to Āmul and then reached Āfr*n, the outpost of Ṭāhir ibn ʿAlī, on the other side of the Jayḥūn.[6]

We traveled via Baykand to Bukhara, where we went straight to al-Jayhānī, 5
the chancellor of the emir of Khurasan, known there as the chief *shaykh*. *Bukhara*
He had ordered a residence for us and had appointed someone to attend to all our needs and concerns and make sure that we experienced no difficulty in getting what we wanted. After a few days, he arranged an audience with Naṣr ibn Aḥmad. We discovered that he was still a boy and did not even have a beard. We greeted him as befits an emir. He commanded us to be seated. His very first words were: "How was my patron, the Commander of the Faithful, when you left him? May God give him long life and cherish him, his retinue, and his spiritual companions." "He was well," we replied. He said, "May God increase his well-being!" The letter was then read out to him. It gave the following instructions: the estate of Arthakhushmīthan was to be handed over by al-Faḍl ibn Mūsā al-Naṣrānī, Ibn al-Furāt's agent, to Aḥmad ibn Mūsā al-Khwārazmī; we were to be provided with funds, with a letter to his governor in Khwārazm ordering him not to hinder us, and with a letter to the garrison at the Gate of the Turks, who were to provide us with an escort and not detain us. "Where is Aḥmad ibn Mūsā?" he asked. "We left the City of Peace without him, and he set off four days later,"[7] we replied and he said, "I hear and obey the commands of my patron, the Commander of the Faithful, may God give him long life!"

Ibn Faḍlān said: al-Faḍl ibn Mūsā al-Naṣrānī, Ibn al-Furāt's agent, got wind 6
of this and came up with a plan to deal with Aḥmad ibn Mūsā. He wrote to the deputies of the superintendent of the Khurasan highway, in the military

رجل من صفته ونعته فمن ظفر به فليعتلقه إلى أن يَرِد عليه كتابنا بالمُثْلة[١] فأُخِذَ بمرو واعتُقِل وأقمنا نحن ببخارى ثمانية وعشرين يوما وقد كان الفضل بن موسى أيضا واطأ عبد الله بن باشتوا وغيره من أصحابنا يقولون إن أقمنا هجم الشتاء وفاتنا الدخول وأحمد بن موسى إذا وافانا[٢] لحق بنا.

٧ قال ورأيت الدراهم ببخارى ألوانا شتّى منها دراهم يقال لها الغِطْرِيفيّة وهي نحاس وشَبَه وصُفْر يؤخذ منها عدد بلا وزن مائة منها بدرهم فضّة وإذا شروطهم في مهور نسائهم تزوّج فلان بن فلان فلانة بنت فلان على كذا وكذا ألف درهم غطريفيّة وكذلك أيضا شراء عقارهم وشراء عبيدهم لا يذكرون غيرها من الدراهم ولهم دراهم أخرصفر وحده أربعون منها بِدانَقٍ ولهم أيضا دراهم صفر يقال لها السَمَرْقَنْديّة ستّة منها بدانق.

٨ فلمّا سمعت كلام عبد الله بن باشتوا وكلام غيره يحذّروني من هجوم الشتاء رحلنا من بخارا راجعين إلى النهر فتكارينا سفينة إلى خوارزم والمسافة إليها من الموضع الذي اكترينا منه السفينة أكثر من مائتي فرسخ فكنّا نسير بعض النهار ولا يستوي لنا سيره كلّه من البرد وشدّته إلى أن قدمنا خوارزم فدخلنا على أميرها محمّد بن عراق[٣] خوارزم شاه فأكرمنا وقرّبنا وأنزلنا دارا فلمّا كان بعد ثلاثة أيّام أحضرنا وناظرنا في الدخول إلى بلد الترك وقال لا آذَنُ لكم في ذلك ولا يحلّ إليّ تركُكم تغرّرون بدمائكم وأنا أعلم أنّها حيلة أوقعها هذا الغلام يعني تكين لأنّه كان عندنا حدّادا وقد وقف على بيع الحديد ببلد الكفّار وهو الذي غرّ نذيرا[٤] وحمله على كلام أمير المؤمنين وإيصال كتاب ملك الصقالبة إليه والأمير الأجلّ يعني أمير خراسان كان أحقّ بإقامة الدعوة لأمير المؤمنين في ذلك البلد لو وجد محيصا ومن بعد فبينكم وبين هذا البلد الذي تذكرون ألف قبيلة من الكفّار وهذا تمويه على السلطان وقد نصحتكم ولا بدّ من الكتاب إلى الأمير الأجلّ[٥] حتّى يراجع السلطان أيّده الله في المكاتبة

١ الأصل: فالمتثله. ٢ الأصل: وافتنا. ٣ الأصل: اميرها ومحمد بن عراق. ٤ الأصل: نذير.
٥ الأصل: امير الاجل.

district of Sarakhs-Baykand, as follows: "Tell your spies to keep a lookout for Aḥmad ibn Mūsā in the caravanserais and the lookout posts. Enclosed is his description. The man who catches him is to detain him until we specify the punishment in writing." Aḥmad ibn Mūsā was later arrested in Marw and put in chains. We stayed twenty-eight days in Bukhara. ʿAbdallāh ibn Bāshtū and other members of our party kept saying, "If we tarry, the winter onslaught will mean we will miss the crossing. Aḥmad ibn Mūsā will catch up with us and will join us." Al-Faḍl ibn Mūsā encouraged this.

Ibn Faḍlān said: I noticed in Bukhara that the dirhams were made of dif- 7
ferent colored metals. One of them, the *ghiṭrīfī* dirham, is made of red and yellow brass. It is accepted according to numerical value rather than weight: one hundred *ghiṭrīfī* dirhams equals one silver dirham. In the dowries for their womenfolk they make the following stipulations: so-and-so, the son of so-and-so, marries so-and-so, the daughter of so-and-so, for so many thousand *ghiṭrīfī* dirhams. This also applies to the purchase of property and the purchase of slaves—they specifically mention *ghiṭrīfī* dirhams. They have other dirhams, made only of yellow brass, forty of which equal one *dānaq*, and a further type of yellow-brass dirham called the *samarqandī*, six of which equal one *dānaq*.

I listened to the warnings of ʿAbdallāh ibn Bāshtū and the others about the 8
onslaught of winter. We left Bukhara and returned to the river, where we *Khwārazm*
hired a boat for Khwārazm, more than two hundred *farsakh*s from where we hired the boat. We were able to travel only part of the day. A whole day's travel was impossible because of the cold. When we got to Khwārazm, we were given an audience with the emir, Muḥammad ibn ʿIrāq Khwārazm-Shāh, who gave us a warm and hospitable reception and a place to stay. Three days later, he summoned us, quizzing us about wanting to enter the realm of the Turks. "I cannot let you do that," he said. "I am not permitted to let you risk your lives. I think all this is a ploy devised by this soldier." (He meant Takīn.)[8] "He used to live here as a blacksmith, when he ran the iron trade in the land of the infidels. He is the one who beguiled Nadhīr and got him to speak to the Commander of the Faithful and to bring the letter of the king of the Ṣaqālibah to him. The exalted emir," (he meant the emir of Khurasan) "has more right to have the name of the Commander of the Faithful proclaimed out there, if only he could find a safe way to do it.[9] And then there are a thousand infidel tribes in your path. This is clearly

وتقيمون أنتم إلى وقت يعود الجواب فانصرفنا عنه ذلك اليوم ثمّ عاودناه ولم نزل نرفق به ونداريه ونقول هذا أمر أمير المؤمنين وكتابه فما وجه المراجعة فيه حتّى أذن لنا فانحدرنا من خوارزم إلى الجرجانيّة وبينها وبين خوارزم في الماء خمسون فرسخا.

٩ ورأيت دراهم خوارزم مزيَّفة ورصاصا وزيوفا وصفرا[١] ويسمّون الدرهم طازجة ووزنه أربعة دوانيق ونصف والصيرفيّ منهم يبيع الكِعاب والدُوّامات[٢] والدراهم وهم أوحش الناس كلاما وطبعا كلامهم أشبه شيء بصياح الزرازير وبها قرية على يوم يقال لها أردكوا أهلها يقال لهم الكرديّة كلامهم أشبه شيء بنقيق الضفادع وهم يتبرّءون من أمير المؤمنين عليّ بن أبي طالب رضي الله عنه في دُبُر كلّ صلاة.

١٠ فأقمنا بالجرجانيّة أيّاما وجمد نهر جيحون من أوّله إلى آخره وكان سُمْك الجمد سبعة عشر شبرا[٣] وكانت الخيل والبغال والحمير والعجل تجتاز عليه كما تجتاز على الطرق وهو ثابت لا يتخلخل[٤] فأقام على ذلك ثلاثة أشهر فرأينا بلدا ما ظننّا إلّا أنّ بابا من الزمهرير قد فُتح علينا منه ولا يسقط فيه الثلج إلّا ومعه ريح عاصف شديدة.

١١ وإذا أتحف الرجل من أهله صاحبه وأراد برّه قال له تعال إليّ حتّى نتحدّث فإنّ عندي نارا[٥] طيّبة هذا إذا بلغ في برّه وصِلته إلّا أنّ الله تعالى قد لطف بهم في الحطب وأرخصه عليهم حمل عجلة من حطب الطاغ بدرهمين من دراهم[٦] تكون زهاء ثلاثة آلاف رَطل ورسم سؤّالهم أن لا يقف السائل على الباب بل يدخل إلى دار الواحد[٧] منهم فيقعد ساعة عند ناره يصطلي ثمّ يقول بَكَنْد يعني الخبز[٨].

١٢ وتطاول مقامنا بالجرجانيّة وذاك أنّا أقمنا بها أيّاما من رجب وشعبان وشهر رمضان وشوّال وكان طول مقامنا من جهة البرد وشدّته ولقد بلغني أنّ رجلين ساقا[٩] اثني عشر جملا ليحملا عليها حطبا من بعض الغياض فنسيا أن يأخذا معهما قدّاحة وحُراقة وأنّهما باتا بغير نار فأصبحا والجمال موتى لشدّة البرد ولقد رأيت لهواء

١ كما في ياقوت وفي الأصل: مزنفة ورصاص وزيوف وصفر. ٢ الأصل: الداوامات. ٣ ياقوت: تسعة عشر شبرا. ٤ ياقوت: لا يتحلحل. ٥ الأصل: نار. ٦ ياقوت: من دراهمهم. ٧ الأصل: الدار الواحد. ٨ ياقوت: ثمّ يقول پكند وهو الخبز فإن أعطوه شيئا أخذ وإلّا خرج. ٩ كما في نصّ الدهّان وفي الأصل: ان اثنا.

an imposture foisted upon the caliph. Such is my counsel. I now have no recourse but to write to the exalted emir, so that he can write to the caliph (God give him strength!) and consult with him. You will remain here until the answer comes." We left things at that but came back later and pressured him. "We have the orders and the letter of the Commander of the Faithful, so why do you need to consult?" we said. In the end, he granted us permission and we sailed downriver from Khwārazm to al-Jurjāniyyah. The distance by water is fifty *farsakh*s.

I noticed that the dirhams in Khwārazm are adulterated and should not 9
be accepted, because they are made of lead and brass. They call their dirham a *ṭāzijah*. It weighs four and a half *dānaq*s. The money changers trade in sheep bones, spinning tops, and dirhams. They are the strangest of people in the way they talk and behave. When they talk they sound just like starlings calling. There is a village one day away called Ardkwā, whose inhabitants are called al-Kardaliyyah. When they talk they sound just like frogs croaking. At the end of the prayer they disavow the Commander of the Faithful, ʿAlī ibn Abī Ṭālib, God be pleased with him.

We stayed several days in al-Jurjāniyyah. The River Jayḥūn froze over com- 10
pletely, from beginning to end. The ice was seventeen spans thick. Horses, *Al-Jurjāniyyah*
mules, donkeys, and carts used it like a road and it did not move—it did not even creak. It stayed like this for three months. We thought the country we were visiting was an «infernally cold»[10] portal to the depths of Hell. When snow fell, it was accompanied by a wild, howling blizzard.

When people here want to honor each other and be generous they say, 11
"Come to my house so we can talk, for I have a good fire burning." This is their custom for expressing genuine generosity and affability. God the exalted has been kind to them by making firewood plentiful and very cheap: a cart load of *ṭāgh* wood costs only two local dirhams, and their carts can hold about three thousand *raṭl*s. Normally, their beggars do not stand outside at the door but go into the house, sit for a while, and get warm by the fire. Then they say, "Bakand" meaning "bread."

We were in al-Jurjāniyyah for a long time: several days of Rajab and 12
all of Shaʿban, Ramadan, and Shawwal.[11] We stayed there so long because the cold was so severe. Indeed, I was told that two men had driven twelve camels to transport a load of firewood from a particular forest but had forgotten to take their flint and tinderbox and passed the night without a fire.

بردها أنّ[١] السوق بها والشوارع لتخلو حتّى يطوف الإنسان أكثر الشوارع والأسواق فلا يجد أحدا ولا يستقبله إنسان ولقد كنت أخرج من الحمّام فإذا دخلت إلى البيت نظرت إلى لحيتي وهي قطعة واحدة من الثلج حتّى كنت أدنيها إلى النار ولقد كنت أنام في بيت جَوْفَ بيت وفيه قُبّة لُبُود تركيّة وأنا مدثّر بالأكسية والفرى فربّما التصق خدّي على المخدّة ولقد رأيت الجباب بها تُكسى البُوستِينَاتِ من جلود الغنم لئلّا تتشقّق وتتكسر فلا يغني ذلك شيئا ولقد رأيت الأرض تنشقّ وبها أودية عظام لشدّة البرد وأنّ الشجرة العظيمة العاديّة لتنفلق بنصفين لذلك.

١٣ فلمّا انتصف شوّال من سنة تسع وثلاثمائة أخذ الزمان في التغيير وانحلّ نهر جيحون وأخذنا نحن في ما نحتاج إليه من آلة السَفَر واشترينا الجمال التركيّة واستعملنا السُفَر من جلود الجمال لعبور الأنهار التي نحتاج أن نعبرها[٢] في بلد الترك وتزوّدنا الخبز والجاوَرْس والنمكسود لثلاثة أشهر وأمرَنا من كنّا نأنس به من أهل البلد بالاستظهار في الثياب والاستكثار منها وهوّلوا علينا الأمر وعظّموا القصّة فلمّا شاهدنا ذلك كان أضعاف ما وصِف لنا فكان كلّ رجل منّا عليه قرطق وفوقه خفتان وفوقه بوستين وفوقه لبّادة وبرنس لا تبدو منه إلّا عيناه[٣] وسراويل طاق وآخر مبطّن وران وخفّ كِيمُخْت وفوق الخفّ خفّ آخر فكان الواحد منّا إذا ركب الجمل لم يقدر أن يتحرّك لما عليه من الثياب وتأخّر عنّا الفقيه والمعلّم والغلمان الذين خرجوا معنا من مدينة السلام فزعا من الدخول إلى ذلك البلد وسرت أنا والرسول وسلف له والغلامان تكين وبارس[٤].

١٤ فلمّا كان في اليوم الذي عزمنا فيه على المسير قلت لهم يا قوم معكم غلام الملك وقد وقف على أمركم كلّه ومعكم كتب السلطان ولا أشكّ فيها ذكر توجيه أربعة آلاف دينار المُسَيَّبيّة له وتصيرون إلى ملك أعجميّ فيطالبكم بذلك فقالوا لا تخش من هذا فإنّه غير مطالب لنا فحذّرتهم وقلت أنا أعلم أنّه يطالبكم فلم يقبلوا واستدفّ

---

١ الأصل: وان. ٢ الأصل: من الحلو والجمال لعيون الانهار التي تحتاج ان نعيرها. ٣ الأصل: عصيناه.
٤ الأصل: وفارس.

In the morning it was so cold that they had frozen to death, as had their camels. The weather was so cold that you could wander round the markets and through the streets and not meet anyone. I would leave the baths, and, by the time I got home, I would look at my beard and see a block of ice. I would have to thaw it at the fire. I would sleep inside a chamber, inside another chamber,[12] with a Turkish yurt of animal skins inside it, and would be smothered in cloaks and pelts, and even then my cheek would sometimes freeze and stick to the pillow. I noticed containers wrapped in sheepskins, to stop them shattering and breaking, but this did them no good at all. I even saw the ground open up into great rifts and mighty, ancient trees split in two because of the cold.

Halfway into Shawwal of 309 [February, 922], the season began to change and the Jayḥūn melted. We set about acquiring the items we needed for our journey. We purchased Turkish camels, constructed the camel-skin rafts for crossing all the rivers we had to cross in the realm of the Turks, and packed provisions of bread, millet, and cured meat to last three months. The locals who knew us told us in no uncertain terms to wear proper clothing outdoors and to wear a lot of it. They gave us a terrifying description of the cold and impressed upon us the need to take the matter very, very seriously. But when we experienced it ourselves, it was so much worse than what they had described, even though we each wore a tunic, a caftan, a sheepskin, a horse blanket, and a burnoose with only our eyes showing, a pair of trousers, another pair of lined trousers, leggings, and a pair of animal skin boots with yet another pair on top of them. Mounted on our camels, we wore so many heavy clothes we couldn't move. The jurist, the instructor, and the retainers who had left the City of Peace with us stayed behind, too scared to enter the realm of the Turks. I pushed on with the envoy, his brother-in-law, and the two soldiers, Takīn and Bārs.[13] 13

On the day we planned to set off, I said to them, "The king's man accompanies you. He knows everything. And you carry the letters of the caliph. They must surely mention the four thousand *musayyabī* dinars intended for the king. You will be at the court of a non-Arab king, and he will demand that you pay this sum." "Don't worry about it," they replied, "he will not ask us for them." "He will demand that you produce them. I know it," I warned. But they paid no heed. The caravan was ready to depart, so we hired a guide 14

أمر القافلة واكترينا دليلا يقال له فَلُوس من أهل الجرجانيّة ثمّ توكّلنا على الله عزّ وجلّ وفوّضنا أمرنا إليه.

١٥ ورحلنا من الجرجانيّة يوم الاثنين لليلتين خلتا من ذي القعدة سنة تسع وثلاثمائة فنزلنا رباطا يقال له زَمَّجان[١] وهو باب الترك ثمّ رحلنا الغد فنزلنا منزلا يقال له جِيت[٢] وجاءنا الثلج حتّى مشت الجمال إلى ركبها فيه فأقمنا بهذا المنزل يومين ثمّ أوغلنا في بلد الترك لا نلوي على شيء ولا يلقانا أحد في بريّة قفر بغير جبل فسرنا فيها عشرة أيّام ولقد لقينا من الضرّ والجهد والبرد الشديد وتواصل الثلوج الذي كان برد خوارزم عنده مثل أيّام الصيف ونسينا كلّ ما مرّ بنا وأشرفنا على تلف الأنفس.

١٦ ولقد أصابنا في بعض الأيّام برد شديد وكان تكين يسايرني وإلى جانبه رجل من الأتراك يكلّمه بالتركيّة فضحك تكين وقال إنّ هذا التركيّ يقول لك أيّ شيء يريد ربّنا منّا هو ذا يقتلنا بالبرد ولو علمنا ما يريد لرفعناه إليه فقلت له قل له يريد منكم أن تقولوا لا إلٰه إلّا الله فضحك وقال لو علمنا لفعلنا.

١٧ ثمّ صرنا بعد ذلك إلى موضع فيه من حطب الطاغ شيء عظيم فنزلناه وأوقدت القافلة واصطلوا ونزعوا ثيابهم وشرّروها ثمّ رحلنا فما زلنا[٣] نسير في كلّ ليلة من نصف الليل إلى وقت العصر أو إلى الظهر[٤] بأشدّ سير يكون وأعظمه ثمّ ننزل فلمّا سرنا خمس عشرة ليلة وصلنا إلى جبل عظيم كثير الحجارة وفيه عيون تنخرف عَبَرَه وبالجفرة الماء[٥].

١٨ فلمّا قطعناه وأفضينا[٦] إلى قبيلة من الأتراك يُعرَفون بالغُزّيّة وإذا هم بادية لهم بيوت شعر يحلّون ويرتحلون ترى منهم الأبيات في مكان ومثلها في مكان آخر على عمل البادية وتنقُّلهم وإذا هم في شقاء وهم مع ذلك كالحمير الضالّة لا يدينون لله بدين ولا يرجعون إلى عقل ولا يعبدون شيئا بل يسمّون كبراءهم أربابا فإذا استشار أحدهم رئيسه في شيء قال له يا ربِّ إيش أعمل في كذا وكذا ﴿وَأَمۡرُهُمۡ شُورَىٰ بَيۡنَهُمۡ﴾ غير

١ الأصل: زمحان. ٢ الأصل: خبب. ٣ الأصل: فما زلتنا. ٤ الأصل: او الى لظهر. ٥ الأصل: عيون ىحرق غير وبالجفرة المآ. ٦ الأصل: فلم قطعنا واقضينا.

called Falūs, an inhabitant of al-Jurjāniyyah. We trusted in almighty God, putting our fate in His hands.

We left al-Jurjāniyyah on Monday, the second of Dhu l-Qaʿdah, 309 15
[Monday, March 4, 922], and stopped at an outpost called Zamjān, the Gate of the Turks. The following morning we traveled as far as a stopping post called Jīt. The snow had fallen so heavily that it came up to the camels' knees. We had to stay there two days. Then we kept a straight course and plunged deep into the realm of the Turks through a barren, mountainless desert. We met no one. We crossed for ten days. Our bodies suffered terrible injuries. We were exhausted. The cold was biting, the snowstorms never-ending. It made the cold of Khwārazm seem like summertime. We forgot all about our previous sufferings and were ready to give up the ghost.

One day, the cold was unusually biting. Takīn was traveling beside me, 16
talking in Turkic to a Turk at his side. He laughed and said, "This Turk wants to know, 'What does our Lord want from us? He is killing us with this cold. If we knew what He wanted, then we could just give it to Him.'" "Tell him," I replied, "that He wants you to declare 'There is no god but God.'" "Well, if we knew Him, we'd do it," he said with a laugh.[14]

We came to a place where there was a huge quantity of *ṭāgh* wood and 17
stopped. The members of the caravan lit fires and got them going. They took their clothes off and dried them by the fires.[15] Then we departed, traveling as quickly and with as much energy as we could manage, from midnight until the midday or afternoon prayer, when we would stop for a rest. After fifteen nights of this,[16] we came to a huge rocky mountain. Springs of water ran down it and gathered to form a lake at its foot.

The Ghuzziyyah

We crossed the mountain and reached a Turkic tribe known as the Ghuzzi- 18
yyah. Much to our surprise,[17] we discovered that they are nomads who live in animal-hair tents that they pitch and strike regularly. Their tents were pitched with some in one place and the same number in another place, as is the practice of transhumant nomads. They lead wretched lives. They are like roaming asses.[18] They practice no recognizable form of monotheism, they do not base their beliefs on reason, and they worship nothing—indeed they call their own chiefs "lord."[19] When one of them consults his chief on a matter, he says to him, "My lord, what shall I do about such and such?" «They decide matters by consultation»,[20] though it is quite possible for the lowliest and most worthless individual in their community to turn up and overturn the consensus they

أنّهم متى اتّفقوا على شيء وعزموا عليه ثمّ جاء أرذلهم وأخسّهم فنقض ما قد أجمعوا[١] عليه وسمعتُهم يقولون لا إلٰه إلّا الله محمّد رسول الله تقرّبًا بهذا القول إلى من يجتاز بهم من المسلمين لا اعتقادا لذلك وإذا ظُلِم أحد منهم أو جرى عليه أمر يكرهه رفع رأسه إلى السماء وقال بِير تَنكِري وهو بالتركيّة بالله بالواحد لأنّ بير بالتركيّة واحد وتنكري الله بلغة الترك ولا يستَنجون من غائط ولا بول ولا يغتسلون من جنابة ولا غير ذلك وليس بينهم وبين الماء عمل خاصّةً في الشتاء.

١٩ ولا يستتر نساؤهم من رجالهم ولا من غيرهم وكذلك لا تستر المرأة شيئا من بدنها عن أحد من الناس ولقد نزلنا يوما على رجل منهم فجلسنا وامرأة الرجل معنا فبينا هي تحدّثنا إذ كشفت فرجها وحكّته ونحن ننظر إليها فسترنا وجوهنا وقلنا أستغفر الله فضحك زوجها وقال للترجمان قل لهم نكشفه بحضرتكم فترونه وتصونه فلا يُوصَل إليه هو خير لِمَنْ أن تُغَطِيه وتُمَكِن منه وليس يعرفون الزنا ومن ظهروا منه على شيء من فعله شقّوه بنصفين وذلك أنّهم يجمعون بين أغصان شجرتين ثمّ يشدّونه بالأغصان ويرسلون الشجرتين فينشقّ الذي يُشَدّ إليهما[٢].

٢٠ وقال بعضهم وسمعني قرآنا فاستحسن القرآن وأقبل يقول للترجمان قل له لا تسكت وقال لي هذا الرجل يوما على لسان الترجمان قل لهذا العربيّ أَلِرَبّنا عزّ وجلّ امرأة فاستعظمت ذلك وسبّحت الله واستغفرته فسبّح واستغفر كما فعلت وكذلك رسم التركيّ كلّما سمع المسلم يسبّح ويهلّل قال مثله.

٢١ ورسوم تزويجهم وهو أن يخطب الواحد منهم إلى الآخر بعض حرمه إمّا ابنته[٣] أو أخته أو بعض من يملك أمره على كذا وكذا ثوب خوارزميّ فإذا وافاه حملها إليه وربّما كان المهر جمالا[٤] أو دوابّ أو غير ذلك وليس يصل الواحد إلى امرأته حتّى يوفي الصداق الذي قد واقف وليّها عليه فإذا وافاه إيّاه جاء غير محتشم حتّى يدخل إلى المنزل الذي هي فيه فيأخذها بحضرة أبيها وأمّها وإخوتها فلا يمنعونه من ذلك.

---

١ الأصل: جمعوا. ٢ الأصل: نشياليهما. ٣ الأصل: انا ابنته. ٤ الأصل: جمال.

have reached. To be sure, I have heard them declare, "There is no god but God! Muḥammad is God's emissary." But this was a way of ingratiating themselves with the Muslims passing through their lands and not out of conviction. When one of them is wronged or something unpleasant happens to him, he raises his head to the heavens and shouts, "Bīr Tankrī," which in Turkic means "By God, by the One!" *Bīr* means "one" and *Tankrī* is "God" in the language of the Turks. They do not clean themselves when they defecate or urinate, and they do not wash themselves when intercourse puts them in a state of ritual impurity. They avoid contact with water, especially in the winter.

Their womenfolk do not cover themselves in the presence of a man, whether he be one of their menfolk or not. A woman will not cover any part of her body in front of anyone, no matter who. One day we stopped at a tent and sat down. The man's wife sat with us. During conversation, she suddenly uncovered her vulva and scratched it, right in front of us. We covered our faces and exclaimed, "God forgive us!" but her husband simply laughed and said to the interpreter,[21] "Tell them: we might uncover it in your presence and you might see it, but she keeps it safe so no one can get to it. This is better than her covering it up and letting others have access to it." Illicit intercourse is unheard of. If they catch anyone attempting it in any way, they tear him in half, in the following manner: they join the branches of two trees, tie the culprit to the branches and then let the trees loose. The man tied to the trees is torn in two. 19

One of them heard me reciting the Qur'an and found it beautiful. He approached the interpreter and said, "Tell him not to stop." One day, this man said to me via the interpreter, "Ask this Arab, 'Does our great and glorious Lord have a wife?'" I was shocked by his words, praised God and asked His forgiveness. He copied my actions. Such is the custom of the Turk—whenever he hears a Muslim declare God's glory and attest His uniqueness, he copies him. 20

Their marriage customs are as follows. One man asks another for one of his womenfolk, be it his daughter, sister, or any other woman he possesses, in exchange for such and such a number of Khwārazmī garments. When he is paid in full, he hands her over. Sometimes the dowry is in camels, horses, or the like. The man is not granted access to his future wife until he has paid the full dowry that he has agreed with her guardian. Once paid, he shows up unabashedly, enters her dwelling, and takes possession of her right there and then, in the presence of her father, mother, and brothers. No one stops him. 21

وإذا مات الرجل وله زوجة وأولاد تزوّج الأكبر من ولده بامرأته إذا لم تكن أُمّه ٢٢
ولا يقدر أحد من التجّار ولا غيرهم أن يغتسل من جنابة بحضرتهم إلّا ليلا من حيث لا يرونه وذلك أنّهم يغضبون ويقولون هذا يريد أن يسحرنا لأنّه قد تغرّس في الماء ويُغرِّمونه مالا.

ولا يقدر أحد من المسلمين[١] يجتاز ببلدهم حتّى يجعل له منهم صديقا ينزل ٢٣
عليه ويحمل له من بلد الإسلام ثوبا ولامرأته مقنعة وشيئا من فلفل وجاورس وزبيب وجوز فإذا قدم على صديقه ضرب له قبّة وحمل إليه من الغنم على قدره حتّى يتولّى المسلم ذبحها لأنّ الترك لا يذبحون وإنّما يضرب الواحد منهم رأس الشاة حتّى تموت وإذا أراد الرجل منهم الرحيل[٢] وقد قام عليه شيء من جماله أو دوابّه أو احتاج إلى مال تَرَكَ ما قد قام عند صديقه التركيّ وأخذ من جماله ودوابّه وماله حاجتَه ورحل فإذا عاد من الوجه الذي يقصده قضاه ماله وردّ إليه جماله ودوابّه وكذلك لو اجتاز بالتركيّ إنسان لا يعرفه ثمّ قال أنا ضيفك وأنا أريد من جمالك ودوابّك ودراهمك دفع إليه ما يريد فإن مات التاجر في وجهه ذلك وعادت القافلة لقيهم التركيّ وقال أين ضيفي فإن قالوا مات حطّ القافلة ثمّ جاء إلى أنبل تاجر يراه[٣] فيهم فحلّ متاعه وهو ينظر فأخذ من دراهمه مثل ماله عند ذلك التاجر بغير زيادة حبّةٍ وكذلك يأخذ من دوابّه وجماله وقال ذلك ابن عمّك وأنت أحقّ مَنْ غَرِمَ عنه وإن فرّ فعل أيضا ذلك الفعل وقال له ذلك مسلم مثلك خذ أنت منه وإن لم يوافق المسلمَ ضيفَه في الجادّة سأل عنه[٤] ثلاثة أين هو فإذا أُرْشِد إليه سار في طلبه مسيرة أيّام حتّى يصير إليه ويرفع ماله عنده وكذلك ما يُهْدِيه له وهذه أيضا سبيل التركيّ إذا دخل الجرجانيّة سأل عن ضيفه فنزل عليه حتّى يرتحل ومتى مات التركيّ عند صديقه المسلم واجتازت القافلة وفيها صديقه قتلوه وقالوا أنت قتلته بحبسك إيّاه ولو لم تحبسه لما مات

١ الأصل: احدهن من المسلمين. ٢ الأصل: الرجل. ٣ الأصل: براة. ٤ الأصل: عن.

When one of them dies and leaves a wife and sons behind, the eldest son 22
marries his dead father's wife, provided she is not his birth mother. No one, merchant or anyone else for that matter, can perform a ritual wash in their presence, except at night when he will not be seen, because they get very angry. They exact payment from him and exclaim, "This man has planted something in the water[22] and wants to put a spell on us!"

No Muslim can pass through their territory without first befriending one 23
of them. He lodges with him and brings gifts from the Muslim lands: a roll of cloth, a headscarf for his wife, pepper, millet, raisins, and nuts. When he arrives, his friend pitches a yurt for him and provides him with sheep, in accordance with his status. In this way, the Muslim can perform the ritual slaughter, as the Turks do not do this but instead beat the sheep on the head until it dies. If someone has decided to travel and uses some of the camels and horses belonging to his friend the Turk, or if he borrows some money, his debt with his friend remains unpaid. He takes the camels, horses, and money he needs from his friend. On his return, he pays the Turk his money and returns his camels and horses.[23] So too, if someone a Turk doesn't know passes through and says, "I am your guest. I want some of your camels, horses, and dirhams," he gives him what he asks for. If the merchant dies on the trip and the caravan returns, the Turk comes to meet the caravan and says, "Where is my guest?" If they say, "He is dead," he brings the caravan to a halt, goes up to the most eminent merchant he sees, unties his goods as the merchant looks on, and takes the exact number of dirhams he had advanced to the first merchant, not a penny more. He also takes back the exact number of camels and horses, saying, "He was your cousin, so you are under the greatest obligation to pay his debt." If the guest runs away, he behaves in the same way, only this time he says, "He was a Muslim like you. You get it back from him." If he does not meet his Muslim guest on the road, he asks three men about him, saying, "Where is he?" When told where he is, he travels, even for days, till he finds him and reclaims his property, along with the gifts he gave him. The Turk also behaves like this when he travels to al-Jurjāniyyah. He asks for his guest and stays with him until he leaves. If the Turk dies while staying with his Muslim friend and the Muslim later passes through this territory as a member of a caravan, they put him to death, with the words, "You imprisoned him and killed him. Had you not imprisoned him, he would not have died." Likewise, they kill

وكذلك إن سقاه نبيذا فتردّى من حائط قتلوه به فإن لم يكن في القافلة عمدوا إلى أجلّ من فيها فقتلوه.

٢٤ وأمر اللواط عندهم عظيم جدّا ولقد نزل على حيّ كوذركين وهو خليفة ملك الترك رجل من أهل خوارزم فأقام عند ضيف له مدّة في ابتياع غنم وكان للتركيّ ابن أمرد فلم يزل الخوارزميّ يداريه ويراوده عن نفسه حتّى طاوعه[١] على ما أراد وجاء التركيّ فوجدهما في بنيانهما فرفع التركيّ ذلك إلى كوذركين فقال له اجمع الترك فجمعهم فيما اجتمعوا قال للتركيّ[٢] بالحقّ تحبّ أن أحكم أم بالباطل قال بالحقّ قال أَحْضِر ابنك فأَحْضَرَه فقال يجب عليه وعلى التاجر أن يُقتَلا[٣] جميعا فامتعض للتركيّ من ذلك وقال لا أُسلم ابني فقال فيفتدي التاجر نفسه ففعل ودفع للتركيّ غنما للفعل بابنه ورفع إلى كوذركين أربعمائة شاة لِمَا رُفع عنه وارتحل عن بلد الترك.

٢٥ فأوّل من لقينا من ملوكهم ورؤسائهم يِنَال الصغير وقد كان أسلم فقيل له إن أسلمت لم ترؤسنا فرجع عن إسلامه فلمّا وصلنا إلى الموضع الذي هو فيه قال لا أتركم تجوزون لأنّ هذا شيء ما سمعنا به قطّ ولا ظننّا أنّه يكون فرفقنا به إلى أن رضي بخفتان جرجانيّ يساوي عشرة دراهم وشِقّة باي باف وأقراص خبز وكفّ زبيب ومائة جوزة فلمّا دفعنا هذا إليه سجد لنا وهذا رسمهم إذا أكرم الرجل الرجل سجد له وقال لولا أنّ بيوتي نائية عن الطريق لحملت إليكم غنما وبُرّا وانصرف عنّا وارتحلنا.

٢٦ فلمّا كان من غد لقينا رجل واحد من الأتراك ذميم الخلقة رثّ الهيئة قمّيء المنظر خسيس المخبر وقد أخذنا مطر شديد فقال قفوا فوقفت القافلة بأسرها وهي نحو ثلاثة آلاف دابّة وخمسة آلاف رجل ثمّ قال ليس يجوز منكم أحد فوقفنا طاعة لأمره فقلنا له نحن أصدقاء كوذركين فأقبل يضحك ويقول من كوذركين أما أَخْرى على لحية كوذركين؟ ثمّ قال بَكَند يعني الخبز بلغة خوارزم فدفعت إليه أقراصا فأخذها وقال مرّوا قد رحمتكم.

---

١ الأصل: حتّى اطاوعه. ٢ الأصل: قال التركي. ٣ الأصل: ان تقتلا.

the Muslim if he gives the Turk alcohol and he falls and dies. If he does not travel as a member of the caravan, they seize the most important member of the caravan and kill him.

They abhor pederasty. A man from Khwārazm lodged with the tribe of the *kūdharkīn* (the deputy of the king of the Turks) and lived for a while with one of his hosts. He was there to trade in sheep. The Turk had a beardless son, whom the Khwārazmī blandished and tried to seduce[24] until he gave in. The Turk turned up, found the two of them in the act, and brought the matter to the *kūdharkīn*, who said to him, "Muster the Turks," which he did, as was the practice. The *kūdharkīn* said to the Turk, "Do you wish me to rule according to what is true or what is false?" "According to what is true." "Then fetch your son!" The son was fetched. "Both must be put to death together." The Turk was angered and said, "I shall not surrender my son." "Then let the merchant pay a ransom," he said. The Turk paid a number of sheep for what had been done to his son, and four hundred ewes to the *kūdharkīn*, for the punishment that had been averted. Then he left the realm of the Turks. 24

The first king and chief we met was the Lesser Yināl. He had converted to Islam but had been told that, "If you convert to Islam, you will never lead us," so he recanted. When we arrived at his camp, he said, "I cannot allow you to pass. This is unheard of. It will never happen." We gave him some gifts. He was satisfied with a Jurjānī caftan worth ten dirhams, a cut of woven cloth, some flat breads, a handful of raisins, and a hundred nuts. When we handed them over, he prostrated himself before us. This is their custom: when a person is generous to another, the other prostrates himself before him. He said, "Were our tents not far from the road, we would bring you sheep and grain." He left us and we carried on. 25

The next morning we encountered a solitary Turk—a despicable figure, unkempt and really quite repulsive—a man of no worth at all. It had started to rain heavily. "Halt!" the man said. The entire caravan ground to a halt: it numbered about three thousand mounts and five thousand men. "Not one of you will pass," he said. We obeyed and said, "We are friends of the *kūdharkīn*." He approached and said with a laugh, "*Kūdharkīn* who? Do I not shit on the beard of the *kūdharkīn*?" Then he shouted, "Bakand"—"bread" in the language of Khwārazm—and I gave him some flat breads, which he took, saying, "Proceed. I have spared you out of pity." 26

٢٧ قال وإذا مرض الرجل منهم وكان له جوارٍ وعبيد خدموه ولم يقربه أحد من أهل بيته ويضربون له خيمة ناحية من البيوت فلا يزال فيها إلى أن يموت أو يبرأ وإن كان عبدا أو فقيرا رموا به في الصحراء وارتحلوا عنه وإذا مات الرجل منهم حفروا له حفيرة كبيرة كهيئة البيت وعمدوا إليه فألبسوه قرطقه ومنطقته وقوسه . . . .[١] وجعلوا في يده قدحا من خشب فيه نبيذ وتركوا بين يديه إناء من خشب فيه نبيذ وجاءوا بكلّ ماله فجعلوه معه في ذلك البيت ثمّ أجلسوه فيه فسقّفوا البيت عليه وجعلوا فوقه مثل القبّة من الطين وعمدوا إلى دوابّه على قدر كثرتها فقتلوا منها مائة رأس إلى مائتي رأس إلى رأس واحد وأكلوا لحومها إلّا الرأس والقوائم والجلد والذنب فإنّهم يصلبون ذلك على الخشب وقالوا هذه دوابّه يركبها إلى الجنّة فإن كان قتل إنسانا وكان شجاعا نحتوا صورا من خشب على عدد من قتل وجعلوها على قبره وقالوا هؤلاء غلمانه يخدمونه في الجنّة وربّما تغافلوا على قتل الدوابّ يوما أو يومين فيحثّهم شيخ من كبارهم فيقول رأيت فلانا يعني الميّت في النوم فقال لي هوذا تراني وقد سبقني أصحابي وشقّقت رِجلاي من اتّباعي لهم ولست ألحقهم وقد بقيت وحدي فعندها يعمدون إلى دوابّه فيقتلونها ويصلبونها عند قبره فإذا كان بعد يوم أو اثنين جاءهم ذلك الشيخ وقال قد رأيت فلانا وقال عرِّفْ أهلي وأصحابي أنّي قد لحقتهم من تقدّمني واسترحت من التعب.

٢٨ قال والترك كلّهم ينتفون لحاهم إلّا أسبلتهم وربّما رأيت الشيخ الهرم منهم وقد نتف لحيته وترك شيئا منها تحت ذقنه وعليه البوستين فإذا رآه إنسان من بعد لم يشكّ أنّه تيس.

٢٩ وملك الترك الغزّيّة يقال له يَبْغُوا وهو اسم الأمير وكلّ من ملَك هذه القبيلة فبهذا الاسم يسمّى ويقال لخليفته كوذركين وكذا كلّ من يخلف رئيسا منهم يقال له كوذركين.

٣٠ ثمّ نزلنا عند[٢] ارتحالنا من ناحية هؤلاء بصاحب جيشهم[٣] ويقال له أَتْرَك بن

١ في الأصل بياض قدر كلمة. ٢ الأصل: عنه. ٣ الأصل: صاحب جيشهم.

Ibn Faḍlān said: The members of a household do not approach someone who is ill. His slaves, male and female, wait on him. He is put in a tent, away from the other tents, where he remains until he dies or recovers. A slave or a pauper is simply thrown out onto the open plain and left. The Turks dig a large ditch, in the shape of a chamber for their dead. They fetch the deceased, clothe him in his tunic and girdle, and give him his bow.[25] They put a wooden cup filled with alcohol in his hand and place a wooden vessel of alcohol in front of him. They bring all his wealth and lay it beside him, in the chamber. They put him in a sitting position and then build the roof. On top they construct what looks like a yurt made of clay. Horses are fetched, depending on how many he owned. They can slaughter any number of horses, from a single horse up to a hundred or two. They eat the horse meat, except for the head, legs, hide, and tail, which they nail to pieces of wood, saying, "His horses which he rides to the Garden."[26] If he has shown great bravery and killed someone, they carve wooden images, as many as the men he has killed, place them on top of his grave and say, "His retainers who serve him in the Garden." Sometimes they do not kill the horses for a day or two. Then an elder will exhort them: "I have seen So-and-So," (i.e., the deceased) "in a dream and he said to me, 'You see me here in front of you. My companions have gone before me. My feet are cracked from following them. I cannot catch up with them. I am left here, all alone.'" Then they bring his horses, slaughter them, and gibbet them at his graveside. A day or two later, the elder arrives and says, "I have seen So-and-So. He said, 'Inform my household and companions that I have caught up with those who[27] went before me and have recovered from my exhaustion.'" 27

Ibn Faḍlān said: Each and every one of the Turks plucks his beard but does not touch his mustache. I would often see one of their aged elders, clad in a sheepskin, his beard plucked but with a little left under his chin. If you caught sight of him from a distance, you would be convinced he was a billy goat. 28

The king of the Ghuzziyyah Turks is called *yabghū*. This is the title given to the ruler of the tribe and is their name for their emir. His deputy is called *kūdharkīn*. Any one who deputizes for a chief is called *kūdharkīn*. 29

Upon leaving the region where this group of Turks was camped, we stopped with their field marshal, Atrak, son of al-Qaṭaghān. Turkish yurts 30

القَطَغَان[1] فضرب لنا قبابا تركيّة وأنزلنا فيها[2] وإذا له ضَبْنَة[3] وحاشية وبيوت كبيرة وساق إلينا غنما وقادوا دوابّ[4] لنذبح الغنم ونركب الدوابّ ودعا هو جماعةً[5] من أهل بيته وبني عمّه فقتل لهم غنما كثيرة وكنّا قد أهدينا إليه هديّة من ثياب وزبيب وجوز وفلفل وجاورس فرأيت امرأته وقد كانت امرأة أبيه وقد أخذت لحما ولبنا وشيئا ممّا ألحقناه به وخرجت من البيوت إلى الصحراء فحفرت حفيرة ودفنت الذي كان معها فيها وتكلّمت بكلام فقلت للترجمان ما تقول قال تقول هذه هديّة للقطغان[6] أبي أتَرَك أهدوها له العرب.

٣١ فلمّا كان في الليل دخلت أنا والترجمان إليه وهو في قبّته جالس ومعنا كتاب نذير الحرميّ[7] إليه يأمره فيه بالإسلام ويحضّه عليه ووجّه إليه خمسين دينارا فيها عدّة دنانير مسيّبيّة[8] وثلاثة مثاقيل مسك وجلود أديم وثوبين مرويّة وقطعنا له منهما قرطقين وخفّ أديم وثوب ديباج وخمسة أثواب حرير فدفعنا إليه هديّته ودفعنا إلى امرأته مقنعة وخاتما وقرأت عليه الكتاب فقال للترجمان لست أقول لكم شيئا حتّى ترجعون وأكتب إلى السلطان بما أنا عازم عليه ونزع الديباجة التي كانت عليه ليلبس الخلع التي ذكرنا فرأيت القرطق الذي تحتها وتقطّع وسخا لأنّ رسومهم أن لا ينزع الواحد منهم الثوب الذي يلي جسده حتّى ينتثر قطعا.

٣٢ وإذا هو قد نتف لحيته كلّها وسباله فبقي كالخادم ورأيت الترك يذكرون أنّه أفرسهم ولقد رأيت يوما وهو يسايرنا[9] على فرسه إذ مرّت وَزّة طائرة فأوتر قوسه وحرّك دابّته تحتها ثمّ رماها فإذا هو قد أنزلها.

٣٣ فلمّا كان في بعض الأيّام وجّه خلف القوّاد الذين يلونه وهم طرخان وينال وابن أخيهما[10] وَيِغْلِز[11] وكان طرخان أنبلهم وأجلّهم وكان أعرج أعمى أشلّ فقال لهم إنّ هؤلاء رسل ملك العرب إلى صهري أَلْمِش بن شِلْكِي ولم يُخيَّر لي أن أُطلقهم إلّا عن مشورتكم فقال طَرخان هذا شيء ما رأيناه قطّ ولا سمعنا به ولا اجتاز

١ الأصل: القطعان. ٢ الأصل: فيه. ٣ الأصل: صنبة. ٤ الأصل: دوابًا. ٥ الأصل: هو وجماعة.
٦ الأصل: للقطعان. ٧ الأصل: نذير الحرمىن. ٨ الأصل: دنانير مسيتة. ٩ الأصل: وهو سايرنا.
١٠ الأصل: ں حىها. ١١ الأصل: وىغلز.

were pitched, and we were lodged in them. He had a large retinue with many dependents, and his tents were big. He gave us sheep and horses: sheep for slaughter and horses for riding. He summoned his paternal cousins and members of his household, held a banquet and killed many sheep. We had presented him with a gift of clothing, along with raisins, nuts, pepper, and millet.[28] I watched his wife, who had previously been the wife of his father,[29] take some meat, milk, and a few of the gifts we had presented and go out into the open, where she dug a hole and buried everything, uttering some words. "What is she saying?" I asked the interpreter, and he replied, "She says, 'This is a gift for al-Qaṭaghān, the father of Atrak. The Arabs gave it to him.'"

That night the interpreter and I were granted an audience in Atrak's yurt. 31 We delivered the letter from Nadhīr al-Ḥaramī, instructing him to embrace Islam. The letter specifically mentioned that he was to receive fifty dinars (some of them *musayyabīs*), three measures of musk, some tanned hides, and two rolls of Marw cloth. Out of this we had cut for him two tunics, a pair of leather boots, a garment of silk brocade, and five silk garments. We presented his gift and gave his wife a headscarf and a signet ring. I read out the letter and he told the interpreter, "I will not respond until you have returned. Then I shall inform the caliph of my decision in writing." He removed the silk shirt he was wearing and put on the robe of honor we have just mentioned. I noticed that the tunic underneath was so filthy that it had fallen to pieces. It is their custom not to remove the garment next to their body until it falls off in tatters.

He had plucked all of his beard and mustache, so he looked like a eunuch. 32 Even so, I heard the Turks state that he was their most accomplished horseman. In fact, I was with him one day, on horseback. A goose flew past. I saw him string his bow, move his horse into position under the bird, and fire. He shot the goose dead.

One day he summoned the four commanders of the adjacent territory: 33 Ṭarkhān, Yināl, the nephew of Ṭarkhān and Yināl, and Yilghiz. Ṭarkhān was blind and lame and had a withered arm, but he was by far the most eminent and important. Atrak said, "These are the envoys from the king of the Arabs to my son-in-law, Almish, son of Shilkī. I cannot rightfully allow them to go any further without consulting you." Ṭarkhān said, "Never before have we

بنا رسول سلطان مذ كنّا نحن وآباؤنا وما أظنّ إلّا أنّ السلطان قد أعمل الحيلة ووجّه هؤلاء إلى الخزر ليستجيش بهم علينا والوجه أن يُقطَع هؤلاء الرسل نصفين نصفين ونأخذ ما معهم وقال آخر منهم لا بل نأخذ ما معهم ونتركهم عراة يرجعون من حيث جاءوا وقال آخر لا ولكنّ لنا عند ملك الخزر أسراء فنبعث بهؤلاء نفادي بهم أولئك فما زالوا يتراجعون بينهم هذه الأشياء سبعة أيّام ونحن في حالة الموت حتّى أجمع دأبهم على أن يخلوا سبيلنا ونمضي فخلعنا على طَرْخان خفتانا مرويّا[1] وشقّتين بابي باف وعلى أصحابه قرطقا قرطقا[2] وكذلك على يِنَال ودفعنا إليهم فلفلا وجاورس وأقراصا من خبز وانصرفوا عنّا.

٣٤ ورحلنا حتّى صرنا إلى نهر بغندي[3] فأخرج الناس سُفَرَهم وهي من جلود الجمال فبسطوها وأخذوا بأثاث[4] الجمال التركيّة لأنّها مدوّرة فجعلوها في جوفها حتّى تمتدّ ثمّ حشوها بالثياب والمتاع فإذا امتلأت جلس في كلّ سفرة جماعة من خمسة وستّة وأربعة وأقلّ وأكثر ويأخذون بأيديهم خشب الخَدَنْك فيجعلونه كالمجاريف ولا يزالون يجذِفون والماء يحملها وهي تدور حتّى نعبر فأمّا الدوابّ والجمال فإنّه يُصاح بها فتعبر سباحة ولا بدّ أن تعبر جماعة من المقاتلة ومعهم السلاح قبل أن يعبر شيء من القافلة ليكونوا طليعة للناس خيفة من الباشغرد[5] أن يكبسوا الناس وهم يعبرون فعبرنا بغندي على هذه الصفة التي ذكرنا ثمّ عبرنا بعد ذلك نهرا يقال له جام في السفر أيضا ثمّ عبرنا جاخش ثمّ اذل ثمّ اردن ثمّ وارش ثمّ اختي ثمّ وبنا[6] وهذه كلّها أنهار كبار.

٣٥ ثمّ صرنا بعد ذلك إلى البجَنَاك وإذا هم نزلوا[7] على ماء شبيه بالبحر غير جارٍ وإذا هم سمر شديدو السمرة[8] وإذا هم محلّقو[9] اللحى فقراء خلاف الغزّيّة لأنّي رأيت من الغزّيّة من يملك عشرة آلاف دابّة ومائة ألف رأس من الغنم وأكثر ما ترعى من الغنم ما

[1] الأصل: خفتان مروي. [2] الأصل: ~~قرطق~~ قرطق. [3] كما في الأصل. [4] الأصل: بالاناث. [5] الأصل: (خلفه من للباشغرد) وحرف الجرّ (من) مكتوب فوق (خلفه). [6] رسمت أسماء هذه الأنهار كما هي موجودة في الأصل. [7] الأصل مطموس قدر كلمة واحدة: هم ... على. [8] الأصل: شديدي السمرة. [9] الأصل: محلقى.

seen or heard of a thing like this. Never before has an envoy from the caliph passed through our realm, even when our fathers were alive. I suspect that it is the caliph's design to send these men to the Khazars and mobilize them against us. Our only option is to dismember these envoys and take what they have." Someone else said, "No. We should take what they have and let them go back naked where they came from." Another said, "No. We should use them as ransom for our fellow tribesmen taken prisoner by the king of the Khazars." They debated like this for seven long days. We were in the jaws of death. Then, as is their wont, they came to a unanimous decision: they would allow us to continue on our way. We presented Ṭarkhān with a robe of honor: a Marw caftan and two cuts of woven cloth. We gave a tunic to his companions, including Yināl. We also gave them pepper, millet, and flat breads as gifts. Then they left.

We pushed on as far as the Bghndī River, where the people got their 34
camel-hide rafts out, spread them flat, put the round saddle frames from their Turkish camels inside the hides, and stretched them tight. They loaded them with clothes and goods. When the rafts were full, groups of people, four, five, and six strong, sat on top of them, took hold of pieces of *khadhank* and used them as oars. The rafts floated on the water, spinning round and round, while the people paddled furiously. We crossed the river in this manner. The horses and the camels were urged on with shouts, and they swam across. We needed to send a group of fully armed soldiers across the river first, before the rest of the caravan. They were the advance guard, protection for the people against the Bāshghird. There was a fear they might carry out an ambush during the crossing. This is how we crossed the Bghndī River. Then we crossed a river called the Jām, also on rafts, then the Jākhsh, the Adhl, the Ardn, the Wārsh, the Akhtī, and the Wbnā. These are all mighty rivers.

Then we reached the Bajanāk. They were encamped beside a still lake as big 35
as a sea. They are a vivid brown color, shave their beards, and live in miser- *The Bajanāk*
able poverty, unlike the Ghuzziyyah. I saw some Ghuzziyyah who owned ten thousand horses and a hundred thousand head of sheep. The sheep graze mostly on what lies underneath the snow, digging for the grass with their hooves. If they do not find grass, they eat the snow instead and grow

بين الثلج تبحث بأظلافها تطلب الحشيش فإذا لم تجده قضمت الثلج فسمنت غاية السمن فإذا كان الصيف وأكلت الحشيش هزلت.

٣٦ فنزلنا على الجناك يوما واحدا ثمّ ارتحلنا فنزلنا على نهر جيخ[١] وهو أكبر نهر رأيناه وأعظمه وأشدّه جرية ولقد رأيت سُفْرة انقلبت فيه فغرق من كان فيها وذهبت رجال كثير من الناس وغرقت عدّة جمال ودوابّ[٢] ولم نعبره إلّا بجهد ثمّ سرنا أيّاما وعبرنا نهر جاخا ثمّ بعده نهر ازخن ثمّ باجاع ثمّ سمور[٣] ثمّ كنال ثمّ نهر سوح ثمّ نهر كيجلوا[٤].

٣٧ فوقفنا[٥] في بلد قوم من الأتراك يقال لهم الباشغرد فحذرناهم أشدّ الحذر وذلك أنّهم شرّ الأتراك وأقذرهم وأشدّهم إقداما على القتل يلقى الرجل الرجل فيقور هامته[٦] ويأخذها ويتركه وهم يحلقون لحاهم ويأكلون القمل يتتبّع الواحد منهم درز قرطقه فيقرض القمل بأسنانه ولقد كان معنا منهم واحد قد أسلم وكان يخدمنا فرأيته وجد قملة[٧] في ثوبه فقصعها بظفره ثمّ لحسها وقال لمّا رآني جيّد[٨].

٣٨ وكلّ واحد منهم ينحت خشبة على قدر الإحليل[٩] ويعلّقها عليه فإذا أراد سفرا أو لقي عدوّا[١٠] قبّلها وسجد لها وقال يا ربّ افعل فيّ كذا وكذا[١١] فقلت للترجمان سل بعضهم ما حجّتهم في هذا ولِمَ جعله ربّه قال لأنّي خرجت من مثله وليس أعرف[١٢] لنفسي خالقا غيره ومنهم من يزعم أنّ له اثني[١٣] عشر ربّا للشتاء ربٌّ وللصيف ربّ وللمطر ربّ وللريح ربّ وللشجر ربّ وللناس ربّ وللدوابّ ربّ وللماء ربّ ولليل ربّ وللنهار ربّ وللموت ربّ[١٤] وللأرض ربّ والربّ الذي في السماء أكبرهم إلّا أنّه يجتمع مع هؤلاء باتّفاق ويرضى كلّ واحد منهم بما يعمل شريكه تعالى الله عمّا يقول الظالمون علوّا كبيرا ورأينا طائفة منهم تعبد الحيّات وطائفة تعبد السمك وطائفة تعبد الكراكيّ فعرّفوني أنّهم كانوا يحاربون قوما من أعدائهم فهزموهم وأنّ الكراكيّ صاحت وراءهم

---

١ الأصل: حجج. ٢ الأصل: والدواب. ٣ رسمت أسماء هذه الأنهار كما هي موجودة في الأصل. ٤ الأصل: كنال ثمّ نهر سوح ثمّ نهر كجلوا. ٥ الأصل: فوفقنا. ٦ الأصل: فيتور همانه؛ ياقوت: فيفزر هامته. ٧ الأصل: وقد قملة. ٨ الأصل: وقال الراى حيد. ٩ ياقوت: الإكليل. ١٠ ياقوت: أو لقاء عدوّ. ١١ ياقوت: افعل بي كذا وكذا. ١٢ ياقوت: ولست أعرف. ١٣ الأصل: ان له اثنا. ١٤ ياقوت: و للموت ربّ وللحياة ربّ.

inordinately fat. During the summer, when they can eat grass, they become very thin.[30]

We spent a day with the Bajanāk, continued on our way, and stopped beside the Jaykh River. This was the biggest and mightiest river we had seen and had the strongest current. I saw a raft capsize in the river and all the passengers on board drown. A great many died, and several camels and horses drowned, too. It took the greatest effort to get across. Several days' march later, we crossed the Jākhā, the Azkhn, the Bājāʿ, the Smwr, the Knāl, the Sūḥ, and the Kījlū. 36

The Bāshghird

We stopped in the territory of a tribe of Turks called the Bāshghird. We were on high alert, for they are the wickedest, filthiest, and most ferocious of the Turks. When they attack, they take no prisoners. In single combat they slice open your head and make off with it. They shave their beards. They eat lice by carefully picking over the hems of their tunics and cracking the lice with their teeth. Our group was joined by a Bāshghird who had converted to Islam. He used to wait on us. I saw him take a louse he found in his clothing, crack it with his fingernail, and then lick it. "Yum!" he said, when he saw me watching him. 37

Each carves a piece of wood into an object the size and shape of a phallus and hangs it round his neck. When they want to travel or take the field against the enemy, they kiss it and bow down before it, saying, "My lord, do such and such with me." I said to the interpreter, "Ask one of them to explain this. Why does he worship it as his lord?" "Because I came from something like it and I acknowledge no other creator," he replied. Some of them claim that they have twelve lords: a lord for winter, a lord for summer, a lord for rain, a lord for wind, a lord for trees, a lord for people, a lord for horses, a lord for water, a lord for night, a lord for day, a lord for death, a lord for the earth. The lord in the sky is the greatest, but he acts consensually, and each lord approves of the actions of his partners. «God is exalted above what the wrongdoers say!»[31] We noticed that one clan worships snakes, another fish, and another cranes. They told me that they had once been routed in battle. Then the cranes cried out behind them, and the enemy took fright, turned tail, and fled, even though they had routed the Bāshghird. They said, "These are his actions: he has routed our enemies." 38

ففزعوا وانهزموا بعدما هزموا فعبدوا الكراكيّ لذلك وقالوا هذه ربّنا لأنّه[1] هزم أعداءنا فهم يعبدونها لذلك قال وسرنا من بلد هؤلاء فعبرنا نهر جرمشان ثمّ نهر اورن ثمّ نهر اورم[2] ثمّ نهر بايناج[3] ثمّ نهر وتيع ثمّ نهر بناسنه ثمّ نهر جاوشين[4] وبين النهر والنهر ممّا ذكرنا اليومان والثلاثة والأربعة وأقلّ من ذلك وأكثر.

٣٩ فلمّا كنّا من ملك الصقالبة وهو الذي قصدناه[5] على مسيرة يوم وليلة وجّه لاستقبالنا الملوك الأربعة الذين تحت يده وإخوانه وأولاده فاستقبلونا ومعهم الخبز واللحم والجاورس وساروا معنا فلمّا صرنا منه على فرسخين تلقّانا هو بنفسه فلمّا رآنا نزل فخرّ ساجدا شكرا لله جلّ وعزّ وكان في كمّه دراهم فنثرها علينا ونصب لنا قبابا فنزلناها[6] وكان وصولنا إليه يوم الأحد لاثنتي عشرة ليلة خلت من المحرّم سنة عشر وثلاثمائة فكانت المسافة من الجرجانيّة إلى بلده سبعين يوما فأقمنا يوم الأحد ويوم الاثنين ويوم الثلاثاء ويوم الأربعاء في القباب التي ضربت لنا حتّى جمع الملوك والقوّاد وأهل بلده ليسمعوا قراءة الكتاب.

٤٠ فلمّا كان يوم الخميس واجتمعوا نشرنا المِطْرَدَيْن اللذين كانا معنا وأسرجنا الدابّة بالسرج الموجّه إليه[7] وألبسناه السواد وعمّمناه وأخرجت كتاب الخليفة وقلت له لا يجوز أن نجلس والكتاب يقرأ فقام على قدميه هو ومن حضر من وجوه أهل مملكته وهو رجل بدين بطين جدّا وبدأت فقرأت صدر الكتاب فلمّا بلغت منه سلام عليك فإنّي أحمد إليك الله الذي لا إله إلّا هو قلت رُدّ على أمير المؤمنين السلام فردّ وردّوا جميعا بأسرهم ولم يزل الترجمان يترجم لنا حرفا حرفا فلمّا استتممنا[8] قراءته كبّروا تكبيرة ارتجّت لها الأرض.

٤١ ثمّ قرأت كتاب الوزير حامد بن العبّاس وهو قائم ثمّ أمرته بالجلوس فجلس عند قراءة كتاب نذير الحرميّ فلمّا استتممته[9] نثر أصحابه عليه الدراهم الكثيرة ثمّ أخرجت

١ الأصل: سالاته؛ ياقوت: هذه ربّنا لأنّها هزمت. ٢ رسمت أسماء هذه الأنهار كما هي موجودة في الأصل.
٣ الأصل: بانناج. ٤ رسمت أسماء هذه الأنهار كما هي موجودة في الأصل. ٥ ياقوت: وهو الذي قصدنا إليه.
٦ كما في ياقوت وفي الأصل: فنزلها. ٧ الأصل: الينا. ٨ الأصل: استتمنا. ٩ الأصل: استتمته.

This is why they worship cranes. We left their territory and crossed the following rivers: the Jrmsān, the Ūrn, the Ūrm, the Bāynāj, the Wtīʿ, the Bnāsnh, and the Jāwshīn.[32] It is about two, three, or four days travel from one river to the next.

39 *The Bulghārs*

We were a day and night's march away from our goal. The king of the Ṣaqālibah dispatched his brothers, his sons, and the four kings under his control to welcome us with bread, meat, and millet. They formed our escort. When we were two *farsakh*s away, he came to meet us in person. On seeing us, he got down from his horse and prostrated himself abjectly, expressing thanks to the great and glorious God! He had some dirhams in his sleeve and showered them over us. He had yurts pitched for us, and we were lodged in them. We arrived on Sunday the twelfth of Muharram, 310 [May 12, 922]. We had been on the road for seventy days since leaving al-Jurjāniyyah.[33] From Sunday to Wednesday we remained in our yurts, while he mustered his kings, commanders, and subjects to listen to the reading of the letter.

40 When they had gathered on the Thursday, we unfurled the two standards we had brought with us, saddled the horse with the saddle meant for the king, dressed him in black, and placed a turban on his head. I brought out the letter of the caliph and said, "We are not permitted to remain seated during the reading of the letter." He stood up, as did the chiefs in attendance. He was big and corpulent. I read the beginning of the letter, and, when I reached the phrase, "Peace be upon you! On your behalf, I praise God—there is no god but Him!" I said, "Return the greetings of the Commander of the Faithful." They did so, without exception. The interpreter translated everything, word by word. When we had finished the letter, they shouted "God Almighty!" at the top of their voices. The ground under our feet shook.

41 I next read the letter of the vizier Ḥāmid ibn al-ʿAbbās. The king continued to stand. I told him to be seated, so he sat down for the reading of the letter of Nadhīr al-Ḥaramī. When I had finished, his companions showered him with many dirhams. Then I produced the gifts meant for him and his wife: unguents,[34] clothes, and pearls. I presented one gift after another until I had handed over everything. Then, in front of his people, I presented a robe of honor to his wife, who was seated by his side. This is their customary

الهدايا من الطيب والثياب واللؤلؤ له ولامرأته[1] فلم أزل أعرض عليه وعليها شيئا شيئا حتّى فرغنا من ذلك ثمّ خلعت على امرأته بحضرة الناس وكانت جالسة إلى جنبه وهذه سنّتهم وزيّهم فلمّا خلعت عليها نثر النساء عليها الدراهم وانصرفنا.

٤٢ فلمّا كان بعد ساعة وجّه إلينا فدخلنا إليه وهو في قبّته والملوك عن يمينه وأمرنا أن نجلس عن يساره وإذا أولاده جلوس بين يديه وهو وحده على سرير مغشّى بالديباج الروميّ فدعا بالمائدة فقدِّمت وعليها اللحم المشويّ وحده فابتدأ هو فأخذ سكّينا وقطع لقمة وأكلها وثانية وثالثة ثمّ احتزّ قطعة دفعها إلى سوسن الرسول فلمّا تناولها جاءته مائدة صغيرة فجعِلت بين يديه وكذلك الرسم لا يمدّ أحد يده إلى الأكل حتّى يناوله الملك لقمة فساعة يتناولها قد جاءته مائدة ثمّ ناولني فجاءتني مائدة ثمّ ناول الملك الرابع فجاءته مائدة ثمّ ناول أولاده فجاءتهم الموائد وأكلنا[2] كلّ واحد من مائدته لا يشركه فيها أحد ولا يتناول من مائدة غيره شيئا فإذا فرغ من الطعام حمل[3] كلّ واحد منهم ما يبقى[4] على مائدته إلى منزله.

٤٣ فلمّا أكلنا[5] دعا بشراب العسل وهم يسمّونه السُجُو ليومه وليلته فشرب قدحا ثمّ قام قائما فقال هذا سروري بمولاي أمير المؤمنين أطال الله بقاءه وقام الملوك الأربعة وأولاده لقيامه وقمنا نحن أيضا حتّى إذا فعل ذلك ثلاث مرّات ثمّ انصرفنا من عنده.

٤٤ وقد كان يُخَطَب له على منبره قبل قدومي اللّٰهمّ وأَصلِح الملك يلطوار ملك بلغار فقلت أنا له إنّ الله هو الملك ولا يسمّى على المنبر بهذا الاسم غيره جلّ وعزّ وهذا مولاك أمير المؤمنين قد رضي لنفسه أن يقال على منابره في الشرق والغرب اللّٰهمّ أصلِح عبدك وخليفتك جعفر الإمام المقتدر بالله أمير المؤمنين وكذا من كان قبله من آبائه الخلفاء وقد قال النبيّ صلّى الله عليه وسلّم لا تُطروني كما أَطَرَت النصارى عيسى بن مريم فإنّما أنا عبد الله ورسوله فقال لي فكيف يجوز أن يخطب لي قلت

١ الأصل: وللولولو لامراته. ٢ ياقوت: ثم ناولها الملك الثاني فجاءته المائدة وكذلك حتى قدم إلى كلّ واحد من الذين بين يديه مائدة وأكل. ٣ الأصل: وحمل. ٤ ياقوت: ما بقي. ٥ ياقوت: فلمّا فرغنا.

practice. The womenfolk showered dirhams on her after I had presented the robe. Then we left.

An hour later, he sent for us, and we were shown into his tent. The kings 42
were on his right. He ordered us to sit on his left. His sons were seated in front of him. He sat alone, on a throne draped in Byzantine silk. He called for the table. It was carried in, laden with roasted meat and nothing else. He picked up a knife, cut off a piece of meat, and ate it, then a second piece and a third, before anyone else. Then he cut off a piece and handed it to Sawsan, the envoy, who had a small table placed in front of him in order to receive it. Such is their custom. No one reaches for the food before the king hands him a portion and a table is provided for him to receive it—the moment he receives it, he gets a table. He handed me a piece next, and I was given a table. He handed a piece to the fourth king, and he was given a table.[35] Then he handed some meat to his sons, and they were given tables. Each of us ate from the table intended for his sole use. No one took anything from any other table. When the king was done with the food, everyone took what remained on his own table back to his lodging.

After the meat, he called for the honey drink *sujū*, which he drinks night 43
and day,[36] and drank a cupful. Then he stood up and said, "Such is my joy in my patron the Commander of the Faithful, may God prolong his life!" The four kings and his sons stood up when he did. So did we. When he had done this three times, we were shown out.

Before I turned up, the phrase "Lord God, keep in piety the king Yilṭawār, 44
king of the Bulghārs!"[37] was proclaimed from the *minbar* during the Friday oration. I told the king, "God is the king, and He alone is to be accorded this title from the *minbar*. Great and glorious is He! Take your patron, the Commander of the Faithful. He is satisfied with the phrase, 'Lord God, keep in piety the imam Jaʿfar al-Muqtadir bi-llāh, your humble servant, caliph, and Commander of the Faithful!' This is proclaimed from his *minbar*s east and west. His forefathers, the caliphs before him, did the same. The Prophet (God bless and cherish him!) said, 'Do not exaggerate my importance the way the Christians exaggerate the importance of Jesus, the son of Mary, for I am simply ʿAbdallāh: God's bondsman and His emissary.'"[38] He asked me, "What proclamation can I rightly use for the Friday oration?" and I said, "Your name and that of your father." "But my father was an unbeliever," he said, "and I do not wish to have his name mentioned from the *minbar*.

باسمك واسم أبيك قال إنّ أبي كان كافرا ولا أحبّ أن أذكر اسمه على المنبر وأنا أيضا فما أحبّ أن يُذكَر اسمي إذا كان الذي سمّاني[1] كافرا ولكن ما اسم مولاي أمير المؤمنين قلت جعفر قال فيجوز أن أتسمّى باسمه قلت نعم قال قد جعلت اسمي جعفرا واسم أبي عبد الله فتقدّمْ إلى الخطيب[2] بذلك ففعلتُ فكان يخطب له اللّٰهمّ وأصلح عبدك جعفر بْن عبد الله أمير بلغار مولى أمير المؤمنين.

٤٥ ولمّا كان بعد قراءة الكتاب وإيصال الهدايا بثلاثة أيّام بعث[3] إليّ وقد كان بلغه أمر الأربعة آلاف دينار وما كان من حيلة النصرانيّ في تأخيرها وكان خَبَرُها في الكتاب فلمّا دخلت إليه أمرني بالجلوس فجلست ورمى إليّ كتاب أمير المؤمنين فقال من جاء بهذا الكتاب قلت أنا ثمّ رمى إليّ كتاب الوزير فقال وهذا أيضا قلت أنا قال فالمال الذي ذُكِر فيهما ما فُعِل قلت تعذّر جمعه وضاق الوقت وخشينا فوت الدخول فتركنا ليلحق بنا فقال إنّما جئتم بأجمعكم وأنفق عليكم مولاي ما أنفق لحمل هذا المال إليّ حتّى أبني به حصنا يمنعني من اليهود الذين قد استعبدوني فأمّا الهديّة فغلامي قد كان يحسن أن يجيء بها قلت هو كذاك إلّا أنّا قد اجتهدنا فقال للترجمان قل له أنا لا أعرف هؤلاء إنّما أعرفك أنت وذلك أنّ هؤلاء قوم عجم ولو علم الأستاذ أيّده الله أنّهم يبلغون ما تبلغ ما بعث بك حتّى تحفظ عليّ وتقرأ كتابي وتسمع جوابي وليس أطالب غيرك بدرهم فاخرج من المال فهو أصلح لك فانصرفت من بين يديه مذعورا مغموما وكان رجلا[4] له منظر وهيبة بدين عريض كأنّما يتكلّم من خابية فخرجت من عنده وجمعت أصحابي وعرّفتهم ما جرى بيني وبينه[5] وقلت لهم من هذا حذرت.

٤٦ وكان مؤذّنه يثنّي الإقامة إذا أذّن فقلت له إنّ مولاك أمير المؤمنين يُفْرِد في داره الإقامةَ فقال للمؤذّن اقبل ما يقوله لك ولا تخالفه فأقام المؤذّن على ذلك أيّاما وهو يسائلني عن المال ويناظرني فيه وأنا أويسه منه وأحتجّ فيه فلمّا يئس منه تقدّم إلى

---

١ ياقوت: الذي سمّاني به. ٢ الأصل: الخاطب. ٣ الأصل: ابعث. ٤ الأصل: وكان رجل. ٥ الأصل: بنه وبينه.

Indeed, I do not wish to have even my own name mentioned, because it was given me by an unbeliever. What is the name of my patron, the Commander of the Faithful?" "Jaʿfar," I replied. "Am I permitted to take his name?" "Yes." "Then I take Jaʿfar as my name, and ʿAbdallāh as the name of my father. Convey this to the preacher." I did so. The proclamation during the Friday oration became, "Lord God, keep in piety Your bondsman Jaʿfar ibn ʿAbdallāh, the emir of the Bulghārs, whose patron is the Commander of the Faithful!"

Three days after I had read out the epistle and presented the gifts, he summoned me. He had learned of the four thousand dinars and of the subterfuge employed by the Christian in order to delay their payment.[39] The dinars had been mentioned in the letter. When I was shown in, he commanded me to be seated. I sat down. He threw the letter from the Commander of the Faithful at me. "Who brought this letter?" "I did." Then he threw the vizier's letter at me. "And this one?" "I did," I replied. "What has been done," he asked, "with the money they refer to?" "It could not be collected. Time was short, and we were afraid of missing the crossing. We left the money behind, to follow later." "You have all arrived," he said. "My patron has given you this sum to be brought to to me, so I can use it to build a fort to protect myself against the Jews who have reduced me to slavery. My man could have brought me the gifts." "Indeed he could have. We did our best." Then he said to the interpreter, "Tell him that I do not acknowledge any of the others. I acknowledge only you. They are not Arabs. If my master (God give him support!) thought that they could have read the official letter as eloquently as you, he would not have sent you to keep it safe for me, read it, and hear my response. I do not expect to receive one single dirham from anyone but you. Produce the money. This would be the best thing for you to do."[40] I left the audience, dazed and in a state of terror. I was overawed by his demeanor. He was a big, corpulent man, and his voice seemed to come from inside a barrel. I left the audience, gathered my companions, and told them about our conversation. "I warned you about this," I said.[41] 45

At the start of the prayer, his muezzin would repeat the phrases announcing the start of prayer twice.[42] I said to him, "These phrases are announced only once in the realm of your patron the Commander of the Faithful." So he told the muezzin, "Accept what he tells you and do not contravene him." The muezzin performed the call to prayer as I had suggested for several days. During this time the king would interrogate me and argue about the money. 46

المؤذّن أن يثنّي الإقامة ففعل وأراد بذلك أن يجعله طريقا إلى مناظرتي[١] فلمّا سمعت تثنيته للإقامة نهيته وصحت عليه فعرف الملك ذلك فأحضرني وأحضر أصحابي.

٤٧ فلمّا اجتمعنا قال للترجمان قل له يعنيني[٢] ما يقول في مؤذّنين أفرد أحدهما وثنّى الآخر ثمّ صلّى كلّ واحد منهما بقوم أتجوز الصلاة أم لا قلت الصلاة جائزة فقال باختلاف أم بإجماع قلت بإجماع قال قل له فما يقول في رجل دفع إلى قوم مالا لأقوام ضعفى محاصرين مستعبدين فخانوه فقلت هذا لا يجوز وهؤلاء قومُ سُوءٍ قال باختلاف أم بإجماع قلت بإجماع فقال للترجمان قل له تعلم أنّ الخليفة أطال الله بقاءه لو بعث إليّ جيشا كان يقدر عليّ قلت لا قال فأمير خراسان قلت لا قال أليس لبُعْد المسافة وكثرة مَنْ بيننا من قبائل الكفّار قلت بلى قال قل له فوالله إنّي لبمكاني البعيد الذي[٣] تراني فيه وإنّي لخائف من مولاي أمير المؤمنين وذلك أنّي أخاف أن يبلغه عنّي شيء يكرهه فيدعو عليّ فأهلك بمكاني وهو في مملكته وبيني وبينه البلدان الشاسعة وأنتم تأكلون خبزه وتلبسون ثيابه وترونه في كلّ وقت خنتموه في مقدار رسالة بعثكم بها إليّ إلى قوم ضعفى وخنتم المسلمين لا أقبل منكم أمر ديني حتّى يجيئني[٤] من ينصح لي في ما يقول فإذا جاءني إنسان بهذه الصورة قبلت منه فألجمنا وما أحرنا جوابا وانصرفنا من عنده قال فكان بعد هذا القول يؤثرني ويقرّبني ويباعد أصحابي ويسمّيني أبا بكر الصدّيق[٥].

٤٨ ورأيت في بلده من العجائب ما لا أحصيها كثرة من ذلك أنّ أوّل ليلة بتناها في بلده رأيت قبل مغيب الشمس بساعة قياسيّة أفق السماء وقد احمرّت احمرارا شديدا وسمعت في الجوّ أصواتا شديدة[٦] وهَمْهَمة عالية فرفعت رأسي فإذا غيم أحمر مثل النار قريب منّي وإذا تلك الهمهمة والأصوات منه وإذا فيه أمثال الناس والدوابّ وإذا في الأشباح[٧] التي فيه تشبه الناس رماح وسيوف أتبيّنها وأتخيّلها وإذا قطعة أخرى مثلها أرى فيها أيضا رجالا ودوابّ وسلاحا فأقبلت هذه القطعة

١ الأصل: مناظري. ٢ الأصل: يعيني. ٣ الأصل: لمكاني البعيد الذين. ٤ الأصل: يجبني. ٥ الأصل: ابو بكر الصدوق. ٦ الأصل: صوتا شديدة؛ ياقوت: أصواتا عالية. ٧ الأصل: واذا في الاستباخ؛ ياقوت: وإذا في أيدي الاشباح.

I would try to persuade him to give up his hopes and explained our reasons. When he despaired of receiving the money, he instructed the muezzin to revert to a repeated announcement. The muezzin did so. The king meant it as a pretext for debate. When I heard the muezzin announce the start of prayer twice, I shouted to him to stop. The muezzin informed the king. The king summoned me and my companions.

He said to the interpreter, "Ask him (he meant me), what is his opinion 47
on two muezzins, one of whom announces the call once, the other twice, both of whom lead the people in prayer? Is the prayer permissible or not?" "The prayer is permissible," I said. "Is there any disagreement on this, or is there consensus?" "There is consensus," I said. "Ask him, what is his opinion about someone who has given to one group of people a sum of money intended for another group of people, weak people, sorely beset and reduced to slavery, betrayed by the first group?" "This is impermissible," I replied, "and they are wicked people." "Is there any disagreement, or is there consensus?" "There is consensus," I said. Then he said to the interpreter, "Ask him, do you think that if the caliph—God give him long life!—were to send an army against me he would be able to overpower me?" "No," I answered. "What about the emir of Khurasan, then?" "No." "Is it not because we are separated by vast distance and many infidel tribes?" he asked. "Of course," I answered. "Tell him, by God—here I am, in this far-off land where we are now, you and I both, yet still I fear my patron the Commander of the Faithful. I fear his curse, should he learn anything displeasing about me. I would die on the spot, though his kingdom is a great distance away. Yet you who eat his bread, wear his clothes, and look on him constantly have betrayed him in the matter of a letter he commanded you to bring to me, to my weak people. You have betrayed the Muslims. I shall accept no instruction from you on how to practice my religion until a sincere counselor arrives. I will accept instruction from such a man." He had dumbfounded us—we had no answer. We left. Ibn Faḍlān said: From then on, he would show me favor and be affable towards me, addressing me as Abū Bakr the Veracious.[43] But he was aloof from my companions.

I lost count of the number of marvels I witnessed in his realm. For 48
example, on our first night in his territory, at what I reckoned was about an hour before sunset,[44] I saw the horizon turn a bright red. The air was filled with a mighty uproar, and I heard the din of many voices. I looked up and

تحمل على هذه[١] كما تحمل الكتيبة على الكتيبة ففزعنا من ذلك وأقبلنا على التضرّع والدعاء وهم يضحكون منّا ويتعجّبون من فعلنا قال وكنّا ننظر إلى القطعة تحمل على القطعة[٢] فتختلطان جميعا ساعة[٣] ثمّ تفترقان فما زال الأمر كذلك ساعة من الليل ثمّ غابتَا[٤] فسألنا الملك عن ذلك فزعم أنّ أجداده كانوا يقولون إنّ هؤلاء من مؤمني الجنّ[٥] وكفّارهم وهم يقتتلون في كلّ عشيّة وأنّهم ما عدموا هذا مذ كانوا في كلّ ليلة.

٤٩ قال ودخلت أنا وخيّاط كان[٦] للملك من أهل بغداد قد وقع إلى تلك الناحية قبّتي لنتحدّث فتحدّثنا بمقدار ما يقرأ إنسان أقلّ من نصف سُبْع[٧] ونحن ننتظر أذان العَتَمَة فإذا بالأذان فخرجنا من القبّة وقد طلع الفجر فقلت للمؤذن أيّ شيء أذّنت قال أذان الفجر قلت فالعشاء الآخِرة[٨] قال نصلّيها مع المغرب قلت فالليل قال كما ترى وقد كان أقصر من هذا إلّا أنّه قد أخذ في الطول وذكر أنّه منذ شهر ما نام خوفا أن تفوته صلاة الغداة وذلك أنّ الإنسان يجعل القدر على النار وقت المغرب ثمّ يصلّي الغداة وما آن لها أن تنضج قال ورأيت النهار عندهم طويلا جدّا وإذا أنّه يطول عندهم مدّةً من السنة ويقصر الليل ثمّ يطول الليل ويقصر النهار.

٥٠ فلمّا كانت الليلة الثانية جلست خارج القبّة وراقبت السماء فلم أر فيها[٩] من الكواكب إلّا عددا يسيرا ظننت أنّه نحو الخمسة عشر كوكبا متفرّقة وإذا الشفق الأحمر الذي قبل المغرب لا يغيب بتّة وإذا الليل[١٠] قليل الظُلْمة يعرف الرجل الرجل فيه من أكثر من غَلْوة سهم قال ورأيت القمر لا يتوسّط السماء بل يطلع في أرجائها ساعة ثمّ يطلع الفجر فيغيب القمر وحدّثني الملك أنّ وراء بلده بمسيرة ثلاثة أشهر قوم يقال لهم وِيسُو[١١] الليل عندهم أقلّ من ساعة قال ورأيت البلد عند طلوع الشمس يحمرّ كلّ شيء فيه من الأرض والجبال وكلّ شيء ينظر الإنسان إليه وتطلع

---

١ ياقوت: هذه القطعة على هذه. ٢ كما في ياقوت وفي الأصل: القطعة تحمل القطعة. ٣ الأصل: جميعا ~~ذلك~~ ساعة. ٤ ياقوت: غابتا. ٥ كما في ياقوت وفي الأصل: مؤمن الجنّ. ٦ الأصل: (كان) مكتوبة فوق (الخيّاط).
٧ ياقوت: نصف ساعة. ٨ ياقوت: فعشاء الأخيرة. ٩ كما في ياقوت وفي الأصل: السما فلم ... من.
١٠ الجملة من (متفرّقة) حتّى (الليل) ناقصة في الأصل وهي موجودة في رواية ياقوت. ١١ ياقوت: وِيسو.

was surprised to see fiery-red clouds close by. Loud voices came from the clouds, where there were shapes that looked like soldiers and horses. These shapes brandished swords and spears. I could form a clear image of them in my mind. Then another group, similar to the first, appeared. I could make out men, animals, and weapons. This second group charged the first, one squadron attacking the other. We were scared and began to pray to God and entreat Him. The locals were astonished at our reaction and laughed at us. Ibn Faḍlān said: We watched as one unit charged the other, engaged in combat for an hour and then separated. After an hour they disappeared. We asked the king about this, and he told us that his forebears used to say, "These are two groups of jinn, believers and unbelievers, who do battle every evening." He added that this spectacle had occurred every night for as long as they could remember.

Ibn Faḍlān said: I went into my yurt with the king's tailor, a man from Baghdad who had ended up there. We were chatting but did not chat for long—less time than it takes you to read halfway through one seventh of the Qur'an.[45] It was beginning to grow dark, and we were waiting for the call to prayer at nightfall. When we heard it we went outside the yurt and noticed that the morning sun had already arisen. So I said to the muezzin, "Which prayer did you call?" "The daybreak prayer." "And what about the last call, the night call?" "We perform that along with the sunset prayer." So I said, "And what of the night?" "The nights are as short as you observed. They have been even shorter but now they have started to grow long." He said that he had not slept for a month, afraid he would miss the morning prayer. You can put a cooking-pot on the fire at the time of the sunset prayer, and by the time you have performed the morning prayer, the pot will not have started to boil. Daylight was very long. I observed that, for part of the year, the days were long and the nights short. Later on I observed the nights grow long and the days short.[46] 49

On our second night, I sat down outside the yurt and watched the sky. I could make out only a few constellations, I think about fifteen. I noticed that the red glow that precedes sunset did not disappear—night was hardly dark at all. In fact you could identify another person at more than a bow-shot away. The moon did not reach the middle of the sky. It would rise in one part of the sky for an hour, then dawn would break, and the moon 50

الشمس[1] كأنّها غمامة كبرى فلا تزال الحمرة كذلك حتّى تتكبّد السماء وعرّفني أهل البلد أنّه إذا كان الشتاء عاد الليل في طول النهار وعاد النهار في قصر الليل حتّى أنّ الرجل منّا ليخرج إلى موضع يقال له إِتِل[2] بيننا وبينه أقلّ من مسيرة فرسخ وقت طلوع الفجر فلا يبلغه إلى وقت العتمة وتطلع الكواكب[3] كلّها حتّى تطبق السماء فما برحنا من البلد حتّى امتدّ الليل وقصر النهار.

ورأيتهم يتبرّكون بعواء الكلاب جدّا ويفرحون به ويقولون سنة خصب وبركة ٥١
وسلامة ورأيت الحيّات عندهم كثيرة حتّى إذا[4] الغصن من الشجرة لتلتفّ عليه العشرة منها والأكثر ولا يقتلونها ولا تؤذيهم حتّى لقد رأيت في بعض المواضع شجرة طويلة يكون طولها أكثر من مائة ذراع وقد سقطت وإذا بدنها عظيم جدّا فوقفت أنظر إليه إذ تحرّك فراعني ذلك وتأمّلته فإذا عليه حيّة قريبة[5] منه في الغلظ والطول فلمّا رأتني سقطت عنه وغابت بين الشجر فجئت فزعا فحدّثت الملك ومن كان في مجلسه فلم يكترثوا لذلك وقال لا تجزع فليس تؤذيك.

ونزلنا مع الملك منزلا فدخلت أنا وأصحابي تكين وسوسن وبارس ومعنا رجل ٥٢
من أصحاب الملك بين الشجر فإذا أنا بعود صغير[6] أخضر كرِقّة المِغْزَل وأطول فيه عرق[7] أخضر على رأس العرق ورقة عريضة مبسوطة على الأرض مفروش عليها مثل النابت فيها حَبّ لا يشكّ من يأكله أنّه رُمّان أَمْلِيسيّ فأكلنا منه فإذا به من اللذّة أمر عظيم فما زلنا نتبعه ونأكله.

ورأيت لهم تفّاحا أخضر شديد الخضرة وأشدّ حموضة من خلّ الخمر[8] تأكله ٥٣
الجواري فتسمّى[9] عليه ولم أر في بلدهم أكثر من شجر البندق لقد رأيت منه غياضا تكون الغيضة أربعين فرسخا في مثلها ورأيت لهم شجرا لا أدري ما هو مفرط الطول وساقه[10] أجرد من الورق ورؤوسه كرؤوس النخل له خوص دقاق[11] إلّا أنّه مجتمع

---

١ ياقوت: حين تطلع الشمس.

٢ الأصل: اتل. ٣ ياقوت: إلى وقت طلوع الكواكب. ٤ الأصل: حتى ~~امتد الليل~~ إذا. ٥ الأصل: حيّة قريب.

٦ الأصل: فاذا انا عودا صغيرا. ٧ الأصل: عروا. ٨ الأصل: متن خل الخمر. ٩ الأصل: يسمى؛ ياقوت: فيسمن. ١٠ الأصل: وساقيه. ١١ كما في ياقوت وفي الأصل: حوص وقال.

would set. The king told me that a tribe called the Wīsū lived three months from his territory, where night lasted less than an hour. Ibn Faḍlān said: I noticed that, at sunrise, the whole country, the ground, the mountains, anything you cared to look at, grew red. The sun rose like a giant cloud. The red persisted until the sun was at its zenith. The inhabitants of Bulghār informed me, "In winter, night is as long as day is now and day is as short as night. If we set out at sunrise for a place called Itil less than a *farsakh* away, we will not get there before nightfall, when all the constellations have risen and cover the sky." When we left Bulghār territory, night had grown long and day short.[47]

They consider the howling of dogs to be very auspicious, I observed. 51
They rejoice and say, "A year of fertility, auspiciousness, and peace." Snakes, I noticed, are so numerous that ten, maybe even more, could be coiled around just one branch of a tree. The Bulghārs do not kill them, and the snakes do not harm them. There was one place where I saw a felled tree more than one hundred cubits in length. I noticed that it had a very thick trunk, so I stopped to examine it. All of a sudden it moved. I was terrified. When I looked closely, I noticed a snake of almost the same length and bulk lying on top of it. When it saw me, it slid off the trunk and disappeared among the trees. I left in a state of alarm and told the king and his companions, but they were unimpressed. The king said, "Have no fear. It will do you no harm."

When we were traveling in the company of the king, we halted at a place 52
where my comrades Takīn, Sawsan, Bārs, one of the King's companions, and I entered a copse. We saw a small piece of dark wood, slender as the staff of a spindle, though a bit longer, with a dark shoot. A broad leaf from the top of the shoot spread on the ground. What looked like berry-bearing calyxes were scattered on it. You could easily mistake the taste of these berries for sweet seedless pomegranates. We ate them, and they were delicious. We spent the rest of our time there looking for them and eating them.

The apples, I noticed, are dark. In fact, they are extremely dark and more 53
acidic than wine vinegar. The female slaves eat them, and they get their name from them.[48] Hazel trees grow in abundance. I saw hazel woods everywhere. One wood can measure forty by forty *farsakh*s. There is another tree that grows there, but I don't know what it is. It is extremely tall, has a leafless trunk, and tops like the tops of palm trees, with slender fronds, but bunched

يجوزون[1] إلى موضع يعرفونه من ساقه فيثقبونه ويجعلون تحته إناء فتجري إليه من ذلك الثقب ماء أطيب من العسل إن أكثر الإنسان منه أسكره كما يسكر الخمر[2].

٥٤ وأكثر أكلهم الجاورس[3] ولحم الدابّة على أنّ الحِنْطة والشعير كثير وكلّ من زرع شيئا أخذه لنفسه ليس للملك فيه حقّ غير أنّهم يؤدّون إليه في كلّ سنة من كلّ بيت جلدَ سمّورٍ وإذا أمر سريّة بالغارة على بعض البلدان فغنمت كان له معهم حِصّة ولا بدّ لكلّ من يعترس أو يدعو دعوة من زلّة للملك على قدر الوليمة وساخْرَج من نبيذ العسل وحنطة رديّة لأنّ أرضهم سوداء منتنة.

٥٥ وليس لهم مواضع يجمعون فيها طعامهم ولكنّهم يحفرون في الأرض آبارا ويجعلون الطعام فيها فليس يمضي عليه إلّا أيّام يسيرة حتّى يتغيّر ويريح فلا يُنتفع به وليس لهم زيت ولا شَيْرَج ولا دهن بتّة وإنّما يقيمون مقام هذه الأدهان دهن السمك فكلّ شيء يستعملونه فيه يكون زفرا ويعملون من الشعير حَساء يُحْسونه الجواريَ والغلمانَ وربّما طبخوا الشعير باللحم فأكل الموالي اللحم وأطعموا الجواري الشعير إلّا أن يكون رأس تيس[4] فيُطعَمَ من اللحم.

٥٦ وكلّهم يلبسون القلانس فإذا ركب الملك ركب وحده بغير غلام ولا أحد يكون معه فإذا اجتاز في السوق لم يبق أحد إلّا قام وأخذ قلنسوته عن رأسه فجعلها تحت إبطه فإذا جاوزهم ردّوا قلانسهم إلى رؤوسهم وكذلك كلّ من يدخل إلى الملك من صغير وكبير حتّى أولاده وإخوته ساعة ينظرون إليه قد أخذوا قلانسهم فجعلوها تحت آباطهم ثمّ أوموا إليه برؤوسهم وجلسوا ثمّ قاموا حتّى يأمرهم بالجلوس وكلّ من يجلس بين يديه فإنّما يجلس باركا ولا يخرج قلنسوته ولا يظهرها حتّى يخرج من بين يديه فيلبسها عند ذلك.

٥٧ وكلّهم في قباب إلّا أنّ قبّة الملك كبيرة جدّا تسع ألف نفس وأكثر مفروشة بالفرش الأرمنيّ وله في وسطها سرير مغشّى بالديباج الروميّ.

---

١ الأصل: يجوز؛ ياقوت: يعمدون. ٢ الأصل: كما يسكر الخمر وأكثر. ٣ الأصل: اكلهم الجاورس.
٤ الأصل: نفس.

together. The locals know where to make a hole in the trunk. They place a container underneath it. Sap, sweeter than honey, flows from the hole. If someone drinks too much sap, he gets as intoxicated as he would from drinking wine.

Their diet consists chiefly of millet and horse meat, though wheat and 54
barley are plentiful. Crop-growers keep what they grow for themselves. The king has no right to the crops, but every year they pay him one sable skin per household. When he orders a raid on a given territory, he takes a share of the booty they bring back. For every wedding feast or banquet the king is given a jug of honey wine, some wheat (of very poor quality, because the soil is black and so foul-smelling), and a gift of food. The amount of food depends on the size of the banquet.

They have nowhere to store their food, so they dig holes in the ground 55
as deep as wells to store it. It only takes a few days for it to rot and give off such an odor that it becomes inedible. They do not use olive oil, sesame oil, or any other vegetable oil. They use fish oil instead. Everything they prepare in it is unwholesome and greasy. They make a broth from barley and give it to slaves of both sexes. Sometimes they cook the barley with some meat. The owners eat the meat, and feed the female slaves the barley, unless the broth is made with the head of a goat, in which case the female slaves are given the meat.

They wear peaked caps. The king rides out alone, unaccompanied by 56
his men or anyone else. If he passes through the market, everyone stands, removes his cap from his head, and places it under his arm. When the king has passed, they put their caps back on. The same is true of those who are given an audience with the king, the great and the lowly—even his sons and his brothers. The moment they are in his presence, they remove their caps and place them under their arms. Then they bow their heads, sit down, and stand up again, until he commands them to be seated. Those who sit in his presence, do so in a kneeling position. They keep their hats under their arms until they have left. Then they put them back on again.

They live in yurts. The king's yurt is enormous and can hold more than a 57
thousand people. It is carpeted with Armenian rugs. In the middle the king has a throne bedecked with Byzantine silk.

٥٨ ومن رسومهم أنّه إذا وُلِدَ لابن الرجل مولود[١] أخذه جدّه دون أبيه وقال أنا أحقّ به من أبيه في حضنه حتّى يصير رجلا وإذا مات منهم الرجل ورثه أخوه دون ولده فعرّفت الملك أنّ هذا غير جائز وعرّفته كيف المواريث حتّى فهمها.

٥٩ وما رأيت أكثر من الصواعق في بلدهم وإذا وقعت الصاعقة على بيت لم يقربوه ويتركونه على حالته وجميع ما فيه من رجل ومال وغير ذلك حتّى يتلفه الزمان ويقولون هذا بيت مغضوب عليهم.

٦٠ وإذا قتل الرجل منهم الرجل عمدا أقادوه به وإذا قتله[٢] خطأً صنعوا له صندوقا من خشب الخَذَنْك وجعلوه في جوفه وسمّروه عليه وجعلوا معه ثلاثة أرغفة وكوز ماء ونصبوا له ثلاث خشبات مثل الشبائح وعلّقوه بينها وقالوا نجعله بين السماء والأرض يصيبه المطر والشمس لعلّ الله أن يرحمه فلا يزال معلّقا حتّى يبليه الزمان وتهبّ به الرياح.

٦١ وإذا رأوا[٣] إنسانا له حركة ومعرفة بالأشياء قالوا هذا حقّه أن يكون يخدم[٤] ربّنا فأخذوه وجعلوا في عنقه حبلا وعلّقوه في شجرة حتّى ينقطع[٥] ولقد حدّثني ترجمان الملك أنّ سنديّا سقط إلى ذلك البلد فأقام عند الملك برهة من الزمان يخدمه وكان خفيفا فهِما فأراد جماعة منهم الخروج في مجازات[٦] لهم فاستأذن السنديّ الملكَ في الخروج معهم فنهاه عن ذلك وألحّ عليه حتّى أذن له فخرج معهم في سفينة فرأوه حركا كيّسا فتآمروا بينهم وقالوا هذا يصلح لخدمة ربّنا فنوجّه به إليه واجتازوا في طريقهم بغيضة فأخرجوه إليها وجعلوا في عنقه حبلا وشدّوه في رأس شجرة عالية وتركوه ومضوا.

٦٢ وإذا كانوا يسيرون في طريق فأراد أحدهم البول فبال وعليه سلاحه انتهبوه وأخذوا ثيابه وجميع ما معه وهذا رسم لهم ومن حطّ عنه سلاحَه وجعله ناحية وبال لم يعرضوا له.

---

١ الأصل: مولودا. ٢ الأصل: واذا قتلوه. ٣ الأصل: واذ راوا. ٤ ياقوت: أن يخدم. ٥ الأصل: ينقطع؛ ياقوت: يتقطّع. ٦ الأصل: مجازات.

One of their customs is for the grandfather, rather than the father, to pick up a new-born boy and declare, "It is my right to care for him and raise him to manhood. It is not the father's right to do so." The brother, not the son, inherits the estate of a deceased man. I told the king that this was impermissible, and I taught him clearly how the inheritance laws work. He understood them. 58

I observed more lightning there than anywhere else. They do not approach a household struck by lightning but let it be, with all of its contents, people, and possessions—everything, in fact—until time destroys it. They say, "This household has incurred divine wrath." 59

They impose capital punishment upon anyone who kills on purpose. For manslaughter, they make a box out of *khadhank*, put the perpetrator inside and nail it fast. They give him three loaves of bread and a flagon of water, erect three pieces of wood in the shape of the frame of a camel saddle and suspend him inside, saying, "We set him between heaven and earth, exposed to the rain and the sun. Perhaps God will have pity on him." He remains there until his body rots over time and is scattered to the winds. 60

If they notice that someone is clever and able, they say, "This man is fit for the service of our lord." They take hold of him, place a rope around his neck and hang him from a tree until he decomposes. The king's interpreter told me that a man from Sind turned up once and served him for a while. This man was clever and able. A group of Bulghārs decided to go on one of their journeys. The man from Sind asked the king's permission to accompany them, but he refused. The man persisted until the king relented and gave his permission. So the man set sail with them. They noticed that he was quick-witted and clever and conspired as follows: "This man is fit for the service of our lord. Let us send him to him." Their route took them past a forest, so they took hold of the man, placed a rope around his neck, tied it to the top of a big tree, and left him there. Then they went on their way. 61

If one of them urinates on a march while still in full armor, everything he has with him, weapons and clothes, is removed as plunder. This is one of their customs. But they leave him alone if he undoes his weapons and puts them aside while urinating. 62

٦٣ وينزل الرجال والنساء إلى النهر فيغتسلون جميعا عراة لا يستتر بعضهم بعضا ولا يزنون بوجه ولا سبب ومَنْ زنا منهم كائنا من كان ضربوا له أربع سكك وشدّوا يديه و رجليه إليها وقطّعوا بالفأس من رقبته إلى فخذيه وكذلك يفعلون بالمرأة أيضا ثمّ يعلق كلّ قطعة منهم ومنها على شجرة وما زلت أجتهد أن يستتر النساء من الرجال فما استوى لي ذلك ويقتلون السارق كما يقتلون الزاني.

٦٤ وفي غياضهم عسل كثير في مساكن النحل يعرفونها فيخرجون لطلب ذلك فربّما وقع عليهم قوم من أعدائهم فقتلوهم.

٦٥ وفيهم تجّار كثير يخرجون إلى أرض الترك فيجلبون الغنم وإلى بلد يقال له وِيسُوا فيجلبون السمّور والثعلب الأسود.

٦٦ ورأينا فيهم أهل بيت يكونون خمسة آلاف نفس من امرأة ورجل قد أسلموا كلّهم يعرفون بالبَرَنْجار وقد بنوا لهم مسجدا من خشب يصلّون فيه ولا يعرفون القراءة فعلّمتُ جماعةً ما يصلّون به ولقد أسلم على يديّ رجل يقال له طالوت فأسميته عبد الله فقال أريد أن تسمّيني باسمك محمّدا ففعلت وأسلمت امرأته وأمّه وأولاده فسُمُّوا كلّهم محمّدا[1] وعلّمته ﴿الحَمْدُ لِلّهِ﴾ و﴿قُلْ هُوَ اللّهُ أَحَدٌ﴾ فكان فرحه بهاتين السورتين أكثر من فرحه إن[2] صار ملك الصقالبة.

٦٧ وكنّا لمّا وافينا الملك وجدناه نازلا على ماء يقال له خلجه[3] وهي ثلاث بحيرات منها اثنتان كبار وواحدة صغيرة إلّا أنّ ليس في جميعها شيء يُلحَق غورُه وبين هذا الموضع وبين نهر لهم عظيم يصبّ إلى بلاد الخزر يقال له نهر إتل نحو الفرسخ[4] وعلى هذا النهر موضع سوق تقوم في كلّ مديدة ويباع فيها المتاع الكثير النفيس.

٦٨ وكان تكين حدّثني أنّ في بلد الملك رجلا عظيم الخلق جدّا فلمّا صرت إلى البلد سألت الملك عنه فقال نعم قد كان في بلدنا ومات ولم يكن من أهل البلد ولا من الناس أيضا وكان من خبره[5] أنّ قوما من التجّار خرجوا إلى نهر إتل[6] كما يخرجون

---

١ الأصل: محد. ٢ الأصل: فرحه الى. ٣ كما في الأصل. ٤ الأصل: آتل تحو الفرس. ٥ كما في ياقوت وفي الأصل: من خبر . . . ٦ الأصل: اتل.

Men and women wash naked together in the river without covering themselves, and yet under no circumstance do they commit adultery. When they catch an adulterer, they set four rods in the ground and tie his hands and his feet to them, no matter who he may be. Then they take an axe, and cut him up, from neck to thigh. They treat the woman in the same manner. They hang the pieces from a tree. I spared no effort to exhort the women to cover themselves in the presence of the men, but that proved impossible. They kill a thief in the same way as they kill an adulterer. 63

There are bees in the woods, and honey is abundant. They know where the bees are to be found and gather the honey. Sometimes they are surprised by an enemy tribe who kills them. 64

Many merchants live there. They travel to the territory of the Turks and bring back sheep and travel to another land, called Wīsū, and bring back sable and black fox. 65

There was one household of five thousand individuals, men and women. They had all converted to Islam and are known as the Baranjār. They had built a wooden mosque to pray in but did not know how to read the Qur'an. I taught one group how to conduct their prayers. A man named Saul converted to Islam under my supervision, and I gave him the name ʿAbdallāh, but he said, "I want you to give me your name—Muḥammad." I did so. His wife, mother, and children also converted. They all took the name Muḥammad.[49] I taught him the suras «Praise be to God» and «Say, He is God, One.»[50] He took greater delight in these suras than if he had been made king of the Ṣaqālibah. 66

We first encountered the king in an encampment at Khljh, a group of three unfathomable[51] lakes, two large, one small. It was about a *farsakh* away from a large river called the Itil, which they used and which flowed to the realm of the Khazars. On the bank of this river there is a market, open from time to time, where many valuable goods are sold.[52] 67

Takīn had told me that a giant lived in the king's territory. When I arrived, I asked the king about this, and he replied, "Yes, he used to live among us, but he died. He was not one of the local inhabitants—in fact, he was not really human. This is his story. A group of merchants went to the Itil, one day away, as is their custom. Now, this river was in spate and had 68

وهذا النهر قد مدّ وطغى ماؤه فلم أشعر يوما إلّا وقد وافاني جماعة من التجّار فقالوا أيّها الملك قد قفا على الماء[١] رجل إن كان من أمّة بقرب[٢] منّا فلا مقام لنا في هذه الديار وليس[٣] غير التحويل فركبت معهم حتّى صرت إلى النهر فإذا أنا بالرجل وإذا هو بذراعي اثنا عشر ذراعا[٤] وإذا له رأس أكبر ما يكون[٥] من القدور وأنف أكثر[٦] من شبر وعينان عظيمتان وأصابع تكون أكثر[٧] من شبر شبر فراعني أمره وداخلني ما داخل القوم من الفزع وأقبلنا نكلّمه ولا يكلّمنا إلّا ينظر[٨] إلينا فحملته إلى مكاني وكتبت إلى أهل ويسوا وهم منّا على[٩] ثلاثة أشهر أسألهم عنه فكتبوا إليّ يعرّفوني أنّ هذا الرجل من ياجوج وماجوج وهم منّا على ثلاثة أشهر عراة يحول بيننا وبينهم البحر لأنّهم على شطّه وهم مثل البهائم ينكح بعضهم بعضا يُخرِج الله عزّ وجلّ لهم كلّ يوم سمكة من البحر فيجيء الواحد منهم ومعه مِدْية فيحتزّ[١٠] منها قدر ما يكفيه ويكفي عياله فإن أخذ فوق ما يقنعهم اشتكى بطنه وكذلك عياله يشتكون بطونهم وربّما مات وماتوا بأسرهم فإذا أخذوا منها حاجتهم[١١] انقلبت ورفعت في البحر فهم في كلّ يوم على ذلك وبيننا وبينهم البحر من جانب والجبال محيطة بهم من جوانب أخر والسُدّ أيضا قد حال بينهم وبين الباب الذي كانوا يخرجون منه فإذا أراد الله عزّ وجلّ أن يخرجهم إلى العمارات سبّب لهم فتح السدّ ونضب البحرُ وانقطع عنهم السمك قال فسألته عن الرجل فقال أقام عندي مدّة فلم يكن ينظر إليه صبيّ إلّا مات ولا حامل إلّا طرحت حملها وكان إن تمكّن من إنسان عصره بيديه حتّى يقتله[١٢] فلمّا رأيت ذلك علّقته في شجرة عالية حتّى مات إن أردت أن تنظر إلى عظامه ورأسه مضيت معك حتّى تنظر إليها فقلت أنا والله أحبّ ذاك فركب معي إلى غيضة كبيرة فيها شجر عظام فقدفني[١٣] إلى شجرة سقطت عظامه[١٤] ورأسه

١ كما في ياقوت وفي الأصل: على ا . . . . ٢ ياقوت: أمّة تقرب. ٣ ياقوت: وليس لنا. ٤ كما في ياقوت وفي الأصل: ذرا . . . . ٥ ياقوت: كأكبر ما يكون. ٦ ياقوت: أكبر. ٧ ياقوت: وأصابعه كلّ واحدة شبر. ٨ ياقوت: وهو لا يتكلّم لا يزيد على النظر. ٩ ياقوت: وهم على. ١٠ الأصل: ومعهما بمديه فنخبر؛ ياقوت: فيجيء الواحد بمدية فيحتزّ. ١١ بياض في الأصل؛ والكلمة موجودة في رواية ياقوت. ١٢ الأصل: حتى تقتله. ١٣ الأصل: فقدفني؛ ياقوت: فتقدّمني. ١٤ وقع بياض في الأصل والجملة (سقطت عظامه) مأخوذة من نصّ الدهّان.

burst its banks. Barely a day later a group of merchants came back and said, 'Your Majesty, there is a man who has followed the course of the river. If he is from a community close by, then we cannot remain in our homes. We will have to migrate.' So I rode to the river with them. I was surprised by what I found when I got there—a man twelve cubits tall, using my forearm as a measure, with a head the size of a huge cooking-pot, a nose more than a span in length, two great eyes, and fingers longer than a span. He unnerved me, and I was gripped by the very terror that had gripped the others. We tried to speak to him, but he did not answer. He just looked at us. So I had him brought to my residence and wrote to the inhabitants of Wīsū, three months distant, asking them for information. They wrote back: 'He is one of the Gog and Magog, who live three months away from us in a state of absolute nakedness. The sea separates us. They live on the far side of the sea, on its shore. They mate with one another, like the beasts of the field. Every day the great and glorious God provides them with a fish from the sea. They come one by one with their knives and cut as much as they need to feed them and their dependents. If they take more than they need, they develop a pain in their stomach. Their dependents also develop a pain in their stomachs. Should he die, then they all die too. When they have what they need from the fish, it flips over and is taken back into the sea. This is how they live day by day. On one side we are separated from them by the sea. They are hemmed in by mountains on all other sides. A wall separates them from the gate from which they will swarm forth.[53] When almighty God intends them to swarm forth into the inhabited lands, He will cause the wall to be breached, the sea will dry up, and the fish will no longer be provided.'"[54] I asked the king about the man. He said, "He stayed with me for a while, but any boys who looked at him died, and pregnant women miscarried. His hands would crush to death anyone he took hold of. When I saw this happening, I hanged him from a tall tree and killed him. If you want to see his bones and skull, I will take you." "By God, I would like that very much," I said. So we rode out to a great wood, and he led me to a tree where the man's bones and skull had fallen. His head was like a bees' nest, and the

تحتها فرأيت رأسه مثل القَفِير الكبير وإذا أضلاعه مثل أكبر عراجين[١] النخل وكذلك عظام ساقيه وذراعيه فتعجّبت منه وانصرفت.

٦٩ قال وارتحل الملك من الماء الذي يسمّى خلجه إلى نهر يقال له جاوشير[٢] فأقام به شهرين ثمّ أراد الرحيل فبعث إلى قوم يقال لهم سواز[٣] يأمرهم بالرحيل معه فأبوا عليه وافترقوا فرقتين فرقة مع خَتَنه[٤] وكان قد تملّك عليهم واسمه ويرغ[٥] فبعث إليهم الملك وقال إنّ الله عزّ وجلّ قد منّ عليّ بالإسلام وبدولة أمير المؤمنين فأنا عبده وهذا الأمر قد قلّدنيه فمن خالفني[٦] لقيته بالسيف وكانت الفرقة الأخرى مع ملك من قبيلة يعرف ملك اَسْكِل وكان في طاعته إلّا أنّه لم يكن داخَلَ في الإسلام فلمّا وجّه إليهم هذه الرسالة خافوا ناحيته فرحلوا بأجمعهم معه إلى نهر جاوشير[٧] وهو نهر قليل العرض يكون عرضه خمسة أذرع وماؤه إلى السُرّة وفيه مواضع إلى التَرْقُوة وأكثره قامة وحوله شجر . . . .[٨] كثير من الشجر الخَذَنْك وغيره.

٧٠ وبالقرب منه صحراء واسعة يذكرون أنّ بها حيوانا دون الجمل في الكبر وفوق الثور رأسه رأس جمل وذنبه ذنب ثور وبدنه بدن بغل وحوافره مثل أظلاف الثور له في وسط رأسه قرن واحد غليظ مستدير كلّما ارتفع دقّ حتّى يصير مثل سنان الرمح فمنه ما يكون طوله خمسة أذرع إلى ثلاثة أذرع إلى أكثر وأقلّ يرتعي ورق الشجر جيّد الخَضَر إذا رأى الفارس قصده فإن كان تحته جواد أمنت منه بجهد وإن لحقه أخذه من ظهر دابّته بقرنه ثمّ زجّ به في الهواء واستقبله بقرنه فلا يزال كذلك حتّى يقتله ولا يعرض للدابّة بوجه ولا سبب وهم يطلبونه في الصحراء والغياض حتّى يقتلوه[٩] وذلك أنّه يصعدون الشجر العالية التي يكون بينها[١٠] ويجتمع لذلك عدّة من الرماة بالسهام المسمومة فإذا توسّطهم رموه حتّى يثخنوه ويقتلوه[١١] ولقد رأيت

---

١ ياقوت: أضلاعه أكبر من عراجين. ٢ كما في الأصل. ٣ الأصل: سوان. ٤ الأصل: خسه. ٥ كما في الأصل. ٦ الأصل مطموس: (هذا الا . . . قل . . . خالفني) فأضفنا الجملة لسياق النصّ. ٧ كما في الأصل.
٨ في الأصل بياض قدر كلمة: . . . ت. ٩ الأصل: حتى يقتلونه. ١٠ الأصل: ىىتها. ١١ الأصل: حتى يثخنونه ويقتلونه.

bones of his ribs, legs, and forearms were larger than the boughs of a palm tree. I departed, filled with wonder.

Ibn Faḍlān said: The king traveled from Khljh to a river called Jāwshīr, where he stayed for two months. When he was ready to leave, he sent a message to a people called Suwāz and commanded them to travel with him. They refused and split into two groups. One sided with his son-in-law W*rʿ, who had become their king. The king sent them a message: "Almighty God has given me the gift of Islam and granted me membership in the kingdom of the Commander of the Faithful. I am His bondsman. He has made me his emir. I will wage war on those who oppose me." The other group aligned themselves with the king of the Askil tribe, who was under the king's sovereignty, though he had not accepted Islam. When the king of the Bulghārs sent the Suwāz this epistle, they were afraid he might attack, so they joined him in his journey to the Jāwshīr river. This is not a very wide river—it is no more than five cubits wide, but the water reaches a man's navel, and comes up to his collar-bone in some places. At its deepest point, it reaches the height of a man. It is surrounded by many trees,[55] including *khadhank* trees. 69

There is a wide plain near the river, where they say an animal smaller than a camel but larger than a bull lives. It has the head of a camel, the tail and hooves of a bull, and the body of a mule. It has a single, round, thick horn in the middle of its head. As the horn grows it becomes narrow and resembles a spearhead. Some of these animals are five cubits tall, some three, with a degree of variation. It eats succulent and tasty leaves from the trees. It charges any horseman it sees. A fleet mare will just about escape, with some effort. But if the animal overtakes the horseman, it unseats him from his horse and tosses him in the air with its horn. Then it rushes him with its horn again and again and kills him, though it pays no heed whatsoever to the horse. They hunt it to death on the plain and in the woods. They climb the tall trees in the wood where the animal lives, and a group of archers with poisoned arrows work together. When the animal is in their midst they shoot it, exhaust it, and kill it. In the king's tent I saw three large bowls that looked as if they were made of Yemeni onyx. The king informed me that they were 70

عند الملك ثلاث طيفوريّات كبار تشبه الجزع اليمانيّ عرّفني أنّها معمولة من أصل قرن هذا الحيوان وذكر بعض أهل البلد أنّه الكركدن.

٧١ قال وما رأيت منهم إنسانا يحمرّ بل[١] أكثرهم معلول وربّما[٢] يموت أكثرهم بالقولنج حتّى أنّه ليكون بالطفل الرضيع منهم وإذا مات المسلم عندهم وإذا امرأة خوارزميّة وغسلوه غسل المسلمين ثمّ حملوه على عجلة تجرّه وبين يديه مِطرَد حتّى يصيروا[٣] به إلى المكان الذي يدفنونه فيه فإذا صار إليه أخذوه عن العجلة[٤] وجعلوه على الأرض ثمّ خطّوا حوله خطّا ونحّوه ثمّ حفروا داخل ذلك الخطّ قبره وجعلوا له لحدا ودفنوه وكذلك يفعلون بموتاهم ولا تبكي النساء على الميّت بل[٥] الرجال منهم يبكون عليه يجوزون[٦] في اليوم الذي مات فيه فيقفون على باب قبّته فيضجّون بأقبح بكاء يبكون وأوحشه هؤلاء للأحرارُ فإذا انقضى بكاؤهم وافى العبيد ومعهم جلود مضفورة فلا يزالون يبكون ويضربون جنوبهم وما ظهر من أبدانهم بتلك السيور[٧] حتّى تصير في أجسادهم مثل ضرب السوط ولا بدّ من أن ينصبوا على باب قبّته[٨] مطردا ويحضرون سلاحه فيجعلونها حول قبره ولا يقطعون البكاء سنتين فإذا انقضت السنتان[٩] حطّوا المطرد وأخذوا من شعورهم ودعا أقرباء الميّت دعوة يعرف بها خروجهم من الحزن وإن كانت له زوجة تزوّجت هذا إذا كان من الرؤساء فأمّا العامّة فيفعلون بعض هذا بموتاهم.

٧٢ وعلى ملك الصقالبة ضريبة يؤدّيها إلى ملك الخزر من كلّ بيت في مملكته جلد سمّور وإذا قدمت السفينة من بلد الخزر إلى بلد الصقالبة ركب الملك فأحصى ما فيها وأخذ من جميع ذلك العُشر وإذا قدم الروس أو غيرهم من سائر الأجناس برقيق فللملك أن يختار[١٠] من كلّ عشرة أرؤس رأسا وابن ملك الصقالبة رهينة عند ملك الخزر وقد كان اتّصل بملك الخزر عن ابنة ملك الصقالبة[١١] جَمال فوجّه يخطبها فاحتجّ عليه وردّه فبعث وأخذها غصبا وهو يهوديّ وهي مسلمة فماتت

١ الأصل: بلى. ٢ الأصل: وبها. ٣ الأصل: س بين نحطرد حتى يصيرون. ٤ (العجلة) غامضة في الأصل.
٥ الأصل: بلى. ٦ الأصل: نكون عليه يجوز. ٧ الأصل: السمور. ٨ الأصل: ينصبو ... باب قبته.
٩ الأصل: السنتين. ١٠ الأصل: فالملك أن يحتار. ١١ الأصل: ابنته ملك الصقالبة.

made out of the base of this animal's horn. Some of the locals claim that this animal is the rhinoceros.

Ibn Faḍlān said: I saw no one in ruddy health. Most of them are sickly, 71
and the majority regularly die from the colic. Even the child at the breast suffers from it. When a Muslim dies and a woman from Khwārazm is present,[56] they wash the body as the Muslims do and then bear him on a cart, preceded by a standard, until they come to his grave. Then they take him from the cart and place him on the ground, draw a line around him, and remove him. They dig his grave, build his tomb, and bury him inside the line they have drawn. This is their burial custom. The women do not weep for the deceased, the men do. They arrive on the day of his death, stand at the entrance to his yurt, and howl and weep in the ugliest and wildest way. And these are freeborn men! When they have finished weeping, the slaves of the deceased bring leather thongs. The men continue to mourn and beat their flanks and exposed parts of their bodies with the leather thongs, leaving weals like those left by the lashes of a whip. At the entrance to his yurt they are required to erect a standard, bring his weapons, and place them around his grave. They weep for two years and then take the standard down and cut off their hair. The deceased's relatives hold a banquet to indicate that they have emerged from mourning. The deceased's wife, if he had one, then takes a husband. Such is their custom for their chieftains. Ordinary folk do not do as much as this for their dead.

The king of the Ṣaqālibah is obliged to pay to the king of the Khazars a 72
tribute of one sable skin for every tent in his kingdom. When the boat from Khazar territory reaches Ṣaqālibah territory, the king goes on board and counts its contents, taking a tenth of its cargo. When the Rūs or any other people come with slaves, the king of the Ṣaqālibah has the right to choose one in every ten. The king of the Khazars holds the son of the king of the Ṣaqālibah as a hostage.[57] The king of the Khazars heard that the daughter of the king of the Ṣaqālibah was beautiful, so he asked for her hand in marriage but was refused. He sent some troops and took her by force, though he is a Jew and she a Muslim. She died at his court, so he demanded a second

عنده فوجّه يطلب سأله أخرى فساعة اتّصل ذلك بملك الصقالبة[١] بادر فزوّجها لملك اَسْكِل وهو من تحت يده خيفة أن[٢] يغتصبه إيّاها كما فعل بأختها[٣] وإنّما دعا ملك الصقالبة أن يكاتب السلطان ويسأله أن يبني له حصنا خوفا من ملك الخزر.

٧٣ قال وسألته يوما فقلت له مملكتك واسعة وأموالك جمّة وخراجك كثير فلم سألت السلطان أن يبني حصنا بمال من عنده لا مقدار له فقال رأيت دولة الإسلام[٤] مُقبِلة وأموالهم يؤخذ من حلّها فالتمست ذلك لهذه العلّة ولو أنّي أردت أن أبني حصنا من أموالي من فضّة أو ذهب لما تعذّر ذلك عليّ وإنّما تبرّكت بمال أمير المؤمنين فسألته ذلك.

٧٤ قال ورأيت الروسيّة وقد وافوا في تجاراتهم ونزلوا على نهر إتل فلم[٥] أر أتمّ أبدانا منهم كأنّهم النخل شقرحمر لا يلبسون القراطق ولا الخفاتين ولكن يلبس الرجل[٦] منهم كساء يشتمل به على أحد شقّيه وتخرُج[٧] إحدى يديه منه ومع كلّ واحد منهم فأس وسيف وسكّين لا يفارقه جميع ما ذكرنا وسيوفهم صفائح مشطّبة[٨] إفرنجيّة ومن حدّ ظفر الواحد منهم إلى عنقه مُخْضِرٌ[٩] شجر وصور وغير ذلك.

٧٥ وكلّ امرأة منهم فعلى ثديها حُقّة[١٠] مشدودة إمّا من حديد وإمّا من فضّة وإمّا نحاس وإمّا ذهب على قدر مال زوجها ومقداره وفي كلّ حقّة حلقة فيها سكّين مشدود على الثدي أيضا وفي أعناقهم أطواق[١١] من ذهب وفضّة لأنّ الرجل إذا ملك عشرة آلاف درهم صاغ لامرأته طوقا وإن ملك عشرين ألفا صاغ لها طوقين وكذلك كلّ عشرة آلاف يزدادها يزداد طوقا لامرأته بما[١٢] كان في عنق الواحدة منهنّ الأطواق الكثيرة وأجلّ الحلي عندهم الخرَز الأخضر من الخزَف الذي يكون على السفن يبايعون[١٣] فيه ويشترون الخرزة بدرهم وينظمونه عقودا لنسائهم.

---

١ في الأصل: الصقال . . . .   ٢ الأصل: وخيفة ان.   ٣ الأصل: باخته . . . .   ٤ الأصل: الاسد . . . .
٥ كما في ياقوت وفي الأصل: نهر .آ. . فلم.   ٦ كما في ياقوت وفي الأصل: الخفاتين . . . الرجل.   ٧ ياقوت: ويخرج.   ٨ الأصل: مشطية.   ٩ الأصل: محضر.   ١٠ كما في ياقوت وفي الأصل: حلقة.   ١١ الأصل: فى اعناقهم اطوار؛ ياقوت: على أعناقهن أطواق.   ١٢ ياقوت: فربّما.   ١٣ ياقوت: يبالغون.

daughter. As soon as the king of the Ṣaqālibah heard this, he was afraid that the king of the Khazars might take her by force, as he had her sister, so he married her to the king of the Askil, who recognizes his authority.[58] It was fear of the king of the Khazars that forced the king of the Ṣaqālibah to write to the caliph and petition him to build him a fortress.

Ibn Faḍlān said: I asked him the following question one day and said, 73
"You have an extensive kingdom, many belongings, and considerable wealth from taxes. Why did you petition the caliph for an unspecified sum of money to build a fortress?" He replied, "I could see that the realm of Islam was flourishing and that the wealth of the Muslims was acquired lawfully. That is why I asked for it. If I had wanted to build a fort using my own silver and gold, I could have. I wanted the money of the Commander of the Faithful to bring me blessings, so I sent him my petition."

Ibn Faḍlān said: I also saw the Rūsiyyah. They had come to trade and had dis- 74
embarked at the Itil River. I have never seen bodies as nearly perfect as theirs. *The Rūsiyyah*
As tall as palm trees, fair and reddish, they wear neither tunics nor caftans. Every man wears a cloak with which he covers half of his body, so that one arm is uncovered. They carry axes, swords, and daggers and always have them to hand. They use Frankish swords with broad, ridged blades. They are dark from the tips of their toes right up to their necks—trees, pictures, and the like.[59]

Every woman wears a small box made of iron, silver, brass, or gold, 75
depending on her husband's financial worth and social standing, tied at her breasts.[60] The box has a ring to which a knife is attached, also tied at her breasts. The women wear neck rings of gold and silver. When a man has amassed ten thousand dirhams, he has a neck ring made for his wife. When he has amassed twenty thousand dirhams, he has two neck rings made. For every subsequent ten thousand, he gives a neck ring to his wife. This means a woman can wear many neck rings. The jewelry they prize the most is the dark ceramic beads they have aboard their boats and which they trade among themselves. They purchase beads for one dirham each and string them together as necklaces for their wives.

٧٦ وهم أقذر[١] خلق الله لا يستحيون[٢] من غائط ولا بول ولا يغتسلون من جنابة ولا يغسلون أيديهم من الطعام بل هم كالحمير الضالّة يجوزون[٣] من بلدهم فيرسون سفنهم بإتل وهو نهر كبير[٤] ويبنون على شطّه بيوتا كبارا من الخشب ويجتمع في البيت الواحد العشرة[٥] والعشرون والأقلّ والأكثر ولكلّ واحد سرير يجلس عليه ومعهم الجواري الرُوقة[٦] للتجّار فينكح الواحد جاريته ورفيقه[٧] ينظر إليه وربّما اجتمعت الجماعة منهم على هذه الحال بعضهم بحذاء بعض ويدخل التاجر[٨] ليشتري من بعضهم جارية فيصادفه ينكحها فلا يزول عنها حتّى يقضي[٩] أربه ولا بدّ لهم في كلّ يوم من غسل وجوههم ورؤوسهم بأقذر[١٠] ماء يكون وأطفسه وذلك أنّ الجارية توافي كلّ يوم بالغداة ومعها قصعة كبيرة فيها ماء فتدفعها إلى مولاها فيغتسل منها يديه ووجهه وشعر رأسه فيغسله ويسرّحه[١١] بالمشط في القصعة ثمّ يمتخط ويبصق فيها ولا يدع شيئا من القذر إلّا فعله في ذلك الماء[١٢] فإذا فرغ ممّا يحتاج إليه حملت الجارية القصعة إلى الذي إلى جانبه ففعل مثل فعل صاحبه ولا تزال ترفعها من واحد إلى واحد حتّى تديرها على جميع من في البيت وكلّ واحد منهم يمتخط ويبصق ويغسل وجهه وشعره فيها.

٧٧ وساعة توافي سفنهم[١٣] إلى هذا المرسى قد خرج[١٤] كلّ واحد منهم ومعه خبز ولحم وبصل ولبن ونبيذ حتّى يوافي خشبة طويلة منصوبة لها وجه يشبه وجه الإنسان وحولها صور صغار وخلف تلك الصور خشب طوال قد نصبت في الأرض فيوافي إلى الصورة الكبيرة ويسجد لها ثمّ يقول لها يا ربّ قد جئت من بلد بعيد ومعي من الجواري كذا وكذا رأسا ومن السمّور كذا وكذا جلدا حتّى يذكر جميع ما قدم معه من تجارته وجئتك بهذه الهديّة ثمّ يترك الذي معه بين يدي الخشبة

١ كما في ياقوت وفي الأصل: وهم اقدر. ٢ ياقوت: يستنجون. ٣ الأصل: بجوز؛ ياقوت: يجيئون. ٤ كما في ياقوت وفي الأصل: بآتل وهو ... كبير. ٥ كما في ياقوت وفي الأصل: الواحد ... شرة. ٦ كما في ياقوت وفي الأصل: الجوار ... روقة. ٧ الأصل: ورقيقه. ٨ ياقوت: وربّما يدخل التاجر عليهم. ٩ كما في ياقوت وفي الأصل: او ببغص. ١٠ كما في ياقوت وفي الأصل: باقدر. ١١ الأصل: فيغتسل منها يديه ووجهه ... ويسرحه؛ ياقوت: فيغسل فيها وجهه ويديه وشعر رأسه ويسرحه. ١٢ كما في ياقوت وفي الأصل: ولا يد ... . في ذلك المآ. ١٣ الأصل: سفينهم. ١٤ ياقوت: المرسى يخرج.

They are the filthiest of all God's creatures. They have no modesty when it comes to defecating or urinating and do not wash themselves when intercourse puts them in a state of ritual impurity. They do not even wash their hands after eating. Indeed, they are like roaming asses.[61] They arrive, moor their boats by the Itil, and build large wooden houses on its banks. They share a house, in groups of ten and twenty, sometimes more, sometimes fewer. Each reclines on a couch. They are accompanied by beautiful female slaves for trade with the merchants. They have intercourse with their female slaves in full view of their companions. Sometimes they gather in a group and do this in front of each other. A merchant may come in to buy a female slave and stumble upon the owner having intercourse. The Rūs does not leave her alone until he has satisfied his urge. They must wash their faces and their heads each day with the filthiest and most polluted water you can imagine.[62] Let me explain. Every morning a female slave brings a large basin full of water and hands it to her master. He washes his hands, face, and hair in the water. Then he dips the comb in the water and combs his hair. Then he blows his nose and spits in the basin. He is prepared to do any filthy, impure act in the water. When he has finished, the female slave carries the basin to the man next to him who performs the same routine as his comrade. She carries it from one man to the next and goes around to everyone in the house. Every man blows his nose and spits in the basin, and then washes his face and hair. 76

They disembark as soon as their boats dock. Each carries bread, meat, onions, milk, and alcohol to a large block of wood set in the ground. The piece of wood has a face on it, like the face of a man. It is surrounded by small figurines placed in front of large blocks of wood set in the ground. He prostrates himself before the large figure and says, "Lord, I have come from a distant land, with such and such a number of female slaves and such and such a number of sable pelts." He lists all his merchandise. Then he says, "And I have brought this offering." He leaves his offering in front of the piece of wood, saying, "I want you to bless me with a rich merchant with many dinars and dirhams who will buy from me whatever I wish 77

فأريد أن ترزقني تاجرا معه دنانير ودراهم كثيرة فيشتري منّي كما أريد[1] ولا يخالفني في ما أقول ثمّ ينصرف فإن تعسّر عليه بيعه وطالت أيّامه عاد بهديّة ثانية وثالثة فإن تعذّر ما يريد حمل إلى كلّ صورة من تلك الصور الصغار هديّة وسألهم[2] الشفاعة وقال هؤلاء نساء ربّنا وبناته وبنوه فلا يزال يطلب إلى صورة صورة يسألها ويستشفع بها ويتضرّع بين يديها فربّما تسهّل له[3] البيع فباع فيقول قد قضى ربّي حاجتي وأحتاج أن أكافيه فيعمد إلى عدّة من الغنم أو البقر فيقتلها ويتصدّق[4] ببعض اللحم ويحمل الباقي فيطرحه بين تلك الخشبة الكبيرة والصغار التي حولها ويعلّق رؤوس البقر أو الغنم على ذلك الخشب المنصوب في الأرض فإذا كان الليل وافت الكلاب فأكلت جميع ذلك ويقول الذي فعله قد رضي ربّي عنّي وأكل هديّتي.

٧٨ وإذا مرض منهم الواحد ضربوا له خيمة ناحية[5] عنهم وطرحوه فيها وجعلوا معه شيئا من الخبز والماء ولا يقربونه ولا يكلّمونه بل لا يتعاهدونه في كلّ أيّام[6] لا سيّما إن كان ضعيفا أو مملوكا فإن برئ وقام رجع إليهم وإن مات أحرقوه فإن كان مملوكا تركوه على حاله تأكله الكلاب وجوارح الطير.

٧٩ وإذا أصابوا سارقا أو لصّا جاءوا به إلى شجرة غليظة وشدّوا في عنقه حبلا وثيقا وعلّقوه فيها ويبقى معلّقا حتّى ينقطع بالرياح والأمطار[7].

٨٠ وكان يقال[8] إنّهم يفعلون برؤسائهم عند الموت أمورا أقلّها الحرق فكنت أحبّ أن أقف على ذلك حتّى بلغني موت رجل منهم جليل فجعلوه في قبره وسقّفوه عليه[9] عشرة أيّام حتّى فرغوا من قطع ثيابه وخياطتها وذلك أنّ الرجل الفقير منهم يعملون له سفينة صغيرة ويجعلونه فيها ويحرقونها والغنيّ يجمعون ماله ويجعلونه ثلاثة أثلاث فثلث لأهله وثلث[10] يقطعون له به ثيابا وثلث[11] ينبذون به نبيذا يشربونه يوم تقتُل

---

١ ياقوت: كلّما أريد. ٢ ياقوت: وسألها. ٣ كما في ياقوت وفي الأصل: فربما يسهل له. ٤ كما في ياقوت وفي الأصل: ويصدّق. ٥ كما في ياقوت وفي الأصل: الواحد ... احة عنهم. ٦ كما في ياقوت وفي الأصل: ولا يكلمونه ... م. ٧ الأصل: وعلقوه ... بدا حتى نقطع بالرياح والأمطار؛ ياقوت: وعلّقوه فيها ويبقى معلّقا حتّى ينقطع من المكث إمّا بالرياح أو الأمطار. ٨ ياقوت: وكان يقال لي. ٩ ياقوت: وسقّفوا عليه. ١٠ الأصل: وثلثا. ١١ الأصل: وثلثا.

and not haggle over any price I set." Then he leaves. If he finds it hard to sell his goods and has to stay there too many days, he comes back with a second and a third offering. If his wishes are not fulfilled, he brings an offering to every single figurine and seeks its intercession, saying, "These are the wives, daughters, and sons of our lord." He goes up to each figurine in turn and petitions it, begging for its intercession and groveling before it. Sometimes business is good, and he makes a quick sale. In that case, he says, "My lord has satisfied my request, so I need to compensate him." He acquires some sheep or cows and kills them, gives a portion of the meat as alms, and places the rest before the large block of wood and the small ones around it. He ties the heads of the cows or the sheep to the piece of wood set up in the ground. When night falls, the dogs come and eat it all up, and the man who has gone to all this trouble says, "My lord is pleased with me and has eaten my offering."

When one of them falls ill, they pitch a tent far away and lay him down 78
inside, with some bread and water. They do not approach him or speak to him. Indeed, they have no contact with him for as long as he is ill, especially if he is a social inferior or a slave. If he recovers and gets back on his feet, he rejoins them. If he dies, they set fire to him. They do not bury dead slaves but leave them as food for the dogs and the birds.

When they catch a thief or a bandit, they take him to a solid tree and put a 79
sturdy rope around his neck. They tie him to the tree and he hangs there until he eventually decomposes from exposure to the rain and the winds.

I was told that they set fire to their chieftains when they die. Sometimes 80
they do more,[63] so I was very keen to verify this. Then I learned of the death of an important man. They had placed him in his grave, with a roof raised over him, for ten days while they finished cutting and sewing his garments. When the deceased is poor, they build a small boat for him, place him inside and burn it. When he is rich, they collect his possessions and divide them into three portions. One-third goes to his household, one-third is spent on his funeral garments, and one-third is spent on the alcohol they drink the day his female slave kills herself and is cremated with her master. They are

جاريتُه نفسَها وتُحرَق مع مولاها وهم مستهترون بالنبيذ يشربونه ليلا ونهارا وربّما مات الواحد[١] منهم والقدح في يده وإذا مات الرئيس قال أهله لجواريه وغلمانه من منكم يموت معه فيقول بعضهم أنا فإذا قال ذلك فقد وجب لا يستوي له أن يرجع ولو أراد ذلك ما تُرِكَ وأكثر من يفعل الجواري[٢].

٨١ فلمّا مات ذلك الرجل الذي قدّمت ذكره قالوا لجواريه من يموت معه فقال أحدهنّ[٣] أنا فوكّلوا بها جاريتين تحفظانها وتكونان معها حيث سلكت حتّى أنّهما ربّما غسلتا رجليها[٤] بأيديهما وأخذوا في شأنه وقطع الثياب له وإصلاح ما يحتاج إليه والجارية في كلّ يوم تشرب وتغنّي فرحة مستبشرة.

٨٢ فلمّا كان في اليوم الذي يُحرَق فيه هو والجارية[٥] حضرت إلى النهر سفينته فيه[٦] وإذا هي قد أُخرِجت وجعل لها أربعة أركان من خشب الخَذَنْك وغيره وجعل أيضا حولها مثل الأنابير الكبار من الخشب ثمّ[٧] مدّت حتّى جعلت على ذلك الخشب وأقبلوا يذهبون ويجيئون ويتكلّمون بكلام لا أفهم وهو بعد في قبره لم يخرجوه[٨] ثمّ جاءوا بسرير فجعلوه على السفينة وغشّوه بالمضرّبات الديباج الروميّ والمساند الديباج الروميّ وجاءت امرأة عجوز يقولون لها ملَك الموت[٩] ففرشت على السرير الفرش التي ذكرنا وهي وَلِيَت خياطته وإصلاحه وهي تقتل الجواري[١٠] ورأيتها جَوَان بيرة ضخمة مكفهرّة.

٨٣ فلمّا وافوا قبره نحّوا التراب عن الخشب ونحّوا الخشب واستخرجوه في الإزار الذي مات فيه فرأيته قد اسودّ لبرد البلد وقد كانوا جعلوا معه في قبره نبيذا وفاكهة وطنبورا فأخرجوا جميع ذلك فإذا هو لم ينتن ولم يتغيّر[١١] منه شيء غير لونه فألبسوه سراويل[١٢] ورانا وخفّا وقرطقا وخفتان ديباج له أزرار ذهب وجعلوا على رأسه

---

١ كما في ياقوت وفي الأصل: الو . . . د. ٢ ياقوت: من يفعل ذلك الجواري. ٣ ياقوت: إحداهن. ٤ كما في ياقوت وفي الأصل: غسلا رجليهما. ٥ الأصل: يحرق فيه والجارية؛ ياقوت: يحرق فيه هو والجارية. ٦ ياقوت: النهر الذي فيه سفينته. ٧ كما في ياقوت وفي الأصل: الكبار من الخ . . . ثم. ٨ كما في ياقوت وفي الأصل: ويتكلمون . . . في . . . جوه. ٩ كما في ياقوت وفي الأصل: على ال . . . ومي والمساند الدساج . . . مي وجآت ا . . . ملك الموت. ١٠ كما في ياقوت وفي الأصل: ا . . . اري. ١١ كما في ياقوت وفي الأصل: لم تغيّر. ١٢ الأصل: سراويلا.

addicted to alcohol. They drink it night and day. Sometimes one of them dies cup in hand. When the chieftain dies, the members of his household ask his female and male slaves, "Who will die with him?" One answers, "I will." At this point the words become binding. There is no turning back. It is not even an option. It is usually the female slaves who offer.

When the man I just mentioned died, they said to his female slaves, 81
"Who will die with him?" One said, "I will." So they put two other female slaves in charge of her, caring for her and accompanying her wherever she went, even to the point of washing her feet with their hands. Then they attended to the chieftain, cutting his garments and setting in order what was required for him. The female slave drank alcohol every day and sang merrily and cheerfully.

I arrived at the river where his boat was moored on the day the chief and 82
the female slave were set on fire. I noticed that the boat had been beached and that it was supported by four *khadhank* props. These props were surrounded by what looked like huge structures of wood. The boat had been hauled on top of the wood. The Rūsiyyah approached, going to and fro around the boat uttering words I did not understand. The chief was still in his grave and had not been exhumed. They produced a couch and placed it on the boat, covering it with quilts and cushions made of Byzantine silk brocade. An aged woman whom they called the Angel of Death turned up. She spread the coverings on the couch. It is her responsibility to sew the chieftain's garments and prepare him properly, and it is she who kills the female slaves. I saw her myself: she was gloomy and corpulent but neither young nor old.[64]

When they arrived at his grave, they removed the soil from the wood. 83
Then they removed the wood and exhumed him, dressed in the garment he was wearing when he died. I noticed that the coldness of the climate had turned him black. They had placed alcohol, fruit, and a *ṭanbūr* in his grave. They removed all of this. Surprisingly, his corpse had not begun to stink. Only his color had deteriorated. They dressed him in trousers, leggings, boots, a tunic, and a silk caftan with gold buttons. They placed a peaked

قلنسوة ديباج سمّوريّة وحملوه حتّى أدخلوه القبّة التي على السفينة وأجلسوه على المضرّبة وسنّدوه[١] بالمساند وجاءوا بالنبيذ والفاكهة والريحان فجعلوه معه وجاءوا بخبز ولحم وبصل فطرحوه بين يديه وجاءوا بكلب فقطعوه بنصفين[٢] وألقوه في السفينة ثمّ جاءوا بجميع[٣] سلاحه فجعلوه إلى جانبه ثمّ أخذوا دابّتين[٤] فأجروهما حتّى عرقتا[٥] ثمّ قطّعوهما بالسيف وألقوا لحمهما[٦] في السفينة ثمّ جاءوا ببقرتين فقطّعوهما أيضا وألقوهما فيها ثمّ أحضروا ديكا ودجاجة فقتلوهما وطرحوهما فيها.

٨٤ والجارية التي تريد تُقْتَل ذاهبةٌ وجائية تدخل قبّة قبّة من قبابهم[٧] فيجامعها صاحب القبّة ويقول لها قولي لمولاك إنّما فعلت هذا من محبّتك فلمّا كان وقت العصر من يوم الجمعة جاءوا بالجارية إلى شيء قد عملوه مثل مَلْبَن الباب فوضعت رجليها على أكفّ الرجال وأشرقت[٨] على ذلك الملبن وتكلّمت بكلام ما[٩] فأنزلوها ثمّ أصعدوها الثانية[١٠] ففعلت كفعلها في المرّة الأولى ثمّ أنزلوها وأصعدوها ثالثة ففعلت فعلها في المرّتين ثمّ دفعوا إليها دجاجة فقطعت رأسها ورمت به وأخذوا الدجاجة فألقوها في السفينة فسألتُ الترجمان عن فعلها فقال قالت في أوّل مرّة أصعدوها هوذا أرى أبي وأمّي وقالت في الثانية[١١] هوذا جميع قرابتي الموتى قعودا وقالت الثالثة هوذا أرى مولاي قاعدا في الجنّة والجنّة[١٢] حسنة خضراء ومعه الرجال والغلمان وهوذا يدعوني فاذهبوا إليه فمرّوا بها نحو السفينة[١٣] فنزعت سوارين كانا[١٤] عليها ودفعتهما إلى المرأة التي تسمّى ملك الموت وهي التي[١٥] تقتلها ونزعت خلخالين كانا عليها ودفعتهما إلى الجاريتين اللتين كانتا تخدمانها وهما ابنتا[١٦] المرأة المعروفة بملك الموت.

---

١ ياقوت: وأسندوه. ٢ ياقوت: نصفين. ٣ كما في ياقوت وفي الأصل: ثم جآوا جميع. ٤ كما في ياقوت وفي الأصل: أخذوا دا . . . ٥ الأصل: غرقتا. ٦ الأصل: لحمها. ٧ كما في ياقوت وفي الأصل: قباتهم. ٨ ياقوت: فأشرفت. ٩ الأصل: بكلام مـ . . . ؛ ياقوت: بكلام لها. ١٠ ياقوت: أصعدوها ثانية. ١١ الأصل: قالت في اول مرة أصعدوها . . . وقالت في الثانية؛ ياقوت: قالت في المرة الأولى هوذا أرى أبي وأمّي وقالت في المرّة الثانية. ١٢ الأصل: الموتى قعـ . . . وقالت الثالثة . . . الجنة؛ ياقوت: الموتى قعودا وقالت في المرّة الثالثة هوذا أرى مولاي قاعدا في الجنّة والجنّة. ١٣ الأصل: والغلمان . . . فاذهبوا الـ . . . نحوا السفينة؛ ياقوت: والغلمان وهو يدعوني فاذهبوا بي إليه فمرّوا بها نحو السفينة. ١٤ الأصل: فنزعت . . . ارن كانا؛ ياقوت: فنزعت سوارين كانتا. ١٥ الأصل: المراة لتي تسـ . . . لتي؛ ياقوت: المرأة العجوز التي تسمّى ملك الموت وهي التي. ١٦ كما في ياقوت وفي الأصل: عليها ودفـ . . . هما ايتنا.

silk cap fringed with sable on his head. They carried him inside the yurt that was on the ship and rested him on a quilt, propping him up with the cushions. They placed the alcohol, fruit, and basil beside him. Then they placed bread, meat, and onions in front of him. They cut a dog in two and threw it onto the boat. They placed all his weaponry beside him. They made two horses gallop into a sweat, cut them into pieces with a sword, and threw the meat onto the boat. They cut two cows into pieces and threw them on board. Then they produced a cock and a hen, killed them, and put them on board too.

Meanwhile, the female slave who had expressed her wish to die came 84
and went, entering one yurt after another. The owner of the yurt would have intercourse with her and say, "Tell your master that I have done this out of love for you." At the time of the Friday late afternoon prayer they brought the female slave to an object they had built that resembled a door-frame. She stood on the hands of the men and rose like the sun above the door-frame. She uttered some words, and they brought her down. They lifted her up a second time, and she did what she had done before. They lowered her and lifted her a third time, and she did what she had done the last two times. Then they handed her a hen. She cut off the head and cast it aside. They picked the hen up and threw it onto the boat. I quizzed the interpreter about her actions and he said, "The first time they lifted her up, she said, 'Look, I see my father and mother.' The second time she said, 'Look, I see all my dead kindred, seated.' The third time she said, 'Look, I see my master, seated in the Garden.[65] The Garden is beautiful and dark-green. He is with his men and his retainers. He summons me. Go to him.'" They took her to the boat and she removed both of her bracelets, handing them to the woman called the Angel of Death, the one who would kill her. She also removed two anklets she was wearing, handing them to the two female slaves who had waited upon her, the daughters of the woman known as the Angel of Death.

٨٥ ثمّ أصعدوها إلى السفينة ولم يُدْخِلوها إلى القبّة وجاء[١] الرجال معهم التراس[٢] والخشب ودفعوا إليها قدحا نبيذا فغنّت عليه وشربته فقال لي الترجمان إنّها تودّع صواحباتها بذلك ثمّ دفع إليها قدح آخر فأخذته وطوّلت الغناء والعجوز تستحثّها على شربه والدخول إلى القبّة التي فيها مولاها فرأيتها وقد تبلّدت وأرادت دخول القبّة فأدخلت رأسها بينها[٣] وبين السفينة فأخذت العجوز رأسها وأدخلته[٤] القبّة ودخلت معها وأخذ الرجال يضربون بالخشب على التراس لأن لا يسمع صوت صياحها فيجزع غيرها من الجواري ولا[٥] يطلبن الموت مع مواليهنّ.

٨٦ ثمّ دخل إلى القبّة ستّة رجال فجامعوا بأسرهم[٦] الجارية ثمّ أضجعوها إلى جانب مولاها وأمسك اثنان رجليها واثنان يديها وجعلت العجوز التي تسمّى ملك الموت في عنقها حبلا مخالِفا ودفعته إلى اثنين ليجذباه[٧] وأقبلت ومعها خنجر[٨] عريض النصل فأقبلت تدخله بين أضلاعها وتخرجه والرجلان[٩] يخنقانها بالحبل حتّى ماتت.

٨٧ ثمّ وافى أقرب الناس إلى ذلك الميّت فأخذ خشبة وأشعلها[١٠] بالنار ثمّ مشى القَهْقَرَى قفاه[١١] إلى السفينة ووجهه إلى الناس والخشبة المشعلة في يده الواحدة[١٢] ويده الأخرى على باب استه وهو عريان حتّى أحرق[١٣] الخشب المعبّأ الذي تحت السفينة ثمّ وافى الناس بالخشب والحطب ومع كلّ واحد[١٤] خشبة قد ألهب رأسها فيلقيها في ذلك الخشب وتأخذ النار في الحطب ثمّ في السفينة ثمّ في القبّة والرجل[١٥] والجارية وجميع ما فيها ثمّ هبّت ريح عظيمة هائلة فاشتدّ لهب النار واضطرم[١٦] تسعّرُها.

١ كما في ياقوت وفي الأصل: ولم يدخلو . . . جآ. ٢ ياقوت: ومعهم التراس. ٣ كما في ياقوت وفي الأصل: فأدخلت . . . بينها. ٤ ياقوت: وأدخلتها. ٥ الأصل: صياحها فيجز . . . ها من الـ . . . .رري ولا؛ ياقوت: صياحها فيجزع غيرها من الجواري ولا. ٦ كما في ياقوت وفي الأصل: رجال . . . باسرهم. ٧ كما في ياقوت وفي الأصل: حبلا . . . الى اثنين ليجذبانه. ٨ ياقوت: ومعها خنجر عظيم؛ الأصل: ومعها جهر. ٩ كما في ياقوت وفي الأصل: النصل فا . . . خل . . . والرجلان. ١٠ كما في ياقوت وفي الأصل: وافى . . . وأشعلها. ١١ ياقوت: القهقرى نحو قفاه. ١٢ كما في ياقوت وفي الأصل: ووجهه . . . المشعلة في يده واحدة. ١٣ كما في ياقوت وفي الأصل: عريان . . . ى أحرق. ١٤ الأصل: ومع . . . واحدة. ١٥ كما في ياقوت وفي الأصل: الحطب . . . والرجل. ١٦ كما في ياقوت وفي الأصل: فيها . . . ريح عظيمة هائلة . . . صطرم.

They lifted her onto the boat but did not take her into the yurt. The men approached with shields and sticks and handed her a cup of alcohol. Before drinking it she chanted over it. The interpreter said to me, "Now she bids her female companions farewell." She was handed another cup which she took and chanted for a long time. The crone urged her to drink it and to enter the yurt where her master was lying. I could see she was befuddled. She went to enter the yurt but missed it, placing her head to one side of the yurt, between it and the boat. The crone took hold of her head and entered the yurt with her. The men began to bang their shields with the sticks, so that the sound of her screaming would be drowned out. Otherwise, it would terrify the other female slaves, and they would not seek to die with their masters. 85

Six men entered the yurt. They all had intercourse with the female slave and then laid her beside her master. Two held her feet, two her hands. The crone called the Angel of Death placed a rope around her neck with the ends crossing one another and handed it to two of the men to pull on. She advanced with a broad-bladed dagger and began to thrust it in between her ribs, here and there, while the two men strangled her with the rope until she died. 86

The deceased's nearest male relative came forward. He picked up a piece of wood and set it alight. He was completely naked. He walked backwards, the nape of his neck towards the boat, his face towards the people. He had the ignited piece of wood in one hand and had his other hand on his anus. He set fire to the wooden structures under the boat. The people came forward with sticks and firewood. They each carried a lighted stick that they threw on top of the wood. The wood caught fire. Then the boat, the yurt, the dead man, the female slave, and everything else on board caught fire. A fearsome wind picked up. The flames grew higher and higher and blazed fiercely. 87

٨٨ وكان إلى جانبي رجل من الروسيّة فسمعته يكلّم[1] الترجمان الذي معي فسألته عمّا قال له فقال[2] إنّه يقول أنتم يا معاشر العرب حمقى فقلت لِمَ ذلك قال إنّكم تعمدون[3] إلى أحبّ الناس إليكم وأكرمهم عليكم فتطرحونه في التراب[4] وتأكله التراب والهوامّ والدود ونحن نحرقه في لحظة فيدخل الجنّة من وقته[5] وساعته فسألت عن ذلك فقال من محبّة ربّه له قد بعث الريح حتّى تأخذه في[6] ساعة فما مضت[7] على الحقيقة ساعة حتّى صارت السفينة والحطب والجارية والمولى رمادا ثمّ رِمْدِدًا ثمّ بنوا على موضع السفينة قد أخرجوها[8] من النهر شبيها بالتلّ المدوّر ونصبوا في وسطه خشبة[9] كبيرة خَذَنْك وكتبوا عليها اسم[10] الرجل واسم ملك الروس وانصرفوا.

٨٩ قال ومن رسم[11] ملك الروس[12] أن يكون معه في قصره أربعمائة رجل من صناديد أصحابه وأهل الثقة عنده فهم يموتون[13] بموته ويُقتَلون دونه ومع كلّ واحد[14] منهم جارية تخدمه وتغسل رأسه وتضع له ما يأكل ويشرب وجارية أخرى يطؤها وهؤلاء[15] الأربعمائة يجلسون[16] تحت سريره وسريره عظيم مرصّع بنفيس الجوهر ويجلس معه على السرير أربعون جارية له وربّما وطئ الواحدة منهنّ بحضرة أصحابه الذين ذكرنا ولا ينزل عن سريره[17] فإن أراد قضاء حاجة قضاها[18] في طشت وإذا أراد الركوب قدّم دابّته إلى السرير فركبها منه وإذا النزول[19] قدّم دابّته حتّى نزل من دابّته[20] وله خليفة يسوس الجيوش ويواقع الأعداء ويخلفه في[21] رعيّته.

١ كما في ياقوت وفي الأصل: . . . يكلم. ٢ كما في ياقوت وفي الأصل: فسألته . . . فقال. ٣ الأصل: حمقى . . . لك قال إنّكم تعمدون؛ ياقوت: حمقى لأنّكم. ٤ كما في ياقوت وفي الأصل: واكرمهم . . . في ا . . . راب. ٥ كما في ياقوت وفي الأصل: فيدخل . . . وقته. ٦ كما في ياقوت وفي الأصل: الريح حـ . . . في. ٧ كما في ياقوت وفي الأصل: فما قصت. ٨ ياقوت: وكانوا أخرجوها. ٩ كما في ياقوت وفي الأصل: في . . . خشبة. ١٠ كما في ياقوت وفي الأصل: وكتبوا . . . اسم. ١١ كما في ياقوت وفي الأصل: ر . . . م. ١٢ ياقوت: ملوك الروس. ١٣ كما في ياقوت وفي الأصل: منهم يموت. ١٤ كما في ياقوت وفي الأصل: ومع . . . واحد منهم. ١٥ كما في ياقوت لأنّ الجملة غامضة جدّا في الأصل. ١٦ كما في ياقوت لأنّ هذه الكلمة غامضة جدّا في الأصل. ١٧ كما في ياقوت لأنّ الكلمة مطموسة في الأصل. ١٨ كما في ياقوت وفي الأصل: حا . . . ها. ١٩ الأصل: السرير . . . وإذا النزول؛ ياقوت: السرير فركبها منه وإذا أراد النزول. ٢٠ ياقوت: حتّى يكون نزوله عليه. ٢١ كما في ياقوت وفي الأصل: الجيوش . . . في.

One of the Rūsiyyah was standing beside me. I heard him speaking to the interpreter who was with me. I asked him what he had said, and he replied, "He said, 'You Arabs, you are a lot of fools!'" "Why is that?" "Because you purposefully take your nearest and dearest and those whom you hold in the highest esteem and put them in the ground, where they are eaten by vermin and worms. We, on the other hand, cremate them there and then, so that they enter the Garden on the spot." I asked about this and he said, "My lord feels such great love for him that he has sent the wind to take him away within an hour." In fact, it took scarcely an hour for the boat, the firewood, the female slave, and her master to be burnt to ash and then to very fine ash. The Rūsiyyah then built a structure like a round hillock over the beached boat, and placed a large piece of *khadhank* in the middle. They wrote the man's name and the name of the king of the Rūsiyyah on it. Then they left. **88**

Ibn Faḍlān said: It is one of the customs of the king of the Rūsiyyah to keep in his palace four hundred of his bravest comrades and most trusted companions beside him. They die when he dies and sacrifice themselves to protect him. Each one has a female slave to wait on him, wash his head, and provide him with food and drink, and a second to have intercourse with. These four hundred companions sit below his huge couch, studded with precious stones. Forty concubines who belong to the king also sit on his couch. Sometimes he has intercourse with one of them in the presence of his comrades. He never steps off his throne. When he wants to satisfy an urge, he does so in a salver. When he wants to ride, he has his horse brought to the throne and mounts it from there. When he wants to dismount, he rides the horse to the throne so he can dismount there. He has a deputy, who leads the armies, fights the enemy, and represents him among his subjects. **89**

٩٠ فأمّا ملك الخزر واسمه خاقان فإنّه لا يظهر إلّا في كلّ أربعة أشهر متنزّها ويقال[١] له خاقان الكبير ويقال لخليفته خاقان بِهْ وهو الذي يقود الجيوش[٢] ويسوسها[٣] ويدبّر أمر المملكة ويقوم بها ويظهر ويغزو وله تذعن الملوك الذين يصاقبونه ويدخل . . . .[٤]

قال ياقوت الحمويّ في كتاب معجم البلدان إنه نقل هذا الفصل في وصف الخزر من كتاب ابن فضلان

٩٠أ فأمّا ملك الخزر واسمه خاقان فإنّه لا يظهر إلّا في كلّ أربعة أشهر متنزّها ويقال له خاقان الكبير ويقال لخليفته خاقان بِهْ وهو الذي يقود الجيش ويسوسها ويدبّر أمر المملكة ويقوم بها ويظهر ويغزو وله تذعن الملوك الذين يصاقبونه ويدخل في كلّ يوم إلى خاقان الأكبر متواضعا يظهر الإخبات والسكينة ولا يدخل عليه إلّا حافيا وبيده حطب فإذا سلّم عليه أوقد بين يديه ذلك الحطب فإذا فرغ من الوقود جلس مع الملك على سريره عن يمينه ويخلفه رجل يقال له كُنْدُر خاقان ويخلف هذا أيضا رجل يقال له جَاوَشِيغَر ورسم الملك الأكبر أن لا يجلس للناس ولا يكلّمهم ولا يدخل عليه أحد غير من ذكرنا والولايات في الحلّ والعقد والعقوبات وتدبير المملكة على خليفته خاقان به.

٩١ ورسم الملك الأكبر إذا مات أن يُبْنَى له دار كبيرة فيها عشرون بيتا ويحفر له في كلّ بيت منها قبر وتكسّر الحجارة حتّى تصير مثل الكحل وتفرش فيه وتطرح النُورة فوق ذلك وتحت الدار نهر والنهر نهر كبير[٥] يجري ويجعلون القبر فوق ذلك النهر ويقولون حتّى لا يصل إليه شيطان ولا إنسان ولا دود ولا هوامّ وإذا دفن ضربت أعناق الذين يدفنونه حتّى لا يُدْرَى أين قبره من تلك البيوت ويسمّى قبره الجنّة ويقولون قد دخل الجنّة وتفرش البيوت كلّها بالديباج المنسوج بالذهب.

---

١ كما في ياقوت وفي الأصل: كل اربـ . . . يقال. ٢ ياقوت: الجيش. ٣ كما في ياقوت وفي الأصل: ويشو . . . .
٤ قد انتهى الأصل هنا ويتلو في الورق سطران ولكنّهما مطموسان. ٥ كما في طبعة الدهّان وفي ياقوت: وتحت الدار والنهر نهر كبير.

90 The title of the king of the Khazars is *khāqān*. He appears in public only once every four months, at a distance. He is called the Great Khāqān. His deputy is called Khāqān Bih, who leads and commands the army, manages and conducts the affairs of the kingdom, and appears in public and leads the raids. The neighboring kings obey him.[66] He enters . . . .

The Khazars

Continuation: A Quotation from Ibn Faḍlān in the Entry on the Khazars in Yāqūt's *Geographical Dictionary*

90A The title of the king of the Khazars is *khāqān*. He appears in public only once every four months, at a distance. He is called the Great Khāqān. His deputy is called Khāqān Bih, who leads and commands the army, manages and conducts the affairs of the kingdom, appears in public, and leads the raids. The neighboring kings obey him. He enters the presence of the Great Khāqān every day, abasing himself in a show of humility and meekness. He must enter his presence barefoot, with a piece of firewood in his hand. When he greets him, he lights the firewood in front of him and then sits on the couch with the king at his right hand. He is represented by a man called Kundur Khāqān, who is, in his turn, represented by a man called Jāwashīghar.[67] According to custom, the Great Khāqān does not sit before the people or speak to them. Only those functionaries we have mentioned are admitted into his presence. Executive power, the meting out of punishment, and the general management of the kingdom are the responsibility of the deputy, the Khāqān Bih.

91 It is the custom that, when the Great Khāqān dies, a large dwelling is constructed for him. It houses twenty tents,[68] in each of which a grave is dug. Stones are pounded to a kohl-like powder and spread on the ground. Lime is thrown on top. A river flows under the dwelling—a fast, powerful river. They[69] construct the grave above the river, saying, "This way, no devil, man, worm, or vermin can reach him!" Those who bury him in his grave are beheaded, so no one knows which tent houses his grave. His grave is called the Garden, and they say, "He has entered the Garden." All of the tents are carpeted with silk woven with gold.

ورسم ملك الخزر أن يكون له خمس وعشرون امرأة كلّ امرأة منهنّ ابنة ملك ٩٢
من الملوك الذين يحاذونه يأخذها طوعا أو كرها وله من الجواري السراري لفراشه ستّون ما منهنّ إلّا فائقة الجمال وكلّ واحدة منها الحرائر والسراري في قصر مُفْرَد لها قبّة مغشّاة بالساج وحول كلّ قبّة مِضْرَب ولكلّ واحدة منهنّ خادم يحجبها فإذا أراد أن يطأ بعضهنّ بعث إلى الخادم الذي يحجبها فيوافي بها في أسرع من لمح البصر حتّى يجعلها في فراشه ويقف الخادم على باب قبّة الملك فإذا وطئها أخذ بيدها وانصرف ولم يتركها بعد ذلك لحظة واحدة.

وإذا ركب هذا الملك الكبير ركب سائر الجيوش لركوبه ويكون بينه وبين المواكب ٩٣
ميل فلا يراه أحد من رعيّته إلّا خرّ لوجهه ساجدا له لا يرفع رأسه حتّى يجوزه.

ومدّة مُلكهم أربعون سنة إذا جاوزها يوما واحدا قتلته الرعيّة وخاصّته وقالوا ٩٤
هذا قد نقص عقله واضطرب رأيه.

وإذا بعث سريّة لم تولّ الدبر بوجه ولا بسبب فإن انهزمت قتل كلّ من ينصرف ٩٥
إليه منها فأمّا القوّاد وخليفته فمتى انهزموا أحضرهم وأحضر نساءهم وأولادهم فوهبهم بحضرتهم لغيرهم وهم ينظرون وكذلك دوابّهم ومتاعهم وسلاحهم ودورهم وربّما قطع كلّ واحد منهم قطعتين وصلبهم وربّما علّقهم بأعناقهم في الشجر وربّما جعلهم إذا أحسن إليهم ساسة.

ولملك الخزر مدينة عظيمة على نهر إتل وهي جانبان في أحد الجانبين المسلمون ٩٦
وفي الجانب الآخر الملك وأصحابه وعلى المسلمين رجل من غلمان الملك يقال له خَز وهو مسلم وأحكام المسلمين المقيمين في بلد الخزر والمختلفين إليهم في التجارات مردودة إلى ذلك الغلام المسلم لا ينظر في أمورهم ولا يقضي بينهم غيره.

وللمسلمين في هذه المدينة مسجد جامع يصلّون فيه الصلاة ويحضرون فيه ٩٧
أيّام الجمع وفيه منارة عالية وعدّة مؤذّنين فلمّا اتّصل بملك الخزر في سنة ٣١٠ أنّ المسلمين هدموا الكنيسة التي كانت في دار البابونج أمر بالمنارة فهدمت وقتل

It is the custom of the king of the Khazars to possess twenty-five women, daughters of the neighboring kings, taken either with their compliance or by force.[70] He has sixty concubines, slaves beautiful beyond compare. The freeborn women and the concubines live in a separate palace. Each has a chamber with a vault of teak paneling and surrounded by a pavilion. Each concubine is served by a eunuch as her chamberlain. When the king wants to have intercourse, he sends for the eunuch who places the woman in the king's bed in the blink of an eye. The eunuch stands by the door of the king's yurt. When the king is done with her, the eunuch takes her by the hand and departs. He does not leave her there for one moment longer. 92

When this great king goes out riding, the entire army rides with him. There is a mile between him and his retinue. When his subjects see him, they lie down on their faces and remain prostrate before him. They do not lift their heads until he has passed. 93

His kingship lasts forty years. When it is just one day past forty years he is put to death by his subjects, including the elite, who say, "His mind is defective and his judgement is impaired." 94

No squadron he dispatches will turn back or retreat, no matter what. Those who come back after a defeat are killed. If his generals and the deputy are defeated, he has them brought into his presence, along with their women and children, and gives the women and children to another man before their very eyes. He does the same with their horses, belongings, weapons, and residences. Sometimes he cuts them in two and gibbets them. Sometimes he hangs them by the neck from a tree. Sometimes he makes them stable hands—if he means to be kind to them, that is. 95

The king of the Khazars has a mighty city on both banks of the Itil. The Muslims are on one bank, the king and his retinue on the other. One of the king's men, a Muslim whose title is Khaz, is in charge of the Muslims. The legal rulings of all the Muslims, both those who reside in the realm of the Khazars and those who go there regularly to trade, are referred to this Muslim retainer. No one else looks into their affairs or judges among them. 96

The Muslims have a congregational mosque in this city. This is where they perform the prayer and gather on Friday, the day of congregation. It has a tall minaret and several muezzins. In the year 310 [AD 922–23],[71] the king of the Khazars was informed that the Muslims had razed the synagogue in Dār al-Bābūnj. He gave orders for the minaret to be razed and for the muezzins 97

المؤذّنين وقال لولا أنّي أخاف أن لا يبقى في بلاد الإسلام كنيسة إلّا هدمت لهدمتُ المسجد والخزر وملكهم كلّهم يهود وكان الصقالبة وكلّ من يجاورهم في طاعته ويخاطبهم بالعبوديّة ويدينون له بالطاعة.

وقد ذهب بعضهم إلى أنّ ياجوج وماجوج هم الخزر. ٩٨

to be killed. He said: “I would not have razed the mosque, were I not afraid that every synagogue in the territory of Islam would be razed!” The Khazars and their king are Jews. The Ṣaqālibah and those who live on the Khazar border are under his rule. He addresses them as slaves, and they owe him their obedience.

Some claim that the Khazars are the tribes of Gog and Magog. **98**

Notes

1 In his entry on the "Bulghār" Yāqūt gives this name as Asad, though his other references to Ibn Faḍlān's full name use Rāshid. Presumably "Asad" is a scribal error.

2 The word *mawlā* that I have translated, in this instance, as "patron" expresses a central feature of Islamic social organization known as *walā'*. The term covers several relationships, including the ownership and manumission of slaves, the patronage of clients, and the protection and support of freeborn men and membership of a person's household. In our text *mawlā* is used to express patronage and clientage, as here (and also §§5, 43–47), ownership of a slave, as in §§55, 76, 80, 84, 85, 86, and the status of being a manumitted slave, a freedman who would continue under the patronage of their manumitters, as in §3: see Crone, "Mawlā."

3 Many Arabic works from the classical period were dictated, and we often find indications of this. Even when books were written down by their author (as opposed to being dictated to an amanuensis), they often preserve this gesture of orality by continuing the practice of using indications of orality such as "he (i.e., the author) said." See §§2, 6, 7, 27, 28, 47, 48, 49, 50, 69, 71, 73, 74, 89, for the instances of this use of "he said" in the text.

4 The word rendered as "representative" is *safīr*, the modern Arabic for "ambassador." It seems that Nadhīr, a high-ranking member of the caliphal court, presented the letter from the king of the Volga Bulghārs to the caliph and so acted in an ambassadorial role, as the king's representative or go-between. His *mawlā* (freedman, manumitted slave) Sawsan, in turn, represents Nadhīr on the embassy and is therefore called the "envoy" (*rasūl*). Ibn Faḍlān represents the caliph.

5 This "medication" is presented to the king in §41 ("unguents"). It later featured prominently as the reason for the king's conversion to Islam: see DeWeese, *Islamization*, 72–81, especially 76–78.

6 Ibn Faḍlān records some thirty days of stopover time at the fourteen halting posts at this stage of their journey.

7 Literally, "five days." Presumably, Ibn Faḍlān means that Aḥmad ibn Mūsā—who was to sell the estate of Arthakhushmīthan and provide the embassy with the money required by the Bulghār king to build the fort—left Baghdad on the fifth day (reckoning inclusively) after the party's departure, on the sixteenth of Safar (June 25).

8 The word translated as "soldier" is *ghulām*. It can denote any man, free or slave, closely bound in service to his master. I have rendered it variously as "soldier," "retainer," "man," and "male slave." See Sourdel, "G͟hulām: 1," and Bosworth, "G͟hulām: 2."

9 A curious echo of Q Nisāʾ 4:121: «Their destination is Jahannam. They will find no way to escape.»

10 See Q Insān 76:13. *Zamharīr* is explained as the burning cold of Hell.

11 From late November–early December, 921 to the end of February, 922.

12 This is the first occurrence of an awkward term in the text, *bayt*, which can designate variously a "tent," a "chamber," or a "house." Here the word *bayt* is contrasted with the other predominant term for "tent" in the text, *qubbah*, properly a "domed structure," rendered here and elsewhere as "yurt." I am unsure what, exactly, is descibed by the phrase "a chamber inside another chamber." The alternative is to render the phrase as "a tent inside another tent, with a Turkish yurt of animal skins inside it."

13 This is the only mention in the extant text of the involvement of Sawsan's "brother-in-law." The "jurists and instructors" mentioned in §3 are here reduced to one jurist and one instructor.

14 I take the point to be that the Turk does not recognize God as a member of the Turkic pantheon. According to Canard, *Voyage*, 102, n. 74, the caliph is intended by the word *rabb*.

15 It is possible that Ibn Faḍlān is drawing a more exact picture, so the phrase may mean that they used their clothes to fan the flames, causing sparks to leap from the fire. I thank Professor Philip Kennedy for this suggestion.

16 That is, on the morning of 17 Dhu l-Qaʿdah, 309 (Tuesday, March 19, 922).

17 I translate the phrase *idhā bi-* with this and similar expressions, of varying emphasis. I want to bring out the strong presence of eyewitness testimony, which predominates in Ibn Faḍlān's account.

18 An allusion to Q Muddaththir 74:50–51. See also §76.

19 This is the first instance in the text of an ambiguous use of the Arabic term *rabb* in Ibn Faḍlān's account of the Turks and the Rūsiyyah. As a form of address, *rabb* can be applied to a human in a position of leadership, but is often reserved for addressing God. The point Ibn Faḍlān makes about monotheism and reason is that the Ghuzziyyah Turks have neither revealed law nor a set of social customs based upon natural law determined through the use of reason. Ibn Faḍlān's picture of them reveals that they are henotheists who base their social practices on a strict code, though he apparently does not think this qualifies as *ʿaql*, reason.

20 Q Shūrā 42:38.

21 This is the first mention in the text of an interpreter.

22 The Mashhad MS reading *tagharrasa* is an unattested form. I suspect it conveys a notion that the bather has "planted" something in the water he washes in.

23 I thank Professor Geert Jan van Gelder for explaining this use of *qāma ʿalā* to me.

24 An echo of Q Yūsuf 12:23.

25 There is a lacuna of one word in the manuscript.

26 The term used is *al-jannah*, a standard Arabic term for Paradise. It recurs regularly throughout the treatise when reference is made to the Turkic or Rūsiyyah otherworld. In §91, the structure in which the Khazar *khāqān* is buried is called "the Garden."

27 The Arabic expression rendered as "those who" is highly irregular: *-hum man* (pronominal suffix with *man* as relative), for the relative pronoun *alladhīna* or simply *man* without the suffix *-hum*.

28 In accordance with the custom described in §23.

29 But not his birth mother, in accordance with the custom described in §22.

30 This statement seems to imply that Ibn Faḍlān was not familiar with the practice of sheep shearing.

31 A paraphrase of Q Isrāʾ 17:43.

32 The last two rivers listed are normally identified as follows: the Jāwshīn is changed to Jāwshīz and is thought to be either the Aqtāy or the Gausherma, and the Bnāsnah is usually written as Niyāsnah. However, all these rivers are located north of the region in which Ibn Faḍlān encounters the king of the Bulghārs. McKeithen observes that: "Ibn Faḍlān here takes the opportunity to account for all the rivers that were crossed by him during his stay in the land of the Ṣaqālibah" (*Risālah*, 82, n. 232). It is possible, of course, that completely different rivers may be intended and that Ibn Faḍlān may not be in a rush at this point in the text to list all the rivers he traversed irrespective of their geographical locations, so I have not altered the spelling of the river names.

33 Ibn Faḍlān is reckoning inclusively, counting the day the caravan departed, the second of Dhu l-Qaʿdah, and the day it arrived.

34 The medication referred to in §3.

35 Presumably the other kings get their share of the meal also.

36 The translation of this phrase is conjectural. It is usually explained in terms of fermentation—that is, letting it sit for a day and a night means the drink does not develop intoxicating properties and so would be permissible for Muslims to drink. If this is the meaning, then I would translate: "so called because it takes a day and a night to make." But Ibn Faḍlān's text does not say that he and the envoys drank the wine but that they

rose to their feet three times while the king drank and delivered his oath. It is Yāqūt's quotation of the passage that adds the verb *wa-sharibnā*, "and we drank."

37 This is one of two places in the text where the title "king of the Bulghārs" is used, rather than "king of the Ṣaqālibah": see also §69.

38 "God's bondsman" is the meaning of the name ʿAbdallāh. For the fuller version of the hadith, see *Risālat Ibn Faḍlān*, ed. al-Dahhān, 118 and n. 1.

39 As explained in §6.

40 Commentators and translators rarely agree that the king's remarks imply that Ibn Faḍlān was an Arab. Canard, *Voyage*, 109, n. 163, thinks that the term *ustādh*, "master," cannot refer to the caliph but only to the vizier. I suspect that the king intends Nadhīr al-Ḥaramī by the term.

41 This was in §14.

42 The *iqāmah* is a second call to stand in prayer, uttered after the *adhān* by the muezzin, as he stands behind the imam, when the latter is about to begin leading prayer. It consists of the text of the *adhān*, with the addition of the phrase *qad qāmat al-ṣalāt*, "prayer has begun." According to Shāfiʿī practice as observed by the caliphal court, the formulae taken from the *adhān* were uttered once in the *iqāmah*, and *qad qāmat al-ṣalāt* was uttered twice, whereas, according to Ḥanafī practice—the practice (*madhhab*) followed by the Samanids of Bukhara and to which the Bulghārs and the other steppe Turks converted—all the formulae were uttered twice. See the detailed note by Canard, *Voyage*, 110–11, n. 165. My thanks go to Professor Shawkat Toorawa for explaining this to me.

43 What the king means by this reference to the first caliph, renowned for his honesty, is unclear.

44 The *sāʿah qiyāsiyyah* refers to a practice of dividing night and day into twelve hours: "the clock worked on 'unequal' hours, that is, the hours of daylight or darkness were divided by twelve to give hours that varied in length from day to day" (Hill, "Sāʿa," 655). A proportional hour may thus be longer or shorter than an astronomical hour, depending on latitude and time of the year. I am grateful to Professor van Gelder for this explanation.

45 The Qur'an was divided into seven equal portions for recitation over the seven days of the week: see von Denffer, *ʿUlūm al-Qur'ān*, 69–70. My thanks go to Professor Toorawa for the reference.

46 This is an indication that Ibn Faḍlān remained with the Bulghārs until the end of the summer and so presumably would not have made the crossing of the Ustyurt back to Khwārazm until the following spring, at the earliest. Markwart, "Ein arabischer Bericht über die arktischen (uralischen) Länder," 279–80 and 331–32, argues, in terms

of astronomical data, that Ibn Faḍlān's claim (that this took place on the night of May 12–13) cannot be an accurate assessment of the hours of daylight in May. He prefers to see this as taking place in July. According to Czeglédy, "Zur Meschheder Handschrift," 225–27, Ibn Faḍlān is organizing his narrative by type of observation. See also McKeithen, *Risālah*, 97, n. 283. The "boiling cooking pot" is a trope of geographical lore concerning the northern regions in Arabic texts. The conversation with the muezzin revolves around the organization of the day in terms of the five ritual prayers: see Monnot, "Ṣalāt."

47 This is the only allusion to the return of the embassy I can detect in the account (aside from the fact of the preservation of the account itself).

48 The passage is obscure and can mean either that the Bulghār word for "female slaves" is the same as that for "apples" or that the apples are called something like "slave apples." Perhaps Ibn Faḍlān picked up a smattering of Bulghār or else acquired this information from the interpreter or a local informant.

49 The Prophet Muḥammad was also known as Aḥmad: see Q Ṣaff 61:6. Both names derive from the same triliteral root pattern in Arabic. The Bulghār's name is Ṭālūt, the Qur'anic name for Saul: Q Baqarah 2:247–49. McKeithen, *Risālah*, 111, n. 335, suggests that Ibn Faḍlān may be endeavoring to represent a Turkic name.

50 These are Q 1, Sūrat al-Fātiḥah and 112, Sūrat al-Ikhlāṣ, respectively.

51 The Arabic states: "there is not one of them whose bottom can be attained."

52 This is the market the Rūsiyyah use in §74.

53 It seems that Gog and Magog are separated from the outside world by both a gate and a wall.

54 It seems that the Wīsū are surprisingly knowledgeable about the Muslim apocalyptic legends of Gog and Magog. The reference to "the Wall" is to the wall that the Qur'an says the Horned Man (Alexander the Great) built to imprison Gog and Magog. For analogues in Arabic sources to the fabulous fish that feeds Gog and Magog, see Canard, *Voyage*, 116, n. 228. The *qāla* that occurs at this point in the text is the *qāla* that indicates that someone has finished speaking.

55 There is a lacuna of one word in the manuscript.

56 The text of the Mashhad manuscript is obscure. Lunde and Stone, *Ibn Fadlān*, 43, translate: "and if a woman from Khwārazm is present." I have adopted their rendering. They explain this in terms of the requirement that a corpse must be washed by a Muslim woman; as the nearest source of Muslim women was Khwārazm, they infer that "Islam had not extended to Bulghār females" (228, n. 79).

57 See §33, where the Ghuzziyyah are forced to pay the same tribute.

58 See §92, for how these hostage brides fair at the Khazar court.

59 This phrase is obscure and the Arabic syntax is far from clear. Ibn Faḍlān is thought by many to be describing tattoos of trees and other forms, but the practice of tattooing is unattested for the Vikings and he may mean that they have the images of trees and other shapes painted on them, perhaps using a plant dye.

60 Viking women often wore a scoop for ear-wax, together with other items for personal grooming, attached to a chain worn around the neck or under a broach. It is this scoop that Ibn Faḍlān calls a knife.

61 A second occurrence of this allusion to Q Muddaththir 74:50–51; see the account of the Ghuzziyyah at §18.

62 Ibn Faḍlān's Arabic implies that, for the Rūsiyyah, this communal wash is a binding ritual.

63 Ibn Faḍlān shows that he is aware that the funerary practice of the Rūsiyyah is not fixed but admits variation based upon wealth. See §71 for a similar recognition of variation in Bulghār funerary ritual based upon tribal status. Variations in the funerary practice of the Ghuzziyyah seem to depend on tribal membership and wealth: see §27.

64 Professor van Gelder refers me to al-Tanūkhī's *Nishwār al-muḥāḍarah*, 2:184.1–185.4 for an anecdote that revolves around the term *jawānbīrah*, an arabicized borrowing from Persian which appears to mean a "middle-aged" woman. I suspect, though I have no hard evidence, that, with this unusual phrase, Ibn Faḍlān may be trying to communicate a more menacing aspect of the Angel of Death than simply telling us her age.

65 See §27 for the "Garden" of the Ghuzziyyah and §91 for the "Garden" of the *khāqān* of the Khazars.

66 See, e.g., §72 for the vassalage of the king of the Bulghārs.

67 Klyashtorny, "About One Khazar Title," argues that this word is an abbreviation of a Turkic honorific that he explains as "head of the royal falcon hunting."

68 In view of the association in the rest of the treatise between tents, illnesses, death, and burial practices I have opted here to render *bayt* as "tent," though "chamber" may equally be intended. See above, n. 12.

69 The identity of "they" is not specified in the text. Presumably Ibn Faḍlān intends the Khazars generally and not, as in the following sentence, the men who actually place the *khāqān* in his grave.

70 Noonan, "Some Observations," 208, infers from this number that the Khazar *khāqān* ruled "over 25 distinct peoples."

71 The year 310 H began on May 1, 922.

Glossary of Names and Terms

ʿAbdallāh ibn Bāshtū al-Khazarī (§§3, 6, 8) the name of the Khazar who serves as the envoy from the king of the Bulghārs to the caliphal court. To judge by his name, ʿAbdallāh, he is a Muslim, a fact that has led some to suspect that he was a political activist working against the Khazar khaqanate.

Abū Bakr (§47) Abū Bakr al-Ṣiddīq (r. 11–13/632–34), the first of the four rightly-guided caliphs, dubbed "the Veracious" (al-Ṣiddīq).

Adhl (§34) the fourth river crossed by the caravan, on portable, collapsible camel-skin rafts, after its departure from the territory of the Ghuzziyyah. It is transcribed as "Oḏïl" by Togan (*Reisebericht*, 32, n. 6), who identifies it as the modern river Uyil.

*Āfr*n* (§4) an otherwise unattested name of the Ṭāhirid outpost which the embassy reaches after crossing the Āmul desert. It is probably a scribal error for Firabr.

Aḥmad ibn ʿAlī (§4) a member of the caliphal force sent to combat Yūsuf ibn Abī l-Sāj, the ruler of Azerbaijan who had, in 304/916, ousted Muḥammad ibn ʿAlī Ṣuʿlūk, the Samanid governor of Rayy, Aḥmad's own brother. Baghdad later recognized Aḥmad as the Abbasid governor of Rayy. He died in 311/924.

Aḥmad ibn Faḍlān ibn al-ʿAbbās ibn Rāshid ibn Ḥammād (§§1, 3, 14, 40–41, 44–47, 48–53, 58–59, 61, 63, 66–68, 70–71, 73–74, 80, 82, 88) the representative of the caliph al-Muqtadir on the embassy, delegated to read the official correspondence from Baghdad, to superintend the presentation of gifts to the Bulghār king and other local dignitaries, and to supervise the jurists and instructors sent with the embassy to instruct the Volga Bulghārs. Before the mission, he had been under the sponsorship of the powerful military commander Muḥammad ibn Sulaymān.

Aḥmad ibn Mūsā al-Khwārazmī (§5) an otherwise unknown person, whose role in the embassy was to take over the running of the estate in

Arthakhushmīthan and, presumably, provide the envoys with the money required by the Bulghār king to build his fort.

Akhtī (§34) the seventh river crossed by the caravan, on portable, collapsible camel-skin rafts, after its departure from Ghuzziyyah territory. Frye (*Ibn Fadlan's Journey*, 97) identifies it as the modern "Ankaty or Buldurti," which corresponds to the Ankati in Róna-Tas's map (*Hungarians and Europe*, 223).

ʿAlī ibn Abī Ṭālib (§9) cousin and son-in-law of the Prophet Muḥammad and the fourth, and last, of the rightly-guided caliphs (r. 35–40/656–61), greatly revered by Shiʿis. The cursing of ʿAlī referred to in the text may be a survival from the days of Umayyad rule.

Almish, Son of Shilkī see al-Ḥasan, Son of Yilṭawār.

Āmul (§4) not to be confused with Āmul, the capital of Ṭabaristān, this is a city on the river Jayḥūn (Oxus, modern Amu Darya), present-day Chardzhou or Turkmenabat. Āmul marks an important crossing-place of the Jayḥūn on the historic route from Nishapur and Marw to Transoxania and beyond. The town of Farab (or Farabr/Firabr), a dependency of Bukhara, lay on the opposite bank.

Ardkwā (§9) a place in Khwārazm otherwise unattested, the inhabitants of which are known as al-Kardaliyyah.

Ardn (§34) the fifth river crossed by the caravan, on portable, collapsible camel-skin rafts, after its departure from Ghuzziyyah territory. It is the "Erden," according to Canard (*Voyage*, 48, 107, n. 134), and the modern "Zhaqsibay or Kaldigayti," according to Frye (*Ibn Fadlan's Journey*, 97).

Arthakhushmīthan (§§3, 5) one of the estates of Ibn al-Furāt in Khwārazm, according to Ibn Faḍlān. Barthold (*Turkestan*, 148) suggests that it corresponds to modern Khojayli, in the Karakalpakstan region of Uzbekistan.

Askil (§§69, 72) the name of a clan subject to the Bulghār king, given as Asghl by Ibn Rustah (*Kitāb al-Aʿlāq*, 141.11). Their king is allied to the Bulghār king through marriage. The clan seems to seek to dissociate itself from the Bulghār king's conversion to Islam.

Atrak, Son of al-Qaṭaghān (§§30–33) the military commander (*sü-baši*) of the Ghuzziyyah Turks, who receives a letter from Nadhīr al-Ḥaramī, the embassy's representative in Baghdad.

Azkhn (§36) the third river crossed by the caravan, on portable, collapsible camel-skin rafts, after its departure from Bajanāk territory. In Róna-Tas's map (*Hungarians and Europe*, 223) it is the Irgiz.

Bājāʿ (§36) the fourth river crossed by the caravan, on portable, collapsible camel-skin rafts, after its departure from Bajanāk territory. Togan (*Reisebericht*, 34, n. 4) suggests it is the modern river Mocha. Most scholars propose that the last letter should be a *ghayn*: *Bājāgh*.

Bajanāk (§§35–36) Petchenegs, a nomadic or semi-nomadic Turkic people first reported east of the Caspian Sea and the second Turkic tribe encountered by the embassy on its route to the Volga Bulghārs. During the third/ninth century, they migrated west, under pressure from the Ghuzziyyah.

bakand (§§11, 26) according to Ibn Faḍlān, he heard this Khwārazmian word for "bread" in Khwārazm and among the Ghuzziyyah.

Baranjār, al- (§66) the name of a clan whose conversion to Islam was supervised by Ibn Faḍlān. The name has been associated with the Khazar settlement in the Caucasus known as Balanjār: see e.g. McKeithen, *Risālah*, 111, n. 334; Golden, *Khazar Studies*, 1, 221–24; Zimonyi, *Origins*, 49).

Bārs al-Ṣaqlābī (§§3, 13, 52) one of the *ghulāms*, presumably a slave-soldier who accompanied the embassy. In the context of the account, his affiliation, indicated by the name al-Ṣaqlābī, would not necessarily identify him as a Bulghār but possibly as a member of the subject population of the Bulghār king.

Bāshghird (§§37–38) Bashkirs, the last tribe encountered before the embassy arrives at the confluence of the Volga and Kama. Not much is known about the Bashkirs in the fourth/tenth century, although they are mentioned in several Arabic-language geographical treatises as occupying territory in the Ural mountains.

Baykand (§5) a town between Āmul and Bukhara, some two *farsakh*s from the latter (Le Strange, *Lands*, 463; Barthold, *Turkestan*, 117–19).

Bāynāj (§38) the fourth river crossed by the caravan after its departure from Bāshghird territory. Kovalevskiĭ (*Kniga*, 194, n. 342) thinks it is the modern river Mayna.

Bghndī (§34) the first river crossed by the caravan, on portable, collapsible camel-skin rafts, after its departure from Ghuzziyyah territory. Togan (*Reisebericht*, 32, n. 3) suggests it may be the modern Zhayïndï, near the river Emba.

Bīr tankrī (§18) a Turkic phrase translated and explained by Ibn Faḍlān as meaning "By God, by the One." Tengri was the Turkic sky-god.

Bnāsnh (§38) the sixth river crossed by the caravan after its departure from Bāshghird territory. Several scholars suggest it be read "Nyāsnah" (e.g., Kovalevskiĭ, *Kniga*, 194).

Bukhara (§§5–8) capital of the Samanid dynasty.

Bulghār/Bulghārs (§§39–73) the destination of the embassy. The Turkic Volga Bulghārs established their state at the confluence of the Volga and Kama rivers during the third/ninth century. By the beginning of the fourth/tenth century they had entered into a dynamic trading relationship with the Samanids in Central Asia, whereby their territory became one of the principal emporia of the period, rivaling and, ultimately, outlasting those of the Khazars. The Volga Bulghārs adopted Islam in the early fourth/tenth century and remained Muslims until the demise of their state in the wake of the attacks of the Mongols and their subsequent integration into the Golden Horde.

City of Peace (§§4, 5, 13) the name used in the text for Baghdad, properly speaking the original Round City of Baghdad, founded by the caliph al-Manṣūr.

Commander of the Faithful (§§2, 5, 8, 9, 40, 43–47, 69, 73) a rendering of *amīr al-mu'minīn*, a title held by the caliphs.

dāʿī (§4) a reference in our text to the Zaydī al-Ḥāsan ibn al-Qāsim (d. 316/928). The title is used among several Muslim groups for their principal propagandists and missionaries. It became especially important in Shiʿi movements, where it was used as the title of the authorized spokesman of the spiritual leader, the Imam.

Dāmghān, al- (§4) the capital of the province of Qumis, on Ibn Faḍlān's route between Simnān and Nishapur; at the time of the mission it was under Zaydī control.

dānaq (§§7, 9) a weight measure, one sixth of the *dīnār mithqāl*, the dinar used as a unit of weight; also here one-sixth of a dirham (see Hinz, *Islamische Masse*, 11 [Persian, *dāng*]).

Dār al-Bābūnj (§97) the unidentified location of a synagogue. Togan (*Reisebericht*, 102–3, n. 4) speculates that it may have to do with the name Alphons or Adalphuns, thus "the house/dwelling of Alphons or Adalphuns."

Daskarah, al- (§4) a town on Ibn Faḍlān's route between Nahrawān and Ḥul-wān. It probably originated as a caravan post that, at the time of the mission, had developed later into an important town on the Khurasan road.

dinar (§§14, 31, 45, 77) an Islamic gold coin.

dirham (§§7, 9, 11, 23, 39, 41, 45, 75, 77) a silver coin weighing usually about three grams and produced in enormous numbers. They circulated within the Islamic caliphate and were exported as payment for goods in long-distance trade. About half a million whole or fragmentary dirhams have been found across the vast trading networks of eastern and northern Europe. It is estimated that, during the first half of the fourth/tenth century alone, about 120 million dirhams were transported along the route taken by Ibn Faḍlān from the territory of the Samanids to the Volga Bulghārs (see Miles, "Dirham").

Faḍl ibn Mūsā al-Naṣrānī, al- (§§5–6) an otherwise unknown person. The account notes that he was the fiscal agent of the estate in Arthakhushmīthan owned by the ousted vizier Ibn al-Furāt, which was to provide the envoys with the money required by the king of the Bulghārs to build his fort.

Falūs (§14) the name of the guide hired by the embassy in al-Jurjāniyyah and possibly representing *qılavuz*, a Turkic word for guide (see, e.g., Togan, *Reisebericht*, 17, n. 5).

farsakh (§§8, 39, 50, 53, 67) a measure of distance, usually just short of six kilometers.

Gate of the Turks (§§5, 15) the name of a garrison outpost maintained at Zamjān by the Samanid emirate, on the edge of Turkic territories.

ghiṭrīfī dirham (§7) a low-value dirham that became the common currency in the region from the third/ninth century on. In theory, six *ghiṭrīfī* dirhams equaled one silver dirham, but there was considerable fluctuation in value. It was named after al-Ghiṭrīf ibn ʿAṭāʾ al-Jurashī who from 175 to 177 (ca. AD 791–93) was governor of Khurasan (see Frye, *Notes on the Early Coinage*, 29–31; Bosworth, "al-Ghiṭrīf b. ʿAṭāʾ").

Ghuzziyyah (§§18–34) the Oghuz, also known in Arabic as the Ghuzz, the first Turkic tribe encountered by the embassy after crossing the Ustyurt. They were an important tribe, whose earliest recorded home was northeast of the Caspian Sea. In the fourth/tenth century, they began moving west into the Khazar khaqanate and ultimately played a role in its downfall.

Gog and Magog (§§68, 98) a ferocious people, trapped, according to the Qurʾan, by Dhū l-Qarnayn (Alexander the Great) behind a great wall

(Q 18, Sūrat al-Kahf). The collapse of the wall signaled the onset of the End Time, when Gog and Magog would wreak destruction on the earth.

Hamadhān (§4) modern Hamadhan in Iran, a major town, the capital of the province known as the Jibāl, on Ibn Faḍlān's route between Qirmīsīn and Sāwah.

Ḥāmid ibn al-ʿAbbās (§41) a financier (223–311/837–923) who became especially prominent as vizier (306–11/918–23) during the reign of al-Muqtadir, a post he occupied at the time of the embassy.

Ḥammawayh Kūsā (§4) Ḥammawayh ibn ʿAlī, Samanid general and military commander of Khurasan. "Kūsā" is a nickname meaning "beardless." His formal title, *ṣāḥib jaysh Khurāsān* (field marshal of Khurasan), was the Arabic equivalent of the Persian title *sipahsālār*.

Ḥasan, Son of Yilṭawār, al- (§2) the name of the Bulghār king of the Ṣaqālibah, in the context of his letter to al-Muqtadir's court. Almish, son of Shilkī, is the name by which Atrak, son of al-Qaṭaghān, refers to him in a Turkic context in §33, when the Ghuzziyyah leaders are debating the fate of the embassy. Atrak also refers to the king as his "son-in-law." The quotation of §2, given by Yāqūt (*Muʿjam al-buldān*, 1.743.11), refers to the king in a third variant: Almis, son of Shilkī Bilṭawār (*blṭwār* is either a misreading of Yilṭawār by the scribe of the Mashhad manuscript or an Arabic attempt to represent a Bulghār pronunciation of the Turkic title *elteber*). The king acquires a fourth name in our text, Jaʿfar, son of ʿAbdallāh, and two new titles, "king of the Bulghārs" and "emir of the Bulghārs" (§44). This is when Ibn Faḍlān sanctions the king's conversion to Islam by approving his Muslim name and gubernatorial title for the Friday oration.

Ḥulwān (§4) a town on Ibn Faḍlān's route between al-Daskarah and Qirmīsīn.

Ibn Faḍlān see Aḥmad ibn Faḍlān.

Ibn al-Furāt (§§3, 5, 6) Abū l-Ḥasan ʿAlī ibn Muḥammad ibn Mūsā ibn al-Furāt (241–312/855–924), an important financier and politician in the early fourth/tenth century who had been deprived of the office of vizier at the time of the embassy and imprisoned. This is the reason that one of his mulcted estates could be used to provide the funding designated for building the Bulghār fort.

Ibn Qārin (§4) Sharwīn ibn Rustam ibn Qārin, the *ispahbad* (local governor) of Firrīm, encountered by the embassy in al-Dāmghān; a descendant of the Qarinid dynasty of Ṭabaristān and ally of the Zaydī ruler al-Ḥasan ibn

ʿAlī al-Uṭrūsh, in territories around the Caspian. He would have been no friend of the mission.

Itil (§§50, 67, 68, 74, 96) the usual Arabic name for the river Volga and for the capital city of the Khazars on the banks of the Volga delta. It is used in the text also for the Bulghār trading emporium on the bank of the Volga (see Golden, *Khazar Studies*, 1, 224–29).

Jaʿfar (§44) the given name of the caliph al-Muqtadir (Abū l-Faḍl Jaʿfar ibn Aḥmad al-Muʿtaḍid), given to the king of the Volga Bulghārs by Ibn Faḍlān to mark his membership in the Islamic polity.

Jākhā (§36) the second river crossed by the caravan, on portable, collapsible camel-skin rafts, after its departure from Bajanāk territory. Togan (*Reisebericht*, 34, n. 2) and others identify it as the river Chagan, a tributary of the Ural.

Jākhsh (§34) the third river crossed by the caravan, on portable, collapsible camel-skin rafts, after its departure from Ghuzziyyah territory. Togan (*Reisebericht*, 32, n. 5) and others identify it as the Sağïz, in Kazakhstan.

Jām (§34) The second river crossed by the caravan, on portable, collapsible camel-skin rafts, after its departure from Ghuzziyyah territory. Togan (*Reisebericht*, 32, n. 4) and others identify it as the Emba.

Jāwashīghar (§90A) the title given to the deputy of the *kundur khāqān* among the Khazar. According to Klyashtorny, "About One Khazar Title," the word is an abbreviation of an honorific that he explains as "head of the royal falcon hunting."

Jāwshīn (§38) the seventh river crossed by the caravan, after its departure from Bāshghird territory. Frye (*Ibn Fadlan's Journey*, 97) gives it as the "Aqtay or Gausherma." Most scholars locate this river in Bulghār territory and note that Ibn Faḍlān here purports to have crossed a river before he could have reached it.

Jāwshīr (§69) a river in Bulghār territory, presumed to be the river referred to earlier in the Mashhad manuscript as Jāwshīn.

Jayhānī, al- (§5) several viziers of Bukhara had this affiliation. Ibn Faḍlān may be referring to the Jayhānī credited with a famous geographical work entitled *The Book of the Routes and the Realms* (*Kitāb al-Masālik wa-l-mamālik*), which has not survived.

Jayḥūn (§§4, 10, 13) the Oxus, an important river in Turkestan, known today as the Amu Darya.

Jaykh (§36) the first river crossed by the caravan, on portable, collapsible camel-skin rafts, after its departure from Bajanāk territory. Frye (*Ibn Fadlān's Journey*, 97) and others identify it as the modern Ural.

Jīt (§15) a way station known to some Arabic geographers, after the entry into the Ustyurt, via the Gate of the Turks, at Zamjān.

Jrmsān (§38) the first river crossed by the caravan after its departure from Bāshghird territory. Togan (*Reisebericht*, 37, n. 1) and others identify it as the river Cheremshan (or Chirimshan).

Jurjāniyyah, al- (§§8, 10, 12, 14, 15, 23, 39) Gurganj, Khwārazm's second city (commercially more vibrant than Kāth), probably corresponding, to some extent, to modern Konya-Urgench.

Kardaliyyah, al- see Ardkwā.

Khadhank (§§34, 60, 69, 82, 88) a type of tree thought by many to be the birch (see, e.g., Róna-Tas, *Hungarians and Europe*, 226).

khāqān (§§90–91) in Ibn Faḍlān's account, the title of the ruler of the Khazars. It is a well-known Turkic title of obscure origin. Among the Khazars the *khāqān* became increasingly a sacral and taboo figure (see Golden, *Khazar Studies*, 1, 192–96).

Khāqān Bih (§90) the title of the deputy of the Khazar *khāqān*. *Bih* is clearly cognate with *beg*, the old Turkic title for a tribal chieftain.

Khaz (§96) the title given to the Muslim *ghulām* of the Khazar *khāqān*, who had executive and judicial authority over the Muslims resident in the Khazar capital.

Khazar/Khazars (§§1, 33, 67, 72, 90–98) the most powerful Turkic group on the Eurasian steppe at the time of the mission, ruled by the *khāqān*. The description of the Khazar polity and regnal customs that exists only in the form of a quotation by Yāqūt seems to have been appended by Ibn Faḍlān (or, according to some, by a later redactor) to his notice on the king of the Rūs. The embassy did not visit the Khazar khaqanate.

Khljh (§§67, 69) the name in the text for the three lakes where the embassy first meets the Bulghār king. The lakes are identified by Kovalevskiĭ (*Kniga*, 218, n. 564) as the modern Chistoe Ozero, Kuryshevskoe Ozero, and Atmanskoe Ozero.

Khurasan (§§4–6, 47) a historical region of Persia and Turkestan. In Ibn Faḍlān's time its borders were marked approximately in the west by the towns of al-Dāmghān and Jurjān and in the northeast by the river Jayḥūn.

Khuwār al-Rayy (§4) a town east of Rayy, on the Khurasan road.

Khwārazm (§§3, 5, 8–9, 24, 26, 71) a region north of Khurasan, extending as far as the southern shore of the Caspian Sea, Khwārazm is used in the text also as the name of the region's capital, Kāth, the residence of the *khwārazm-shāh* (see Le Strange, *Lands*, 446–59; Bosworth, "Kāth"; Bosworth, "Khʷārazm").

khwārazm-shāh (§8) the ancient Iranian title of the rulers of Khwārazm. The Khwārazm-Shāh dynasty ruled the area, remaining in power until the Mongol invasion. In Ibn Faḍlān's time the person holding this title was Muḥammad ibn ʿIrāq, who governed in the name of the Samanid emir.

Kījlū (§36) the eighth river crossed by the caravan, on portable, collapsible camel-skin rafts, after its departure from Bajanāk territory. Togan (*Reisebericht*, 34, n. 8) identifies it as the Kundurcha, pointing out the existence of a nearby village named "Kijläw," on the lesser Cheremshan.

Knāl (§36) the sixth river crossed by the caravan, on portable, collapsible camel-skin rafts, after its departure from Bajanāk territory. Togan (*Reisebericht*, 34, n. 6) and others identify it as the modern river Kinel.

kūdharkīn (§§24, 26, 29) the title given to any Ghuzziyyah noble who acts as deputy (*khalīfah* in the text) of the king of the Ghuzziyyah. There is no agreement on the meaning or etymology of the term. Golden (*Introduction*, 209) traces it to the Turkic phrase *kül erkin*.

Kundur Khāqān (§90A) the title given to the deputy of the *khāqān bih* among the Khazars.

Līlī ibn Nuʿmān (§4) a Daylamī general who served the Caspian Zaydīs al-Ḥasan ibn ʿAlī al-Uṭrūsh and al-Ḥasan ibn Qāsim. The latter appointed him to the governorship of Jurjān. In early 309/921, just before the departure of the embassy, he had occupied al-Dāmghān and Nishapur but was captured and killed by the Samanid field marshal Ḥammawayh Kūsā in Rabiʿ al-Awwal, 309/July–August, 921, as the embassy was moving through Khurasan.

Lesser Yināl see Yināl.

Marw (§§4, 6, 31, 33) a town on Ibn Faḍlān's route between Sarakhs and Qushmahān, which was the source of some of the textiles presented by the embassy to local potentates.

Muḥammad (§66) an alternate version of Ibn Faḍlān's given name Aḥmad. The Prophet Muḥammad was also known as Aḥmad (see Q Ṣaff 61:6).

Muḥammad ibn ʿIrāq see *khwārazm-shāh*.

Muḥammad ibn Sulaymān (§1) the redoubtable secretary of the Army Bureau, who defeated the Qarmaṭians in Syria in 291/903, wrested Egypt from Ṭulunid control in 292/905, and had been trying to maintain order in the eastern empire. He died in the caliphal campaign against Aḥmad ibn ʿAlī, who had seized control of Rayy upon the assassination of the Abbasid governor, ʿAlī ibn Wahsudhān. His death would have meant that Ibn Faḍlān was without a principal patron, though Ibn Faḍlān seems also to have secured the patronage of the caliph in Baghdad. It was possible for a person to enjoy the patronage of more than one patron at the same time, though perhaps Ibn Faḍlān was a member of the caliph's household and functioned under the patronage of Muḥammad ibn Sulaymān.

Muqtadir, al- (§§1–3, 44) the ruling caliph (r. 295–320/908–32) when Ibn Faḍlān's embassy made its journey. His full name was Abū l-Faḍl Jaʿfar ibn Aḥmad al-Muʿtaḍid, and his regnal title al-Muqtadir bi-llāh, "Mighty in God."

musayyabī dinar (§§14, 31) the *musayyabī* was a coin of uncertain value said to have been minted in Transoxania by al-Musayyab, governor of Khurasan, especially common among Turkic peoples in northern Khwārazm. It is odd that they are described in the text as dinars, which were gold coins. Frye (*Ibn Fadlan's Journey*, 88–90) wonders whether Ibn Faḍlān is confusing "real *dinar*s or rare gold coins" with Khwarazmian coins and suggests that Ibn Faḍlān means "equivalents in value of so many *musayyabi* dirhams."

Nadhīr al-Ḥaramī (§§3, 31, 41) a powerful eunuch at al-Muqtadir's court. He presents the Bulghār king's letter to the caliph and organizes the finances of the mission. He is the *mawlā* (patron) of the caliph's envoy, Sawsan al-Rassī, and provides the mission with letters to Atrak, son of al-Qaṭaghān, the Ghuzziyyah military commander, and to the Bulghār king.

Nahrawān (§4) the first town east of Baghdad reached by the mission after their departure.

Naṣr ibn Aḥmad (§5) Naṣr (r. 301–31/914–23) became the Samanid emir of Khurasan as an eight-year-old boy. When Ibn Faḍlān visited him in 309/921 he would have been only fifteen or sixteen years old.

Nishapur (§4) a town in Khurasan under Samanid control at the time of the mission.

Qaṭaghān, al- see Atrak, son of al-Qaṭaghān.

Qirmīsīn (§4) a town, modern Kermanshah, on Ibn Faḍlān's route between Ḥulwān and Hamadhān.

Qushmahān (§4) a town on the edge of the Karakum desert, on Ibn Faḍlān's route between Marw and Baykand.

raṭl (§11) a common, variable measure of weight.

Rayy (§4) an important town on the Khurasan road, between Hamadhān and Khuwār al-Rayy. At the time of the mission, it had been, for many years, the focus of the struggle for regional domination between the caliphate in Baghdad and the Samanids. Its ruins lie in the southern suburbs of present-day Tehran.

Rūsiyyah (§§72, 74–89) also known in Arabic as *al-Rūs*, one of the marvels witnessed by Ibn Faḍlān while in the custody of the king of the Bulghārs, a mysterious group of traders and raiders that continues to fascinate more than a millennium after Ibn Faḍlān encountered them. Their identity in Arabic writings has long been debated, not least with regard to the homonymous state (known as Rus') that emerged during the fourth/tenth century. In Ibn Faḍlān's account, the Rūs are traders who set up camp on the bank of the Itil (Volga) and thus in or near Bulghār lands, and we are given a unique eyewitness description of their community.

Samanids a Persian dynasty, rulers of Transoxania and then of Khurasan (204–395/819–1005). At the time of the mission, the Samanid ruler, Naṣr ibn Aḥmad, acknowledged the suzerainty of the caliph and went by the title of "emir."

samarqandī dirham (§7) a specific type of coin said by Ibn Faḍlān to be made of yellow brass and to equal six *dānaq*s.

Ṣaqālibah (§§1, 2, 3, 8, 39, 66, 72, 97) a name used in Arab-Islamic geographical and historical works, from the third/ninth century on, for certain northern peoples whose ethnic identity is not readily ascertainable. It may refer occasionally to Slavic peoples but seems generally to have a less specific connotation. At §97 it seems to denote the Finno-Ugrian peoples who live in the territories neighboring the Khazar realm. Throughout Ibn Faḍlān's account, the ruler of the Bulghārs is called the "king of the Ṣaqālibah" (§§1, 2, 3, 8, 39, 66, 72).

Sarakhs (§§4, 6) a town on Ibn Faḍlān's route between Nishapur and Marw.

Sāwah (§4) a caravan town (modern Saveh) on Ibn Faḍlān's route between Hamadhān and Rayy.

Sawsan al-Rassī (§§3, 42, 52) eunuch and freedman, under the patronage of Nadhīr al-Ḥaramī; the most important member of the embassy, the envoy of the caliph.

Simnān (§4) a town (modern Semnan) some two hundred kilometers east of present-day Tehran, on Ibn Faḍlān's route between Khuwār al-Rayy and al-Dāmghān; at the time of the mission it was under Zaydī control.

Sind (§61) the region around the lower course of the Indus river.

Smwr (§36) the fifth river crossed by the caravan, on portable, collapsible camel-skin rafts, after its departure from Bajanāk territory. Togan (*Reisebericht*, 34, n. 5) and others identify it as the modern Samara, one of the major tributaries of the lower Volga.

Sūḥ (§36) the seventh river crossed by the caravan, on portable, collapsible camel-skin rafts, after its departure from Bajanāk territory. Togan (*Reisebericht*, 34, n. 7) and others identify it as the modern Sok (or Soq, Suk).

Sujū, al- (§43) apparently a honey drink—perhaps a kind of mead—drunk by the Bulghār king. There is disagreement about whether the drink is intoxicating or not.

Ṣuʿlūk (§4) Muḥammad ibn ʿAlī Ṣuʿlūk, a Daylamī, the Samanid governor of Rayy from 289–304 to 912–16; brother of Aḥmad ibn ʿAlī and, at the time of the mission, the Abbasid governor of Rayy.

Suwāz (§69) name of a Bulghār clan whose members refuse to travel with the king, thus declaring their rejection of his conversion to Islam.

Ṭāgh (§§11, 17) Togan (*Reisebericht*, 13) suggests that this is a tree of the amaranth genus *Haloxylon*, known by the Russian name *saxaul*. The saxaul ranges in size from a large shrub to a small tree, usually 2–8 meters tall. The wood is heavy and coarse and the bark spongy. The saxaul grows throughout the Middle East and Central Asia and is very hardy and drought-resistant. In addition to providing fuel for heating, the thick bark stores moisture, which may be squeezed out for drinking, making it an important source of water in arid regions.

Ṭāhir ibn ʿAlī (§4) Togan (*Reisebericht*, 6, n. 4) speculates that this may be Ṭāhir ibn ʿAlī al-Wazīr, who was in the service of Caliph al-Muktafī (r. 289–95/902–8).

Takīn al-Turkī (§§3, 8, 13, 16, 52, 68) a member of the caliphal embassy, presumably a "slave-soldier" of Turkic origin, who was very knowledgeable about the Turkic steppe peoples and the Volga Bulghārs. The local potentate of Khwārazm recognizes him as a prominent figure in the iron trade, which, in fourth/tenth-century terms, would also have implied that he worked as a weapons dealer.

Ṭanbūr (§83) a long-necked stringed instrument from Central Asia.

Ṭarkhān (§33) the title of the most important member of the delegation of senior Ghuzziyyah figures convened by Atrak in order to consult about whether to permit the embassy to continue on its way.

ṭāzijah (§9) a coin used in Khwārazm. See Frye, *Notes on the Early Coinage*, 16–23 (on the coins of Khwārazm).

Turk/Turks (§§1, 5, 12, 13, 15, 16, 18, 20, 23, 24, 26–30, 32, 37, 65) a generic name for all the Turkic-speaking peoples of Central Asia with whom the Muslims came into contact. In the translation, I use "Turkic" for the language the Turks speak, and "Turkish" for their camels and yurts.

Ūrm (§38) the third river crossed by the caravan after its departure from Bāshghird territory. Kovalevskiĭ (*Kniga*, 194) suggests it is the modern river Urm. Today, there is a village with the name Urm, where Volga Bulghar inscriptions have been found.

Ūrn (§38) the second river crossed by the caravan after its departure from Bāshghird territory. Togan (*Reisebericht*, 37, n. 2) suggests it is the river Ürän, which enters the Volga across from modern Ulyanovsk.

Wārsh (§34) the sixth river crossed by the caravan, on portable, collapsible camel-skin rafts, after its departure from Ghuzziyyah territory. Togan (*Reisebericht*, 33, n. 1) and others identify it as the modern Qaldagayti (or Kandagayti) river.

Wbnā (§34) the eighth river crossed by the caravan, on portable, collapsible camel-skin rafts, after its departure from Ghuzziyyah territory. Kovalevskiĭ (*Kniga*, 192, n. 306) identifies it as the Lesser Ankaty river (Sholek Antaky), which empties into Shalkar lake, in southern Kazakhstan. According to Frye (*Ibn Fadlan's Journey*, 97) it is modern "Utba."

Wīsū (§§50, 65, 68) according to the king of the Bulghārs, the Wīsū live three months' travel north of the Bulghārs and trade with them. Togan (*Reisebericht*, 55, n. 3) and Kovalevskiĭ (*Kniga*, 205, n. 475) agree that the Wīsū are the Veps.

Wtīʿ (§38) the fifth river crossed by the caravan after its departure from Bāshghird territory. Togan (*Reisebericht*, 37, n. 5) and others identify it as the modern river Utka.

*W*r‘* (§69) the name or title of a son-in-law of the Bulghār king, with whom the Suwāz clan ally themselves when they refuse to travel with the king and thus reject his conversion to Islam. According to Togan (*Reiseberi-cht*, 75, n. 2), it reflects a Bulghār form of the ancient Turkic title *buyrug* (modern Turkish *buyruk*).

yabghū (§29) the regal title of the king of the Ghuzziyyah Turks.

Yāqūt Yāqūt ibn ʿAbdallāh al-Rūmī al-Ḥamawī (d. 626/1229), a biographer and geographer renowned for his encyclopedic writings. "Al-Rūmī" ("the man from Rūm") refers to his Byzantine origin, and "al-Ḥamawī" connects him with Ḥamāh, in Syria. In his topographical dictionary *Kitab Muʿjam al-buldān*, he included quotations from Ibn Faḍlān's account, which remained the principal vestiges of the work until Togan's discovery of the Mashhad manuscript in 1923.

Yilghiz (§33) a member of the delegation of senior Ghuzziyyah figures convened by Atrak in order to consult about the embassy.

Yilṭawār (§§2, 44) an arabicized form of a Turkic title *elteber*, written as *blṭwār* once in the Mashhad manuscript and in Yāqūt's quotation of the opening of the text. It seems to have been conferred on the Bulghār king or his father or both, presumably by the Khazars, to indicate a ruler subordinate to the Khazar *khāqān*.

Yināl (§§25, 33) apparently a title of a high-ranking Ghuzziyyah tribesman, used twice in the text. The first occurrence is qualified by the adjective *al-ṣaghīr* ("the younger" or "the lesser"), which may indicate age or status. It is possible that Ibn Faḍlān meets two men, the lesser Yināl (§25) and the Yināl (§33). The position of *yināl* is thought by some to designate the deputy of the *kūdharkīn* or the heir apparent to the *yabghū*.

Zamjān (§15) a garrison post, referred to as the Gate of the Turks, the first stopover taken by the embassy on leaving al-Jurjāniyyah, on the edge of the Ustyurt.

Zaydī/Zaydiyyah a branch of the Shiʿah, whose name comes from Zayd ibn ʿAlī ibn al-Ḥusayn, who led a revolt in Kufa in 122/740. In Ibn Faḍlān's text, the Caspian (and not the Yemeni) Zaydiyyah are meant, in particular the group known as the Nāṣiriyyah, who accepted leadership from among the descendants of al-Ḥasan ibn ʿAlī al-Uṭrūsh (d. 304/917), whose title was al-Nāṣir li-l-Ḥaqq, "he who brings victory to God's Truth."

Bibliography

Barthold, W. *Turkestan down to the Mongol Invasion*. Cambridge: Gibb, 2007.

Bosworth, C. E. "Al-Ghiṭrīf b. ʿAṭāʾ." In *Encyclopaedia of Islam*, 2nd ed. Suppl. fasc. 5–6. Leiden: Brill, 1982, 326–27.

———. "Ghulām, 2. Persia." In *Encyclopaedia of Islam*, 2nd ed. Leiden: Brill, 1991, 2:1081–84.

———. "Kāth." In *Encyclopaedia of Islam*, 2nd ed. Leiden: Brill, 1997, 4:753–54.

———. "Khwārazm." In *Encyclopaedia of Islam*, 2nd ed. Leiden: Brill, 1997, 4:1060–65.

———. "Naṣr b. Aḥmad b. Ismāʿīl." In *Encyclopaedia of Islam*, 2nd ed. Leiden: Brill, 1993, 2:1015.

Brett, Michael. "Egypt." In *The New Cambridge History of Islam*. Vol. 1, *The Formation of the Islamic World Sixth to Eleventh Centuries*, edited by Chase F. Robinson, 541–80. Cambridge: Cambridge University Press, 2010.

Bukharaev, R. *Islam in Russia: The Four Seasons*. Richmond: Curzon, 2000.

Canard, Marius. *Ibn Fadlân: Voyage chez les Bulgares de la Volga*. Paris: Sindbad, 1988.

Coetzee, J. M. *Waiting for the Barbarians*. London: Secker and Warburg, 1980.

Crone, P. "Mawlā." In *Encyclopaedia of Islam*, 2nd ed. Leiden: Brill, 1991, 6:874–82.

Czeglédy, K. "Zur Meschheder Handschrift von Ibn Faḍlāns Reisebericht." *Acta Orientalia* 1 (1951): 217–60.

DeWeese, Devin. *Islamization and Native Religion in the Golden Horde*. University Park, PA: Pennsylvania State University Press, 1994.

Edwards, P. *The Story of the Voyage: Sea-Narratives in Eighteenth-Century England*. Cambridge: Cambridge University Press, 1994.

Frye, Richard N. *Notes on the Early Coinage of Transoxania*. New York: American Numismatic Society, 1949.

———. "Some Early Iranian Titles." *Oriens* 15 (1962): 352–59.

———. *Ibn Fadlan's Journey to Russia: A Tenth-Century Traveler from Baghdad to the Volga River*. Princeton: Markus Wiener, 2005.

Göckenjan, Hansgerd, and Istvan Zimonyi. *Orientalische Berichte über die Völker Osteuropas und Zentralasiens im Mittelalter: Die Ǧayhānī-Tradition*. Wiesbaden: Harrassowitz, 2001.

Golden, Peter B. "The Question of the Rus' Qağanate." *Archivum Eurasiae Medii Aevi* 2 (1982): 76–97.

———. *An Introduction to the History of the Turkic Peoples: Ethnogenesis and State-Formation in Medieval and Early Modern Eurasia and the Middle East.* Wiesbaden: Harrassowitz, 1992.

———. *Khazar Studies: An Historico-Philological Inquiry into the Origins of the Khazars.* Budapest: Akadémiai Kiadó, 1980.

Greenblatt, Stephen. *Marvelous Possessions: The Wonder of the New World.* Oxford: Clarendon Press, 1991.

Hill, Christopher. *The English Bible and the Seventeenth Century Revolution.* London: Penguin, 1994.

Hill, D. R. "Sāʿa." In *Encyclopaedia of Islam*, 2nd ed. Leiden: Brill, 1995, 8:654–56.

Hinz, W. *Islamische Masse und Gewichte.* Leiden: Brill, 1970.

———. "Farsakh." In *Encyclopaedia of Islam*, 2nd ed. Leiden: Brill, 1991, 2:812–13.

Honigmann, E. [C. E. Bosworth]. "Nīshāpūr." In *Encyclopaedia of Islam*, 2nd ed. Leiden: Brill, 1995, 8:62–64.

Ibn Rustah. *Kitāb al-Aʿlāq al-nafīsah.* Edited by M. J. de Goeje. Leiden: Brill, 1967.

Kennedy, Hugh. *The Prophet and the Age of the Caliphates.* London: Longman, 1991.

King, David A. *In Synchrony with the Heavens: Studies in Astronomical Timekeeping and Instrumentation in Medieval Islamic Civilization.* Vol. 1, *The Call of the Muezzin.* Leiden: Brill, 2004.

Kipling, Rudyard. *The Man Who Would Be King: Selected Stories of Rudyard Kipling.* London: Penguin, 2011.

Klyashtornyj, S. G. "The Oguz of the Central Asia and the Guzs of the Aral region." *International Journal of Central Asian Studies* 2 (1997): 1–4.

Kovalevskiĭ, A. P. *Kniga Akhmeda Ibn Faḍlāna o ego puteshestvii na Volgu 921–2.* Kharkiv: Izdatelstvo Gos. Universiteta, 1956.

Le Strange, G. *The Lands of the Eastern Caliphate.* Cambridge: Cambridge University Press, 1930.

Lockhart, L. "Ḥulwān." In *Encyclopaedia of Islam*, 2nd ed. Leiden: Brill, 1986, 3:571–72.

Lunde, Paul, and Caroline Stone. *Ibn Fadlān and the Land of Darkness: Arab Travellers in the Far North.* London: Penguin, 2012.

Macintyre, Ben. *Josiah the Great: The True Story of the Man Who Would Be King.* London: HarperCollins, 2004.

Madelung, Wilferd. "The Minor Dynasties of Northern Iran." In *The Cambridge History of Iran.* Vol. 4, *The Period from the Arab Invasion to the Saljuqs*, edited by R. N. Frye, 198–249. Cambridge: Cambridge University Press, 1999.

———. "Zaydiyya." In *Encyclopaedia of Islam*, 2nd ed. Leiden: Brill, 2002, 11:477–81.

Makdisi, George. "Autograph Diary of an Eleventh-Century Historian of Baghdad." *Bulletin of the School of Oriental and African Studies* 18 (1956): 9–31, 236–60; 19 (1957): 13–48, 281–303, 426–43.

Markwart, J. "Ein arabischer Bericht über die arktischen (uralischen) Länder aus dem 10. Jahrhundert." *Ungarische Jahrbücher* 4 (1924): 261–334.

Massignon, Louis. *Hallāj. Mystic and Martyr.* Translated, edited, and abridged by Herbert Mason. Princeton: Princeton University Press, 1994.

———. [L. Gardet]. "al-Ḥallādj." In *Encyclopaedia of Islam.* 2nd ed. Leiden: Brill, 1986, 3:99–104.

———. "Ḥāmid b. al-ʿAbbās." In *Encyclopaedia of Islam.* 2nd ed. Leiden: Brill, 1986, 3:133.

Masʿūdī, Abū l-Ḥasan al-. *Murūj al-dhahab wa-maʿādin al-jawhar.* Edited by Charles Pellat. 7 vols. Beirut: Manshūrāt al-Jāmiʿah al-Lubnāniyyah, 1965.

McKeithen, J. E. *The Risālah of Ibn Faḍlān: An Annotated Translation with Introduction.* PhD diss., Indiana University, 1979.

Miles, G. C. "Dirham." In *Encyclopaedia of Islam*, 2nd ed. Leiden: Brill, 1991, 2:319–20.

Minorsky, V. *Ḥudūd al-ʿālam.* Edited by C. E. Bosworth. Cambridge: Gibb, 1982.

———. "Abū Dulaf." In *Encyclopaedia of Islam.* 2nd ed. Leiden: Brill, 1986, 1:116.

———. [C. E. Bosworth]. "Al-Rayy, 1. History." In *Encyclopaedia of Islam*, 2nd ed. Leiden: Brill, 1995, 8:471–73.

———. [C. E. Bosworth]. "Sāwa, 1. History." In *Encyclopaedia of Islam*, 2nd ed. Leiden: Brill, 1997, 9:85–87.

Miskawayh. *Tajārib al-umam.* Edited by Abū l-Qāsim Imāmī. Tehran: Dār Surūsh li-l-Ṭibāʿah wa-l-Nashr, 2001.

Monnot, G. "Ṣalāt, 3.A. The Five Daily Prayers." In *Encyclopaedia of Islam*, 2nd ed. Leiden: Brill, 1995, 8:928–29.

Noonan, T. S. "Some Observations on the Economy of the Khazar Khaganate." In *The World of the Khazars: New Perspectives: Selected Papers from the Jerusalem 1999 International Conference*, edited by P. B. Golden, H. Ben-Shammai, and A. Róna-Tas, 207–44. Leiden: Brill, 2007.

Olsson, J. "Coup d'état, Coronation and Conversion: Some Reflections on the Adoption of Judaism by the Khazar Khaganate." *Journal of the Royal Asiatic Society* 23, no. 4 (2013): 495–526.

Pellat, Ch. "Al-Djayhānī." In *Encyclopaedia of Islam.* Suppl. fasc. 5–6. Leiden: Brill, 1982, 265–66.

Rekaya, M. "Ḳārinids." In *Encyclopaedia of Islam*, 2nd ed. Leiden: Brill, 1997, 4:644–47.

Reynolds, Dwight., ed., *Interpreting the Self: Autobiography in the Arabic Literary Tradition.* Berkeley: University of California Press, 2001.

Riley-Smith, J. "The State of Mind of Crusaders to the East, 1095–1300." In *The Oxford Illustrated History of the Crusades*, edited by J. Riley-Smith, 66–90. Oxford: Oxford University Press, 1997.

Risālat Ibn Faḍlān. Edited by Sāmī al-Dahhān. Damascus: al-Majmaʿ al-ʿIlmī al-ʿArabī, 1959.

Róna-Tas, A. *Hungarians and Europe in the Early Middle Ages*. Budapest: Central European University Press, 1999.

Shaban, M. A. *Islamic History: A New Interpretation*. Vol. 2, *A.D. 750–1055 (A.H. 132–448)*. Cambridge: Cambridge University Press, 1981.

Sourdel, D. "Ghulām, 1. The Caliphate." In *Encyclopaedia of Islam*, 2nd ed. Leiden: Brill, 1991, 2:1079–81.

Spuler, B. "Gurgandj." In *Encyclopaedia of Islam*, 2nd ed. Leiden: Brill, 1986, 3:1141–42.

Strothmann, R. "Al-Ḥasan al-Uṭrūsh." In *Encyclopaedia of Islam*, 2nd ed. Leiden: Brill, 1986, 3:254–55.

Subrahmanyam, Sanjay. *The Career and Legend of Vasco da Gama*. Cambridge: Cambridge University Press, 1997.

Tanūkhī, al-Muḥassin ibn ʿAlī al-. *Nishwār al-muḥādarah wa-akhbār al-mudhākarah*. Edited by ʿAbbūd al-Shaljī. 8 vols. Beirut: Dār Ṣādir, 1971.

Togan, A. Zeki Velidi. *Ibn Faḍlān's Reisebericht*. Abhandlungen für die Kunde des Morgenlandes 24, no. 3. Leipzig: Brockhaus, 1939.

van Berkel, Maaike, Nadia El Cheikh, Hugh Kennedy, and Letizia Osti, eds. *Crisis and Continuity at the Abbasid Court: Formal and Informal Politics in the Caliphate of al-Muqtadir (295–320/908–32)*. Leiden: Brill, 2013.

von Denffer, Ahmad. *ʿUlūm al-Qurʾān. An Introduction to the Sciences of the Qurʾān*, 2nd ed. Markfield: The Islamic Foundation, 2003.

Yāqūt al-Ḥamawī al-Rūmī. *Kitāb Muʿjam al-buldān*. Edited by F. Wüstenfeld. Leipzig: Brockhaus, 1866.

Zamora, Margarita. "Christopher Columbus's 'Letter to the Sovereigns': Announcing the Discovery." In *New World Encounters*, edited by Stephen Greenblatt, 1–10. Berkeley: University of California Press, 1993.

Zetterstéen, K. V. [C. E. Bosworth]. "Al-Muḳtadir." In *Encyclopaedia of Islam*, 2nd ed. Leiden: Brill, 1993, 7:541–42.

———. [C. E. Bosworth]. "Al-Muktafī." In *Encyclopaedia of Islam*, 2nd ed. Leiden: Brill, 1993, 7:542–43.

Zimonyi, I. *The Origins of the Volga Bulghars*. Szeged: Attila József University, 1990.

Further Reading

Works prefixed with an asterisk are either popular writings or useful overviews from which those unfamiliar with the subject might benefit.

Reproduction of the Mashhad Manuscript

Majmūʿ fī l-jughrāfiyā: mimmā allafahu Ibn al-Faqīh wa-Ibn Faḍlān wa-Abū Dulaf al-Khazrajī. Edited by Fuat Sezgin, with M. Amawi, C. Ehrig-Eggert, and E. Neubauer. Frankfurt am Main: Institute for the History of Arabic-Islamic Science at the Johann Wolfgang Goethe University, 1994 [additional photographic reproductions are to be found in Kovalevskiĭ, *Kniga*, and Czeglédy, *Zur Meschheder Handschrift*].

Editions of the *Kitāb*

Togan, A. Zeki Velidi. *Ibn Faḍlān's Reisebericht.* Abhandlungen für die Kunde des Morgenlandes 24, no. 3. Leipzig: Brockhaus, 1939 (a classic of twentieth-century scholarship, containing an edition and extensive and detailed commentary).

Risālat Ibn Faḍlān. Edited by Sāmī al-Dahhān. Damascus: al-Majmaʿ al-ʿIlmī al-ʿArabī, 1959.

Riḥlat Ibn Faḍlān. Edited by Ḥaydar Muḥammad Ghaybah. Beirut: al-Sharikah al-ʿĀlamiyyah li-l-Kitāb, 1994.

Risālat Ibn Faḍlān. Edited by Shakīr Luʿaybī. Abu Dhabi and Beirut: Dār al-Suwaydī li-l-Nashr wa-l-Tawzīʿ and al-Muʾassasah al-ʿArabīyah li-l-Dirāsāt wa-l-Nashr, 2003.

Selected Translations of the *Kitāb*

Danish

Simonsen, J. B. *Vikingerne ved Volga: Ibn Faḍlāns rejsebeskrivelse.* Højberg: Wormianum, 1997 [a partial translation].

English

McKeithen, J. E. *The Risālah of Ibn Faḍlān: An Annotated Translation with Introduction.* PhD diss., Indiana University, 1979.

*Frye, Richard N. *Ibn Fadlan's Journey to Russia: A Tenth-Century Traveler from Baghdad to the Volga River.* Princeton: Markus Wiener, 2005.

*Lunde, Paul, and Caroline Stone. *Ibn Fadlān and the Land of Darkness: Arab Travellers in the Far North.* London: Penguin, 2012.

French

Canard, Marius. *Ibn Fadlân: Voyage chez les Bulgares de la Volga.* Paris: Sindbad, 1988. First published as "La Relation du Voyage d'Ibn Fadlân chez les Bulgares," *Annales de l'Institut d'Études Orientales* 5 (1958): 41–145.

*Charles-Dominique, Paul. *Voyageurs arabes: Ibn Faḍlân, Ibn Jubayr, Ibn Baṭṭûṭa et un auteur anonyme.* Paris: Gallimard, 1995.

German

Fraehn, C. M. *Ibn Fozlan's und andere Araber Berichte über die Russen älterer Zeit.* St. Petersburg: Kaiserl. Akademie der Wissenschaften, 1823.

Togan, A. Zeki Velidi. *Ibn Faḍlān's Reisebericht.* Abhandlungen für die Kunde des Morgenlandes 24, no. 3. Leipzig: Brockhaus, 1939 [a classic of twentieth-century scholarship, containing an edition and extensive and detailed commentary].

Norwegian

Birkeland, Harris. *Nordens Historie i Middelalderen etter Arabiske Kilder.* Oslo: Jacob Dybwad, 1954 [a partial translation].

Persian

Ṭabāṭabā'ī, Abū l-Fażl. *Safarnāmah az Aḥmad ibn Fażlān ibn al-ʿAbbās ibn Rāshid ibn Ḥammād.* Manābiʿ-i tārīkh va-jughrāfiyā-yi Īrān 2. Tehran: Intishārāt-i Bunyād-i Farhang-i Īrān, 1966.

Polish

Kmietowicz, A., F. Kmietowicz, and T. Lewicki. *Źródła arabskie do dziejów słowiańszczyzny.* Wroclaw: Zakład im. Ossolińskich, 1985 [edition, translation, and commentary].

Russian

Kratchkovskiĭ, I. *Puteshestvie Ibn-Fadlana na Volgu.* Moscow and Leningrad: Izdatelstvo Akademii Nauk SSSR, 1939 [translation, with notes and commentary, under the general editorship of Kratchkovskiĭ].

Kovalevskiĭ, A. P. *Kniga Akhmeda Ibn Faḍlāna o ego puteshestvii na Volgu 921–2*. Kharkiv: Izdatelstvo Gos. Universiteta, 1956 [also contains a commentary and a facs. reprod. of the Mashhad manuscript].

Collections of Articles

The following books contain many articles that will be of interest to those wanting to know more about Ibn Faḍlān, or the Turkic world of the period, or the tradition of Arabic geographical writing.

Bosworth, C. E., ed. *The Turks in the Early Islamic World*. Aldershot UK and Burlington VT: Ashgate, 2007.

Golden, Peter B. *Nomads and their Neighbours in the Russian Steppe: Turks, Khazars and Qipchaqs*. Aldershot: Variorum, 2003.

———. *Turks and Khazars: Origins, Institutions, and Interactions in Pre-Mongol Eurasia*. Aldershot: Variorum, 2010.

Golden, Peter B., H. Ben-Shammai, and A. Róna-Tas, eds. *The World of the Khazars: New Perspectives*. Selected Papers from the Jerusalem 1999 International Conference. Leiden: Brill, 2007.

Khazanov, Anatoly M., and Andre Wink, eds. *Nomads in the Sedentary World*. Richmond: Curzon, 2000.

Netton, I. R., ed. *Islamic and Middle Eastern Travellers and Geographers*. London: Routledge, 2007.

Noonan, T. S. *The Islamic World, Russia and the Vikings, 750–900: The Numismatic Evidence*. Aldershot: Variorum, 1998.

Sezgin, F., with M. Amawi, C. Ehrig-Eggert, and E. Neubauer, eds. *Texts and Studies on the Historical Geography and Topography of Northern and Eastern Europe*, vol. 3. Frankfurt am Main: Institute for the History of Arabic-Islamic Science at the Johann Wolfgang Goethe University, 1994.

On Ibn Faḍlān and his *Kitāb*

Bosworth, C. E. "Aḥmad. b. Fażlān." In *Encyclopaedia Iranica*. London: Routledge and Kegan Paul, 1985, 1:640.

Canard, M. "Ibn Faḍlān." In *Encyclopaedia of Islam*, 2nd ed. Leiden: Brill, 1986, 3:759.

Czeglédy, K. "Zur Meschheder Handschrift von Ibn Faḍlān's Reisebericht." *Acta Orientalia* 1 (1950–51): 217–43.

Dunlop, D. M. "Zeki Validi's Ibn Faḍlān." *Die Welt des Orients* 1 (1947–52): 307–12.

Frye, R. N., and R. P. Blake. "Notes on the Risala of Ibn-Fadlan." *Byzantina Metabyzantina* 1, no. 2 (1949): 7–37 [repr. in *The Turks in the Early Islamic World*, edited by C. E. Bosworth, 229–59, Aldershot UK and Burlington VT, Ashgate, 2007].

*Gabriel, J. "Among the Norse Tribes: The Remarkable Account of Ibn Fadlan." *Aramco World* 50, no. 6 (1999): 36–42.

Graf, H.-J. "Die Bedeutung des Ibn Faḍlān für die germanische Altertumskunde." In *Zeki Velidi Togan'a Armağan. Symbolae in honorem Z.V. Togan*, 397–404. Istanbul: Maarif Basımevi, 1950–55.

Kowalska, M. "Ibn Faḍlān's Account of His Journey to the State of the Bulġārs." *Folia Orientalia* 14 (1972–73): 219–30.

Manylov, Y. P. "O puti Ibn Faḍlāna iz Khorezma cherez Plato Ustyurt [On Ibn Faḍlān's route from Khorezm through Plato (sic) Ust Yurt]." *Sovetskaya Arkheologiya* 2 (1979): 92–100.

Miquel, André. *La géographie humaine du monde musulman jusqu'au milieu du XIe siècle: Géographie et géographie humaine dans la littérature arabe des origines à 1050*, Paris and The Hague: Mouton, 1967 [especially relevant is the discussion of Ibn Faḍlān on pp. 132–39].

Montgomery, J. E. "Pyrrhic Scepticism and the Conquest of Disorder: Prolegomenon to the Study of Ibn Faḍlān." In *Problems in Arabic Literature*, edited by M. Maroth, 43–89. Piliscsaba: The Avicenna Institute of Middle Eastern Studies, 2004.

———. "Travelling Autopsies: Ibn Faḍlān and the Bulghār." *Middle Eastern Literatures* 7, no. 1 (2004): 3–32.

———. "Spectral Armies, Snakes, and a Giant from Gog and Magog: Ibn Faḍlān as Eyewitness Among the Volga Bulghars." *The Medieval History Journal* 9 (2006): 63–87.

Ritter, H. "Zum Text von Ibn Faḍlān's Reisebericht." *Zeitschrift der Deutschen Morgenländischen Gesellschaft* 96 (1942): 98–126.

Safwat, N. F. "The First Arab Diplomatic Envoy to Russia from Baghdad." *Ur* 2 (1981): 10–18.

Sobolevskii, A. I. "Zápiska Ibn-Faḍlāna [Le mémoire d'Ibn-Faḍlān]." *Comptes rendus de l'Académie des sciences de Russie, B* (1929): 223–27.

Zakhoder, B. N. "Ibn Faḍlān i al-Masʿūdī." *Kratkie Soobshcheniya Instituta Vostokovedeniya* 38 (1960): 15–18.

Al-Muqtadir's Reign and Early Fourth/Tenth-Century Administration

van Berkel, M. *Accountants and Men of Letters. Status and Position of Civil Servants in Early Tenth Century Baghdad*. PhD diss., Amsterdam University, 2003.

van Berkel, Maaike, Nadia El Cheikh, Hugh Kennedy, and Letizia Osti, eds. *Crisis and Continuity at the Abbasid Court: Formal and Informal Politics in the Caliphate of al-Muqtadir (295–320/908–32)*. Leiden: Brill, 2013.

Zetterstéen, K. V. [C. E. Bosworth]. "Al-Muḳtadir." In *Encyclopaedia of Islam*, 2nd ed. Leiden: Brill, 1993, 7:541–42.

Geography and Routes

To acquire a sense of the geography and itineraries mentioned in Ibn Faḍlān's account, the following studies, arranged according to the route of the mission, are useful:

Le Strange, Guy. *The Lands of the Eastern Caliphate*. Cambridge: Cambridge University Press, 1930 [an indispensable gazetteer for the topography of the route from Baghdad to the Ustyurt].

Minorsky, V. [C. E. Bosworth]. "Al-Rayy." In *Encyclopaedia of Islam*, 2nd ed. Leiden: Brill, 1995, 8:471–73.

Bosworth, C. E. "Khurāsān." In *Encyclopaedia of Islam*. 2nd ed., Leiden: Brill, 1986, 5:55–59.

Barthold, W. [R. N. Frye]. "Bukhārā." In *Encyclopaedia of Islam*, 2nd ed. Leiden: Brill, 1986, 2:1293–96.

Bosworth, C. E. "Khʷārazm." In *Encyclopaedia of Islam*. 2nd ed, Leiden: Brill, 1997, 4:1060–65.

Spuler, B. "Gurgandj." In *Encyclopaedia of Islam*. 2nd ed, Leiden: Brill, 1991, 2:1141–42.

Planhol, X. de. "Caspian Sea." In *Encyclopaedia of Iran*. Costa Mesa: Maza, 1992, 5:48–61.

Róna-Tas, A. *Hungarians and Europe in the Early Middle Ages*. Budapest: Central European University Press, 1999 [on p. 223, there is a detailed map of Ibn Faḍlān's reconstructed riverine route from Ghuzziyyah territory to Bulghār].

Spuler, B. "Itil." In *Encyclopaedia of Islam*. 2nd ed, Leiden: Brill, 1997, 4:280–81.

On Trade and Trade Routes

Ducène, J.-Ch. "Le commerce des fourrures entre l'Europe orientale et le Moyen-Orient à l'époque médiévale (IXe-XIIIe siècle): pour une perspective historique." *Acta Orientalia* 58, no. 2 (2005): 215–28.

Kovalev, R. "The Infrastructure of the Northern Part of the 'Fur Road' between the Middle Volga and the East during the Middle Ages." *Archivum Eurasiae Medii Aevi* 11 (2000–1): 25–64 [deals specifically with the part of the trade route traversed by Ibn Faḍlān, from Khwārazm to Bulghār on the Volga].

*Martin, Janet. *Treasure of the Land of Darkness: The Fur Trade and its Significance for Medieval Russia*. Cambridge: Cambridge University Press, 1986.

Peoples and Tribes in the *Kitāb*

The territories north of the caliphate, from the realm of the Samanids east of the Caspian to Bulghār on the middle Volga, are not well documented for the period in question. They were inhabited predominantly by nomadic or semi-nomadic Turkic tribes, and large-scale migrations were frequent. In the early fourth/tenth century an important trade route emerged between the Samanids and the Bulghārs of the middle Volga, along which caravans transported great quantities of goods in exchange for Arabic silver dirhams, some of which were produced specifically for export via this trading relationship.

*Christian, David. *A History of Russia, Central Asia and Mongolia*. Vol. 1, *Inner Eurasia from Prehistory to the Mongol Empire*. Oxford: Blackwell, 1998 [a useful historical overview with a section on the Samanids].

Dolukhanov, Pavel. *The Early Slavs: Eastern Europe from the Initial Settlement to the Kievan Rus*. London and New York: Longman, 1996 [valuable archaeological study].

*Frye, Richard N. *The Golden Age of Persia*, London: Orion, 2000.

Göckenjan, Hansgerd, and Istvan Zimonyi. *Orientalische Berichte über die Völker Osteuropas und Zentralasiens im Mittelalter: Die Ǧayhānī-Tradition*. Wiesbaden: Harrassowitz, 2001 [analyzes and discusses texts by other Arabic writers on some of the peoples encountered by Ibn Faḍlān].

*Golden, Peter B. *An Introduction to the History of the Turkic Peoples: Ethnogenesis and State-Formation in Medieval and Early Modern Eurasia and the Middle East*. Wiesbaden: Harrassowitz, 1992 [essential reading].

*———. *Central Asia in World History*. New York: Oxford University Press, 2011 [the best place to start for an overview of the region, from ancient to modern].

Khazanov, A. *Nomads and the Outside World*. Madison: University of Wisconsin Press, 1994.

Minorsky, V. *Ḥudūd al-ʿālam*. Edited by C. E. Bosworth. Cambridge: Gibb, 1982 [a translation of this important early anonymous Persian geography, with excellent commentary].

Pritsak, O. "The Turcophone Peoples in the Area of the Caucasus from the Sixth to the Eleventh Century." In *Il Caucaso: Cerniera fra culture dal Mediterraneo alla Persia (secoli IV–XI) 20–26 aprile 1995*, vol. 1, 223–45. Spoleto: Sede dello Centro, 1996.

Sinor, Denis. *Introduction à l'étude de l'Eurasie Centrale*. Wiesbaden: Harrassowitz, 1963 [a useful if outdated bibliographic resource].

*———, ed. *The Cambridge History of Early Inner Asia*, Cambridge: Cambridge University Press, 1990 [excellent survey articles on the Turkic peoples of the steppes].

*Soucek, S. *A History of Inner Asia*, Cambridge: Cambridge University Press, 2000.

Roux, J.-P. *La mort chez les peuples altaïques anciens et médiévaux*. Paris: Librairie d'Amérique et d'Orient, 1963.

———. *Faune et flore sacrées dans les societés altaïques*. Paris: Librairie d'Amérique et d'Orient, 1966.

———. "Tengri." In *The Encyclopedia of Religion*. New York: MacMillan, 1987, 14:401–3.

———. "Turkic Religions." In *The Encyclopedia of Religion*. New York: MacMillan, 1987, 15: 87–94.

Shboul, A. M. H. *Al-Masʿūdī and His World: A Muslim Humanist and His Interest in Non-Muslims*. London: Ithaca Press, 1979 [al-Masʿūdī's work of human geography, dating from several decades after Ibn Faḍlān's mission, provides notices on many of the peoples and places Ibn Faḍlān visited].

*Whittow, Mark. *The Making of Byzantium, 600–1025*. Berkeley and Los Angeles: University of California Press, 1996 [excellent account of Byzantium's dealings with many of the peoples encountered by Ibn Faḍlān].

The Ghuzziyyah

The Ghuzziyyah (Ghuzz/Oghuz) were an important Turkic tribe, whose earliest recorded abode was northeast of the Caspian Sea. In the fourth/tenth century they began moving west into the Khazar realm and ultimately played a role in its downfall.

Adamović, M. "Die alten Oghusen." *Materialia Turcica* 7–8 (1981–82): 26–50.

Agajanov, S. G. "The States of the Oghuz, the Kimek and the Kïpchak." In *History of Civilizations of Central Asia*. Vol. 4, *The Age of Achievement: AD 750 to the End of the Fifteenth Century. Part One, The Historical, Social and Economic Setting.*, edited by M. S. Asimov and C. E. Bosworth, 61–76. Paris: Unesco, 1998.

Cahen, Cl. "Ghuzz." In *Encyclopaedia of Islam*, 2nd ed. Leiden: Brill, 1991, 2:1106–10.

Golden, P. B. "The Migrations of the Oğuz." *Archivum Ottomanicum* 4 (1972): 45–84 [reprinted as Article IV in his *Nomads and Their Neighbours*].

Gömeç, S. "The Identity of Oguz Kagan. The Oguz in the History and the Epics of Oguz Kagan." *Oriente Moderno* 89, no. 1 (2009): 57–66.

Gündüz, T. "Oguz-Turkomans." In *The Turks*. Vol. 1, *Early Ages*, edited by Hasan Celâl Güzel, C. Cem Oğuz, and Osman Karatay, 463–75. Ankara: Yeni Türkiye, 2002.

Husseinov, R. "Les sources syriaques sur les croyances et les moeurs des Oghuz du VIIe au XIII siècle." *Turcica* 8, no. 1 (1976): 21–27.

Koca, S. "The Oghuz (Turkoman) Tribe Moving from Syr Darya (Jayhun) Region to Anatolia." In *The Turks*. Vol. 2, *Middle Ages*, edited by Hasan Celâl Güzel, C. Cem Oğuz, and Osman Karatay, 129–43. Ankara: Yeni Türkiye, 2002.

Klyashtornyj, S. G. "The Oguz of Central Asia and the Guzs of the Aral region." *International Journal of Central Asian Studies* 2 (1997): 1–4.

Salgado, F. M. "El Arabismo Algoz (al-guzz): contenido y uso." *Historia, Instituciones, Documentos* 26 (1999): 319–28.

Nagrodzka-Majchrzyk, T. "Les Oghouz dans la relation d'Aḥmad Ibn Faḍlān." *Rocznik Orientalistyczny* 49, no. 2 (1994): 165–69.

Zachariadou, E. A. "The Oğuz Tribes: The Silence of the Byzantine Sources." In *Itinéraires d'Orient: Hommages à Claude Cahen*, edited by R. Curiel and R. Gyselen, 285–89. Bures-sur-Yvette: Groupe pour l'Étude de la Civilisation du Moyen-Orient, 1994.

The Bajanāk

The Bajanāk (Pechenegs) were a nomadic or semi-nomadic Turkic people first reported east of the Caspian Sea. In the third/ninth century they migrated west, under pressure from the Ghuzziyyah (Ghuzz/Oghuz). As allies of the Byzantines, the Pechenegs were an important force on the Pontic steppes and further west, near Kievan Rus', and, by the end of the century, they had driven the Magyars to the Pannonian lowlands, where the state of Hungary was established.

Romashov, S. A. "The Pechenegs in Europe in the Ninth-Tenth Centuries." *Rocznik Orientalistyczny* 52, no. 1 (1999): 21–35.

Takács, B. Z. "Khazars, Pechenegs and Hungarians in the Ninth Century." In *The Turks*. Vol. 1, *Early Ages*, edited by Hasan Celâl Güzel, C. Cem Oğuz, and Osman Karatay, 524–32. Ankara: Yeni Türkiye, 2002.

Wozniak, F. E. "Byzantium, the Pechenegs, and the Rus': The Limitations of a Great Power's Influence on its Clients in the Tenth Century Eurasian Steppe." *Archivum Eurasiae Medii Aevi* 4 (1984): 299–316.

The Bāshghird

Not much is known about the Bāshghird (Bashkirs) in the fourth/tenth century, although they are mentioned by several Arab geographers. They were apparently an independent people occupying territories on both sides of the Ural mountain range in the region of the Volga, Kama, and Tobol Rivers.

Togan, Z. V. "Ba<u>shd</u>ịirt." In *Encyclopaedia of Islam*, 2nd ed. Leiden: Brill, 1986, 1:1075–77.

The Bulghār

The Turkic Volga Bulghārs established their state on the confluence of the Volga and Kama rivers in the third/ninth century. Early in the fourth/tenth century they entered into a dynamic trading relationship with the Samanids in Central Asia, as a result of which the territory of the Volga Bulghārs became one of the principal emporia of the period, rivaling and ultimately outlasting those of the Khazars. The Bulghārs adopted Islam in the early fourth/tenth century, and it remained their religion until the demise of their state in the wake of the attacks of the Mongols and their subsequent integration into the Golden Horde.

Bennigsen, E. "Contribution à l'étude du commerce des fourrures russes. La route de la Volga avant l'invasion mongole et le royaume des Bulghars." *Cahiers du Monde russe et soviétique* 19 (1978): 385–99.

Erdal, M. *Die Sprache der wolgabolgarischen Inschriften*. Wiesbaden: Harrassowitz, 1993.

Hakimzjanov, F. S. "New Volga Bulgarian Inscriptions." *Acta Orientalia* 40, no. 1 (1986): 173–77.

Hrbek, I. "Bulghār." In *Encyclopaedia of Islam*, 2nd ed. Leiden: Brill, 1986, 1:1304–08.

Khalikov, A. H., and J. G. Muhametshin. "Unpublished Volga Bulgarian Inscriptions." *Acta Orientalia* 31, no. 1 (1977): 107–25.

Mako, G. "The Islamization of the Volga Bulghars: A Question Reconsidered." *Archivum Eurasiae Medii Aevi* 18 (2011): 199–223.

Noonan, Thomas S. "Volga Bulghāria's Tenth-Century Trade with Sāmānid Central Asia." *Archivum Eurasiae Medii Aevi* 11 (2000–2001): 140–218.

Smirnov, A. P. *Volzhskie Bulgary*. Moscow: Izdatelstvo Gosudarstvennogo istoricheskogo muzeĭà, 1951.

Vladimirov, G. "Histoire et culture de la Bulgarie de Volga (traits spécifiques)." *Bulgarian Historical Review/Revue Bulgare d'Histoire* 34, nos. 3–4 (2006): 3–24.

Zimonyi, I. *The Origins of the Volga Bulghars*. Szeged: Attila József University, 1990.

———. "Volga Bulghars and Islam." In *Bamberger Zentralasienstudien*, edited by Ingeborg Baldauf and Michael Friederich, 235–40. Berlin: Schwarz, 1994.

The Rūsiyyah/Rūs

The identity of the people called al-Rūsiyyah or al-Rūs in Arabic writings has long been debated, not least with regard to the Slavic state that emerged in the course of the fourth/tenth century. In Ibn Faḍlān's account, the Rūs are traders who set up camp in or near Bulghār territory, and he gives us a unique eyewitness description of their community that has inspired several studies.

Danylenko, A. "The Name 'Rus'': In Search of a New Dimension." *Jahrbücher für Geschichte Osteuropas* 52 (2004): 1–32.

Duczko, W. *Viking Rus: Studies on the Presence of Scandinavians in Eastern Europe*. Leiden: Brill, 2004.

*Franklin, S., and J. Shepard. *The Emergence of Rus, 750–1200*. London and New York: Longman, 1996.

Golden, P. B. "The Question of the Rus' Qağanate." *Archivum Eurasiae Medii Aevi* 2 (1982): 77–97 [reprinted as Article V in his *Nomads and Their Neighbours*].

———. "Rūs." In *Encyclopaedia of Islam*, 2nd ed. Leiden: Brill, 1995, 8:618–29.

Hraundal, Th. J. *The Rūs in Arabic Sources: Cultural Contacts and Identity*. PhD diss., University of Bergen, 2013.

Montgomery, J. E. "Ibn Faḍlān and the Rūsiyyah." *Journal of Arabic and Islamic Studies* 3 (2000): 1–25.

*———. "Arabic Sources on the Vikings." In *The Viking World*, edited by S. Brink and N. Price, 550–61. Oxford and New York: Routledge, 2008.

———. "Vikings and Rus in Arabic Sources." In *Living Islamic History*, edited by Y. Suleiman, 151–65. Edinburgh: Edinburgh University Press, 2010.

Noonan, Thomas S. "When Did Rūs/Rus' Merchants First Visit Khazaria and Baghdad?" *Archivum Eurasiae Medii Aevi* 7 (1987–91): 213–19.

A large part of Ibn Faḍlān's description of the Rūs describes an intriguing, if violent, funerary ceremony:

Lewicki, T. "Les rites funéraires païens des Slavs occidentaux et des anciens russes d'après les relations—remontant surtout aux IX-Xe siècles—des voyageurs et des écrivains arabes." *Folia Orientalia* 5 (1963): 1–74.

Price, N. "Passing into Poetry: Viking Age Mortuary Drama and the Origins of Norse Mythology." *Medieval Archaeology* 54 (2010): 123–57.

Sass, T., and M. L. Warmind. "Mission Saqaliba." *Chaos* 11 (1989): 31–49.

Schjødt, J. P. "Ibn Faḍlān's Account of a Rus Funeral: To What Degree Does It Reflect Nordic Myths?" In *Reflections on Old Norse Myths*, edited by P. Hermann, J. P. Schjødt, and R. T. Kristensen, 133–48. Turnhout: Brepols, 2007.

*Taylor, T. *The Buried Soul: How Humans Invented Death*. London: Beacon Press, 2002 [the relevant sections are pp. 86–112 and 170–93].

The Khazars

The empire of the Khazar *khāqān* emerged in the early first/seventh century and remained the most important entity on the Eurasian steppe for many centuries. Occasional allies of Byzantium, the Khazars fought off Muslim advances via the Caucasus in the first/seventh and second/eighth centuries, subsequently maintaining a more peaceful relationship with the caliphate, conducted mainly through trade. The Arabic sources state that, at some point, the elite surrounding the house of the *khāqān* converted to Judaism.

Barthold, W., and P.B. Golden. "Khazar." In *Encyclopaedia of Islam*, 2nd ed. Leiden: Brill, 1997, 2:1172–81.

*Brook, Kevin A. *The Jews of Khazaria*. Northvale, NJ: Aronson, 1999.

———. "Khazar-Byzantine Relations." In *The Turks*. Vol. 1, *Early Ages*, edited by Hasan Celâl Güzel, C. Cem Oğuz, and Osman Karatay, 509–14. Ankara: Yeni Türkiye, 2002.

Czeglédy, K. "Khazar Raids in Transcaucasia in AD 762–764." *Acta Orientalia* 11, no. 1 (1960): 75–88.

———. "Notes on Some Problems of the Early Khazar History." In *Trudy Dvadtsat' pyatogo Mezhdunarodnogo Kongressa Vostokovedov, Moskva 1960*, edited by B. G. Gafurov, vol. 3, 336–38. Moscow: Izdatelstvo Vostochnoi Literatury, 1963.

*Dunlop, D. M. *The History of the Jewish Khazars*. Princeton: Princeton University Press, 1954.

Flyorova, V.E. *Obrazy i siuzhety mifologii Khazarii [The Images and Topics of Khazarian Mythology]*. Jerusalem: Gesharim and Moscow: Mosty Kul'tury: Evreĭskiĭ universitet v Moskve, 2001.

Golden, Peter B. *Khazar Studies: An Historico-Philological Inquiry into the Origins of the Khazars*. Budapest: Akadémiai Kiadó, 1980.

———. "Khazaria and Judaism." *Archivum Eurasiae Medii Aevi* 3 (1983): 127–56 [reprinted as Article III in his *Nomads and their Neighbours*].

———. "Some Notes on the Comitatus in Medieval Eurasia with Special Reference to the Khazars." *Histoire Russe* 28, no. 1 (2001), 153–70.

———. *Nomads and Their Neighbours in the Russian Steppe: Turks, Khazars and Qipchaqs*. Aldershot: Variorum, 2003.

———. "Irano-Turcica: The Khazar Sacral Kingship Revisited." *Acta Orientalia* 60, no. 2 (2007): 161–94 [reprinted as Article X in his *Turks and Khazars*].

———. *Turks and Khazars: Origins, Institutions, and Interactions in Pre-Mongol Eurasia*. Aldershot: Variorum, 2010.

Klyashtorny, S.G. "About One Khazar Title in Ibn Faḍlān." *Manuscripta Orientalia* 3, no. 3 (1997): 22–23.

Mako, G. "The Possible Reasons for the Arab-Khazar Wars." *Archivum Eurasiae Medii Aevi* 17 (2010): 45–57.

Mason, R. A. E. "The Religious Beliefs of the Khazars." *Ukrainian Quarterly* 51, no. 4 (1995): 383–415.

Naimushin, B. "Khazarskii kaganat i vostochnaia Evropa: Stolkovenia mezhdu 'kochevnikami stepei' i 'kochevnikami rek'" [The Khazar Kaghanate and Eastern Europe: Collision between the "Nomads of the Steppe" and the "Nomads of the Rivers"]. In *Bâlgari i Xazari: Prez Rannoto Srednovekovie*, edited by Tsvetelin Stepanov, 142–58. Sofia: TANGRA, 2003.

Noonan, T. S. "What Does Historical Numismatics Suggest about the History of Khazaria in the Ninth Century?" *Archivum Eurasiae Medii Aevi* 3 (1983): 265–81.

———. "Why Dirhams First Reached Russia: The Role of Arab-Khazar Relations in the Development of the Earliest Islamic Trade with Eastern Europe." *Archivum Eurasiae Medii Aevi* 4 (1984): 151–282 [reprinted as Article II in his *The Islamic World*].

———. "Khazaria as an Intermediary between Islam and Eastern Europe in the Second Half of the Ninth Century: The Numismatic Perspective." *Archivum Eurasiae Medii Aevi* 5 (1985): 179–204.

———. "Byzantium and the Khazars: A Special Relationship?" In *Byzantine Diplomacy: Papers from the Twenty-Fourth Spring Symposium of Byzantine Studies, Cambridge, March 1990*, edited by J. Shepard and S. Franklin, 109–32. Aldershot: Variorum, 1992.

———. "The Khazar Economy." *Archivum Eurasiae Medii Aevi* 9 (1995–97): 253–318.

———. "The Khazar-Byzantine World of the Crimea in the Early Middle Ages: The Religious Dimension." *Archivum Eurasiae Medii Aevi* 10 (1999): 207–30.

———. "Nomads and Sedentarists in a Multi-Ethnic Empire: The Role of the Khazars in the Khazar Khaganate." *Archivum Eurasiae Medii Aevi* 15 (2006–7): 107–24.

Olsson, J. "Coup d'état, Coronation and Conversion: Some Reflections on the Adoption of Judaism by the Khazar Khaganate." *Journal of the Royal Asiatic Society* 23, no. 4 (2013): 495–526.

Pletneva, S. *Ocherki Khazarskoĭ arkheologii [Essays on Khazar Archaeology]*. Jerusalem: Gesharim and Moscow: Mosty Kul'tury, 1999. [A collection of Pletneva's important contributions to Khazar archaeology, with an afterword in English by Vladimir Petrukhin.]

Polgár, S. "A Contribution to the History of the Khazar Military Organization: The Strengthening of the Camp." *Acta Orientalia* 58, no. 2 (2005): 197–204.

Romashov, S. A. "Istoricheskaya geografia khazarskogo kaganata (V-XIII vv) [The Historical Geography of the Khazar Kaghanate (5th-13th c.)]." *Archivum Eurasiae Medii Aevi* 11 (2000–1): 219–338.

Shapira, D. "Two Names of the First Khazar Jewish Beg." *Archivum Eurasiae Medii Aevi* 10 (1999): 231–41.

Shepard, J. "The Khazars' Formal Adoption of Judaism and Byzantium's Northern Policy." *Oxford Slavonic Papers* 31 (1998): 11–34.

Togan, A. Zeki Velidi. "Völkerschaften des Chazarenreiches im neunten Jahrhundert." In *Texts and Studies on the Historical Geography and Topography of Northern and Eastern Europe*, edited by Fuat Sezgin, with M. Amawi, C. Ehrig-Eggert, and E. Neubauer, vol. 3, 302–38. Frankfurt am Main: Institute for the History of Arabic-Islamic Science at the Johann Wolfgang Goethe University, 1994.

Zadeh, M. S. "Khazars in Islamic Sources." *Amu Darya* 4, no. 6 (2000): 273–96.

Zuckermann, C. "On the Origin of the Khazar Diarchy and the Circumstances of Khazaria's Conversion to Judaism." In *The Turks*. Vol. 1, *Early Ages*, edited by H. Celâl Güzel, C. Cem Oğuz, and O. Karatay, 516–23. Ankara: Yeni Türkiye, 2002.

Index

About the NYU Abu Dhabi Institute

NYU
ABU DHABI
INSTITUTE

The Library of Arabic Literature is supported by a grant from the NYU Abu Dhabi Institute, a major hub of intellectual and creative activity and advanced research. The Institute hosts academic conferences, workshops, lectures, film series, performances, and other public programs directed both to audiences within the UAE and to the worldwide academic and research community. It is a center of the scholarly community for Abu Dhabi, bringing together faculty and researchers from institutions of higher learning throughout the region.

NYU Abu Dhabi, through the NYU Abu Dhabi Institute, is a world-class center of cutting-edge research, scholarship, and cultural activity. The Institute creates singular opportunities for leading researchers from across the arts, humanities, social sciences, sciences, engineering, and the professions to carry out creative scholarship and conduct research on issues of major disciplinary, multidisciplinary, and global significance.

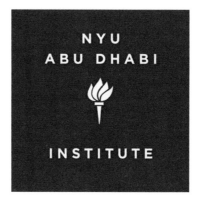

About the Typefaces

The Arabic body text is set in DecoType Naskh, designed by Thomas Milo and Mirjam Somers, based on an analysis of five centuries of Ottoman manuscript practice. The exceptionally legible result is the first and only typeface in a style that fully implements the principles of script grammar (*qawāʿid al-khaṭṭ*).

The Arabic footnote text is set in DecoType Emiri, drawn by Mirjam Somers, based on the metal typeface in the naskh style that was cut for the 1924 Cairo edition of the Qur'an.

Both Arabic typefaces in this series are controlled by a dedicated font layout engine. ACE, the Arabic Calligraphic Engine, invented by Peter Somers, Thomas Milo, and Mirjam Somers of DecoType, first operational in 1985, pioneered the principle followed by later smart font layout technologies such as OpenType, which is used for all other typefaces in this series.

The Arabic text was set with WinSoft Tasmeem, a sophisticated user interface for DecoType ACE inside Adobe InDesign. Tasmeem was conceived and created by Thomas Milo (DecoType) and Pascal Rubini (WinSoft) in 2005.

The English text is set in Adobe Text, a new and versatile text typeface family designed by Robert Slimbach for Western (Latin, Greek, Cyrillic) typesetting. Its workhorse qualities make it perfect for a wide variety of applications, especially for longer passages of text where legibility and economy are important. Adobe Text bridges the gap between calligraphic Renaissance types of the 15th and 16th centuries and high-contrast Modern styles of the 18th century, taking many of its design cues from early post-Renaissance Baroque transitional types cut by designers such as Christoffel van Dijck, Nicolaus Kis, and William Caslon. While grounded in classical form, Adobe Text is also a statement of contemporary utilitarian design, well suited to a wide variety of print and on-screen applications.

About the Editor-Translators

Tim Mackintosh-Smith is an independent scholar specializing in Arabic travel literature and is the author of several books of his own travels. Of these, his trilogy on Ibn Baṭṭūṭah (*Travels with a Tangerine, The Hall of a Thousand Columns,* and *Landfalls*) retraces the fourteenth-century Moroccan's journeys across three continents. His work has earned him the 1998 Thomas Cook/*Daily Telegraph* Travel Book Award and, appropriately, the Ibn Baṭṭūṭah Prize of Honour, awarded in 2010 by the Arab Centre for Geographical Literature. He has been based for over thirty years in the Yemeni capital, Sanaa.

James E. Montgomery is currently The Sir Thomas Adams's Professor of Arabic and Fellow of Trinity Hall at the University of Cambridge. He juggles many obsessions. Some of them he has had for many years now though he has probably discarded even more over the years. His current obsessions are: the body of writings attributed to al-Jāḥiẓ (d. 255/868–69); Arabic hunting poetry of the third/ninth century; the novels of Kurt Vonnegut and J. M. Coetzee; the Library of Arabic Literature. He is lucky to have a wonderful wife, three amazing children, and two brilliant dogs. He likes to get out of Cambridge and go to Yorkshire as often as possible.